MORE ADVANCE PRAISE FOR
THREE SQUARES

"Combining scholarly rigor with lively storytelling, Abigail Carroll offers a fresh look at American culinary history. Resisting the nostalgia often associated with discussion of family meals, Carroll argues that American dining rituals are relatively modern and are constantly evolving to meet contemporary needs and values. This masterful synthesis will delight both professional scholars as well as newcomers to the exciting new field of food history. Highly recommended!"
—Warren Belasco, author of *Meals to Come: A History of the Future of Food*, and Visiting Professor of Gastronomy, Boston University

"With *Three Squares*, Abigail Carroll gives us a very long view of American dining habits, beginning with life in colonial times and ending in the 21st century. With sometimes startling descriptions of the ad hoc eating that occurred on either side of a main noon meal in our earliest years, we witness the impact of away-from-home work in industry and commerce that appropriated the middle of the day and left us with 'cold, quick, and cheap lunches.' The story of breakfast cereal and snack foods and the erosion of the properly set, middle-class dinner table with everyone minding their manners caps this fascinating narrative." —Sandy Oliver, author of *Saltwater Foodways: New Englanders and Their Food at Sea and Ashore in the 19th Century*

"You will never look at your three meals a day, or snacks throughout the day, the same way after you read this fascinating, well-researched book. For anyone interested in food, this book is a must. It tells the historical stories and elucidates the business forces that underpin our current eating practices." —Anne Fishel, Associate Clinical Professor of Psychology, Harvard Medical School, and consultant to The Family Dinner Project

THREE SQUARES

Copyright © 2013 by Abigail Carroll

Published by Basic Books,
A Member of the Perseus Books Group

Books published by Basic Books are available at special discounts for bulk purchases in the United States by corporations, institutions, and other organizations. For more information, please contact the Special Markets Department at the Perseus Books Group, 2300 Chestnut Street, Suite 200, Philadelphia, PA 19103, or call (800) 810-4145, ext. 5000, or e-mail special.markets@perseusbooks.com.

Composition by Cynthia Young

Library of Congress Cataloging-in-Publication Data
Carroll, Abigail.
    Three squares : the invention of the American meal / Abigail Carroll.
        pages cm
    Includes bibliographical references and index.
    ISBN 978-0-465-02552-7 (hardcover) — ISBN 978-0-465-04096-4 (ebook)
1. Food habits—United States—History.   2. Diet—United States—History.
3. Dinners and dining—United States—History.   4. Luncheons—United States—
History.   5. Breakfasts—United States—History.   6. National characteristics,
American.   7. United States—Social life and customs.   I. Title.

    GT2853.U5C38 2013
    394.1'20973—dc23

                                                                    2013008929

10 9 8 7 6 5 4 3 2 1

Three Squares

The Invention of the American Meal

Abigail Carroll

BASIC BOOKS

A Member of the Perseus Books Group

New York

To my family—
John, Diana, Cozette, and Julian
—who always make dinner special.

CONTENTS

INTRODUCTION

We Are How *We Eat*

THIS BOOK WAS not supposed to be about the American meal. I had intended to write about the American snack: peanuts, pretzels, popcorn, and all those salty (and sometimes sweet) pleasures we munch at parties, use to nurse our boredom on airplanes, and indulge ad infinitum in front of the television. I had been gathering research for the Indiana State Museum on the relationship between snacking and obesity for a collaborative exhibition with the Science Museum of Minnesota, and as an historian by training, I could not help but wonder about snacking trends before the 1970s, prior to which the data sharply dropped off. So I embarked on my own investigative journey, probing historical newspapers, magazines, novels, letters, cookbooks, and memoirs. I learned a great deal about American snacking habits before my lifetime, but to my surprise, I also discovered something that focused my attention more squarely on the American meal: the snack and the meal cannot be understood apart from one another. They emerged out of the same historical moment, and, as this book reveals, their stories are wholly intertwined.

My investigative journey into the history of snacking, and then into the evolution of the modern meal, started with a simple question: "Why?" I first began to interrogate my eating habits as a teenager: Why do I always eat cereal in the morning? Why do we say grace at dinner but not at lunch or breakfast? Why do we condemn, or at least scorn, snacking? Of course, the question of why is as much a question of why not. When it comes to the morning meal, why do people choose toast and coffee or biscuits, bacon, and eggs? Why not fries and a hamburger? Or a salad, nachos, mashed potatoes, fish chowder, stir fried broccoli, marinated tofu, or a slice of lemon meringue pie? The more I thought about why we eat as we do, the more I realized how difficult finding the answers would be. They are not spelled out in nutrition texts, explained in cooking manuals, or revealed in advertisements. Nor are they to be found in food-industry trade journals (though here one can garner some clues). Instead, they lie deeply embedded in popular assumptions about what is normal, good, fashionable, healthy, and American. Perhaps no other aspect of our lives is as saturated with popular assumptions as the way we eat. When it comes to meals, our habits have become so deeply engrained that we hardly wonder why we adhere to them. As writing this book has taught me, though, there are reasons.

A certain logic dictates why we eat three meals a day, not two or four; why table manners are standard at dinner when hardly any social rules apply to breakfast; why we consume orange juice in the morning and sandwiches at lunch; why people snack on peanuts at circuses and hot dogs at baseball parks. There are even reasons for garnishing casseroles with potato chips and calling TV dinners "TV dinners," even though manufacturers did not originally intend for consumers to eat them in front of a TV. This book is about those reasons.

Most of us think we know why we eat the way we do. We weigh taste against nutrition and nutrition against price, and we make thoughtful decisions about not only what we put into our bodies but also how much, how frequently, and in whose company. In fact, we make many more food-related decisions than we think we do—approximately two hundred every day—and most of them are not deliberate; we simply make them on autopilot. It turns out that environmental factors like the color of a room, the aroma wafting from a kitchen, the wording on a menu, the size of a snack-food package, the depth of a mug, and the radius of a plate all influence the way we eat, whether we realize it or not. But although conscious choice plays a role in shaping how we eat, and environmental influences do so all the more, another factor has a surprisingly powerful effect on our food habits: the past.[1]

More than mere sources of nourishment, our meals are gifts from our ancestors and the cultures in which they lived. We have, to a large extent, inherited the way we eat. Take breakfast, for example. When we pour milk into a bowl heaped with rice puffs or bran flakes, we probably don't realize that this morning meal has a lot to do with nineteenth-century religious health reforms and the belief that a grain-based breakfast was the biblically sanctioned solution to a national case of indigestion. Lunch and dinner are also living artifacts that say as much about the cultures and ideals of the eras in which they were born as they do about our modern lives today.

We may come together as family over a hot meal in the evening to catch up on the day's events because we like to, but we also do this because the past prescribes it. When the Industrial Revolution upended the agricultural work schedules of countless farmers-turned-factory workers in the mid-nineteenth century and made it unfeasible for them to eat their main meal in the middle of the day, dinner shifted to the evening. Until then, dinner had not been a particularly social affair. Though food was generally consumed in the presence of family, talking was minimal, as was concern for table manners. But once evening became the only significant portion of the workday when siblings and parents could reconnect, dinner became special, and it still is.

Lunch—the sandwiches we slap together and throw into a brown paper bag or the soup we ladle into cardboard containers and balance on cafeteria trays—is a relic of the same shift: these quick, simple staples came to the rescue when the noontime feed assumed its new identity as an away-from-home routine. Cold staples that do not require utensils and no-frill, low-cost prepared foods at quick-service venues gained popularity largely for reasons of practicality. They were practical then, and they remain practical now.

In recent years, Americans have become obsessed with food like never before. Though we spend far less time cooking than previous generations, we spend more time reading, talking, and watching shows about food. Authors, journalists, bloggers—all have taken to writing about it with relish, and even historians have begun tackling this fascinating aspect of American life. But so far, no one has written the story of what brought various foods together three times a day, seven days a week, to become something more than nourishment—a meal, and in particular, the American meal.

Like pasta, pork, and pinot noir, the American meal has a history. The everyday conventions that define breakfast, lunch, and dinner have evolved over time and been shaped by characters from all walks of life. Men and women from industrialists to slaves, from inventors, entrepreneurs, and scientists to reformers, poets, and politicians—even quacks—have left their mark on the American meal. Of course no single person is responsible for a cultural habit as far-reaching and complex as dinner, and historical circumstances such as weather, wars, and economic slides have certainly played their part. Still, more than anything else, people have shaped the meal as we know it. Their discoveries have broadened our palates, their voices have swayed our decisions, and their products have showed up on our plates.

Their products have also appeared in our pantries, backpacks, and freezers—the places we raid when, between meals, we suddenly desire something crispy and salty or creamy and sweet. Individuals' morals, ideas, politics, and pocketbooks, it turns out, have also shaped snacking, which is an important part of American history because it speaks to Americans' inventiveness, quick pace of life, entrepreneurial spirit, fondness for childhood, and stubborn sense of freedom. Snacking reveals so much about American culture that it deserves its own book— or so I thought until I tried to write it. To tell the full story, we must place the snack within the context of the meal, and of course the story of the meal would be incomplete if we didn't also shine a spotlight on the snack. This is because the meal and the snack are merely two sides of the same coin.

The modern snack and the modern meal arose from the same circumstances. They emerged out of the tumult that was life during the Industrial Revolution, and ever since then, tension has marked their relationship. Prior to the Industrial Revolution, most peoples' meals were informal, haphazard, practical affairs, and if someone swallowed a slice of pie between them, no one raised an eyebrow. But when meals—especially dinner—became more social, more mannerly, and more rigidly defined, snacking became transgressive. For a child, a pastry from the cake shop after school was no longer an innocent treat but an offense to all that dinner had come to represent: family, home, and middle-class propriety. Rules about snacking reinforced the sacredness of the meal, and the sacredness of the meal further sanctioned rules against snacking.

Although social rules about eating are more relaxed today, personal decisions about whether and with what to satiate the stomach's mid-morning or late-evening grumbles remain fraught. To snack or not to snack; to unwrap the candy bar and snatch a gratifying, chocolaty bite or to wait out the irksome craving in hopes that it will pass quickly. When we ponder such a dilemma, countless shoulds and shouldn'ts related to health, weight, moral strength, reputation, and the importance of eating proper meals rear their ugly heads. (I can still hear my grandmother scolding, "You'll ruin your appetite!" whenever I'm tempted to indulge between meals.) Some have attempted to shirk these stuffy parameters altogether adapting unconventional approaches to eating such as "grazing," a continual snacking throughout the day that some consider preferable for digestion and metabolism. Such an approach frees the eater from a tyranny of outdated dietary strictures—or so it would seem. In reality, grazing adheres to a different set of rules, but a set of rules all the same. Whichever direction one takes—to snack, not to snack, or simply to moderate between-meal consumption—it is impossible to escape fully the eating injunctions the Victorians prescribed.

If nineteenth-century eating injunctions still color our relationship with snacking, they do so all the more with regard to dinner, especially as we watch this cherished cultural invention enter into a state of decline. Twenty-first-century Americans worry about the deterioration of family meals, and some feel guilty about their failure to reverse this trend in their own homes. Local and national newspapers frequently print articles with headlines like "Families Dine Together Less Often," "Giving Up on Family Dinner," and "The Pangs of Family Mealtime Guilt." Mealtime has been set on a pedestal as the ultimate occasion for parenting, one that, once missed, we cannot replace. And because the idea of cooking has so imbued our notions of mothering, we often perceive alternatives to the family dinner as neglect. Headlines like those above may give the impression that we are losing our grip on a tradition that has served as a harbor and leaven for our values, but the pages of this book will remind readers that the family dinner as we think of it is relatively new—only about 150 years old. The ritual of coming together around a table in the evening is not a natural phenomenon; it is a social construction.

For as long as family dinner has been around, it has thrived as a myth as much as (if not more than) a reality. Depictions of family meals in literature, film, art, advertisements, magazines, sitcoms, and television commercials present (or critique) a Victorian ideal, one that we all too often confuse with the real. Although many families do gather regularly to eat, many do not. And for those families that would, numerous obstacles can all too easily block the way—work schedules, commutes, sports matches, play rehearsals, business trips, and dates. In other cases, family dinner is subverted by social friction, interrupted by texts and phone calls, or diluted by the distraction of a television. Given that dinner is a social construction and our lifestyles are changing and becoming more frenetic, surely we can and will adapt, as we've always done in the past. So what's the big deal?

Here's the big deal: statistics pointing to dwindling participation in family meals also reveal an alarming rise in snack consumption. Obesity rates are increasing faster than ever, and the connection between obesity and the unraveling of meal patterns becomes more compelling every year. Initiatives such as the grassroots Family Dinner Project and First Lady Michelle Obama's Let's Move bring national attention to these trends and beg us to ask some fundamental questions about the role of the meal in society—its health benefits, its educational value, and its function in family life. Perhaps the family meal is worth saving, even if it is only a cultural heirloom, not an ordinance of nature. And if we are going to save it, why not revise and improve it?

Certainly, we are not the first to ask this question. American culture makers have debated the meal for years. Their voices echo throughout this book, offering a channel into the past as well as an instructive perspective on the present. They amuse, provoke, enlighten, and critique. And for the visionary who cares about the American meal and perhaps even wants a hand in determining its course, these voices offer a compass with which to navigate the future.

French gastronome Jean Anthelme Brillat-Savarin famously argued that we are what we eat. This book contends that we are also how we eat. Not only do the foods with which we satiate our appetites reveal secrets about our identities, but so do the forms into which we shape those foods, the order in which we consume them, the places where we sit down to partake of them (if we sit down at all), and the people we surround ourselves with when we enjoy them. Whether we cook or order takeout, install ourselves at a table or plop down in front of the television, join with others for a formal meal or grab a snack to chomp on in the car speaks to the deep, often tacit relationships we have with our families, our sustenance, our society, and ourselves. Of course this connection between how we eat and who we are is nothing new. When European colonists first encountered the tribal peoples of North America, how natives ate became central to European notions of who natives were. The American meal began to take shape in the heat of this cultural collision.

1

WHY COLONIAL MEALS
WERE MESSY

ON A COLD, biting day in the winter of 1704, the Reverend John Williams of Deerfield, Massachusetts, trekked forty-five miles through the snow on a foot journey from his hometown to Québec three hundred miles north. During this arduous hike, he had nothing to eat but a slab of frozen meat, which he kept in his pocket and gnawed on throughout the day. Though food, this was far from a meal, and Williams would have preferred to stop, build a fire, and enjoy the pleasure of a proper dinner at the usual dinnertime—in the middle of the day. "From break of dawn till dark, [we] never so much as sat down at noon to eat warm victuals," he complained. But stopping to prepare a meal was simply out of the question because this journey was not voluntary.[1]

Mohawk Indians had taken Williams captive during the infamous Deerfield Raid organized by the French as part of Queen Anne's War. During his ordeal, he had no choice but to eat in the manner of his captors and to make do without his usual English fare. Subsisting on groundnuts, roots, cranberries, and the occasional ration of dried moose flesh, he pined for Deerfield's customary staples. "For three weeks," he lamented, "I [ate] no bread." For at least three weeks he also had to forego the comfort of regular meals. These were import-ant to him, especially having hot food in the middle of the day, but the

1

foreign culture into which Williams had been plunged approached food in an altogether different—and, to the colonists, downright startling—fashion. As long as his fate rested in the hands of his captors, he had to live—and eat—by their rules.[2]

ENCOUNTERING THE TRIBAL PEOPLES of North America, European explorers and settlers found themselves forced to question an institution they had long taken for granted: the meal. "[They] have no such thing as set meals breakfast, dinner or supper," remarked explorer John Smith. Instead of eating at three distinct times every day, natives ate when their stomachs cued them, and instead of consuming carefully apportioned servings, they gleaned a little from the pot here and there. English colonists deplored this unstructured approach. They believed in eating according to rules and patterns—standards that separated them from the animal world. But when it came to structure, colonists were hardly in a position to boast. Though they believed in ordered eating, their meals were rather rough around the edges, lacking the kind of organization and form that typifies the modern meal today. Hardly well defined or clean-cut, colonial eating occasions were messy in more ways than one. Perhaps this partially explains why explorers and colonists were so quick to criticize native eating habits—in doing so, they hid the inconsistencies in their own.[3]

Colonists found Native American eating habits wanting because they judged them by the European standard. For Europeans, a meal combined contrasting components—usually cereals, vegetables, and animal protein. Heat offered an additional desirable contrast. Swedish traveler Peter Kalm noted that many "meals" consumed by the natives of the mid-Atlantic, where he traveled in the mid-eighteenth century, consisted simply of "[maple] sugar and bread." With only two ingredients and a distinct lack of protein, not to mention heat, this simplistic combination fell short of European criteria; it was more of a snack. Other typical nonmeals included traveling foods such as *nocake* (pulverized parched cornmeal to which natives added water on the go) and *pemmican* (a dense concoction of lean meat, fat, and sometimes dried berries). Hunters, warriors, and migrants relied on these foods, designed to be eaten in that particularly un-meal-like way in which John Williams ate his frozen meat on his journey to Québec: as the stomach required it and on the go.[4]

Jerked venison and fat, chewed as one traversed the wilderness, was not most colonists' idea of a proper meal, and if natives' lack of sufficient contrasting components and the absence of a formal eating schedule puzzled colonists, even more mystifying was natives' habit of going without meals, and often without any food at all, for extended periods. Jesuit missionary Christian LeClercq portrayed the Micmac of the Gaspé Peninsula in Canada as a slothful people, preserving and storing only a token winter's supply: "They are convinced that fifteen to twenty lumps of meat, or of fish dried or cured in the smoke, are more than enough to support them for the space of five to six months." LeClercq and many others did not realize that if natives went hungry, they did so not from neglect but by choice. Fasting was a subsistence strategy, and Native Americans were proud of it.[5]

Throughout the year, Native Americans prepared for times of dearth by honing their fasting skills. They practiced hunger as a kind of athletic exercise, conditioning their bodies for the hardships of hunting, war, and seasonal shortages. According to artist George Catlin, the Mandan males in what are now the Dakotas "studiously avoided . . . every kind of excess." An anthropologist among the Iroquois observed that they were "not great eaters" and "seldom gorged themselves." To discourage gluttony, they even threatened their children with a visit from Sago'dakwus, a mythical monster that would humiliate them if it caught them in the act of overeating.[6]

Native and European approaches to eating came to a head in the vice of gluttony. Many tribal peoples condemned overeating as a spiritual offense and a practice sure to weaken manly resolve and corrupt good character. Europeans also condemned it, largely for religious reasons, but more fundamentally because it represented a loss of control over the animal instincts. In the European worldview, overindulgence was precisely the opposite of civility, and the institution of the meal guarded against gluttony and a slippery descent into savagery. The meal gave order to and set boundaries around the act of eating, boundaries that Europeans felt native practices lacked. As explorers and colonists defended the tradition of the meal, the institution took on new meaning. For them, it became a subject of pride, serving as an emblem of civilization and a badge of European identity.[7]

Europeans viewed Native Americans largely as gluttons. Because whites caught only fleeting glimpses of the complex and continually shifting lives of Native Americans, they were liable to portray the native way of life according to a single cultural snapshot, which, when it came to food, was the posthunt feast. It was well known that natives ate much and frequently during times of abundance. John Smith recorded that when natives returned from the hunt with large quantities of bear, venison, and oil, they would "make way with their provision as quick as possible." For a short time, he explained, "they have plenty and do not spare eating." White witnesses popularized the image of just such moments of plenty as typical.[8]

Although Native Americans were hardly gluttons, Europeans, fascinated by the idea of a primitive people with a childlike lack of restraint, embraced the grossly inaccurate stereotype of the overeating Indian. William Wood portrayed the natives of southern New England as gorging themselves "till their bellies stand forth, ready to split with fullness." A decidedly strange Anglo-American amusement involved watching Native Americans relish a meal. "Why," asked George Catlin, "[is it] that hundreds of white folks will flock and crowd round a table to see an Indian eat?" With a hint of disappointment, William Wood recorded the appetites of tribespeople invited to an English house to dine as "very moderate." Wood was uncertain whether to interpret this reserve as politeness or timidity, but clearly he and his fellow English spectators had not expected shy and tempered eaters.[9]

One culture's perception of another often says more about the perceiver than the perceived. Although settlers lambasted natives for gluttony, whites may have been the real gluttons. According to more than one observer, many a native blushed at Europeans' bottomless stomachs. "The large appetites of white men who visited them were often a matter of surprise to the Indians who entertained them," wrote a nineteenth-century folklorist among the Iroquois. Early anthropologist Lewis Morgan concluded that natives required only about one-fifth of what white men consumed, and he was skeptical of his own ability to survive on such a paucity of provisions.[10]

Through their criticisms, exaggerations, and stereotypes, colonists distanced themselves from a population whose ways appeared savage and unenlightened, and the organized meal provided a touchstone in this clash of cultures. It became a yardstick by which Europeans measured culture and a weapon by which they defended their definition of it. They had long known what a meal was, but now, by contrast, they knew firsthand what it was not. Encountering the perceived meal-less-ness of the natives brought the colonists' esteemed tradition into question and gave them an opportunity to confirm their commitment to their conventions. They refused to approve of, let alone adapt to, the loose food-ways of Native Americans and instead embraced all the more heartily a structured, meal-centered European approach to eating.

WHEN THEY APPLIED the European concept of the meal to the apparently haphazard eating habits of Native Americans as a measure of civilization, explorers and colonists set a standard they themselves could hardly live up to. Although Native Americans failed to organize their consumption of food according to the European tradition of meals, the meals that most colonists enjoyed were much less methodical than their rhetoric implied. For all the emphasis on civility, colonists' daily eating routines were hardly a picture of propriety. Their habits were not clean-cut, and their meals hardly reached the twin benchmarks of structure and regularity. Eating in seventeenth- and early-eighteenth-century America was a precarious, imbalanced, and surprisingly rustic affair, in this sense, colonial meals were messy. They were also messy by today's standards, as they were consumed quite primitively. The humble dinner of a rural Maryland ferryman and his family supplies a compelling case in point.

When distinguished Annapolis physician Alexander Hamilton reached the Susquehanna River on a journey to New England in 1744, the ferryman, whom he found having dinner at home with his family, invited him to share their sustenance. The meal consisted of "a homely dish of fish without any kind of sauce." Despite his hunger, Hamilton declined to partake. "They desired me to eat, but I told them I had no stomach." The meal's presentation and the manner of its consumption probably had something to do with Hamilton's sudden lack of appetite. "They had no cloth upon the table, and their mess was in a dirty, deep, wooden dish which they evacuated with their hands, cramming down skins, scales, and all. They used neither knife, fork, spoon, plate, or napkin because, I suppose, they had none to use." The scene was crude but, at the same time, curiously quaint. Hamilton might have condemned the inelegant habits of these coarse country folk, but he chose instead to idealize them. "I looked upon this as a picture of that primitive simplicity practiced by our forefathers." By recording the details of the scene, he preserved it as a relic revealing what a typical slice of colonial American life might have looked like a century earlier.[11]

Until the mid-nineteenth century—and for some, well beyond— most Americans' meals were not what we would think of as meals today. Instead of family gatherings around food-laden tables at usual times of day, meals were generally informal, variable, and socially unimportant affairs. Americans during this time ate frequently and irregularly, with little concern for mealtime conventions or social decorum. Eating had often been a casual, ad hoc, and untidy nonevent that made little use of tables and chairs, required no utensils, and bore few if any social expectations. This approach to food lasted well into the nineteenth century in some households. Booker T. Washington, who grew up a slave in Virginia in the 1850s and 1860s, recalled that his family supped without the benefit of utensils or table, balancing tin plates on their knees or eating directly from the skillet or pot. "I cannot remember a single instance during my childhood," he wrote, "when our family entire sat down at the table together and . . . ate a meal in a civilized manner."[12]

During the colonial era and even, to a certain extent, into the nineteenth century, meals were not only rustic but unbalanced. As the central and by far most important meal, dinner set the course for the day. Taken hot around noon, it was both the main meal and, in a sense, the only one. The others, breakfast and supper, were frequently spontaneous and often monotonous, typically relying on standbys such as pie, toast, cheese, mush, or any meat or fish remaining from dinner the day before. This recycling of meals remained typical for generations. Lyndon Freeman of Sturbridge, Massachusetts, customarily ate meat and sauce left over from dinner as "hash-up for breakfast the next morning." On the day of the grisly 1892 Lizzie Borden murders in Fall River, Massachusetts, the family breakfasted on mutton soup and cold mutton left over from (at least) the day before.[13]

Breakfast and supper featured fare whose main function was to keep the stomach satisfied until the next decent filling—to bridge the gap from dinner one day to dinner the next. Often the morning and evening meals were merely glorified snacks, especially as they were frequently taken cold. This interchangeability stemmed from preindustrial Americans' informal approach to eating and their generally pragmatic view of food. For most, food was fuel, and eating was less about enjoying the pleasures of the palate or family fellowship than replenishing work-weary bodies and fitting them for the next round of arduous chores. Whether the refueling took place in company or alone, with or without regard for etiquette, using utensils or fingers, at a regular time or spontaneously, seated at a table or leaning against a wall, what mattered most was that it took place. Food meant survival; it was energy and sustenance, and obtaining one's fill was serious business. No surprisingly, the shape and social trappings of the meal meant comparably little.[14]

PRIOR TO THE VICTORIAN ERA, the everyday meal in America was fluid. The line between a meal and a snack was blurred, as neither form of eating could be pinned down and definitively distinguished from the other. Eating occasions in the preindustrial era evaded categorization for the simple reason that life itself was less categorized, boxed, and delineated. The informality and spontaneity with which Americans approached eating conformed to and accommodated an organic, preindustrial, agricultural existence.

Most colonists farmed and inhabited a world shaped by seasonal rhythms. Late summer was a time for "putting up" the crop: drying fruit, preserving berries, and pickling vegetables. Butchering came in late fall when daytime temperatures hovered around freezing and fresh meat could be safely salted, smoked, dried, submerged in barrels of brine, or ground into sausage. Mending, candle dipping, and maintenance activities were saved for the winter, and with spring came the time for plowing, cleaning, planting, and calving. Just as the season had its wheel of activities, so did the weeks and days. Typically, Monday was wash day, Tuesday ironing day, Saturday baking day, and Sunday the Sabbath—with a cleaning day and a market day somewhere in between. Whether it was washing day or baking day, there were cows to milk (in both the morning and the evening), milk to strain and set for cheese or churn into butter (while it was still fresh), fires to tend, wood to haul, ash to clear, infants to nurse, and, of course, food to cook.[15]

At the heart of this agricultural existence was the hearth, a cooking mechanism that turned out what might look to modern eyes like a lopsided parade of meals, but one that nonetheless complemented the organic rhythms of a life lived off the land. Since working the land meant early mornings in order to take advantage of the light, stomachs were ready for dinner by noon, and homemakers spent a good deal of the morning preparing the midday meal. With so much time and effort devoted to the midday meal, supper was necessarily smaller and frequently cold, as was breakfast the next morning.

Like their kin laboring in fields and barns, homemakers also coordinated their schedules with the sun. Cooking a hot meal over a hearth involved numerous tasks difficult to conduct by the limited brightness of candles or grease lamps. And since candles and lamp fuel were precious, it only made sense to wind down activities, including cooking, when (or well before) the sun dipped below the horizon. The rhythm of the day's meals reflected that of the day's work, and both mirrored the rhythms of the sun.[16]

Although colonists of various regions and backgrounds relied on the hearth, not all hearths were the same. Early New England and southern examples featured an oven tucked into the back wall accessed by stepping into the interior of the hearth. In the late eighteenth century, the oven migrated to the front, which was safer and more convenient and shored up extra cooking space. German settlers in Pennsylvania were known for their raised hearths, designed to contain ceramic stew pots for the slow cooking of soups, stocks, and broths. Visitors to Dutch homes in the Hudson River Valley took note of the "hung," or jamb-less, fireplaces, which, rather than being recessed, were simply flush with the back of the room and had a remarkably open feel. "It looked as though they made a fire against the wall itself," remarked Swedish traveler Peter Kalm while passing through the Albany region in 1748. Spanish colonists introduced *hornos*, large adobe bake ovens, to the Southwest, and in the mid-Atlantic and the South, outdoor ovens and bake houses were not uncommon.[17]

On southern plantations, "big house" kitchens sported enormous, state-of-the-art hearths up to ten feet wide and usually located in detached, two-story structures sometimes connected to the plantation house by a covered walkway. The separation of the kitchen from the main residence served a dual purpose: it kept the mess and odor of cooking far from the master and mistress's space, and in warm weather it protected that space from stifling bursts of heat. More importantly, it demarcated social boundaries, reinforcing the hierarchy of the plantation. Not just architecture but gastronomy reinforced these boundaries: in the big house kitchen, the cook typically prepared two sets of dishes, one for the master's family and guests and one for the field hands and house slaves, who spent their days tending tobacco and laundering clothes. The spacious, well-outfitted hearths that typified plantation kitchens were designed specifically to accommodate such a task. At night, the cook and other slaves climbed up to the loft where they slept on straw mats with wool blankets.[18]

Whether in a big house kitchen or a New England hall, the process of preparing food over hot embers required a host of specialized skills. It started with building a fire, a task undertaken early in the morning and which more than one nineteenth-century commentator described as an "architectural" achievement. Usually, the homemaker kindled the morning fire from the banked remains of the previous night's blaze, but if that blaze had gone out completely, a child could be sent to a neighbor's house with some tongs to retrieve a live coal. Less preferably, she could strike an iron against sharp flint and, aiming the resulting stream of sparks into a tinderbox, set some flax strands or an old rag to smoldering. The smoldering rag or flax strands could then be applied to a candle wick, which in turn, once ignited, was used to light the small twigs that served as kindling for the new kitchen fire. Because such a task required considerable skill and often some additional luck, colonial cooks invested much effort in keeping the hearth fire burning.[19]

Managing a hearth required a nuanced understanding of the different kinds of fires necessary for preparing various types of dishes. As part of her skill set, the cook needed to master the construction of a "tender" fire for some dishes, a "clear" fire for others, and "moderate," "solid," "quick," "slow," "brisk," or "soaking" fires for yet others. Early nineteenth-century directions for roasting a suckling pig called for contrasting temperatures for the spitted carcass: "The ends must have more fire than the middle." One cookbook author likened the art of hearth cooking to a scientific profession: "A cook must be as particular to proportion her fire to the business she has to do as a chemist." After achieving the right kind of fire, the cook regulated it attentively. "Care should be taken that the fire do not slacken," warned the author of an 1808 recipe for boiling a leg of salt pork. She also had to guard against singeing the hem of a sleeve or skirt or inadvertently bumping a kettle or knocking over a pot, as the contents could be scalding.[20]

Although a blazing fire had its uses, cooks often preferred down-hearth cooking, which required less wood and gave the cook more temperature control. About forty minutes after starting a fire, cooks shoveled cinders into small piles on the brick, stone, or packed dirt that formed the hearth floor. These glowing beds of charcoals served as burners on which were placed footed skillets, called "spiders," as well as pots set on trivets. Cooks could augment temperatures using different types of wood, manipulating air flow, and lowering the position of hanging pots and kettles on the trammel, a notched rod suspended from a lug pole or an iron crane, which could be swung away from or closer to the flames.[21]

Not only did boiling, simmering, and frying take place at the hearth over the embers, but so did baking. In fact, baking sometimes also took place directly in the embers. Corn breads and root vegetables were common candidates for this method, which, thanks to an ad hoc oak-leaf wrap or a liberal dusting of cornmeal, often emerged from the cinders surprisingly clean. Alternatively, cooks could mat dough on a plank, or bannock board, and prop it near the fire to catch the heat. Thomas Hazard of Rhode Island reminisced about his mother's "fire-cakes" prepared in this fashion: the cake paste was "spread on a smooth piece of board, and set up with a flat iron before the blaze, browned on one side, and then turned over to be browned on the other." Flipping the paste, he noted, required some "sleight of hand." The Dutch oven, the most common down-hearth cooking implement in early America, used hot coals on the brick or stone apron jutting out from the fireplace and demanded less dexterity. Nestled in a bed of embers with hot charcoals blanketing the top, this squat, three-footed, cast-iron pot with a flat, heavy lid that curved slightly upward along the edge turned out stewed meat, steamed puddings, baked beans, and faithfully biscuits, corn cakes, and pies between baking days when the bricks of the beehive oven remained cold.[22]

The cook fired up the beehive oven, a domed enclosure tucked into the hearth (later, built into its front side), only once a week—and for good reason: it was a burdensome contrivance to operate. To begin with, the cook constructed a fire directly in the clay or brick enclosure and let it burn for about two hours. To measure the relative temperature, she might throw in a handful of flour and observe the speed with which it turned brown or submit her own arm to the heat and test how long she could hold it there. "If you cannot hold your hand in longer than to count to twenty moderately," advised Catharine Beecher, "it is hot enough." If one could count to thirty, she explained, the heat was not yet sufficient. After achieving the correct temperature, the cook raked out what remained of the fire and entrusted a succession of breads, pies, and pots of beans (ordered according to the temperatures they required) to the chamber. A cook with a small household conducted this routine once a week, but if she had more than a few mouths to feed, she would repeat the process up to three times on the same day or, alternatively, hold a second baking day in the middle of the week. With all the trouble required to heat the oven, baking-day dinners were not surprisingly simple and light, but a fresh pie compensated for the scaled-down meal nicely.[23]

Cooking in the colonial era was laborious and could also be painstakingly slow, though homemakers accepted this as part of life. Combined with the tasks of food preservation, it probably occupied more of an early American housewife's time than any of her other chores. Reconstituting dried and salted goods, which comprised a large percentage of winter fare, also took significant time. An 1808 recipe for dried fish requires the cook, once she has prepared the fire, to "hang" the fish in a pot of scalding water for "six hours followed by another hour in fresh water." "To be in perfection," wrote Miss Lee in her instructions for roasting a suckling pig, "it should be killed in the morning to be eaten at dinner." With such effort and so many hours involved in the hearth-cooking process, homemakers prepared considerable amounts of food at a time, resulting in a sizeable noontime meal that they could recycle into smaller meals in the evening and then the next morning. Like tending the land, which required care and generous amounts of time to produce crops in season, tending the hearth required patience and skill. In its way, it produced a rich harvest.[24]

IF THE DAILY unfolding of meals in early America seems lopsided, with a heavy dinner in the middle of the day and lesser, colder feeds in the morning and evening, the physical scaffolding of the meal was frequently crude and make-do. In his description of the ferryman's dinner, Alexander Hamilton failed to note many of the material details of the dinner, and these gaps may be telling. There is no mention, for instance, of the family's table or chairs. The partakers may have been seated around a board, but because of their humble circumstances, we cannot safely make this assumption. Dinner in the colonial era did not always involve sitting down. In some households, children were expected to stand. Women sometimes ate on their own after they had fed their kin. Only about a third of families in seventeenth-century Virginia had chairs or benches, and only one in seven had both. Most individuals scraped by at mealtimes by sitting on any furniture available. Visitors to a cabin on the western frontier "sat down on the bed, for chairs and stools there were none." Some eaters chose to lean or squat rather than to sit.[25]

In addition to doing without chairs, many early colonists ate their meals without the benefit of tables. No more than one in four seventeenth-century Virginia households featured this basic category of furniture. Early colonists typically put together makeshift tables by laying a board across two trestles. They also relied on other surfaces—a trunk, a chest, even the head of a cradle. Many simply did without the benefit of a surface altogether and held their bowls in hand, and when it came to preparing food, cooks simply chopped vegetables on a cutting board balanced on the lap. At his death in 1646, William Googe of Lynn, Massachusetts, left his wife and three children a one-room house containing two chairs. He also left them a stool, a chest, and a trunk. The children had probably eaten meals sitting on these or on wooden boxes common in colonial households. These items often went unrecorded in inventories because they were of so little value. Apparently, there was no table in Googe's household.[26]

Colonists not only subsisted with few or no chairs and tables but also frequently did without knives, forks, and plates, as Hamilton's account poignantly illustrates. Like the Maryland ferryman's family, early Americans would not have served meals on porcelain or even, for the most part, on pewter but rather in wooden bowls called trenchers, originally thick slices of stale, hardened bread. Although the gentry of medieval Europe collected trenchers in baskets after a meal to distribute as food to the poor, humbler folk would have eaten theirs sopped with gravy or sauce. By the end of the sixteenth century, it was custom to place a wooden platter beneath the bread, and eventually the platter assumed the bread's function. The earliest trenchers in America may have been made of bread, but wooden bowls—often mere blocks of poplar with shallow, hollowed-out depressions—would quickly have replaced them. Those households that could afford pewter plates were more likely to display them in open cabinets than to sully them with the juices of their midday meal.[27]

Hamilton did not record whether the ferryman and his family members each ate from a wooden bowl, but it would not have been out of place for the rustic elder and his wife to share one trencher and his children another. Eating with a trencher mate was standard until the late eighteenth century. Siblings paired off and took turns helping themselves not only from a mutual trencher but from a common wooden, leather, or ceramic drinking vessel as well. Some ceramic vessels sported two or more handles to ease the passing from one thirsty drinker to the next. Eaters were less likely to share spoons and knives, but if they did pass a utensil back and forth, standard etiquette called for the diner to wipe it with a napkin before handing it over. Knives were personal items, and colonists frequently carried their own; they used it, and not their host's, when eating in another's household. But utensils were not always part of the picture, as in the case of the ferryman and his wife. Bread, efficient at sopping up gravy and sauce, frequently sufficed in place of spoons, and fingers commonly substituted for knives, which, with their pointed tips, functioned less to cut food than to carry it to the mouth.[28]

Most colonists ate their dinners forkless. Forks did not appear in American households until the early eighteenth century, though a few seventeenth-century elites, including Governor John Winthrop, owned them as novelties and status symbols. Invented in Italy, forks were not popular among middling folk in England until at least the mid-sixteenth century. When they appeared, forks had two tines and functioned to secure food for the knife to cut. Soon the tines became a means to spear food and pick it up as well. Thanks to the fork, the knife no longer had to do double duty as a cutting implement and food transporter; as a result, its sharp tip gave way to a rounded edge. Anecdotal evidence suggests that a movement against the crude practice of picking one's teeth with the knife point after a meal also engendered this change. The newly rounded edge created additional space on the blade for sweeping food, spoon-like, to the mouth. Peas were shoveled with the flat of the knife, though some insisted on spiking them individually with fork tines, a practice an early-nineteenth-century commentator likened to "eat[ing] soup with a knitting needle." Although forks were common in middle-class American households by the early nineteenth century, many continued to rely on knives to do what we would use a fork for today. The French traveler Frances Trollope was astonished to witness that the generals, colonels, and majors traveling with her on a Mississippi steamboat in 1828 had the "frightful manner of feeding themselves with their knives, till the whole blade seemed to enter the mouth."[29]

Before the introduction of the fork, when fingers frequently served as a utensil, napkins played a central dinnertime role. Today they are largely peripheral and often only ceremonial; then, they could prove quite critical. The lack of napkins at the ferryman's dinner may have come as a bit of a surprise, but there are more ways than one to clean hands. Dipping them in a bowl of water or, if there were servants, having water poured over them was one option. Alternately, one could wipe fingers on the tablecloth—a communal napkin writ large—or on any number of personal garments. Erasmus's sixteenth-century warning against the temptation to "lick greasy fingers" and "wipe them on one's tunic" suggests that the practice was not uncommon in his day, and if napkins were absent from a meal a century later, the temptation to use such alternatives must have been formidable. When the fork appeared, some saw the new utensil as a way to save napkins. Others saw forks as entirely superfluous precisely because of the napkin: What was the necessity of having a fork when God gave us fingers to eat with and napkins for cleaning them? Or so the logic went. The debate would have had little meaning for the ferryman and his wife, who humbly supped without the benefit of either napkins or forks. In the absence of a tablecloth, personal handkerchiefs may have served as the couple's napkin alternative, and the meal would likely have ended with a thorough washing of hands and face.[30]

Perhaps the lack of scaffolding to support the kinds of mealtime customs most modern Americans are used to can help us better understand why early American eating was often rushed and notoriously unsocial. Alexander Hamilton did not comment on the sociality of the ferryman's dinner, but it is hard to imagine a family eating fish with their hands engaging in a nuanced conversation. Until the mid-nineteenth century, except among the elite, meals were less social affairs and more about the business of eating. Although diners may have eaten together and even spoken to each other, they likely remained focused on the task at hand: refueling. Perhaps the paucity of mealtime conversation in America stemmed from a fixation on the food, or perhaps it stemmed from a general sense of hurry, which nineteenth-century travelers would later comment on at length. "I had been some time in America before I was able to keep up to my neighbours in their rapidity of despatching [*sic*] their meals," remarked Scotsman John Duncan. When British major general James Edward Alexander dined at an inn in Nashville, Tennessee, he remarked that several gentlemen had eaten so fast that they rose from the table, wiping their mouths with their hands, before he had even taken his first bite. Although travel narratives may represent a class divide—upper-class diners commenting on the habits of middling and poorer folks—when it came to the dinner table, there is little evidence that average Americans took their time.[31]

Hamilton's encounter with the ferryman on the Susquehanna River illuminates a stark but fascinating contrast between his urban, sophisticated world and that of the rural poor inhabiting colonial villages and hamlets. It is telling that of all the differences between these two worlds, the doctor found eating customs the most intriguing. He might have commented on the family's rustic clothes, country accents, or provincial mannerisms, but he chose to record their approach to a meal, and his preference speaks to the meal's function as an important cultural marker. Although the contrast between the two worlds intersecting on the ferry that day in 1744 was poignant, perhaps even more poignant was their similarity. As foreign as these primitive eaters were to Hamilton, they presented a picture of his heritage, and thus, a distant reflection of himself.

ALEXANDER HAMILTON did not call what the ferryman and his family ate a dish or even a meal. He called it a "mess." This was no comment on aesthetics, though Hamilton's words would have fully qualified as such. In his day, "mess" simply meant "food." The term derives from the Latin *missum,* or "something sent," as in something sent to the table. Because anything at all could be sent to the table, be it appealing or unappetizing, the term came to connote ordinary or lowly fare and eventually even animal fodder. Later, "mess" came to mean "jumbled," just like the foods on most ordinary colonists' trenchers in the seventeenth and early eighteenth centuries. "Jumbled" would have also described many of the foods Native Americans stewed in earthen pots and served in wooden bowls. Colonists too were known to eat in wooden bowls, but as it turns out, they had something else in common with the aboriginals: their "messy" way of eating.[32]

If one kind of "mess" typified colonial eating in the first century of European settlement, it was pottage. When Edward Winslow of Mayflower fame visited the ailing Wampanoag sachem Massasoit, the native chief asked the Englishman to hunt some fowl and make him an "English pottage." Massasoit had tasted English fare during earlier visits to the Plymouth settlers, and apparently he liked it. The fact that he sent Winslow hunting speaks to the kind of pottage he had in mind. But Winslow knew that Massasoit, in his sickly condition, would not be able to stomach meat, so he had a tribal woman "bruise" some corn while he foraged for herbs. Winslow boiled the cornmeal with strawberry leaves and sassafras root, the only suitable wild plants he could find in the Massachusetts forest in early spring. He strained the broth through his handkerchief and fed it to the chief. The concoction proved restorative, and before long Massasoit had fully regained his health, though not without a setback from overindulging in a second pottage that Winslow made from a fatty duck.[33]

Seventeenth-century English settlers brought with them a predilection for pottage. The word "pottage" derives from the French *potage*, meaning "made in a pot"; in England, it would have consisted of boiled meat and grain with the addition of herbs or vegetables for flavor. A simpler pottage might have had little or no meat, consisting merely of stewed grains, not unlike oatmeal. "Frumenty" was a kind of sweetened gruel made from wheat. The simplest pottage of all was merely broth or milk poured over pieces of stale bread.[34]

Gervase Markham's 1615 cookbook, *The English Housewife*, offers a recipe for pottage under the title "Of Boiled Meats Ordinary"; it calls for mutton, oatmeal, and greens: "Take a leg of mutton cut into pieces. . . . Put into a clean pot with fair water and set on the fire. . . . [Add] strawberry leaves, spinach, scallions, a little parsley, oatmeal well beaten. . . . Let it boil with a quick fire . . . then season with salt and serve either with sippets or without." Sippets were decorative slices of fried bread or toast—a relative of sops, pieces of bread soaked in soup or stew. Markham's pottage may have constituted the entire meal: it had the necessary contrasting elements of protein, starch, and vegetables, though it is questionable whether seventeenth-century Americans would have considered vegetables necessary to a complete meal.[35]

In the colonies, recipes in British cookbooks would have required ad hoc adjustments on the part of transplanted English cooks, who could not procure in North America all the ingredients Markham and other British cookbook authors called for. These cookbooks also left voids that colonial cooks needed to fill because the authors did not provide recipes for such abundant North American staples as corn and squash. Edward Winslow displayed New World culinary ingenuity when, in lieu of oatmeal or another familiar Old World grain, he added ground cornmeal, a Native American staple, to Massasoit's dish. Not until the 1796 appearance of Amelia Simmons's *American Cookery*, the first printed American cookbook, did colonists have access to published recipes for the "pompion," or pumpkin, which seventeenth-century observer John Josselyn called an "ancient New England Standing Dish." Because pumpkins have a consistency similar to apples, cooks often put them to use in traditional apple dishes such as pies or sauces. Swedish explorer Peter Kalm enjoyed them mashed with milk "in about the same way we do turnips." In the New World, colonists simply applied their knowledge of one food to the next, and cookbooks were unnecessary when it came to the art of substitution, though they would in time codify that art and, in doing so, help legitimize an emerging American cuisine.[36]

With numerous English foodstuffs unavailable in the colonies, squash and root vegetables filled in many gaps. Although life was precarious, it would have been even more so without an abundance of pumpkins. Lifesavers when other supplies were low, they proved, not surprisingly, monotonous. Eighteenth-century Moravian missionaries on the Indiana frontier lived for a time largely on pumpkin. They boiled it, mixed it with cornmeal, and baked it. Englishman Jonathan Carver noted that colonists used pumpkin "partly as a substitute for bread." New Englanders also relied heavily on pumpkins when more desirable staples were scarce. An anonymous seventeenth-century poem relays a sense of what it was like to live on the orange gourd—both the dreary prospect of endless servings as well as a sense of relief for a needed appetite appeaser: "We have pumpkins at morning and pumpkins at noon; / If it were not for pumpkins we should be undone."[37]

Vegetables played two roles in the early American diet: they served either as a garnish and appeared on the periphery of the meal or as a substitute for another food and constituted the core of the meal. For the Moravian missionaries in Indiana, pumpkins functioned as a stomach filler, occupying the center of the meal in place of more traditional staples, such as meat or grain. When not driven to rely on vegetables as a kind of ballast, colonists relegated what they grew in their gardens to the margins of their eating, employing vegetables primarily as a flavoring to add interest to an otherwise bland or unvarying meal. Equally as important, vegetables offered welcome medicinal qualities. Prolonged consumption of meat without accompanying vegetables inevitably led to illness, scurvy in particular, though early Americans did not know precisely why. They did know that a little onion or leek cast into a stew or broth kept illness at bay.[38]

The various herbs and greens that Gervase Markham called for in his recipe for pottage—including strawberry leaves, which show up in the cornmeal concoction Edward Winslow prepared for Massasoit—functioned as a garnish, lending a meal flavor and basic protective qualities. They represented few calories, though their nutritional contribution was more than negligible. In early colonial America, most vegetables were consumed as "green sauce"; that is, they were harvested fresh, added to stews and pottages, and boiled down to a pulpy, sauce-like consistency. Part of dinner, the sauce was a secondary element. If vegetables were the center of the meal, this was due to necessity, not fancy.[39]

Raw fruits and vegetables occupied perhaps the lowest rung in the hierarchy of colonial foodstuffs. Although medieval suspicions of these edibles as dangerous, even poisonous, may have lingered, seventeenth-century Americans overlooked raw fruits and vegetables mostly because they believed them to offer little or nothing to the human constitution. At the heart of this conviction was a widespread understanding at that time that good health was a fragile balance of humors. The body functioned best, according to this theory, when it maintained a proper harmony of moist, dry, warm, and cold elements, and the ideal physiological state was slightly warm and somewhat moist. Beef, considered mildly warm and moist, met the requirements perfectly. Vegetables and fruit did not. They fell on the cold end of the spectrum, posing a threat to the critical balance that determined well-being. Apples, cold in nature, were bad for the nerves when eaten raw, and lettuce was so cold and moist that it could extinguish lust. Cooking could neutralize the offending characteristics of less desirable foods, so when consumed, fruits and vegetables were customarily boiled in stews and puddings, baked in pies, or converted into condiments with the help of vinegar, sugar, or brine.[40]

There were other reasons for avoiding raw fruits and vegetables. These comestibles had at times been associated with poverty. In Europe, peasants ate onions both raw and cooked, and their breath bore witness. Certain fruits and vegetables caused flatulence or could be difficult to digest. Jerusalem artichokes, noted Virginian gardener John Randolph in 1764, caused "commotions in the belly." Raw fruits and vegetables were also associated with disease. Overindulging oneself when the berry crop ripened or peaches came into season could produce a laxative effect that, if not sufficiently regrettable in and of itself, mirrored the symptoms of a more serious malady, dysentery. These associations provided sufficient ground for wariness.[41]

It is hard to know whether colonists truly avoided fruits and vegetables as much as some historians have claimed, or whether these foods are relatively absent in early accounts because they played such an ordinary culinary role that they largely went unrecorded. Whatever the case, in the late eighteenth and early nineteenth centuries, more references to vegetables and fruit began to appear. Their general consumption likely increased during this time, but their more frequent mention in travel notes, memoirs, and cookbooks may also stem from the emergence of a more modern approach to food.[42]

The art of substitution was not merely a matter of apples and pumpkins; it also applied to meat. Although Markham's pottage recipe calls for mutton, colonists might have used game or salt pork. Mutton was not easy to come by in the early years of North American settlement. Sheep require open pasture and protection from predators, but neither was very feasible for early subsistence farmers, who carved their holdings out of woodland and had little time to devote to building proper fences. Besides, sheep's wool was often more in demand than sheep's meat. In the decade leading up to the Revolutionary War, when the colonies boycotted English imports and pledged to wear homespun in resistance to the Stamp Act, eating mutton was shunned, and some communities even outlawed killing a sheep for meat. Of course, settlers and their descendants did eat mutton, especially in the Southwest, where it was introduced in the 1800s, but in America it never became the staple that it had been in England.[43]

When it came to raising livestock in colonial America, pork fit the bill. Pigs accommodated the New World landscape as well as small farmers' lifestyles much better than sheep and game. Able to feed on nuts, underbrush, berries, and roots, pigs roamed about in the woodlands and required no pasture or fences. They could even fend for themselves against wild animals, including wolves and bears. As natural rooters and foragers, they helped till fields and clear forest for pasture. They provided the staple meat on the frontier and continued to do so even as it edged west. Following slaughter in the fall, cuts were salted, smoked, or pickled in brine, and the fullness of the proverbial pork barrel became the measure of a family's subsistence.[44]

A colonial pottage would more likely have featured pork than Markham's mutton, but most early American families did not have such robust pork barrels that they could make that meat the center of daily dinners. Most could not partake frequently of any meat for that matter. Flesh would have crowned the main meal of the day on special occasions, such as slaughtering time and the Sabbath; otherwise, at least in the seventeenth century, it was likely to serve more as a flavoring that offered a good dose of fat and a little token protein. The most common of these flavorings, salt pork, made from the side, belly, or fatback of a pig, was an early American staple. It had long been associated with sailors' fare because, like hardtack, it lasted for months, if not years, in a ship's hold. Its long shelf life and portability also made it a typical ration for soldiers during the Civil War.[45]

Markham's pottage called for "oatmeal well beaten," but traditional English grains were not available to early colonists, including oats as the English knew them. In the 1670s, John Josselyn noted that colonists boiled "naked oats," or silpee, a close relative of common oats that made a decent hot cereal as well as bread. New Hampshire settlers had their own silpee tradition, called "sowens," consisting of ground oats left to ferment in water and then boiled to a jelly. Although European oats were not initially prevalent in New England agriculture, they eventually became the third most widely planted grain in the region and grew abundantly in other regions. By the second half of the eighteenth century, the Middle Colonies were not only producing enough oats for their own needs but exporting the grain to other colonies and abroad. During the seventeenth century, however, the New World cousin of European oats would have to do.[46]

Wheat was so hard to come by that it remained nothing short of a luxury for many years in New England. Its scarcity on the frontier led to a tradition of consuming it only on Sabbaths, and in New Netherland rules prohibited bakers from selling white bread and cakes to Native Americans because the supply of wheat was limited. By the eighteenth century, wheat was making some inroads. In the 1730s, it was successfully cultivated in the Chesapeake, and around the same time, it began flourishing in the mid-Atlantic, which served as the breadbasket of the colonies before the closing decades of the eighteenth century. The Dutch recognized the wheat-growing capacity of what is now New York early on: "Our Netherlanders raise good wheat," wrote voyager David DeVries in 1642. He also noted healthy harvests of rye, barley, oats, and peas. But the scarcity of wheat in parts of the colonies for extended periods (due in large part to a persistent fungus known as wheat blast) set up the conditions for a variety of substitutes to take its place.[47]

When they ran out of grain, colonists often employed the humble pea. Stewed grain was common in Britain, sometimes eaten on its own like hot cereal and sometimes served as a base for meat in a more substantial meal. Regional and class differences determined which grains a person generally consumed: wheat, barley, or rye. Peas had been standing in for all these grains in less affluent English households for centuries. The dried legumes were typically ground into meal, which sometimes served as flour for bread. (When peas ran out, acorns and beans might take their place.) Perhaps more common than bread was pease porridge—the ground meal boiled into a pudding. "Pease porridge hot, pease porridge cold," from a famous medieval nursery rhyme, speaks to the seemingly endless round of the dull green gruel on which English peasants and later colonial subsistence farmers heavily relied.[48]

Despite the monotony it represented, pease porridge supplied a cheap, starchy, and filling protein that was ideal for North American winters not only because it was hot but because peas stored well when dried and could keep throughout the winter. Potatoes did not become popular garden crops in New England until the 1720s, and colonists did not start digging root cellars to store them—along with carrots, turnips, cabbages, and onions—until around the same time. Before the early- to mid-eighteenth century, peas were commonly the main, if not the only, "vegetable" available during the colder months. Pease porridge eventually morphed into baked beans when beans, which were native to North America, proved hardier than English pea plants. As far as a replacement for wheat, barley, oats, and rye, peas had done their job well, but they could not compete with a particular New World grain that proved to be a promising alternative.[49]

IF ONE SUBSTITUTION characterized settlers' New World foods more than any other, it was the replacement of wheat and other European grains with corn. The word "corn" was originally synonymous with "seed" or "grain." In Europe, "corn" had referred to the predominant local grain of a given area: oats in one place, rye in another. So when European settlers needed a name for the yellow kernels of maize that Native Americans relied on so heavily, they called it "Indian corn" or simply "Indian." According to this logic, corn pudding was reduced to "Indian pudding" and corn and rye bread to "rye and Indian." Although the colonists called maize "Indian corn" because Native Americans relied on that grain most, they might as well have called it "settlers' corn" because it quickly became the grain they counted on most heavily too, though at first they were none too proud of their alliance with this primitive native staple.[50]

One use of corn by the early colonists was in the making of a provision they simply could not live without: beer. Calorie dense and nutrient rich, this restorative beverage helped fuel the hard work of agriculture, blacksmithing, and carpentry—and eventually the establishment of a new nation. Colonists relied on beer for warmth in winter and refreshment in summer. It functioned as a kind of food but was also an effective thirst quencher. At a time when water was often contaminated and more likely than not to make a person sick, beer proved to be a safe form of hydration. It was so important as a potable source of hydration that in 1620 the so-called Pilgrims disembarked from the Mayflower in what became known as Plymouth instead of holding out for their original destination, the Hudson River. The reason, according to William Bradford, was that their barrels had run dangerously low: "We could not take time for further search or consideration, our victuals being much spent, especially our beer."[51]

By the time the Mayflower passengers decided to end their voyage in New England, other European settlers in the New World had already ventured into the realm of corn brews. Although the 1580s Roanoke Colony, or the "Lost Colony," off the coast of Virginia failed, Roanoke settlers' attempt to brew alcohol from maize did not. Thomas Harriot declared the result of their experiment "as good ale as was to be desired." A few decades later, the Jamestown colonists were innovatively crafting beer out of maize, even preferring the New World alternative to the barley-malted beverage they had brought with them from England. In 1662, John Winthrop Jr. described the maize-brewing process for readers back in England and defended beer made from corn as "very wholesome." In addition to corn kernels, cornstalks and corn bread, molasses, wild rice, pumpkins, Jerusalem artichokes, persimmons, green peas, potatoes, and maple syrup were all used for malt.[52]

Even though it made a decent beer, corn was controversial, and there was a strong bias against it from early on. In his late sixteenth-century history of plants, the English herbalist John Gerard maintained that maize offered little or no nourishment while proving difficult to digest: bread made from it, he observed, was hard and dry, and he warned that because it contained no bran, "it bindeth the belly." Such a staple, he concluded, was "a more convenient food for swine than for man"; indeed, it had been a major component in the slops farmers fed their hogs in England. Somewhere between the two categories of men and hogs, according to Gerard, fell "the barbarian Indians." They relied on corn simply because they "know no better." Primed by these notions, if not these precise words, colonists were predictably uncomfortable with the idea of eating like the tribal peoples they encountered, not to mention hogs, but if they wanted to survive, they had to swallow their pride. For the settlers, eating maize meant blurring the lines between themselves and those they saw as savages. Whether they wanted to or not, by consuming corn they were, in effect, going native.[53]

Despite corn's dubious reputation, colonists made liberal use of it, both as a substitute ingredient in English dishes and in the various Native American preparations they adopted and transformed. One historian has described settlers' diets as "colonial creole," an amalgamation of native and English culinary traditions. A particularly common "creole" corn-based dish was samp. Derived from the native *nasaump*, which Roger Williams called "a kind of meal pottage, unparched," samp consisted of hominy made from dried kernels that were soaked and, in the words of John Winthrop Jr., beaten to "the biggness of rice," then boiled till tender and served with milk or butter and perhaps sugar. Johnny cakes (likely once called "journey cakes") were large round breads baked on a board in front of the fire, not unlike Native American corn breads. Because they resembled oatcakes from the Scottish highlands, these were also called "Indian bannocks." "Rye and Injun," alternatively called "brown bread" (not to be confused with Boston brown bread, a sweeter, more pudding-like concoction developed in the nineteenth century), relied on both corn and rye and was the most common brick-oven-baked bread in New England for over a century.[54]

Ironically, one of the most ubiquitous and iconic colonial American foods was a corn-based dish that, although a modification of a traditional English dish, was not unlike a Native American staple. Pennsylvanians called the popular dish of porridge made from ground and boiled cornmeal "mush," New Netherlanders called it "suppawn," Louisianans called it "coush coush," and New Englanders called it "hasty pudding." Mush was a Native American staple, but English settlers chose to eat it in the British tradition as sweetened porridge rather than in the native tradition as the foundation for a savory, meat-and-vegetable stew. New Englanders called it hasty pudding as a euphemism for the English "stirabout" porridges of the same name made from ground oats or grated bread. John Josselyn articulated the resemblance between the two early on, explaining that colonists "boyl" the cornmeal "upon a gentle Fire till it be like a Hasty Pudden." Before long, the need to qualify the meal through comparison to its English counterpart faded away. By the eighteenth century, the boiled cornmeal was no longer like hasty pudding; it simply was hasty pudding.[55]

Cornmeal mush not only shared striking similarities with Native American food but also overlapped with African food. A nineteenth-century traveler in western Africa called "fufu," a millet preparation he encountered, "the common paste or hasty pudding." In South Carolina, this dish, which came to rely on cornmeal, was sometimes called "turn meal and flour"; eighteenth- and nineteenth-century enslaved Africans commonly ate it as a porridge or baked it into bread. Dinner for field hands often required cooking in the fields, and cornmeal fit the bill. It could be boiled into mush or made into flat breads known as "ashcakes" by placing the paste between oak or cabbage leaves and inserting them into the hot coals and ash of a campfire in the field. "Hoe cakes" were essentially the same, though presumably heated on the flat of a hoe. A working adult slave would have eaten nine or ten hoe cakes for a meal, sometimes with a little buttermilk, salt pork, or herring—often without. Poor southern whites also relied on ashcakes, though they typically topped them with butter.[56]

Despite cornmeal mush's associations with marginalized popula-
tions, the colonial- and federal-era ruling classes eventually favored
it, as evidenced by "Connecticut Wit" Joel Barlow's mock heroic 1796
poem, "The Hasty Pudding." By the time he penned this charming
lyric, Americans had not only accepted but come to celebrate corn.
Writing nostalgically of his homeland while serving as a diplomat in
France, Barlow commended the simple mixture of cornmeal and milk
as "a wholesome dish, and well deserving praise." The religious tone
with which he honored his favorite breakfast is both humorous and
telling. He called the porridge his "morning incense" and defended it
from those who would "stamp with disrepute / the luscious food, because it feeds the brute." Through references to its native origins and
an insistence on the regional New England name for the cornmeal
dish, Barlow rendered hasty pudding synonymous with American, and
in particular New England, identity. To this dish, his "pure hereditary
taste," he credited his father's brawn, his own robust health, and, by
extension, the vigor of the newly independent nation.[57]

Joel Barlow was not the first to celebrate cornmeal mush or to
frame it as a symbol of American identity. In 1766, Benjamin Franklin publicly defended the virtues of "Indian corn" and its many culinary forms, including hasty pudding, in the *London Gazetteer.* An angry
English gentleman had attacked the reputation of the American staple. In his pointed opinion, the New World grain failed to afford an
"agreeable, or easy digestible breakfast." He considered it so inferior
as to require copious draughts of strong black tea to accompany it
as a digestive aid. Without tea, colonists threatening to boycott the
English-imported brew would no longer be able to stomach their traditional corn-based foods, the Englishman predicted. Their breakfast
habits would surely disintegrate, and with them, their defiant political
resolve.[58]

Franklin begged to differ. He considered "Indian corn" most
pleasing, perhaps even the mainspring of Americans' strength, and
he voiced his opinion on the matter with strong words for his English adversary: "Pray let me, an American, inform the gentleman,
who seems ignorant of the matter, that Indian corn, take it for all in
all, is one of the most agreeable and wholesome grains in the world;
that its green leaves roasted are a delicacy beyond express; that samp,

hominy, succotash, and nokehock, made of it, are so many pleasing varieties; and that Johnny cake or hoecake, hot from the fire, is better than a Yorkshire muffin." By "Yorkshire muffin" Franklin meant what we would call an English muffin, the main difference between it and the "delicacies" that Franklin promoted being that an English muffin was made from wheat, a grain associated with the upper classes and seen for much of history as far superior to corn.[59]

As Franklin's amusingly earnest argument reveals, corn became an object of pride for those colonists who, in distancing themselves from British tyranny, sought new symbols, including culinary symbols, with which to express their emerging national identity. It represented the colonies because it was native to them, but it also expressed the republican simplicity idealized during this era. A republic necessarily depended on the virtue of its citizens to sacrifice their private interests for the public good. Luxury and self-indulgence became politicized as offenses against the state; by contrast, plainness became patriotic. Hardly any breakfast was plainer than milk and maize. Hardly any breakfast was more patriotic.[60]

When Franklin flamboyantly offered his sentiments about Indian corn and American independence, mush still had a promising career ahead of it. It would remain popular for generations, especially in rural areas and on the frontier. At the same time, it had become old-fashioned. Mush had begun to fall out of fashion when Franklin was writing because it was made of corn, which, although an ideologically important food, was less and less consequential as a wheat stand-in since wheat had finally met with success in colonial agriculture. Mush was also becoming old-fashioned because it was a pottage, a type of mess, and the "messy" approach to food that characterized early colonial meals was slowly but surely giving way to new, more modern ideas about eating.

2

THE BRITISH INVASION

FOR THE FIRST century or more of American history, colonists embraced a fluid, organic, and largely medieval way of eating. They favored one-pot dishes, followed a seemingly lopsided sequence of meals, focused more on food than the company with whom they shared it, and made do with the minimum when it came to the physical scaffolding of meals—utensils, plates, drinking vessels, tables, and chairs. For all their criticism of Native Americans' lack of structure when it came to food, European settlers' approach to eating was hardly less "messy."

But sometime in the eighteenth century, colonists began to change their way of eating. They started to embrace English gentility, which showed up in the expansion of kitchens and their wares, heavier reliance on certain cooking techniques such as roasting, adoption of the English afternoon tea ritual, and the eventual transformation of the teatime accompaniment, cake, into a breakfast staple. English gentility also revealed itself on the plate. Colonists' dinners featured more and more meat—as did their breakfasts—and instead of a one-pot meal, dinner increasingly became a harmony of individual foods. Meat distanced itself from vegetables, and vegetables became independent of starches. In this new context, vegetables outgrew the status of mere flavoring or garnish, and meat acquired a new role as the anchor of the meal. Although old-fashioned pottages did not entirely disappear, they gave way to a new food ideal that favored solid over liquid, form over fluidity, and order over chaos. The proverbial pot of "pease porridge hot" yielded to pudding and a roast. It was the birth of a new culinary paradigm.

WHEN SUSAN LESLEY penned her early reminiscences of life in Northampton, Massachusetts, in the 1820s and 1830s, she recalled her mother preparing dinner: "[There was] always a large joint, roasted or boiled, with plenty of vegetables and a few condiments . . . good bread and butter, and a plain pudding or pie." The food was abundant, as Lesley remembered it, and the homey aroma seemed to waft back to her even as she wrote. Such a meal was iconic of New England fare in the eighteenth and early nineteenth centuries. It represented a standard of living an arm and a leg above that of most in the seventeenth century and expressed new culinary sensibilities emerging not just in New England but in the colonies at large.[1]

Pottage fare had comprised a significant portion of early Americans' subsistence. Simple, economical, and filling, if plain, it was well suited to the conditions of the frontier. But it was also peasant fare. As colonists' crops and livestock expanded and their trade became more lucrative, they began to move away from pease porridge and its variations (though many common foods that persisted took their cues from the pottage theme, including baked beans, succotash, and cornmeal mush). Colonists were beginning to prefer foods that stood on their own, held their shape, and bore an individual identity. Pottage ceded some of its territory to puddings, moist, cake-like combinations of flour, milk, eggs, sugar, meat, suet, and fruit that were steamed or boiled in pudding cloths (though at times baked in a pastry). More significantly, pottage yielded ground to meat, which began to dominate dinner, appearing at the center of the meal and in its own capacity as an autonomous dish.

By the early- to mid-eighteenth century, meat had come into its own. No longer just a flavoring for the middling artisan or humble farmer, it had become the focal point of dinner. By the middle to end of the century, it was appearing independently, set apart from the vegetables and grains once combined with it to create a mixed dish. In her description of childhood dinners, Lesley listed the meat dish first;

it played the starring role. She listed vegetables second, as the supporting cast; they accompanied the roast, not the other way around.[2]

The eighteenth-century migration of meat from the edge to the center of the dinner plate stemmed from the more comfortable subsistence colonists had attained by that time, reflecting an increased, though still moderate, prosperity. But it also ensued as a result of that precarious engine of change we often forget existed in centuries past: fashion. For roughly the first century of American settlement, survival was priority number one for everyone except a small handful of elites, and how dinner tasted or was served mattered little. Clothing, fences, and roofs came first, along with calories. There was little room for fashion, culinary or otherwise. But when resources increased and life became less precarious, colonists could afford to consider style and taste. And they had deep and compelling cultural reasons to do so, reasons that had to do with their identity, with how they understood who they were.[3]

The initial colonial settlers were by and large English, and proud of it. We cannot underestimate their deep affiliation with (and affinity for) England. Many saw the New World as a place where Britishness could be perfected in a new, better England. Gentlemen hopefuls who could not inherit property in the Old World because of the land crunch could live out their landholding aspirations in the Chesapeake, where they might grow tobacco on expansive plantations and lead aristocratic lives. Puritans, persecuted for their protest of church corruption in England, could construct a utopian society featuring the best of English ideas and institutions while escaping the heavy hand of a flawed national religion. Perhaps their utopian society would even serve as a model for England, by which she could purify and renew her church. In setting out from England for North America, the colonists left behind constricting circumstances they hoped to exchange for more accommodating ones, but they had no intention of leaving behind their beloved British identity.

As time passed, the tie between colonists and their Old World origins naturally weakened, making the mother country seem farther and farther away, but that distance would soon shorten again. Perhaps this was the result of an identity crisis or more simply a natural expression of class as wealth expanded in the colonies and folks seeking to distinguish themselves looked to England for cues. Whatever the cause, at some point in the eighteenth century, the colonists contracted a veritable case of Anglophilia. Their cultural trajectory away from England reversed, and they began moving toward the homeland, even as it began moving toward them. British imports flooded into the New World as part of a consumer revolution that has also been called "the British invasion"; British styles, whether in dress or architecture, gained new prominence, and British ways became colonial ways, from tea drinking to parlor keeping. The colonial kitchen did not escape this re-anglicization. Thanks to the new trend toward larger and better-equipped kitchens, dinner was transformed from a coarse, unsophisticated pioneer endeavor into a more civilized, genteel, and British affair.[4]

Colonial kitchens expanded during the eighteenth century both in terms of space and implements. Finished lean-tos were often added to the backs of houses to create more room for food preparation (later replaced by ells); fireplaces became smaller and more efficient (thanks to the migration of the oven from the back to the side); and additional areas, including pantries and root cellars, increased preservation and storage capacity. In short, space became more specialized and opened up possibilities for new culinary choices, as did the array of English implements being imported into the colonies: large copper stew pots, wide-bottomed saucepans, and tin-coated tea kettles, to name a few. When one thinks of the cramped hall of an early one- or two-room frontier dwelling in which cooking space was shared with living, sleeping, and working quarters, it is no wonder that one-pot stews and pottages were the norm. Once colonists could spread out their cooking activities and add variety to their wares, their culinary options multiplied.[5]

In her memoir, Susan Lesley remembered meat not only generally as the center of her mother's ample dinners but specifically as boiled or roasted. Of course, there were other ways to prepare meat. Frying was common and the bane of countless travelers who complained of tough, sinewy cuts sizzled in fat at country taverns. By the early eighteenth century, fried chicken had made deep inroads into Virginia foodways. Simmering was a more genteel approach to preparing meat, and compositions of various ingredients simmered together were known as "fricassees." Planter William Byrd regularly dined on fricassee of chicken, veal, rabbit, or game to which the cook sometimes added claret, egg yolks, and oysters. But boiling and roasting would become particularly characteristic of the re-anglicized dinners of the eighteenth century.[6]

Cooks had long relied on boiling as a way to prepare dinner, though the method had previously been associated with one-pot meals like pottages or stews, which may have been brought to a boiling point and then allowed to simmer for a few hours. The boiling that Lesley remembered in her mother's kitchen entailed an altogether different scenario. Lesley recalled cuts of meat submerged in the water, then removed when done. Although stews and pottages incorporated the water into the foodstuff so that the liquid was part of the meal, the joints Lesley remembers were autonomous, the water serving as a medium of food preparation rather than as a component of the meal itself. Boiling had been a predominant mode of cooking and would remain part of American foodways for many years to come, but roasting, a longtime British ideal, became increasingly fashionable in the eighteenth century as fresh meat became more available. Roasting fresh meat was more sophisticated than boiling salt-preserved meat; it yielded subtler textures and flavors. As an added appeal, the roast could incorporate a stuffing. Although colonists roasted poultry, this cooking technique was especially associated with larger joints, cuts that proved less desirable when boiled and, of course, cost more. For those interested in expressing their status through the kinds of foods they ate, a roast fit the bill.[7]

Roasting had traditionally been the prerogative of the elite, as poor and middling folk tended to lack the necessary equipment for it as well as the resources to buy the finer cuts. Preparing meat on a spit over the fire took longer than boiling and required more wood. It also required more work. A homemaker would have to periodically twist the string suspending the meat from the ceiling or turn the spit resting on the andirons. Because this work unfolded over the course of several hours, she might prefer to rely on a child, servant, or slave. (Some mechanisms employed dogs.) With added space and resources in the eighteenth century, more colonists acquired tin kitchens, three-sided enclosures that, when placed in front of the fire, functioned like a portable reflector oven that evened out the heat around the roast (see Figure 2). Though rotating the spit inside the tin kitchen was still necessary, it need not take place as frequently. For the wealthy, a wall-mounted jack further simplified the process. This system of pulleys and weights attached to a clocklike mechanism automated the process. Instead of turning a roast by hand for several hours or relying on someone else to do so, the homemaker merely wound up the jack and let it slowly turn the spitted fowl or leg of lamb.[8]

Relying more on roasted meat raised middling colonists' level of sophistication, bringing them closer to the ways of the elite. It also underscored their English identity, since a proper, juicy roast had long been the dinner ideal in the homeland. In *The Frugal Housewife* (1765), Susannah Carter presents a menu for a simple but filling late winter dinner: "Ham and fowls roasted: marrow puddings." Carter was English, and her cookbook was printed in England, but beginning in the 1740s, English cookbooks were being reprinted in America, and this one, with its multiple editions, proved among the most popular. The emphasis on meat in Carter's March dinner menu is obvious, as is the emphasis on roasting. What also stands out is her emphasis on serving more than one meat.[9]

For centuries, multiple meats had been standard at European banquets. The lavish feasts of fifteenth-century Burgundy were known for outlandish heaps of food served in a sequence of several courses and often including calves, pigs, and even oxen, all roasted whole. Three centuries later, in 1780, the English country parson James Woodforde celebrated the entry of one of his congregants' children into the church with a three-course dinner that continued the tradition of multiple meats at celebratory meals. The spread included a calf's head, boiled fowl and tongue, a roasted saddle of mutton, larks, wild dung fowls, and a swan. Instead of whole large animals, this event featured a combination of birds and cuts, echoing the extravagance of the grander medieval feasts in a modified, if still profuse form.[10]

A typical dinner for Woodforde and his wife may not have included swan or calf's head, but it did frequently feature two separate kinds of meat. One afternoon in December 1799, the couple shared a meal of fish and roasted leg of mutton, a typical weekday dinner in their household. This meal reflected the prescriptions in Carter's cook-book, which not only included dinners of "ham and fowls roasted" but "forequarter of a lamb; fresh salmon," "a roasted shoulder of veal stuffed; a leg of pork boiled," "green goose with gravy sauce; neck of veal boiled," and "roasted pig with proper sauce of gravy and brains pretty well seasoned; mackerel boiled with melted butter and herbs."[11]

Following in the footsteps of the British elite, well-to-do colo-nists seated themselves at spreads of meat not unlike those record-ed by Reverend Woodforde. An anonymous Virginia manuscript cookbook from 1700 suggested that the dinner hostess's role in part was to supply what she called a "riot of meat." French general Fran-cois Jean Chastellux partook of just such a riot when he dined with George Washington and other Revolutionary War generals on a re-past of "eight or ten large dishes of butchers meat and poultry" sup-plemented by vegetables and followed by pastry and puddings. On a smaller but still remarkable scale, Philip Vickers Fithian, the tutor at Robert Carter's Nomini Hall in Virginia, attended an Easter dinner in 1774 that included beef, roast pig, and boiled rockfish. Later that year, while traveling to Maryland, he enjoyed a tavern dinner of fried chicken and ham. John Harrower, also a tutor at a Virginia plantation, recalled dinner at Belvedere as consisting of "smoack'd bacon or what we call pork ham . . . either warm or cold; when warm we have also either warm roast pig, lamb, ducks, or chicken."[12]

Colonists measured their prosperity in part by the quantity and va-riety of meat they consumed, but abundance at a colonial table served another purpose as well: it set the partakers apart from a not-so-distant past marked by scarcity and monotony, when endless rounds of pease porridge typically substituted for meat and flesh functioned as little more than a fatty flavoring for boiled legumes, grain-based stews, and broth. Perhaps the well-to-do colonists were making up for the dearth suffered by the generations that preceded them, or perhaps they were reinforcing their British identity, reminding themselves that they were not frontiersmen and pioneers but well-established Englishman who had succeeded in their New World experiment. Whatever the case, by the early- to mid-nineteenth-century less prestigious folk had adopted the ideal of multiple meats at the table, as seen at Thanksgiving when the holiday dinner featured at least two different birds, turkey and chicken being the most common, and often a leg of pork or mutton to boot.[13]

Although meat featured more centrally at dinner than it once had, it also acquired a prominent position on the breakfast table beginning in the mid-eighteenth century. Peter Kalm noted that by the 1750s, the Dutch in New York regularly supplemented their bread, butter, and round cheeses with slices of dried beef. In 1822, Timothy Dwight commented that in the country towns of New England and New York, "smoke-dried beef" or "some species of fish or flesh broiled" now accompanied the traditional bread and butter. According to Dwight's observations, meat was consumed two to three times a day. "So universal is this custom," he remarked, "that a breakfast without such an addition is considered as scarcely worth eating." Young Mainer Richard Tucker, who was used to eating meat at least once a day at home, gave evidence for Dwight's observation when he wrote to his parents from his new boarding school in Bethlehem, Pennsylvania, that sometimes he ate meat three times in a day. Nineteenth-century cookbooks featured breakfast recipes for dried beef, turkey ragout, fried veal liver, mincemeat, spare ribs, broiled chicken, meat loaf, and even wild duck.[14]

Fish, too, was a common breakfast staple, at least in coastal areas. Caroline King, remembering her Salem, Massachusetts, childhood, wrote of the "inevitable fish-balls" accompanied by baked beans for breakfast on Sundays. This menu reflected the Puritan New England tradition of baking on Saturdays in preparation for the Sabbath: the beans cooked slowly in the oven after the breads and pies were finished, ensuring that on Sunday, the day of rest, no cooking had to be done. Fish balls were often made from the leftovers of Saturday dinner, it being the habit of New Englanders to consume fish for dinner once a week, though, for Protestant purposes, not usually on Fridays. Many nineteenth-century cookbooks offered fish recipes for breakfast. Marion Harland's 1873 *Common Sense in the Household* included instructions for morning servings of codfish balls, boiled salt shad, fried sea bass, and fried trout. One could also find recipes for oyster fritters or rockfish relish to be spread on toast.[15]

Meat for breakfast, and to a lesser extent fish, was de rigueur at taverns, and tavern goers rarely had the freedom to pass it up even if they preferred lighter fare. English traveler Adam Hodgson wrote with emphasis in 1820 that "in stopping to breakfast in the Southern states, you must never calculate on a detention of less than two hours, as your entertainers *will* prepare dishes of meat or poultry for you." Thomas Ashe might have benefited from this warning. In a rush, he stopped by a tavern for breakfast one morning in Kentucky and attempted to expedite the meal by requesting only tea or coffee, but the tavern matron would hear nothing of it. "Children were dispatched after fowls," he explained. Once caught, the birds were plucked and put on the fire where ham had been frying and bread baking. Two hours later, a frustrated Ashe sat down to an ample but unasked for spread of hot and cold meats along with pickles, tea, and bread.[16]

Despite the frustration of Hodgson, Ashe, and others, many travelers celebrated, even reveled in, the meat-laden breakfasts they partook of in taverns, hotels, and the residences of hospitable friends or strangers. One gentleman crossing the interior approved enthusiastically of a breakfast featuring "hot beef steaks, roast and boiled chickens, and various sorts of cold meat." British traveler Thomas Hulme, passing through Kentucky and Illinois in the early nineteenth century, ate "bacon, beef, eggs, honey bread, with tea and coffee" for breakfast and remarked with regard to the food, "I never liked my living in England more than I do here."[17]

Regional differences were often evident in meats and meat preparations. Scrapple, a sausage traditionally made on butchering day from pig's haslet (the heart, liver, and other edible organs), offal (the entrails), and a mixture of cornmeal and buckwheat, was common in Pennsylvania and has been associated particularly with Philadelphia. Although the Pennsylvania Germans had a tradition of pork sausage for breakfast, they also took a liking to English-style beefsteak, which they readily incorporated into their breakfast routine. Ham, although fairly pervasive, was particularly associated with the South. "It is the custom to have a plate of cold ham upon the table," noted one late eighteenth-century traveler, "and there is scarcely a Virginian lady who breakfasts without it." On the frontier, game was not uncommon. Traveling in the western prairies, author Washington Irving feasted one morning on venison ribs and another on buffalo meat. Here, however, one could also encounter meats that eluded categorization.

One traveler, served steak for breakfast by the missionary family he was staying with, discovered that it was not beef or even buffalo; it was horse.[18]

THE EMPHASIS on meat beginning in the eighteenth century often cast vegetables into the shadows. Susan Lesley, the Northampton memoirist, remembered "plenty" of them at her mother's table, but other accounts hardly mention vegetables. Susannah Carter's menu for a suitable March dinner simply features roasted meats and marrow pudding; vegetables are conspicuously absent, though most vegetables would have been scarce at that time of year. When Philip Vickers Fithian dined at a tavern on his way from Virginia to Maryland in October 1774, he simply recorded having ham and chicken. Fresh roots like turnips, beets, and carrots would have been plentiful during this time, and some heartier greens would still be growing in the gardens of this part of the country, but there is no evidence they appeared at his dinner. Perhaps he deemed any vegetables accompanying his meal too minor in importance to note, or possibly there were none.[19]

Mention of fruits and vegetables was minimal in texts of this period with one glaring exception: potatoes. Often referred to as "Irish potatoes," the white tubers made their appearance in colonial gardens during the eighteenth century, and gardeners who grew them began digging root cellars to preserve them along with other root vegetables such as onions, turnips, and carrots. Though Robert Turner of Philadelphia planted a potato patch as early as 1685 and hoped to have a "brave increase" for transplanting the following year, the potato did not become a staple crop in the North until the 1720s and in the South until the 1750s. This versatile starch proved a favorite companion for meats and a practical substitute for grain in stews. What is more, it was surprisingly democratic. George Washington grew potatoes in his garden as early as 1767, and by the time of the American Revolution, members of the colonial navy ate rations of the tubers three days a week. Slaves in the South also grew potatoes, though they favored the sweet variety, which they substituted for the African yam in their cookery. Slaves even derived small incomes from potatoes. When George Washington ran short, he bought some from his neighbor's slave as well as from one of his own, the "old Negroe fellow Jupiter."[20]

Unlike whites of European descent, who may have clung to archaic perceptions of fresh vegetables as inferior, Africans brought with them a rich tradition of vegetable and fruit cultivation and consumption, a heritage that would eventually help shape American cuisine. In addition to potatoes, slaves grew okra, an African vegetable transported to the colonies, which became a common ingredient in gumbo, a stew developed in French Louisiana that took its name from the Bantu word for the pointed green seedpods. In the 1780s, William Feltman observed "snaps and collards" in slaves' gardens, and others recorded cowpeas, pumpkins, squash, watermelon, sorghum, corn, and millet. Slaves also grew gourds and bottle pumpkins, which, when hardened, served as drinking vessels.[21]

In the eighteenth century the colonial kitchen garden came into its own, and directions for putting up vegetables began to appear in print. Amelia Simmons's *American Cookery* (1796) provided instructions for cultivating cabbage, carrots, asparagus, artichokes, cucumbers, and lettuce, as well as recipes for boiling several vegetables, including broad beans, which she suggested garnishing with boiled parsley and serving with butter. She also offered recipes for pickling cucumbers and artichokes in her section on preserves. Soon after 1800, New England household inventories began referring to what they once termed "sauce" as "roots and vegetables," revealing a change in perception of vegetables from a mere flavoring or garnish to an autonomous foodstuff that held merit of its own.[22]

Occasionally a plate of vegetables even served as an entire meal: a dish of asparagus in early spring was not unheard of, asparagus being a fashionable food in Europe and colonial America at the time, but this was the exception rather than the norm. Although Americans of the eighteenth and early nineteenth centuries did enjoy vegetables, they did not embrace them wholeheartedly, as John Adams attested: "How beneficial it would be," he noted, "if more of our countrymen thought as freely as does Mr. Thomas Jefferson about fruits and vegetables." The second president admired his friend and successor's appreciation for what a well-cultivated garden could produce, and he lamented that the broader American public failed to share this perspective.[23]

Making up for their limited appearance in fresher forms, some fruits and vegetables appeared on the dinner table well hidden as part of the ancient English pudding. They also arrived on the table via an enduring American favorite: pie. Puddings and pies were mixed dishes given a solid form. They were essentially pottage encased in a crust and baked in an oven or in the case of puddings, wrapped in a cloth and boiled, then sliced like a round of moist, dense bread. Neither was new, but both were on rise, in part due to their practical advantages. Although making pottage required its own cooking pot, a thrifty homemaker short on iron vessels could simply wrap a pudding in a piece of recycled cloth and submerge it in a pot already in use. Pottage was perishable and did not last long, but encased in a piecrust and baked, it was sealed from the air and suddenly had a shelf life. In addition to their practicality, these dishes held appeal because of their strong ties to England.[24]

The pudding is an Anglo-Saxon invention with roots in the Roman era. Black pudding, perhaps the earliest version of this food, was simply a way of preserving blood, the most perishable of animal products of which there was no shortage on slaughtering day. Blood was boiled in an animal gut along with fat, vegetable matter, and grain, and the result was *botullus,* or "sausage." And that is precisely what puddings once were: sausages. The French term for sausage, *boudin* (still used in Cajun Louisiana), links the Latin word for sausage with the English word "pudding." A simple definition for pudding is "something enclosed in a sausage skin." During the Middle Ages, white puddings appeared in which the animal offal was accompanied by eggs, breadcrumbs, and milk or cream, setting the stage for sweet puddings and eventually the dessert puddings we are familiar with today.[25]

In the seventeenth century, puddings were a common component of English and colonial dinners, and pease porridge, although a pottage, sometimes took the form of a pudding: the dried peas were ground into a flour-like meal and boiled in a bag for a plain and rustic dinner. Boiled cornmeal made a similarly mundane pudding, one that was commonplace in the colonies from very early on. John Winthrop, first governor of the Massachusetts Bay Colony, may have been thinking of pease porridge and cornmeal pudding when, penning a letter to his wife a few weeks after his arrival in Salem, he described his meals as consisting of "pease, puddings, and fish," a diet that he characterized as "coarse," a commentary less on the food's texture than its lack of sophistication. Puddings were such a central part of colonists' subsistence that when Winthrop wrote to his wife, he reminded her not to forget to bring a "case to boyle a pudding in" when she crossed the ocean to join him. He anticipated the pudding case would be put to good use on board the ship well before she even arrived at her destination.[26]

English medieval puddings had generally contained meat, and until the late eighteenth century, meat puddings were the norm in the colonies as well. Suet, the fatty tissues around the kidneys in cattle and sheep, was often mixed with flour, spices, and sometimes eggs to form a batter that was then boiled for two to five hours. Dried fruit was commonly added beginning in the seventeenth century, making way for the plum pudding, "plum" referring initially to prunes, then later to any type of dried fruit—currents and raisins in particular. Although basic puddings usually relied on the suet itself for richness, more decadent variations were not hard to find. A 1700 recipe for marrow pudding from an anonymous Virginia manuscript cookbook calls for mixing cream and sugar with bone marrow along with grated biscuits, currants, and eggs. Cooks were to bake rather than boil this dish, a puff pastry blanketing the top. An even more decadent recipe from the same cookbook was for calves' foot pudding, a sugar-sweetened suet pudding boiled in a veal caul (intestinal lining) with currants, eggs, cream, bread, and the requisite shredded calves' feet.[27]

In addition to variations in richness, regional differences among puddings surfaced as well. Sweet potato pudding, rice pudding, and chicken pudding became staples in the South, while Indian pudding, with its customary cornmeal and molasses, remained a longtime favorite in New England. Slaves in eighteenth-century South Carolina made an African-inspired sesame, or benne, pudding, while inhabitants of the lower Midwest favored persimmon pudding. In the mid-Atlantic, Pennsylvania Germans enjoyed dumpling puddings: flour boiled with eggs, milk, and currants. *Brod-pudding,* or bread pudding, could be sweet but was often a savory dish made with rye loaf, milk, eggs, onions, chopped bacon, and herbs.[28]

In the colonial era, pudding was not dessert; it was an integral part of dinner. In fact, pudding was so closely associated with dinner that the two became synonymous. "Come at pudding time" initially meant,

"Come over for dinner," though, in actuality, pudding might also appear at supper or breakfast. When Susan Lesley was a child in the 1820s and 1830s, her mother would have likely served the pudding alongside the joint, not following it, as would later become the custom. Had Lesley been born earlier, she might have known pudding as a precursor to the joint. Josiah Quincy remembered Sunday dinners as a schoolboy at John Adams's table as opening with a boiled corn-meal pudding, a "custom of the time,—it being thought desirable to take the edge off one's hunger before reaching the joint." As a matter of thrift, poorer families may have regularly served pudding as a preliminary course, if not the only one. Not until late in the eighteenth century did the custom of pudding for dessert, or of a dessert course in general, begin to take hold.[29]

In its migration from savory to sweet and from main course to dessert, the pudding is not alone; it paralleled pie, that other iconic English food that Lesley remembered her mother preparing. In her memoir, Lesley did not describe the kinds of pies her mother made, and we cannot know whether they included standards like chicken, apple, seafood, or gooseberry pie. Colonists ate plenty of meat pies, just as they ate their fair share of meat puddings. English and American cookbooks sported recipes for pies made from turkey, tongue, calf's head, eel, carp, oyster, mutton, hen, hare, lamb, and pigeon, to name a few. A particularly hearty eighteenth-century specimen that offered a dizzying array of flesh was the battalia pie, a typical recipe for which included chicken, pigeon, rabbit, sheep's tongue, sweetbreads, lambstone, cockscombs, and oysters. More familiar to the modern reader may be mincemeat pie, a medieval dish that originally featured finely hashed beef mixed with dried fruit. Suet later complimented and then simply replaced the beef.[30]

Like puddings, which initially served to preserve perishable animal parts (particularly blood), pies also had their beginnings as a means of food preservation and, like puddings, were essentially mixed dishes, or pottages, enclosed in a crust and given solidity. In the seventeenth and early eighteenth centuries, the crust, which today forms an important part of the pie eater's gustatory experience, was a mere edifice, a tasteless container for the contents, initially referred to, not all that inappropriately, as a "coffin." Often made simply from water and rye or unbolted wheat without the benefit of lard or sugar, crusts were unappetizing and so hard that one traveler quipped of the typical "house-pie" he encountered in rural Delaware that it "is not broken if a wagon wheel goes over it." So they could access pie contents more than once, cooks designed crusts that they could open and close and used clarified butter or other fats to reseal the crust and protect the contents from air.[31]

Another pie tradition in colonial America differed significantly from the one the traveler in Delaware encountered. This was the cobbler, a deep-dish fruit pie made in a pot rather than a brick oven and thus lacking a formal crust. This method of preparation saved both effort and time, and cobblers were especially common on the frontier, where many kitchens did not at first have the luxury of a brick oven. Iterations of cobblers were sundry and included slumps, grunts, crisps, crumbles, buckles, Betties, and pandowdies, to name a few. Each consisted of stewed fruit topped with batter or crumble, which, in the case of slumps and grunts, crowned the surface as a kind of drop biscuit or, as in the case of pandowdies, was inverted into the fruit and its juices after baking to form a kind of dumpling. Supposedly, cobblers owe their name to the crust's resemblance to street cobbles, which speaks to the rusticity of the dish. Only when German and French immigrants infused American eating habits with their more refined pie traditions—the shoofly pie of the Pennsylvania Dutch, the tarts and galettes of the French—did the common American pie become more like the pies we know today, with their buttery crusts and variety of fruit and custard fillings.[32]

THE EVOLUTION OF PIE from a practical form of food preservation to a delicately sweetened dessert and from a nebulous, batter-topped pot of stewed fruit to a carefully shaped work of art mirrors a larger cultural trend, a shift away from frontier rusticity toward a European gentility. Colonists' soft spot for European sophistication, and in particular for all things British, articulated itself through a greater consumption of puddings, pies, and roasted meat as well as through a variety of emerging beverages—tea, coffee, chocolate—and the intricate customs that surrounded them. Because of their cosmopolitan nature as imports, the mannered sociality they implied, and the costly materials on which they depended, these beverages, especially tea, took colonial gentility to new heights.

Tea, coffee, and drinking chocolate entered the colonies by way of England in the late seventeenth century as medicinals and quickly became social drinks among the well-to-do. Considered "quite serviceable for the ill," in the words of an eighteenth-century herbalist, chocolate appeared in one Boston apothecary as early as 1712. Following the fashion of the Spanish and French, elites enjoyed chocolate at breakfast. The distinguished Bostonian Samuel Sewell took chocolate in the morning from time to time. Upon saying his prayers and reading from Homer's *Odyssey* one morning in 1709, Virginia statesman William Byrd "ate chocolate for breakfast," or so his diary records. Although Byrd wrote that he ate chocolate, he more likely drank it—colonists did not yet consume chocolate as a solid. Rather, they grated blocks of it into milk or water, added sugar, spices, and sometimes eggs, warmed the mixture in a chocolate pot, and sipped the thick and often bitter concoction from a ceramic cup.[33]

Perhaps Byrd and others referred to chocolate as a food rather than a drink because, although fluid, it was also quite substantive. The colonists' concoction more closely resembled what the Aztecs consumed than the sweetened, Dutch-processed cocoa that passes for hot chocolate today. The observation of a Spaniard in Mexico might help us appreciate colonial chocolate: "Whoever drinks a cup of this liquor can go through the day without taking anything else." Chocolate and the avid chocolate drinker were forces to contend with. During the Seven Years War and later the Revolutionary War, high-ranking officers such as Moses Greenleaf, who served at Fort Ticonderoga, fortified themselves in the morning with chocolate, and chocolate even became a regular part of rations and an important source of energy for soldiers of the Continental Army during the American Revolution. But chocolate never reached the heights of popularity attained by its caffeinated sisters, and when it came to choosing between coffee and tea, only one proved enduringly synonymous with British prestige.[34]

Long consumed in the Far East and introduced to Europe by the mid-seventeenth century, tea became available in the colonies via England as early as the 1690s. As with chocolate, the upper class first took it for its medicinal properties, then as a social drink. Initially, only the wealthy could afford the costly leaf and the even costlier equipage necessary for brewing, serving, and drinking it. By the mid-eighteenth century, however, tea had become part of everyday life for elite and middling colonists alike. In the morning, George Washington regularly drank two cups, and in the words of Swedish explorer Peter Kalm, tea featured in "even the country people's daily breakfast."[35]

By the mid-eighteenth century, tea had also ingratiated itself into the afternoon, and its consumption in the latter part of the day, especially in the presence of visitors, became a distinctive measure of class. Wealthy folk and later their middling counterparts regularly set aside responsibilities for an hour or so in the afternoon to delicately sip the warm refreshment in the company of guests. Their practiced use of specialized tea furnishings—cups, saucers, trays, pots, strainers, canisters, tea tables, sugar tongs, sugar bowls, slop bowls, tea spoons, and cream jugs—set them apart from those who could not afford such wares or spare the time to employ them. These unique implements served as props in a kind of class ceremonial. Afternoon tea was as much about performing leisure as indulging in it. Despite being a domestic activity that took place largely in private homes, teatime was a form of conspicuous consumption.[36]

Tea was more than a mere afternoon refreshment; it had taken on certain characteristics of a meal. Food was often served—bread and butter, pie, cake, perhaps even a spread of cold cheeses and meats—and the event had meal-like predictability. Although not necessarily a daily affair, teatime was a regular one associated with a particular time of day and often even a particular hour. In 1749, Peter Kalm noted that the residents of Albany took tea at three o'clock. Three decades later, a French officer noted that Bostonians took their tea at five.[37]

Like a formal mealtime, teatime conformed to an abiding protocol, a methodic sequence of events. It started with the careful measuring out of tea leaves from the caddy and the pouring of hot water over them from a steaming kettle into a ready pot. The proper way to hold the teacup was with pinky extended, the right way to discard the dregs was to pass a strainer over the surface of the brew and empty the contents into the slop bowl, and the polite way to decline the offer of a refill was to turn one's cup upside down and place a spoon on it. With the emergence of tea gowns in the late nineteenth century, there was even a proper way to dress for tea.[38]

Teatime bore many trappings of the modern meal, including an emphasis on order and structure, but it resembled a modern meal in at least one more important way: it was inherently social. Partakers entered a delicate dance of words that unfolded in time with the stirring and sipping. Teatime was an excuse as much for hospitality and commensality as for refreshment. In fact, tea was so social that tea parties, usually held later in the evening, were common sites for courtship. At a time when traditional meals—breakfast, dinner, and supper—were informal, loosely structured, and often spontaneous affairs more likely to be marked by silence than sociality, tea stood out as modern, fashionable, and distinctly English. It was also democratic. Unlike at a typical colonial family's dinner, during which matters such as who stood and who sat and who had the prerogative to speak reflected the hierarchy of family members, each tea participant was expected to engage in conversation and play an equal part. The eighteenth- and early-nineteenth- century afternoon tea ritual was a harbinger of consumption trends to come.[39]

Had tea drinking not become so well established in colonial life or been so closely associated with England, it would not likely have proved such an effective tool of civil protest during the Revolutionary era, when, under the Stamp Act, the British imposed taxes on a broad range of articles, among them, colonists' favorite morning and afternoon brew. By boycotting tea, colonists politicized the import. Defying the tyranny of England was as simple as foregoing one's morning cup or, as many chose to do, imbibing an alternative. Creative symbols of revolt, tea substitutes, some of which Benjamin Franklin rattled off to his English antagonist in his defense of Indian corn, became customary. He proudly informed the gentleman that tea-abstaining colonists could brew sage and balm, sweet hickory and walnut leaves, and even pine buds. The most famous substitutes were raspberry leaves, known as "hypernion," and the flowering, four-leafed plant, loosestrife, made famous as "liberty tea." Of course, there was always coffee.[40]

In 1774, Philip Vickers Fithian, the young tutor at Nomini Hall, Robert Carter's eminent Virginia plantation, breakfasted on hominy and milk, sage tea, and coffee. "They are now too patriotic to use tea," he observed. Coffee, which originated in Ethiopia, with cultivation spreading to tropical areas, had arrived in the colonies around the same time as tea, and coffeehouses popped up in colonial cities starting in the late seventeenth century. Unlike London coffeehouses, these doubled as taverns, but similar to their British progenitors, they served as social and intellectual hubs and centers of political foment. In an ironic twist, the Sons of Liberty gathered at a Boston coffeehouse (the Green Dragon, later nicknamed the "Headquarters of the Revolution"), to plot, among other actions, the Boston Tea Party.

Coffee was a less domestic beverage than tea. Like tea, it served a medicinal function. Unlike tea, when it became a social beverage, consumption took place primarily in public, not in the home. The American Revolution may have played some part in grafting it into the domestic lives of colonists, and perhaps Americans drink more coffee than tea today in part as a result of that conflict. It helped that coffee could grow in the West Indies, and colonists need not import it via England. Indeed, coffee consumption grew sevenfold between 1772 and 1799, and by the middle of the nineteenth century, Americans were drinking four times more of the Ethiopian brew than its Chinese rival. Eventually they would discover, with the help of their immigrant neighbors from northern Europe, that coffee not only served as a satisfying tea alternative but went particularly well with cake.[41]

IN THE NINETEENTH century, cake joined the ranks of puddings and pies as a particularly un-pottage-like American staple (at least in its baked form) that could stand proudly on its own. Of course, cake was nothing new. It had appeared on American supper tables and at special celebrations (such as Muster Day, when militia gathered to train, and Election Day, when rural folk flooded into towns to vote) ever since colonists could afford wheat flour and extra eggs. But cake started to show up as something other than a special supper or teatime delicacy: it was becoming an integral part of the American breakfast. In 1849, Henry David Thoreau consumed a morning meal at the home of an oysterman on Cape Cod who served him eel, applesauce, and doughnuts. Thoreau was not terribly interested in the eel, which he passed up for the doughnuts and applesauce. Buttermilk cake commanded his attention as one of the options on the table, and it must have proved to him as tempting as the eel had proved unappetizing.[42]

With the rise of breakfast cakes—sweet breads, muffins, biscuits, and the like—the genteel English custom of afternoon tea and cake was, in a sense, rearticulating itself as a new kind of morning meal, though without the ceremony and pretense of the afternoon ritual. Traditional cakes required an often lengthy, involved, and sometimes precarious process of preparation, but in the mid-nineteenth century, declines in the price of flour, the advent of chemical leavenings, and the invention of the cookstove set the stage for more convenient alternatives. "Quick bread" turned out to be cheaper, less laborious, and, with its increased lightness, particularly pleasing to the palate.

Breakfast cakes had appeared on American tables well before the mid-nineteenth century. Primarily griddle cakes, however, they had lacked the lightness that cooks went to great lengths to achieve; nor were they necessarily eaten at breakfast. Pancakes, waffles, doughnuts, and French toast had migrated across the Atlantic with particular immigrant groups as early as the seventeenth century and mostly started their New World careers as regional foods, only later becoming national favorites. Although variations of pancakes were enjoyed throughout Europe—*crêpes* in France, *plattar* in Sweden—the Dutch form became standard in the New World, and the American word "pancake," from *pannekoen,* reflects this trajectory. The term also reminds us that these were not prepared in an oven but on a griddle. A recipe for buckwheat cakes appeared in the first Dutch cookbook published in the United States, and around 1750 Peter Kalm declared the hearty dish the "most popular winter breakfast in Philadelphia." By the 1850s, pancakes had become standard American fare, no longer associated only with the Northeast. Around the mid-twentieth century, a whiter and distinctly fluffier variety, which one cookbook author called "common pancakes," eclipsed the buckwheat sort.[43]

More likely to show up as dinner or a special festive dessert rather than as an anchor for a morning meal in Europe (both historically and today), pancakes, waffles, and doughnuts were (and to a certain extent remain) associated with particular holidays on the continent.

In fact, pancakes were so popular on Shrove Tuesday that the day of feasting before Lent was nicknamed "Pancake Tuesday." Waffles, also devoured in the days and hours before the Lenten fast, showed up in the Low Countries at Christmas, New Years, and Twelfth Night—a trend to which countless Dutch and Flemish genre paintings attest. In the New World, people ate waffles as a dessert, a holiday snack, or a savory base for meat and gravy dishes. Not until the early nineteenth century did waffles and pancakes appear regularly on the breakfast table with butter and molasses, and even into the early decades of the twentieth century, meal-anchoring waffles, often made with rice or sweet potatoes, proved popular as beds for creamed chicken at tea houses.[44]

Doughnuts also started out as a festive treat, not as part of the American morning routine. The French brought beignets, their own variation of doughnuts with them to Louisiana, and these, like the *fastnachts* introduced to North Carolina by the Moravians, were celebrated Shrove Tuesday indulgences. The Dutch in New York enjoyed *oly koecks* at Christmas and on other holidays, and these would eventually become the American standard that nineteenth-century housewives fried weekly as part of their baking-day routine. *Oly koecks* were small dough rounds, which Washington Irving described in 1806 as "balls of sweetened dough, fried in hog's fat." Although Susannah Carter instructed cooks to "make them in whatever form you please," nineteenth-century recipes frequently called for cutting the dough into diamonds. Rings emerged sometime during that century when cooks began cutting two concentric circles of dough with differently sized tumbler rims. Patented doughnut cutters, appearing in the 1850s, popularized doughnuts with holes and helped make them a national standard.[45]

Just as doughnuts hailed from more than one European country, what we call French toast has roots that span the continent. Despite its name, French toast is hardly (just) French. In fact, people living in the nineteenth century were as likely to credit it to the Germans, typically referring to it to as "German toast" or occasionally *Arme Ritter*. In truth, it hailed from neither France nor Germany exclusively and was merely an old European tradition for using up stale bread by soaking it in milk and eggs and frying it on a griddle. Strictly speaking, this was less breakfast cake than recycled bread, though it proved a favorite even among the upper classes in Europe. Its rich ingredients—eggs, milk, and sugar—leant it an air of sophistication.

The original French name for French toast, *pain perdu*, does not allude to the air of sophistication the dish expressed but rather emphasizes the frugality that it also came to embody. *Pain perdu*, or "lost bread," a term still bandied about in New Orleans, nods to the traditionally stale nature of the main ingredient, and in this spirit home economist Mary Hinman Abel offered a recipe for French, or "fried," toast in her *Practical Sanitary and Economic Cooking* (1890) as a means of rescuing old bread dried for future reconstitution. French toast was known by a few other names: "American toast" and "nun's toast," to name two. For "Mennonite toast" the bread is deep-fried like a doughnut. In *The Carolina Housewife* (1847), a recipe for French toast appears under the title "Queen Esther's bread," perhaps the first printed Jewish recipe in the United States. Jews likely associated the rich, egg-based treat with Purim, just as Christians had once associated it, along with waffles and pancakes, with the days of festivity preceding the fasting period of Lent.[46]

Although pancakes, waffles, doughnuts, and French toast remained popular in the nineteenth century and beyond, softer, lighter alternatives joined them once baking batter in a cookstove oven became a popular alternative to frying it on a griddle. The technical underpinnings of the breakfast cake's success are threefold. First, the cookstove oven provided a more intense, focused heat than the old-fashioned hearth, and it was nearly always "on." Second, new chemical leavens transformed the cook's ability to raise dough, easing the once laborious and time-consuming task while rendering the product lighter and more consistent. Third, and most fundamentally, advances in grain production increased the availability and affordability of wheat, without which Thoreau's buttermilk cake would have been a mere anomaly rather than evidence of an emerging national tradition.

Key to wheat's heightened availability was the construction, beginning in 1817, of a waterway to what would become the nation's breadbasket. The Erie Canal opened up new grain-growing lands in central New York and, soon after, the Midwest. Settlers on the frontier shipped their crops on barges to New York City, inaugurating a veritable flood of grain into the eastern seaboard. Farmers had grown wheat with some success in the mid-Atlantic, but by 1839, Ohio, Illinois, Iowa, and Wisconsin were producing one-fourth of the nation's wheat and corn, and by the Civil War, they were putting out half. What is more, the quality of the wheat produced in these states exceeded that of the wheat grown in the mid-Atlantic due to the interior region's more highly developed, industrialized processing infrastructure, which milled a finer, lighter flour. In 1830, Americans were eating more meat than wheat, but by 1850, they were eating twenty pounds more wheat per year than they had in 1830. Although meat consumption had previously topped that of wheat, the ratio was now reversed. Wheat, you could say, had become the new meat.[47]

The introduction of novel leavening products accompanied wheat's new currency. Bakers had used yeast for centuries to raise bread, and colonists with a little extra money lining their pockets sometimes relied on eggs beaten into the dough to accomplish the same purpose. In the late 1700s, pearl ash, a derivative of potash made from processing burned wood, became a popular time- and money-saving alternative. The Dutch introduced it to the colonies from Europe, where professional bakers had relied on it since the Middle Ages, and it appeared in Amelia Simmons's late-eighteenth-century recipes for gingerbread. Toward the mid-nineteenth century, sodium bicarbonate, or baking soda, emerged along with other kinds of salts derived from minerals and plants, generically referred to as saleratus. Because pearl ash and saleratus are alkaline substances, they require mixture with an acid to produce their leavening effect, so recipes that called for them also called for ingredients such as molasses, sour milk, lemon, or, later, cream of tartar. Companies began marketing agents with the proper combination of alkali and acid around the turn of the twentieth century, and modern baking powder was born.[48]

Although cooks still used yeast in baking, pearl ash and leavening salts were beginning to save them no small amount of time. With these agents, cakes became easier to make, and the cake-like phenomenon of "quick bread" came into its own. Cooks did not call quick breads "quick" for nothing. Colonial homemakers often made their own yeast from ingredients such as hops or potatoes, and this process typically spanned several days. Milk came in handy as a yeast base when, as Lydia Maria Child noted, "one wants to make biscuits suddenly," but this alternative approach still required an hour. A cook relying on eggs as a leaven would first have to whip them "to a snow," and nineteenth-century recipes specify this task as taking between fifteen minutes and half an hour. To beat the ingredients of a proper butter cake sufficiently could require up to a full hour, and fancy preparations sometimes called for two hours or even more. By contrast, the buttermilk cake presented to Henry David Thoreau for breakfast at the Cape Cod oysterman's house did not require a carefully prepared yeast, persistent beating of ingredients, or hours sitting near the fire to rise if it was made from a recipe anything like Elizabeth Lea's 1859 recipe, which called for saleratus. In fact, it did not have to sit at all—the cook only had to beat the dough for a few minutes before putting it in the oven.[49]

One popular quickbread, muffins, are miniature cakes that appeared on the scene in conjunction with the new leavening agents. Early American recipes for muffins made what we would think of as English muffins: flat, round, wheat-based yeast breads originally associated with teatime in Britain. Thomas Jefferson enjoyed these so much at Monticello that when he became president, he requested the recipe so that he could enjoy them at the White House too. First baked in ceramic cups or iron rings, raised muffins were popularly called "gems" after a commercial baking powder, as well as "cup cakes," though this second term initially referred not to cooks baking the batter in individual cups (a meaning that would eventually triumph) but to the unit by which they measured the recipe's main ingredients. "Muffin" derives from "moufle," an old French term for mittens, which, when applied to bread, meant "soft." More precisely, "muffin" plays on the English word "muff," a single, often fur-lined mitt for keeping hands toasty. Most early recipes for these breakfast treats were exceedingly plain. Catharine Beecher's *Treatise on Domestic Economy* (1841) simply included "corn muffins" and "wheat muffins," and the little round cakes only began featuring fruits, such as raisins and dates, in the late 1800s. The blueberry muffin did not surface until well into the twentieth century.[50]

Home economist Sarah Tyson Rorer called the increasingly popular breakfast cakes baked in rings or cups "quick muffins" or "raised muffins," emphasizing their convenience and distinguishing them from their flatter and more time-consuming English predecessors. The miniature raised cakes owed their success not only to saleratus and baking soda (which had become so prominent that recipe titles incorporated the agent names—soda biscuits, for instance) but also to a revolutionary apparatus that entered American kitchens starting in the 1830s: the cookstove. At first, the cast-iron behemoth met with much skepticism. Credited with modernizing the White House, President Millard Fillimore and his wife, Abigail, installed the mansion's first cookstove in 1850, but their staff preferred the original hearth and walked off the job in protest. Only after the president himself went to the patent office to learn how to control the heat distribution did the head chef agree to use it.[51]

Despite their flaws and the many frustrations that hearth-oriented homemakers encountered while transitioning to them, when it came to baking, cookstoves provided practical advantages. Because the oven did not require a separate fire, as did the brick chamber set into the back or side of a fireplace, the homemaker could take advantage of heat produced for other cooking tasks to bake her breads, cakes, and pies. In addition, the cookstove delivered a "fast" heat perfect for muffins and other quick breads made with saleratus, which required an intense and steady high temperature. Cookstove makers capitalized on these advantages, affiliating their appliances with a variety of mouth-watering pastries. In addition to manufacturing the actual appliances, these companies produced muffin rings and gem pans and provided complimentary recipes for ambitious quick breads and cakes, supplying women with hours', if not years', worth of novel baking projects.[52]

Cooks were enamored of the baking possibilities the cookstove and the new types of commercial leavening opened up for them, but these innovations rendered the homemaker far more dependent on cookery literature than she had ever been in the past. Until this point, cooking knowledge had been based on the hearth, and much was left to the cook's discretion. An eighteenth-century recipe for pound cake might read "one pound sugar, one pound butter, one pound flour, one pound eggs," with directions that relied on the cook's experience, such as "Watch it well." Suddenly, seasoned cooks found many of their time-proven skills old-fashioned and their once standard knowledge obsolete. Recipes necessarily became more detailed, and the need for additional instruction, especially when it came to baking, helped set the conditions for a proliferation of recipes for muffins and other quick breads. *Mrs. Lincoln's Boston Cook Book* (1884) alone included recipes for multiple variations of gems, puffs, popovers, soda biscuits, shortcakes, fruitcakes, muffins, and Sally Lunns. Once largely teatime treats, these sweet breads and miniature cakes became regular breakfast delights, imparting an air of refinement to the morning meal while leaving behind the social pretense of the teatime ritual. A new baking era had begun.[53]

WHEN NORTHAMPTON memoirist Susan Lesley dined with her family on pudding, pie, roast meat, and vegetables as a child in the early nineteenth century, the cookstove was just a glimmer on the horizon. By the time she sat down to pen her childhood memories as an adult several decades later, she was likely familiar not only with the kinds of dishes the cookstove produced but with precisely how the apparatus operated. The old-fashioned hearth-prepared dishes she associated with her mother and her youth were comfort foods—plain, down-home, domestic—but during the years when she actually consumed them, they characterized a new level of sophistication, a step up from the more organic, "messy" approach to dinner that had marked colonial life in the seventeenth-century.

Puddings, pies, and roasts were not new foods during the eighteenth century; nor were breakfast cakes in the nineteenth. Their growing popularity, however, displayed a new sensibility about food. So too did the slow but sure emergence of the vegetable as an autonomous aliment, one well worth serving apart from a stew and as more than a mere flavoring. Pottage and other mixed foods did not die out—they persisted and we even continue to enjoy them today—but in the eighteenth century, they began to make room for the more atomized dinner that was coming into its own, one in which the contents of pots appeared separately on the plate. This dinner was more cultured, more rationalized, and distinctly more British, as was the teatime routine that emerged in its shadow. Breakfast cakes, which reflected teatime indulgences, punctuated this trend. With their airy textures and individually molded shapes, they offered an elegant and updated spin on the classic pottage of stewed grain, or mush.

By embracing the new eating fashions, colonists were making a gradual break with the past. They traded in their medieval worldview for Enlightenment thinking and exchanged humble peasant ways for elite British conventions. As this transformation was reaching completion, another gustatory trend began to make its way across the ocean, but this one had less to do with what one ate for dinner and more to do with when.

3

HOW DINNER BECAME SPECIAL

JANE CUNNINGHAM, author of *Jennie June's American Cookery Book* (1870), did not much like what was happening with American meals. The times were changing. People no longer generally ate their first meal of the day in the "early hours," and the main meal now took place at five o'clock or well after, rather than at one or two. Cunningham had a bone to pick with these modern eating habits. "Six o'clock dinners," she warned, "destroy health." Eating the bulk of one's food so late in the day promised nothing but harm to the American stomach. In addition, it was certain to encourage idleness. Freed from the responsibilities of preparing and serving a traditional dinner in the late morning and early afternoon, women would surely "give the day to gossiping and visiting." Shifting the dinner hour would bring Americans to ruin, Cunningham implied, but reality proved just the opposite. As dinner became an evening meal, it became a family meal, and as it became a family meal, it became special.[1]

Dinner in the colonial era had been a midday activity. Rising early—usually between five and six o'clock—suited members of an agrarian society, and by around noon these early risers were ready for a substantial meal. Benjamin Franklin considered it ideal to wake at five o'clock, breakfast by seven, dine between noon and one, and have supper after six. This kind of schedule, typical in the seventeenth and eighteenth centuries, held well into the nineteenth century. A traveler in the 1820s visited a cabin on the Ohio frontier at noon and found its inhabitants eating a hot spread of meat, vegetables, milk, cider, and corn bread. The same traveler partook of an even earlier dinner when he visited a New York Shaker community: "We were summoned to dinner about ten o'clock." Affluent colonists usually got up later, breakfasting at nine or ten and dining between one and three. Dinner may have been later for them, but it was still an afternoon—not an evening—routine.[2]

In the mid-nineteenth century, it became fashionable to eat the main meal of the day later and later. By the 1860s, upscale hotels, which had traditionally served dinner between one and three, began to offer the option of dining well after those hours. The seven-hundred-bed St. Nicolas Hotel on Broadway sat diners at one, four, and five o'clock, accommodating the habits of both traditional patrons and those adhering to the new dining trends. By the 1880s, it was no longer out of the ordinary for a traveler to state, "I found myself comfortably seated at dinner at the usual hour of half-past six." This was precisely the hour at which President Grover Cleveland and his wife dined during their residency in the White House.[3]

As dinner shifted to the evening and became an important family routine—important because it was now the main occasion for spending time together when family members spent their days apart—snacking entered into the crosshairs. Snacking was the antithesis of meals in general and of dinner, the archetypal meal, in particular. During this era, dining became exalted, and snacking taboo. Snacking posed a threat to the meal; it subverted the family's fellowship around the table and the middle-class values that proper evening meals had come to embody. Rhetoric about snacking warned of its dangers and proliferated, serving a dual purpose: it demonized between-meal consumption and glorified the family dinner. Focusing attention on the transgression of snacking elevated the importance of the evening meal, carving a pedestal for the new nightly family gathering.

With snacking as its nemesis, dinner became an evening affair whether Jane Cunningham approved or not, and this change occurred for two reasons. First, the shifting shape of work in the mid-nineteenth century led to new schedules and roles within the family. Second, the rising importance of social class made dinner a classroom for manners and a training ground for worldly success. Both changes in schedule and class structure were the offspring of industrialization.

Although the shape of the modern meal may have little to do with industry, it has everything to do with the Industrial Revolution. The modern meal emerged from the crucible of change that was the nineteenth century, a time of upheaval when the status quo was disrupted and reinvented on every level—social, cultural, technological, economical. The Industrial Revolution not only revolutionized the means of producing goods in this country but altered how ordinary Americans lived, turning everyday life for masses of people on its head in just a few decades.

The crux of the change was the shift from farm to factory. The manufacture of goods, once centered primarily on farms and in homes and artisan workshops, was now becoming centered in mills, where waterpower ran complex machinery that fabricated products like cloth and glass in great quantities and at high speeds. A plethora of consumables suddenly became available for purchase and sale. Individuals could generate new wealth and enjoy novel conveniences—but at a price. As farmers' sons and daughters left family fields for factory floors and embraced a distinctly urban existence, they exchanged small-town life and its normally face-to-face trade for the anonymity of large, class-divided cities, which presented different kinds of opportunities and new forms of danger. Here, their lives came under the dictatorship of the calendar and clock. In the new atmosphere of regimentation, eating would never be the same. Meals underwent a transformation that, for better or worse, was permanent.[4]

WHEN THEY LEFT their family farms and country homes, mill workers submitted themselves to the demands and conditions of the factories. Rigid schedules now determined their lives—their coming and going, their rising and sleeping, their working and relaxing. Even their eating necessarily took place "on time." "She must eat when the iron tongue bids her, or not at all," wrote one nineteenth-century commentator about the life of the typical New England mill girl in the 1840s. "When she will take her meals, and what shall be the articles of food constituting them, are not, with her, matters of choice and rejection." The "iron tongue," of course, was the bell that rang to awaken mill hands in the morning and then again throughout the day to announce the start and finish of work and the beginning and end of meals. Harriet Farley described the typical mill girl's schedule at Lowell: "We go in [to the factory] at five o'clock; at seven we come out to breakfast; at half-past seven we return to our work, and stay till half-past twelve. At one, or quarter past one four months of the year, we return to our work and stay till seven at night." In Massachusetts, the typical mill girl devoted fourteen hours to running machinery with two half-hour breaks for meals until legislation of the ten-hour workday in 1874. The breaks included the time necessary not only for eating but also for traveling between the factory and boarding house.[5]

Most mill girls lodged and ate at company boarding houses, which functioned as homes away from home. Because the girls were generally young and single, they relied on the matrons as substitute parents who cooked for them and saw that they followed boardinghouse rules about curfews, cleanliness, and guests. Fellow boarders became surrogate siblings. In the dining room—or "eating room," as one girl less politely called it, seeing as there wasn't much time for lingering over a meal—the boardinghouse "family" came together three times a day. In some establishments, more than one shift was necessary to accommodate the onslaught of hungry mouths. As to the food, the mill girls ate what the matron placed before them: meat, potatoes, vegetables, porridge, soup, stew, tea, coffee, and plenty of bread. It was not restaurant fare, just simple, plain, down-home sustenance. But it was hearty and usually hot, and with no cooking or cleanup required on the mill workers' part, complaints were relatively few.[6]

Whereas early mill workers typically ate the midday meal at their boardinghouses—their homes away from home—urban middle- and upper-class Americans soon found the tradition of dining at home in the middle of the day impractical. Though their schedules were often more flexible than those of manual laborers, permitting them the time necessary to leave for a meal, the average distance between their residences and workplaces grew, increasingly making a midday excursion home a greater effort than it was worth. As a result of new ways of doing business and the changing landscape these practices shaped, home and workplace underwent a divorce.

In the preindustrial era, artisans and merchants had conducted much of their business in the same buildings that housed them, and the homestead had been the principal site of production. On farms, the processing of raw materials took place on a family's land, under the roof of its house, and in its constellation of outbuildings. In towns and cities, workshops, offices, and shops were commonly attached to private dwellings. If the homestead did not function as a primary workplace, its inhabitants usually labored nearby. Towns and small cities relied on a largely face-to-face economy in which work and home lives necessarily overlapped.

An altogether different geography marked the large, industrializing cities emerging in the mid-nineteenth century. Here, sites of manufacture and commerce tore away from residential areas as production processes became mechanized and commerce fell under the dictatorship of growing companies and, later, corporations. Commercial, industrial, and residential districts emerged. Eventually suburbs, connected to city centers by streetcars, offered an escape from the noise, pollution, and wheeling and dealing of the urban environment for those who could afford them.

Quiet, pastoral neighborhoods in city outskirts served as refuges from the city for businessmen and their families. Here a husband and father could unwind, reconnect with family, and enjoy the simple pleasures of domestic life after a long day in the harsh world of capitalistic trade. And such areas sheltered a wife and her children from the increasingly masculine and capitalistic environment of the urban downtown. Suburbs, by definition, were secluded, usually located "ten to fifteen miles away from the unceasing noise and hurry of the city," according to prominent nineteenth-century landscape architect Andrew Jackson Downing. But distance, the very thing that made suburbs a refuge, compromised their accessibility. The private homes of the elite and growing middle class, safe from the shady faces and dark market forces that infused the downtown with hints of danger, were out of reach during the daytime for inhabitants working in the city. Suburban dwellers found that they could not easily break away from the office or shop for the trip back home. Those for whom returning home to dine in the middle of the workday was no longer a feasible option needed an alternative.[7]

When businessmen could no longer continue the tradition of a midday domestic dinner, they increasingly patronized restaurants and clubs. Here they not only enjoyed fine, leisurely meals but also furthered their business interests by socializing with colleagues and clients. But such a solution had its drawbacks. Pushing papers at desks throughout the morning hardly constituted the kind of physical exertion requiring a heavy meal, and some wondered whether there wasn't physical danger for the white-collar worker in the practice of midday dining. Among the critics of this practice was the author of an 1886 *Good Housekeeping* editorial titled "The Proper Hour for Dinner." In 1870, less than two decades prior to this editorial, *Godey's Lady's Book,* perhaps the most widely read women's periodical of its time, had claimed that "nature has fixed no particular hours for eating." But by the 1880s, the *Good Housekeeping* editorialist and others disagreed.[8]

Good Housekeeping argued that dining in the middle of the day had become distinctly old-fashioned; worse, it was injurious. The author observed that the previous generation—that is, the fathers and grandfathers of her day's businessmen—would have risen early and engaged in the heaviest work before noon. The modern merchant, on the other hand, "gets downtown at about 10 o'clock and is busy till 3 or 4 o'clock in the afternoon." Dinner is consumed in the middle of business rather than after and necessarily "on the jump," with the stomach suffering an unfortunate blow as a result. The enlightened businessman, the editorial proposes, eats this "important meal," by contrast, when he has time, in the evening, and this way he is more likely to eat it "slowly, and with proper regard for the welfare of his digestive apparatus." His work for the day done, after the meal he can smoke a cigar, engage in conversation, or take up a novel. "It is always better to dine late." "Such a practice," the author concludes, "is conducive to happiness and long life."[9]

Although business, not health, concerns drove the midday meal from the afternoon to the evening, the health conscious, including the *Good Housekeeping* editorialist, enthusiastically approved. As long as the late dinner was not exceptionally heavy, it promised to relieve a plethora of middle-class Americans' ailments. As its main benefit, an evening dinner could be consumed at leisure and thus, in the words of cookbook author Christine Terhune Herrick, "digested peacefully."

It was more conveniently balanced with exercise than a midday dinner taken by a businessman whose work tied him to a desk for the rest of the afternoon. A commentator in *Harper's Bazaar* claimed, "Much of the improved physique which is so generally recognized among Americans is due to the increased habit of dining late." One medical doctor regularly prescribed a shift of the main meal for those suffering from insomnia—allegedly, he saw more than a few of his patients who embraced late dinners cured.[10]

As new urban business routines uprooted the traditional midday dinner, the precise hour at which one dined increasingly revealed one as a career-minded urbanite or a rural farmer or artisan. "The varying occupations and residences of families," explained a Chicago newspaper in 1876, "divide the time of dining between noon and six o'clock." Those living in rural areas and small manufacturing towns where workplaces were close to home ate at around noon, the article explained, whereas those in cities dined at around six. In New York City, whose denizens set American dining fashions, eating at seven or later was not unheard of. For a time, not only did rural dinnertimes lag behind urban ones, but certain cities lagged behind others. "Many people in Boston still dine at two," noted *Harper's Bazaar* in 1886. Those who lived in Beantown simply could not keep pace with their hungry counterparts in the Big Apple. Thus, where one's dinner hour fell on the dinner-hour spectrum hinted at the place from which one haled.[11]

The dinner hour also became an indicator of one's class status, though at first some confusion persisted among the middle class regarding whether it was proper to dine at midday rather than in the evening or vice versa. For about two decades, it was common for one family to dine in the evening while its neighbors dined in the afternoon. Even across the week, a family's dinnertimes were not always consistent, the meal being served at one o'clock on one day and at five or six o'clock the next. "Unless you know the habits of a household well," complained a columnist in the mid-1880s, "you are not safe from the awkwardness of stumbling upon [their] meal-time." Sometimes individual family members' preferences were at odds, as in the case of the Bruntons, a fictional household created by author Lucretia P. Hale for her 1885 *Good Housekeeping* story, "The Bruntons'

Family Problem, and How It Was Solved." Erastus, Hector, and Eustace are globe-trotting businessmen whose cosmopolitan ways and long working hours cause them to prefer a late dinner, but when they dine at home under their parents' roof, their habits clash with those of their father, who clings to the tradition of the old-fashioned midday dinner. Such a conundrum presents a challenge for the homemaker, Mrs. Brunton, and her servants. Not surprisingly, business and fashion eventually trump tradition in the story, as they did in history.[12]

Before long, evening became the clear middle- and upper-class dinnertime standard, and its afternoon alternative acquired a reputation as provincial and blue-collar. In 1890, publisher and philanthropist George W. Childs declared, "The late dinner is firmly intrenched [*sic*] in the citadel of American life." By contrast, an early-afternoon dinner branded one as a laborer or country bumpkin. "If you desire to be among the *crème de la crème*," advised *Good Housekeeping* columnist Marian Devereux, "dine no earlier than five." One could sometimes get away with mid-afternoon, she conceded—"Society will tolerate three and will often forgive two"—but dining any earlier would encroach on the hours during which manual workers took their midday break. A noon dinner was necessarily an inelegant one and suggested an unfortunate lack of leisure, that treasured marker of upper-class status that middle-class Americans went out of their way to emulate and display. Once the norm for the average American, the midday dinner now reeked of what Devereux called "plebian necessity," at least to those aspiring to climb the class ladder. To them it was no longer benign; the afternoon dinner had become a definite faux pas.[13]

Driven by business and fashion and reflecting concerns about health, the main meal of middle-class Americans' day anchored itself squarely in the evening during the closing decades of the nineteenth century. With this shift came another, less simple one. In the course of its migration to the evening, dinner had become not only the main meal but also a special one—special because it was shared. In 1894, *Good Housekeeping* called it "the one important meal of the day, both socially and gastronomically." Gastronomy would come to play a central role, especially at formal dinners, which involved entertaining guests and displaying class prerogatives. But the family dinner was about much more than fine food; it was about the people who joined together to partake of it. Dining together in the evening helped the middle-class Victorian family to understand itself as a family, and this new understanding made the meal so much more than a meal. Now it was a ritual.[14]

FAMILY LIFE IN the nineteenth century underwent massive change that eventually redefined what it meant to be a family, and eating dinner together was central to that redefinition. In colonial America, families cooperated to sustain themselves, each member contributing to the work that generated the household's income. Except perhaps for the very young, everyone was expected to be economically productive. In the nineteenth century, though, middle-class roles shifted as gender responsibilities diverged: in general, men took on economic responsibilities, and women shouldered domestic ones. Most middle-class husbands left the household daily to enter the world of manufacturing and trade, while their wives dressed up and made social calls to friends and neighbors or stayed at home to care for infants, manage servants, and tend to household tasks.[15]

No longer laboring together as an economical unit, family members needed a new way to bond, and dinner fit the bill. With husbands, wives, and children inhabiting separate worlds during the day—office, factory, home, school—coming together around a table in the evening took on heightened significance. In 1885, a *Good Housekeeping* columnist called it "a social reunion of no little importance." The dinner hour, she warned, could be the only daily occasion for which the modern urban family assembled. Without it, she feared, family members "might grow up as distant acquaintances." Communal consumption replaced cooperative production as the glue that held the family together. By regularly eating the evening meal in each other's company, close kin renewed their ties and strengthened their sense of mutual belonging.[16]

The emergence of the dining room speaks to the rising importance of dinner as a ritual of family bonding. Although designed to impress guests, this space helped transform family dinner into much more than a casual occasion. Dining rooms first appeared in American homes in the late seventeenth century, but these celebrated chambers were highly formal affairs found only in the houses of the utmost elite. The vast majority of Americans ate not far from the hearth in the "hall," a multipurpose room that housed a variety of activities, from cooking and candle making to sewing and scripture reading. At the end of the eighteenth century, dining rooms were more common but still a feature of the homes of the wealthy. Middle-class Americans, especially those in cities, did not live in houses with a separate room devoted to the formal service of dinner until the mid-nineteenth century.[17]

Along with the emergence of the dining room came an abundance of specialized furnishings. Perhaps the most distinctive furnishing in the Victorian dining room was the often enormous and intricately carved sideboard. This altar-like buffet, with its decorative wooden backboard and paneled cabinets, housed silverware, dishes, glasses, cutlery, water pitchers, and wine and functioned as a serving station during formal dinners, where servants carved the roast, portioned the salad, or plated the dessert. Its gothic design and formidable presence cultured the dining room, lending it a sense of courtly purpose. Naturalistic harvest and hunting motifs sporting sheaves of wheat, grape clusters, deer, game birds, and cornucopias celebrated nature's bounty but also, more importantly, contained it. In some ways, the dining room was a sideboard writ large: it celebrated, or at least accommodated, the appetite, while at the same time ritualizing and thereby refining it as civil, sophisticated, and polite.[18]

Other specialized dining room furnishings appeared as well: a table primarily for eating; matching chairs, one for each family member; and individual rather than shared dishes and drinking vessels. In early America, most families had a makeshift "table-board," a long, narrow plank supported on sawhorse-like trestles (hence the phrase "room and board," with "board" referring to one's meals, or more literally, the table-board on which they were served). These plain, rustic contraptions could be disassembled as needed and served a variety of purposes besides eating. Chairs, generally associated with authority, were somewhat scarce, and men, as heads of household, usually occupied them. Those without chairs sat on stools or backless, bench-like seats called "forms" designed to accommodate several people. Women, often on their feet serving the meal, joined their men folk when they got the chance or else sat separately, eating their share after the others had finished. If allowed at the table at all, children were expected to yield their spots should others require them. Rather than sitting with the adults, children frequently sat at a side table, though it was not unheard of for them to stand. As mentioned in Chapter 1, early American families also tended to share utensils: they passed cups back and forth and shared trenchers, usually between spouses or siblings. That each member of the Victorian middle-class family—male or female, old or young—had his or her own seat, tableware, and designated place at the table shows just how greatly Victorian families differed from their predecessors, not merely in what they could afford but in how much they valued the social aspects of the everyday meal.[19]

By the mid-nineteenth century, family members even faced each other at the table as if, over the course of the meal, they might actually talk. Prior to then, Americans frequently ate in silence and in haste. Food was fuel, and they worked at finishing their meals as soon as possible. Socializing was secondary—if it happened at all. The hungry diners, often including hired help, boarders, guests, and extended kin, usually sat on one side of the narrow table-board, not both. This made conversation awkward at best. But when they had eating to do, conversing was probably the last thing on their minds. A 1744 etiquette manual titled *A Pretty Little Pocket Book* even warned children—lest they be tempted—not to speak unless spoken to. Foreigners frequently commented on Americans' proclivity to consume their fare without speaking. When French traveler Frances Trollope attended an American dinner party, she noted that "the only sounds heard were those produced by knives and forks and an unceasing chorus of coughing." Charles Dickens put it this way: "Nobody says anything, at any meal, to anyone."[20]

Beginning in the mid-nineteenth century, attitudes toward dinnertime conversation changed. Communication among individuals at the table became a standard expectation and eventually a carefully cultivated and highly prized art. That an 1888 popular woman's magazine article titled "A Few Homely Words on the Matter of Conversation" focused mainly on interactions between family members over dinner speaks to the growing prominence of conversation during the domestic evening meal. The dinner table had become not only *a* place to talk but *the* place. Here the mix of generations living under the same roof learned to accommodate each other in the matter of polite social interaction.[21]

A new openness toward weaving the voices of children into the nightly dinnertime conversation emerged during these decades as well, and not merely for the sake of egalitarianism. "Home conversation is an essential part of children's education, [and] the family dinner table is the best place to commence this education," argued the author of "A Few Homely Words." Parents began to question the old adage "Children should be seen and not heard"; silence among the younger set at the table seemed a wasted opportunity for growth and maturation. Adults might instruct children over a meal and expand their learning. Games provided a particularly structured opportunity for educational dinnertime conversation. One Boston family frequently spent the evening meal naming towns and cities or famous historical figures in alphabetical order. This scholastic exercise turned the evening meal into an ad hoc lesson in geography or history. The game, and thus the dinnertime curriculum, sometimes included spelling. Such structured exercises provided more than didactic lessons in classroom subjects. They also furnished occasions for children to practice the back-and-forth of ordinary dinner-table repartee.[22]

Another dinnertime exercise in civic virtues included cordially offering to serve others at the table, a kindness increasingly expected of all family members at the evening meal. "To keep a watchful eye upon the needs of others, to invite them with gentle courtesy to partake of what they may lack in their supply of the different dishes," philosophized conversation expert Ellen Bliss Hooker, "[effects an] unselfishness and harmony for which nothing else gives opportunity." Dinner-table reciprocity became a growing middle-class standard for all ages, and engaging the diplomatic give-and-take of family fellowship, whether in the volunteering of anecdotes or the polite passing of butter and beans, was considered a lesson of inestimable value to youth, who would eventually find their success as adults hinging in part on the sophistication and grace with which they conducted conversation at the dinner tables of colleagues, peers, and notables.[23]

A variety of trappings enhanced dinnertime courtesy and formality and turned the nightly meal into nothing less than a regular domestic ceremony. Lighting derived additional value from the new gathering time, commonly after sunset. "The festal appearance imparted by the gleam of candles, lamps, or gas upon silver and glass cannot be acquired by daylight," reasoned Herrick, who argued for the evening dinner over its afternoon counterpart precisely because of how well the later time leant itself to ceremony. She also encouraged the use of a white tablecloth and the placement of flowers on the table. In more well-to-do families, evening dress further raised the level of the meal's formality. "Each member of the family dons a fresh costume," observed publisher and philanthropist George W. Childs. According to Herrick, this practice helped give the dinner table "the look of a pleasant social gathering instead of a mere stopping-place for food." The ritualizing of dinner as a nightly ceremony emphasized and embodied the family's obligation to itself. It also spoke of class values; the trappings aided the ambitious middle-class family in identifying itself as respectable and successful. And it gave children a chance to try on airs of dignity and to practice their familial and future worldly roles.[24]

For children, playing their parts as respected members of the family at the dinner table was a little like practicing to become respected members of society. "Let the table, when no one is present but the home circle, be the model of what it should be when surrounded by guests," wrote Herrick in 1885. When there were no guests to impress, a butler and waitress often served as in-house audience members who offered a healthy motivation for children to display exemplary speech and behavior. Protocol encouraged propriety and a certain measure of formality in the dining room so that when children found themselves in situations where these virtues counted most, they would be well prepared. And in the world of nineteenth-century America, situations imbued with significant social implications presented themselves regularly.[25]

In an urbanizing and industrializing era, strangers constantly brushed shoulders, and one needed to know how to navigate this unpredictable sea of anonymity. "Refrain from making acquaintance with any strangers unless you are certain of their respectability," warned Eliza Leslie in her 1854 ladies' etiquette manual, *The Behavior Book*. Etiquette served as a basic way to signal and recognize respectability. It helped strangers to "read" each other's class status and thereby judge the safety and suitability of potential social interactions. A lot was at stake for children learning the mores of the society they would one day enter, so it comes as no surprise that food and approaches to consuming it grew into such a highly charged aspect of nineteenth-century middle-class experience. Conducting oneself properly at the table was an acquired skill, and much rode on one's ability to master it. This included learning which habits disgraced the eater and steering well clear of them. Helping oneself first and speaking out of turn were perils young diners learned to avoid from experience and parental guidance. There were many pitfalls when it came to honoring the sacred evening meal, but one trumped all others, especially for children: snacking.[26]

IT IS HARDLY COINCIDENTAL that so many of the stipulations of Victorian eating revolved around snacking. Snacking was a by-product of that Victorian invention, the modern meal, and the modern meal was in turn partially defined by snacking, its transgressive counterpart. Dinner had become heavily infused with social meaning: it represented the family bond and middle-class propriety. Victorians came to see snacking as distinctly hostile to these meanings. It compromised one's ability to participate fully in the family's nightly "household festival," and kin could perceive this as an act of defiance and a personal insult. In addition, snacking spoke poorly of character and called into question one's suitability for membership in middle-class society.[27]

Snacking could undermine the ritual of family dinner in many ways. Its tendency to dampen the appetite might result in picky eating or a desire to postpone or skip the meal altogether. Apathy toward eating might also result in lateness to the table, an intolerable behavior. Mrs. Lincoln Phelps, in her 1876 *The Educator, or Hours with My Pupils,* advised children to "[abstain] from eating between meals" and to "observe all family regulations; not to be late or irregular, at meals." "Everyone should be prompt," advised courtesy writer Alexander Murdoch Gow two years earlier in *Good Morals and Gentle Manners.* "The meal should not be delayed by our tardiness."[28]

Phelps's instruction not to be "late or irregular" at meals and Gow's emphasis on the importance of being "prompt" speak to the centrality of structure and orderliness when it came to Victorian approaches to eating. A rigid regularity marked meals, particularly dinner, at least according to the cultural ideal. Victorians so revered this regularity that when the fictional Mrs. Brunton complains about cooking for a household that is inconsistent in its arrival at the table, the family convenes a parlor meeting to discuss the problem. Snacking jeopardized the structure and orderliness of meals and disturbed the balance that their sequence represented. Imbalance was no more obvious than when diners breeched standards of punctuality. A late child was an offense to the family's fellowship, an empty seat, an affront to the members' mutual association.[29]

To be "late or irregular" at dinner, having eaten between meals, showed disregard for one's family, but perhaps worse, it also demonstrated indifference to one's place in the larger world. The dining room incubated social order and a sense of where one fit within it; here one polished the skills of courtesy and diplomacy necessary for success in the public sphere. A child's behavior at the table spoke to his or her potential to negotiate the world outside the home. Snacking undermined the instructive potential of the meal; the snacker snubbed the important educational institution of dinner. Failure, by snacking, to "observe all family regulations" revealed a character weakness that might, if not corrected, translate to a future social liability of a more serious nature: a failure to maintain middle-class status.[30]

But snacking represented more than one's failure to fulfill a family—and, by extension, worldly—role. It also signaled a failure to live up to certain moral standards. In an *Atlantic Monthly* article, F. B. Perkins recalled his parents' strict refusal to grant him "stomachic reinforcements" during church services in the early part of the nineteenth century. "Neither cooky [*sic*], raisin, nor peppermint lozenge would they dispense. It would violate the important rules—'Attend to the sermon,' and 'No eating between meals.'" Outside church their response to such a request was repeatedly, "My son, if you are hungry, you can eat a piece of good dry bread."[31]

Perkins's parents scolded him for wanting a snack at church for two reasons. First, on religious grounds, to indulge one's appetite while a pastor was delivering a sermon would have been disrespectful at best and sinful at worst. Second, on secular grounds, common wisdom held that one simply should not eat between meals. But this admonition was more than a mere health guideline; it was a down-right test of character. It smacked of moralism, as did Perkins's parents' insistence on the rather ascetic option of dry bread. Adherence to or transgression of the commandment against snacking powerfully revealed a person's inner strength, or lack thereof—it tested one's mettle and showed what a person was made of.

If there was a queen of domestic moralism in the nineteenth century, it was Catharine Beecher. A proponent of female education, Beecher wrote cookbooks and collaborated with her sister, Harriet Beecher Stowe, author of *Uncle Tom's Cabin,* on the widely read domestic manual *American Woman's Home* (1869). For Catharine Beecher, the nuclear family was a microcosm of the Kingdom of God, and the home was a miniaturized heaven. Every detail of domestic work had spiritual significance. When it came to snacking, she condemned it. For her, eating whenever one pleased simply "to gratify the palate" was unjustifiable. "When a tempting article is presented," she instructed, "every person should exercise sufficient self-denial to wait till the proper time for eating arrives." Beecher's word choice reveals the Christian overtones in her advice. She describes foods one might spontaneously consume outside the proper meal schedule as "tempting," linking snacking to sin. For her, eating apart from meals for the purpose of satiating one's cravings represented more than a breach of etiquette: it was a failure of character, a corruption of virtue. The solution was stark and simple: self-denial, a concept with decidedly Christian underpinnings. For Beecher, denying the body its whims was godly. One's response to the weighted dilemma of whether or not to snack demonstrated one's moral fiber.[32]

In addition to serving as a kind of diagnostic tool that revealed character, rules against snacking also provided an antidote to moral weakness. Learning to obey them helped youths develop integrity and virtue and protected them from an array of vices that might compromise their respectability further down the road. The act of eating was thickly laced with social prohibitions because the middle class perceived indulging the appetite at whim as dancing dangerously close to the edge of a variety of character flaws related to an inability to control the animal instincts. Highly suspicious of the body, Victorians saw appetite, like sex, as deeply capricious and best repressed. The temptation to eat between meals, which, for instructive purposes, stood in for other temptations, provided a unique tool for tutoring youth in the ultimate Victorian value: restraint.[33]

Restraint formed the general underlying theme of most nineteenth-century etiquette manuals. The young Victorian needed to learn to negotiate many behaviors that other diners could interpret as code for an unruly appetite: leaving immediately after dinner suggested that the guest came only for the food; complimenting the host on a meal with more than a little enthusiasm framed him as a gourmand; helping himself rather than waiting to be served revealed an appetite-driven impatience. Gow elaborated on the politics of restraint at the table, cautioning that one must not rush to dinner, begin to eat before one's elders, spit or blow one's nose, make unnecessary noise with the lips, ask for coffee when only tea had been provided, tip the chair back when finished, excuse oneself from the table without apologizing, or take any untouched provisions for later. Above all, one must avoid the appearance of desire. He counseled the reader not to show any eagerness when approaching the dinner table. As he put it, "We should not seem hungry." Limiting one's behavior at the table was good training for limiting one's behavior away from it.[34]

In addition to expressing moral failure, snacking was also an offense to the integrity of the human body as nineteenth-century Americans understood it; it compromised physical health. Although popular voices like the Beecher sisters spiritualized snacking, they also medicalized it, drawing on the rhetoric of science—both popular and professional—to persuade readers of this particular habit's dangers. Snacking was a much-derided social blunder, but more than that, it was simply "unsafe." It wreaked havoc with the Victorians' increasingly finicky metabolism.[35]

Americans have long been known for abundance at the table. Prior to industrialization, most Americans ate what might be considered a farmer's diet. They consumed hearty fare that sustained arduous physical labor, agricultural and otherwise. With the affluence industrialization brought and the considerable amount of clerical, desk-bound work it created, fewer Americans were burning the same number of calories as previous generations. Although lifestyles had become more sedentary, dietary patterns were slow to follow. The result was dyspepsia, or chronic indigestion.

If eating too much at meals caused indigestion, then so did eating between meals. In his 1864 book of home remedies, Dr. A. W. Chase condemned the practice of "constantly nibbling at raisins, candy, cheese, apples, and every other edible," a practice, he intimated, was particularly common among grocers. "Stop, until just before the meal, then eat what you like, go to your meal, and return, not touching again until mealtimes, and you are safe." For Dr. Chase, it was not just the "overloading of the stomach at meals" but the "constant eating and drinking between meals" that debilitated the worn out digestive system and brought on dyspepsia. Dr. William Whitty Hall was adamant when it came to snacks: under his care, the dyspeptic must "resolutely and most strictly avoid eating anything whatever between meals," except, he conceded, a slice of lemon, which had a "cooling" medicinal effect.[36]

The problem with snacking was not only that it encouraged gluttony, which led to dyspepsia, but that it overtaxed the digestive organs, which were, in the nineteenth century, desperately in need of some time off. In the words of Catharine Beecher, "Children as well as grown persons are often injured by eating between their regular meals, thus weakening the stomach by not affording it any time for rest." How much rest did the stomach need? In her opinion, it required five hours between regular meals: three for digestion and two for repose. Dr. Chase agreed with her, with the caveat that young children usually need to eat every three hours and those who walked might benefit from an exception to the rule—a cracker for nourishment before going out.[37]

In the opinion of nineteenth-century dietary reformers, snacking held manifold dangers for the digestive system, not the least of which was the rich nature of the foods many people, especially children, chose for snacks. Although we may not think of raisins and apples as unhealthy, they were frequently consumed as dessert in the nineteenth century, so when Dr. Chase warned his readers about nibbling on them throughout the day, he was attacking his readers' sweet tooth. More dubious were sugary pastries and other readily available desserts. "Dyspeptic[s]," according to Dr. Chase, suffered in part because of their proclivity toward taking "puddings or pies at any time." Eliza Leslie counseled her readers to punish a child who "purloin[ed] cakes or sweetmeats by giving him none the next time they [were] on the table."[38]

Beecher criticized such sugary goodies for their "highly concentrated nourishment." Overly "nourishing" foods focused a dangerously high amount of energy in a small, insufficient bulk. Cakes and cookies could be safely consumed, argued Beecher, only when coupled with "more bulky, less nourishing substances," for example, the grains, vegetables, and meats that generally rounded out a meal. Indulged on their own, these energy-dense foods were certain to weaken the digestive powers and skew the delicate balances of the human system. In popular opinion, these foods could also lead to an affinity for alcohol. For this reason, the author of an advice book for young mothers warned that children should be restricted from treating their tongues to "stray morsels of food at irregular times," especially "biscuits, fruit, and sweets." "Just in proportion as we gratify our propensity for excitement at the confectioner's shop," cautioned another parenting manual, "in the same proportion do we expose ourselves to the danger of yielding to temptation, should other gratifications present themselves." In this author's opinion, the confectioner's shop was "the high road to drunkenness," the phrase "other gratifications" being a euphemism for love of the bottle.[39]

Because of children's particular attraction to sweet, rich foods, especially candies, cakes, and cookies (and the moral pitfalls associated with them), dietary reformers warned parents to avert unnecessary temptation. As a preventative measure, they should supply growing sons and daughters with substantial quantities of decidedly prosaic food. "Never tempt their appetites by delicacies when plain food is not relished," wrote Dr. Chase. "Plain food" was a panacea for children's unwieldy appetites, and no food was plainer than a slice of cold, unbuttered bread. "A piece of bread will be a healthy lunch" (read "snack"), he wrote. "A child seldom eats bread to excess." Recall the result of Perkins's childhood request for a snack in church. Refusing him candies and cookies, his parents instead offered a piece of dry loaf. The option was unappealing by design. Proper middle-class

Victorians, his parents drew on the instructive, reforming properties of the ultimate plain food: unadorned bread.[40]

Good, dry bread may not have appealed to Perkins or other hungry children his age, but it certainly appealed to adults who sought to discipline unwieldy children and raise them as respectable middle-class citizens. For these adults, dry bread was good indeed. It was good for putting down cravings and for teaching children to overcome their palates' frivolous whims. It was good for impressing on them the virtue of self-control and the dangers of failed restraint. It spoke to them about their responsibility to family and society and schooled them in the etiquette they would one day need to take their place successfully in the larger world. The prospect of dry bread was also good for protecting the ritual of dinner from corruption and, by extension, strengthening the integrity of familial bonds.

The rhetoric of snacking in nineteenth-century cookbooks, mothers' manuals, advice columns, home remedy references, and medical tomes reveals that eating between meals—a habit that did not previously lift eyebrows—had become a veritable social (and medical) sin, at least among the increasingly scrutinizing middle class. To the extent that dinner had become sacred, snacking had become sinful. One seemed to serve as a barometer of the other.

As industrialization forced families into new working schedules and social roles, eating patterns changed, and dinner shifted to accommodate a variety of practical, social, and psychological needs. In the new context of urban, industrialized America, evening, the time when families came together after the day's separation, became special. Logically, so did dinner. In the mid-nineteenth century, this meal started doing double duty: it fed Americans' spirits as well as their stomachs. It reminded them of who they were as families and affirmed their sense of membership in a growing middle-class society. The evening meal would become even more special when, on top of these uses, it became a way to sense and express belonging to a larger family: the nation.

4

HOW DINNER
BECAME AMERICAN

IN THE FIRST half of the twentieth century, dinner became American, and no artist depicted its American-ness more enduringly than Norman Rockwell. In his famous 1943 *Saturday Evening Post* illustration "Freedom from Want," a family gathers around a plainly set table with a large browned turkey at its center in anticipation of a satisfying Thanksgiving meal. Their purpose is to enjoy this harvest meal together and, it being a time of war, to celebrate the country's heritage of prosperity and freedom. Rockwell painted a picture of patriotism using images of food and domesticity. He portrayed dinner as inherently special, and it was, both in the image and in life. But what had made it special during the nineteenth century was only the foundation for what made it so in the early twentieth. Whereas dinner had served as a vehicle of family cohesion and an expression of middle-class identity in the nineteenth century, in the twentieth, as Rockwell hinted, it became a way to connect with the nation. From the 1880s and especially after 1900, the idea of the family dinner began to fuse with the idea of America, but before this fusion took place, something curious happened. On its way to becoming American, dinner became French.

Dinner traveled a formidable distance on the road to becoming what Norman Rockwell depicted during World War II. As we have seen, it started out in the early years of European settlement as a frontier endeavor that shared many qualities with Old World peasant fare. With its emphasis on one-pot meals, dinner was, in essence, a New World version of a medieval European meal. In the eighteenth century, it became refined and rationalized, featuring English sensibilities and the Enlightenment qualities of symmetry, order, and balance. Even during the decades following the Revolution, the American dinner remained a variation on a distinctly British theme. But sometime in the nineteenth century, diners embraced a decidedly more genteel and significantly fussier and more flamboyant eating tradition than that of England. With much pomp and pageantry, dinner left behind the heavy British dishes that had come to define it and incorporated the delicacies of an altogether different culinary landscape.

In the households and institutions of the privileged, and later in those of the emerging middle class, French foods and dining customs became indispensible for anyone who was, or wanted to be, someone. French food and foodways expressed distinction and aspiration. They served as tools one could use to leverage social status. After all, they embodied sophistication. When Alexander Marjoribanks dined at the Montgomery House during his visit to Boston in the 1850s, the gourmet spread the chefs had laid out for dinner surprised and impressed him: cutlet *de veau,* codfish with Madeira sauce, lamb *en papillote,* mutton with a *sauce piquant,* larded sweetbreads, chicken fricassee, and ham omelet were just a few of the menu items the Scotsman noted in his journal.

Marjoribanks was traveling in the United States just as Americans' taste for such British classics as roasts, puddings, and pies was giving way to a preference for delicacies from the land of fois gras and escargots. "With singular good sense," commented Marjoribanks, Americans have "discarded to a great extent the common English or plain roast and boiled cookery, and adopted the scientific elaborate cuisine of France." He deemed such a cuisine superior to that less-than-French approach to food whereby "taste is mere gross appetite" and "the quantity of solid meat consumed is held to be the test . . . of the excellence of the entertainment." Americans were turning a corner in their approach to dinner, and Marjoribanks approved.[1]

At least three aspects of French dining sensibility penetrated (many would say improved) American eating during the mid- to late

nineteenth century: the division of dinner into a sequence of courses—soup, entrée, salad, dessert; the association of particular kinds of
foods with these courses—lettuce leaves and vinaigrette with the salad
course, for example; and the adoption of a far more intricate dining
room code of etiquette. Each of these aspects of French dining contributed to the new formality associated with dinner, which functioned
as a kind of language for elites and later the middle class. By dining *à
la française,* the privileged and upwardly mobile could set themselves
apart from the rest of society using a vocabulary of silverware and salad greens.

THE MONTGOMERY HOUSE meal that Marjoribanks enjoyed was not
entirely French because it lacked one crucial element of French dining: courses. The Scotsman delighted in the exquisite dishes prepared
by skilled chefs from abroad, but he was appalled at the sight of his
fellow diners partaking of the various dishes at once, "cramming"
their plates, each preparation mixing slightly with the next. Charles
Dickens called those who let the juices of their foods mingle on their
plates "dirty feeders," and Marjoribanks was tempted to apply the
term. The Scotsman could come up with only one possible explanation for this behavior: "the extreme haste [diners were] in to bring
their repast to an untimely end." If Americans were ever going to fully
adopt French dinner-table sensibilities and the tradition of courses,
then they were going to have to develop a habit that did not come naturally to them: slowing down. Thirty years after Marjoribanks's observations, the American middle class was still trying to learn this lesson.[2]
   Leisurely meals had long been a natural part of the upper-class
dining routine, which easily accommodated new European fashions.
Courses, more elegantly referred to as *service à la russe,* became de rigueur at restaurants and hotels, as well as at upper-class dinner parties, and diners devoted no small amount of time and attention to
consuming them. Formal meals commonly included six, eight, and
even ten courses. Cookbook author Fannie Farmer presented an 1896
menu that featured twelve courses. The annual banquet of the Ohio
Society of New York, held at the famed Delmonico's restaurant a decade earlier, featured oysters followed by soup and hors d'oeuvres; a
fish course; a *relevé* consisting of a beef dish and tomatoes au gratin;

an entrée, which included veal croquettes, chicken, green beans, and peas; a roast accompanied by salad; a dessert of Madeira pudding *à la mode*; and a final offering of fruit, petits fours, and coffee. As a courtesy, the bill of fare, printed entirely in French, would have appeared at each table setting; the dinner it outlined must have occupied several hours.[3]

By the 1880s, the vogue for French food and customs was beginning to trickle down. The wealthy were no longer the only ones serving and enjoying their dinners sequentially; those middle-class families willing to slow down were as well. Popular media had been encouraging members of the middle class, always on the lookout for ways to raise their status by imitating the elite, to embrace courses even though they required considerably more time. Although readers of a magazine like *Good Housekeeping* might not be able to afford to serve larded sweetbreads or codfish with Madeira sauce at the family dinner table, they could likely make room in their schedules for courses. Time was dear, but if members of the middle class accommodated this new dining trend with the help of a servant or two, their status could only benefit.[4]

In the increasingly class-conscious climate of late-nineteenth-century America, not serving meals in courses was beginning to look uncultured. "In too many families," chided food writer Christine Terhune Herrick, "the art of dining is entirely unknown, its place being taken by what might be better termed a periodical 'feed.' Dining, in the true sense of the word," she insisted, "is impossible without deliberation." Instead of serving food "jumbled on the table in a helter-skelter fashion," Herrick stated, homemakers should prepare a three-course meal: soup with bread, meat with vegetables, and dessert. An additional salad course preceding the dessert was optional. Though clearly not the simplest way to do dinner, this approach was practically effortless compared to the expectations of a truly formal event. Herrick implied that courses were exceedingly more respectable than the old-fashioned custom of serving all dishes of a meal simultaneously, and as rising numbers of people adopted the new mode, not eating one's dinner in this fashion became a social liability.[5]

The French also influenced American dinner habits by introducing many of the types of dishes for which specific courses would become known. Though they were largely imported, we generally think of many of these dishes as American today. Depending on whether or not oysters opened a meal (a French custom that rapidly permeated American dining culture in the nineteenth century), the first or second course of a respectable Victorian dinner, following the French standard, was almost always soup, or *potage*, as the menu was likely to read. American colonists had never been big soup eaters, though they depended heavily on soup-like dishes such as porridge and stew. In contrast to those concoctions, characterized by considerable (and often more sizeable) solids, soup is a relatively thin preparation with more liquid than solids. Soup became popular among the American elite before the middle class enjoyed it, and its popularization may trace back to the French Revolution, when gastronomes such as Jean Anthelme Brillat-Savarin joined the wave of French emigrants fleeing the Reign of Terror who brought their cooking to American shores. In 1794, Brillat-Savarin opened a "restorateur" in Boston, where he acquired a reputation as the "Prince of soups." An ancient dish also enjoyed by certain other immigrant groups, such as Germans in Pennsylvania (known for potato soups) and Africans (whose peanut soups both master and slave enjoyed on southern plantations), soup did not penetrate the broader American palate until the late nineteenth century. This is also when soup became sophisticated, and serving croutons with it—crisp pieces of fried bread—added to its panache.[6]

Although seen as sophisticated when opening a meal, soup had the opposite reputation when standing in for a meal—perhaps because, when eaten as dinner, soup was a simple, one-pot meal that recalled the seventeenth- and eighteenth-century approach to dinner. Or perhaps soup for dinner was unsophisticated because it was sometimes associated with poverty and thrift. Charitable soup kitchens where the down-and-out could come for a free hot meal served this sometimes watery dish because it was both economical and nutritious. During the two world wars, cookbooks and pamphlets encouraged homemakers to make use of leftovers as a way to free up resources for the troops and the Allies, and adding leftovers to the soup pot—or relying on leftovers as the main ingredient in soup—was an apt way to heed this civic call. So, while soup expressed patriotism for a short time in American history, it was usually perceived as a lesser meal.[7]

Preparation as a separate course in the French fashion transformed soup from a humble, outmoded subsistence food into a respected expression of gentility, heightened by the liberal use of (frequently misspelled) French terminology. Consommé, bisque, and purée are originally French terms for soups that have become naturalized into the English language. Brillat-Savarin is credited with introducing the *potage à la julienne,* a soup of finely chopped vegetables that Mary F. Henderson in *Practical Cooking and Dinner Giving* (1876) simply calls "julienne soup." Because French terminology leant an air of sophistication to a dish, restaurant menus usually listed offerings in part or fully in French. Henderson's cookbook features a glossary of French and English terms for the benefit for those homemakers wishing to present their dinner guests with a written bill of fare in French in keeping with the fashion of the times.[8]

Soup was a standard first or second course for most formal nineteenth- and early-twentieth-century dinners (and increasingly for less formal ones as well); salad, its twin French import, usually featured later in the meal between the entrée and dessert. Though salad was not unheard of in colonial America, references to it in the historical record are sparse, especially with respect to the middling and lower classes. That only the upper classes ate salad consistently before the late nineteenth century may have something to do with the perishability of lettuce. Prized and associated with the fashionable tables of England and France, romaine was highly seasonal and too delicate to travel long distances in train cars. By the 1870s, however, greenhouses on the outskirts of urban areas began to supply cities with lettuce leaves, cucumbers, radishes, and tomatoes, enabling the middle class to make salad a standard course. Just after the turn of the twentieth century, "iceberg" lettuce emerged, a sturdy variety that could stand up to the conditions of cross-continental travel, making salad even more readily available as a dinner-table option.[9]

The most common dressing for salads in the United States was based on the French novelty mayonnaise, a generally made-from-scratch concoction formed by beating together egg yolks and oil. The process required about fifteen minutes, and its success, according to one nineteenth-century British author, depended on "the mode of working it up, which is very elaborate." Mayonnaise was also the key ingredient in other popular late-nineteenth-century forms of salad that persist today: chicken salad, potato salad, ham salad, and so forth. Although staples of summer picnic spreads and deli-counter sandwiches today, these were delicacies in the nineteenth century associated with fashionable ladies' luncheons. Ironically, although mayonnaise is indeed French (some have argued that the condiment was named in honor of the French siege of Mahon in 1756), greens in Paris were more likely to sport vinaigrette, which Americans in turn called "French dressing."[10]

For middle-class Americans of the Victorian era, salad dressing was socially important; in their view, properly combining the ingredients and delicately tossing the greens was an art, not unlike baking a cake. In particular, they considered it a feminine art and usually expected a female to do the honors. An old French tradition not unheard of in the United States during the Victorian era held that a young woman with nimble fingers should toss a salad. (To remark, *elle retourne la salade avec les doigts*, was to describe a lady as youthful and beautiful.) At a dinner party, the hostess customarily dressed the salad while her servants looked on. "It is an accomplishment to know how to dress a salad well," Mary Henderson noted. Such a skill was "especially prized in the fashionable world." Hostesses who wanted to display their skill further might concoct a more decorative dressing, such as Henderson's red mayonnaise sauce, tinted with ground lobster coral. This imaginative recipe anticipated the fanciful salads of the early twentieth century, when appearance trumped taste and innovations in form and hue acquired by a liberal use of gelatin and coloring took the salad into new and surprising territory.[11]

During the Victorian era, no dinner was complete without that other French course Americans took to with flair: dessert. Dessert was special not just because of its sweet taste but because of its separation from the rest of the meal as a uniquely end-of-dinner course. The word "dessert" derives from the French verb *desservir,* meaning to remove what is left on the table—literally, "to unserve." It was what those seated at the table enjoyed after they had finished dinner and the servants had cleared away the dishes.[12]

The concept of a sweet course following a savory entrée was largely foreign to Americans before the mid-nineteenth century. Meals had customarily incorporated sweet foods rather than keeping them separate. There had been no sweet note to look forward to at the end of dinner because the meal itself combined sweet and savory. In the colonial era, an apple pie might accompany a roasted bird, or a rich, cinnamon-spiced suet pudding might precede a pot of pease porridge and salt pork. Some meat pies were simultaneously savory and sweet. Mincemeat, for example, typically consisted of savory ingredients—minced beef and beef suet—and sweet ones, including apples, raisins, currants, sugared preserves, and sometimes sweet wine. Despite its sweet elements, mincemeat was not originally served as a dessert, though it would eventually become one. Mincemeat exemplifies the early American use of sugar as a flavor, not merely as a sweetener. Sugar also functioned as a digestive. Sweet jellies and jams frequently accompanied meats (in the same way that cranberry sauce often accompanies turkey on Thanksgiving or mint jelly often accompanies lamb) because they helped render fatty, sinewy, salt-preserved flesh more palatable.[13]

Before French influence transformed the American table, it had left its mark on the British one, and dessert in America benefited from this early cross-fertilization. In the sixteenth and seventeenth centuries, elite Brits enjoyed collations of fanciful candies accompanied by nuts, fruit, wine, and sometimes cheese in a custom that mimicked the French *voidée*, which the English called a "banquet." (Only in more recent times has the word "banquet" come to signify a feast.) These after-dinner events typically unfolded in separate rooms, garden retreats, or even banqueting houses, where partakers milled about as one would do at a cocktail hour today. The nut-and-fruit aspect of this English tradition crossed the ocean and was not uncommon in American households into the late nineteenth and early twentieth centuries. Author and clergyman Edward Everett Hale remembered "dates, prunes, raisins, figs, and nuts" as typical of a "handsome dessert" enjoyed during his nineteenth-century childhood, and as late as the 1920s, magazines like *Good Housekeeping* published menus for Thanksgiving meals that ended with a postpie course of nuts and fruit.[14]

As sugar became increasingly affordable and serving fashionable food grew more imperative culturally, Americans developed a special affinity for what the French had to offer when it came to dessert. Class-conscious Americans gravitated not only to the taste of sugary French delights but to the sophistication they embodied. Ices, tarts, creams, meringues, soufflés, flans, macaroons—these highly respected preparations closed a dinner party elegantly and expressed a household's gentility deliciously.

One French dessert eclipsed all others and became an icon of the new after-dinner institution. Legendarily invented by French chef Antoine Carême, the charlotte russe was a delicate, molded custard flavored with lemon, vanilla, or sherry, flanked by ladyfingers, and topped with Bavarian cream. Garnishes might include raspberries, strawberries, or almonds, and toward the twentieth century, variations appeared featuring coffee, caramel, and chocolate. In the twentieth century, this dessert would be demoted to a cream-topped round of sponge cake punctuated with a maraschino cherry and sold in cardboard containers as candy-store standbys. Jewish and Italian children in New York especially prized the Charlie Roosh, as it came to be known. Though the charlotte russe became Americanized and democratized just as numerous other French foods and customs would, during the Victorian era it epitomized the French sensibilities that the American upper and middle classes had gone to great lengths to acquire.[15]

WITH THE transformation of dinner into a reflection of French sensibilities in the late nineteenth century, courses and the foods they incorporated become fashionable. Soup, salad, and dessert came to define a proper dinner, and the more French they appeared, the better—which explains why hosts employed French names so conspicuously, though often inaccurately. But for the elite, as well as for middle-class Americans desperately trying to keep up with them, sequential courses, fancy French dishes, and elegant but difficult-to-pronounce words on menus were not enough. Now that they had begun to acquire urbane, Continental food customs, they wanted to display them. The formal dinner party proved the perfect stage.

Proper comportment at a formal dinner party was a perpetual middle-class conundrum. This fancy evening affair was new to this group of Americans, and presenting oneself appropriately at such a genteel occasion was a significant matter. It was essential that guests be entertained properly and that courses be tendered correctly. From this necessity emerged a fastidious set of rules outlining everything from the appropriate order of dishes to the right positioning of silverware. Along with salads, flans, and *service à la russe*, Americans readily embraced another French import: etiquette.

Though not exclusively French, the rules of the new social protocol reflected Americans' new fondness for French taste. Detailed guidelines—many elaborated ad nauseam in countless etiquette manuals—prescribed courtly, aristocratic behavior, and hardly an aristocracy had been courtlier than that of Louis XVI, the Sun King, who built Versailles and raised the twin arts of royal feasting and noble courtesy to unparalleled heights. Adopting a French-inspired mode of etiquette expressed the seriousness with which upper- and then middle-class Americans embraced refinement.[16]

In the spirit of the French court, American dinner parties during the Victorian era adhered to strict social customs when it came to escorting, serving, sitting, and standing. According to one etiquette manual, hostesses determined the male escorts for each female guest in anticipation of the official entrance into the dining room. She informed the gentlemen of their partners by way of written cards placed on a hall table. The host was paired with the lady in whose honor the dinner was being given, and the two made their entrance first, with the hostess and the husband of the guest of honor constituting the tail of the procession. Servants were always to offer food on diners' left side and wine on their right. The lady of the house was not to allow her plate to be removed until everyone else's had been, and she determined the appropriate moment, usually a lull in the after-dinner conversation, at which to signal her female companions to retreat with her to the drawing room, leaving the men free to discuss masculine subjects of interest over liquor and cigars.[17]

Although a host and hostess shouldered the responsibility for following proper protocol, guests had just as many rules to keep in mind. In her 1888 etiquette manual, *The Correct Thing in Good Society,* Florence Howe Hall reminded her male reader not to escort a lady into the dining room without first offering her his arm and to remember to rise when she left the room with her female companions at the close of the meal. Hall instructed guests of both sexes to avoid sitting on the edge of a chair, leaning too far forward during a meal, or setting elbows on the table. While eating, one was to make as little noise as possible (it was essential not to scrape the plate, clear one's throat, or smack one's lips), and as far as the soup and fish courses were concerned, asking for seconds was unacceptable. When it came to silverware, the rules became even more complex.[18]

Whereas flatware lacked variety during the seventeenth and early eighteenth centuries, there was an overabundance of it during the nineteenth century, which made the act of eating at the Victorian dinner party a veritable art. Multiple kinds of forks, knives, spoons, and serving utensils presented themselves to the dinner guest, each with a specific, categorical use. There were oyster forks, asparagus tongs, orange spoons, ice-cream knives, cake servers, grape shears, cheese scoops, soup ladles, nutpicks, and sugar sifters, to name a few. According to Florence Howe Hall, an individual place setting at a dinner party should include "two large knives, a small silver knife and fork for fish, three large forks, a table-spoon for soup, [and] a small oyster fork for eating raw oysters." Faced with "nearly a dozen solid silver articles to be used with the different courses," a fictitious traveler from China at an American dinner party circa 1900 regretted not having availed himself of etiquette lessons.[19]

Along with the multiplicity of flatware came a profusion of rules about how to use it. It was proper, for instance, to hold the fork in the right hand with the tines curving down; however, packing food on the back of the fork would require one to bring it to the mouth "wrong side up," and this was entirely unacceptable (see Figures 6a–b). Silver knives were the appropriate choice for cutting fruit; applying a steel knife to a peach or plum was a definite faux pas. One had to be careful not to inadvertently leave a spoon standing in a teacup or retain a utensil in hand once a plate had been removed. Studying the habits of the diners around him, the Chinese tourist remarked that "soup is eaten with a bowl-like spoon, and it is the grossest breach to place this in your mouth, or approach it endwise." Fish, he remarked, was only to be eaten with forks, and "to use the knife even to cut the fish would be unpardonable."[20]

We cannot underestimate the importance of following the rules of etiquette at a Victorian dinner party. More than the risk of embarrassment rode on one's ability to wield a knife and a fork properly—one's very status could be at stake. "You [can] at once recognize a person of the gentleman class," commented the Chinese traveler, "by his use of his knife or fork. . . . If he is a commoner, he eats with his knife; if a gentleman, with his fork." Whether or not sightings of "knife eaters" were common at upscale dinner parties, the fact that diners were aware of and perhaps even on the lookout for this category of guest underscores how deeply they read into fellow diners' mealtime habits. They expected to recognize elites by the elegance and ease with which they followed dinnertime decorum, and they knew that a distinctly awkward lack of refinement would give away working men and women who had little time or interest, not to mention resources, to devote to such pretentiousness. Most elites were groomed in the complicated ways of formal entertainment, and most working-class folk remained happily uninitiated, but members of the middle class, who were frequently self-taught, treaded a finer line.[21]

When it came to the uses and importance of etiquette, members of the middle class found themselves in a position altogether different from that of laborers or the gentry. Thanks to the Industrial Revolution, Americans of this demographic had grown in their means and status and entertained high hopes of building on their achievements. They found etiquette a particularly apt tool with which to express their aspirations for the future and their emerging image of themselves as successful. By displaying an ability to engage social codes properly, especially at the dinner table, many hoped to negotiate their way into more exclusive circles and prove themselves worthy of association with those of higher rank. For them, adhering to proper etiquette was about more than maintaining social status; often it was also about aggrandizing it, though usually at significant risk.

Etiquette worked in two ways: it offered an "in," an opportunity for inclusion, but because it existed largely to demarcate social boundaries, it could prove ruthlessly exclusive. In his 1880 novel *The Rise of Silas Lapham*, William Dean Howells captures this precariousness brilliantly. Lapham, the protagonist, is a self-made man who courts the higher echelons of Boston society with a clumsiness that betrays his working-class roots. He finds himself at a formal dinner party with much to gain and just as much to lose. The etiquette books he has read inform the way he dresses, talks, and comports himself at the dinner, but somehow they have neglected to prepare him for a particularly delicate situation: declining wine politely. The teetotaler unexpectedly finds himself with his wineglass full and, not wishing to offend his host by refusing it, indulges obligingly. Unfortunately, after several unsolicited refills, he makes a sorry fool of himself when he becomes unforgivably drunk. The mishap threatens to mar his personal reputation, but far worse are the possible repercussions for his business relationships with the men at the table and those in their network, who are sure to hear of his scandalous behavior. For a time, it is unclear whether his professional life and many of his personal relationships will survive. As Howells illustrates in this scenario, a thoughtless dinner table blunder could compromise a man's career and perhaps even destroy it all together.[22]

With the increasing slipperiness of class in the industrialized era, etiquette had become a test. It helped distinguish the elegantly civilized from the folksy and unrefined. Such a test was necessary in a world where urban anonymity made it possible to imitate class status easily. But when it came to the dinner table, the complexity and subtlety of proper decorum proved hard to counterfeit, and the class status of the diner who failed to meet the standards of modern etiquette was quickly—and shamefully—revealed. It didn't take much. If the diner handled the silverware in an antiquated "country" style, sat down to or rose from the table hastily, refused the soup (or asked for seconds), uttered a vulgarism such as the word "stomach" (or any other questionably direct reference to the body), or arrived more than five minutes early or late, he jeopardized his prospects of climbing the social, and consequently the economic, ladder.[23]

CONFORMING TO the new French-inspired standards of a formal dinner party in the mid- to late nineteenth century depended not only on a proper sequence of courses and a savvy knowledge of etiquette but on the deft work of cooks and servants. The elaborateness of an evening event was directly proportional to the number of servants behind the scenes, and when these largely live-in workers were no longer reliable, affordable, or available, American dining standards had to change accordingly. No longer could dinner retain its Victorian formality; no longer could the meal's celebrated French sensibility continue to define it. Servants underpinned French food fashions in America, and when they began to disappear, dinner started to simplify and, in simplifying, to Americanize.

Servants were critical to the success of the Victorian dinner party primarily because of courses. At each stage of the meal, waiters replaced sullied dishes and silverware. They delivered food to the table, refreshed wine glasses, replenished the bread, and, between the meat and the dessert, removed the upper tablecloth to reveal a fresh linen underneath. In the mid- to late nineteenth century, most middle-class households depended on at least one servant, and sometimes three or four. Catharine Beecher called for four servants in her instructions for a middle-class dinner party: two waiters and two cooks. In their absence, she warned, "it is absolute cruelty for a husband to urge, or even allow his wife to go through all the toil, anxiety, and effort needful for such an affair."[24]

Serving dinner *à la russe* was perhaps the ultimate way to exhibit status because it put servants in the spotlight, thereby emphasizing the household's middle-class prestige. Having servants and relying on them visibly in front of guests set hosts apart from laborers and landed them in the same category as the utmost elite: they were now among the served. But unlike the elite household, the middle-class household could only afford a handful of servants, not enough to host a truly extravagant event, and when the pool of reliable servants began to dwindle in the second half of the nineteenth century, the upper class snatched up remaining candidates by offering higher wages, leaving many middle-class households high and dry.[25]

The servant problem had two prongs: dwindling availability and decreasing reliability. In the years following the Civil War, factory jobs became open to women, and later in the century, so did professional positions as typists, stenographers, and shopkeepers. Drawn by these domestic-service alternatives, fewer Anglo-American, Canadian, Irish, and northern European immigrant women were available for hire in homes. Central and eastern European immigrants replaced the initial generation of servants on the East Coast and in the interior, with Asian immigrants coming to the rescue on the West Coast. Like their predecessors, however, the new generation of servants kept an eye out for better jobs, viewing domestic service as a stopgap while they sought more desirable work. Worse, most of the new immigrants lacked proficiency in English and were at a distinct cultural disadvantage when it came to cooking American food. Surely some, perhaps many, made concerted efforts to master their household tasks, but the reigning stereotype was one of ignorance and carelessness, and frustrated homemakers complained widely about irresponsible help.[26]

Unreliable servants were the bane of middle-class households in the mid- to late nineteenth century, and their substandard abilities in the kitchen and dining room proved a liability to the homemaker wishing to display her refinement by way of a formal dinner party. "To give a dinner," wrote an English traveler in 1840, "is to the majority of Americans really an effort, not from disinclination to give one, but from the indifference and ignorance of the servants." Catharine Beecher was careful to warn her readers that in order to succeed in holding the dinner party for which she offered meticulous instructions, the homemaker needed her cooks to be "experienced" and her waiters "well-trained." Only with careful tutelage on the part of the homemaker could her servants fulfill their duties competently. According to cookbook author Marion Harland, such training was the key to "poetic repasts" and the praise they elicited. The homemaker who neglected to train her servants properly would surely be cursed with "vulgar joints and stiff dinner tables." Perhaps worse than a "stiff table" and substandard meat was the risk of a poorly prepared and amateurishly served meal, making the host and hostess look "green" and compromising their standing as members of the middle class.[27]

Magazine columns and newspaper editorials pitched several solutions to the servant problem, and a few were put to the test. One was simply to modify the meal and lower expectations—in short, to informalize—but resistance to this solution ran deep. A French observer noted that when it came to dining, middle-class Americans were "not willing to be themselves"; they refused to entertain and be entertained "in a manner suitable to their modest means." Rather, they lived plainly and frugally so that on special occasions they could hold an extravagant dinner on a scale "utterly unrelated to their everyday life." At such a dinner, Susan Hayes Ward noted, "course follows course, many of them sent away scarce tasted." Meanwhile, "expeditious washings" of the household's limited dishes must take place between courses unless extras were borrowed from the neighbors. Ward believed eradicating that "bane of modern entertainments: the enormous number of courses that style makes essential" would best alleviate the pressure. But modifying expectations was akin to sacrificing a household's reputation, and, not surprisingly, it was a last resort.[28]

The Home Economics Association, established in 1893, presented another solution. It ran schools to train servants and thereby raise the level of skilled labor in the home so that the middle class might maintain its standard of living—formal dinner parties included. But by the early twentieth century, this solution was no longer viable because candidates were so few and far between. Due to its failure to locate sufficient numbers of servants for training, the organization's focus shifted away from disappearing servants and toward their replacement: the middle-class housewife. Thanks to advances in technology, an entourage of newly developed appliances soon assisted the modern American homemaker in her daily routine, and eventually electricity came to her aid. Automatic devices were often advertised as mechanical domestics—even the Kelvinator, an early refrigerator, was hailed as the hostess's "perfectly wonderful helper." But the effect of the new "help" was less a lightening of the workload than a raising of standards. Rather than easing household chores by turning out more properly trained servants, the home economics movement essentially trained the middle-class housewife to take over the work of her help in a smooth and intelligent manner of which she could be proud.[29]

But a single set of hands, no matter how agile and efficient, could not be expected to simultaneously maintain a household and serve formal multicourse meals. Only one of these matters was indispensable, and logic easily determined which. A homemaker could relinquish her ritual of formal dinners, and the family would survive. But by no means could she neglect laundry, cleaning, and the basic feeding of her kin. The decline of servants necessarily meant a decline in dinnertime expectations; the servantless household and Victorian middle-class ideas about proper evening meals were simply incompatible. Thankfully, home economists were giving their full attention to the dilemma. Their contributions, along with those of the food-processing industry, would prove salvific—or devastating, depending on one's perspective—for decades to come.[30]

In the early twentieth century, the home economics approach to cooking focused on helping the housewife save time. For Christine Frederick, this meant cutting out steps. Tired of feeling like a slave to her domestic chores, she tapped into her husband's enthusiasm for Taylorism, a new principle of scientific management that reorganized tasks for the sake of efficiency, and she adapted those principles to her kitchen. The result was a novel approach to cooking that pivoted on rationalism and professionalism. Frederick called the idea "household engineering." She saw the kitchen as a factory writ small, likening the counter to a mechanic's bench and the cook's utensils and ingredients to tools and supplies. She broke down processes into their smallest of parts in order to systematize each discrete kitchen task as well as the space that facilitated it. An omelet, she concluded, is most efficiently prepared when the icebox is near the cabinet, the cabinet close to the stove, and the stove within reach of the serving table. Grouping utensils according to function (preparation, serving, cleanup) further streamlined kitchen operations. Frederick's approach to cooking concerned itself less with the quality of the product than its swift and methodical accomplishment. Such an approach resulted in meals that were bland, pragmatic, and carefully contrived.[31]

In the years following World War I, efficiency found a friend in the food industry, and when Christine Frederick and other home economists started to get cozy with major food-processing companies, a new approach to cooking began to permeate the country, one that centered on processed foods. Packaged food saved steps. A can of soup provided a humble but almost instantaneous meal, and combined with a few ingredients and baked into a casserole, it could go a long way to making a substantial dinner. With a pudding mix, a gelatin packet, or a can of grated pineapple at her fingertips, a housewife could assemble a "homemade" dessert in a matter of minutes. Cooking had become a kind of magic.[32]

But for all the promises of the food industry and the home economists, dinner suffered a demotion as it transitioned away from the French culinary sensibilities so prized in the preceding decades. No longer were middle-class homemakers holding multicourse dinner parties and reading in etiquette books about how to dress for and act at the fashionable affairs to which they anticipated invitations. Instead, they were learning how to cook for themselves in the novel absence of servants and hoping that if their husbands brought a colleague or boss home from work, the contents of a few packages and cans thrown together and doctored up to look homemade would prove satisfactory.

Home economics tackled the servant problem with a solution—training proper servants—but eventually became a support system for those who, in their newfound servantless situations, would have to take up the slack. Rather than resolving the servant problem, the home economics movement accommodated it, and the main accommodator was the housewife, who was now expected to take on the work of the servant, turn it into a domestic science, and embark on it with cheerfulness and proficiency—all without remuneration. What is more, some leaders in the home economics movement called for women to approach their domestic duties as an art, a means of creative self-expression through which they might derive not only satisfaction but personal meaning. Other women who could not stomach this sort of thinking presented a more radical solution: cooperative housekeeping.[33]

Why not centralize cooking? wondered women fed up with inept help who had no intention of assuming kitchen responsibilities themselves. In a cooperative arrangement, each member would take turns preparing an evening meal or contribute resources toward the hiring of a professional cook. Utopians such as the Shakers had done this for generations. Despite a number of floundered attempts, including the ill-fated cooperative housekeeping club of prominent Harvard Square housewives and their husbands organized by Melusina Fay Pierce in the 1860s, the movement gained momentum around the turn of the century. Take, for example, a dining club established in 1907 in Carthage, Missouri. Members rented a clapboard house and outfitted it to accommodate dinner for sixty. Participating households drew lots for tables (not everyone could sit near the windows) and ate as individual family units using their own china brought from home. Rent from two boarders and membership dues covered expenses, including compensation for a manager, two cooks, two waitresses, and a dishwasher. One member praised the experiment, which appealed particularly to those unable to find or afford reliable servants, as a "Home for the Help-less."[34]

Other cooperatives, such as the Twentieth Century Food Company of New Haven, Connecticut, skipped over the home-away-from-home aspect of Carthage-style arrangements and delivered dinner directly to participants' doors. This setup enabled diners to enjoy the benefits of centralized cooking while still partaking of meals as a family in their own homes, but it was not without additional logistical challenges. The problem of how to keep a multicourse meal at a desirably warm temperature plagued the delivery-based system. One solution, proposed by author Charlotte Perkins Gilman in her serial novel *What Diantha Did* (1909–1910), was the asbestos-lined food container. This specially insulated aluminum vessel comes to the rescue in Gilman's story about a woman and her cooked-food service. When a cooperative participant invites a skeptic to dinner, the guest is converted, enthusiastically pronouncing the roast beef "hot and juicy," the salad "crisp," the ice cream "hard," and the coffee—just hot enough to almost burn the tongue—"perfect." "Why—it's like Paris," she proclaims. For many women who took up war work during the 1910s, when cooperative cooked-food services were in their prime, a warm dinner delivered to the door may not have been "Paris," but it was certainly a welcome, if short-lived, luxury.[35]

Cooperative housekeeping, with its feminist and socialist underpinnings, never flourished in the United Stated, but it did receive significant attention in popular media between the 1880s and 1920s. Some Americans would have learned about it through Gilman's novel, others through the utopian fiction of Edward Bellamy, who, along with Gilman, advocated for kitchen-less houses. *Good Housekeeping* published an influential article by Bellamy in 1889, spurring the creation of numerous "Bellamy Clubs" in which women put to practice the writer's experimental ideas. Between 1918 and 1919, *Ladies Home Journal* published a series of articles on cooperative arrangements with titles like "Will the Kitchen Be Outside the Home?" and "One Kitchen Fire for 200 People." In 1923, *Woman's Home Companion* sponsored a contest in which readers could submit cooperative housekeeping plans designed specifically for their towns or neighborhoods and win a $100 prize contingent on the establishment of an actual cooperative.[36]

Had it become mainstream, cooperative housekeeping might have set the American dinner on a very different trajectory than the one that brought the meal to where it is today. Kitchen-less houses might have become the norm; apartment dwellers might have learned to rely on centralized food services included in monthly rent; cooking might have transformed into an occasional leisure activity. At the same time, the family dinner as nineteenth- and early-twentieth-century Americans knew it might have dissolved, along with the institutions that came to be associated with it: proper manners, polite conversation, and familial accountability.

Because cooperative housekeeping ultimately failed, kitchen-less houses and centralized cooking facilities did not become the norm, and the evening dinner remained strictly a family affair. The reasons for the failure are no mystery. From a purely practical perspective, those who supported the idea of cooperative housekeeping could rarely reconcile the cost of three- and four-course dinners—the middle-class standard of the era—with their reluctance to divert a greater portion of their incomes to the cause. From an ideological perspective, cooperative housekeeping disrupted traditional gender roles. Cooking for family had become such an important part of women's identity (even if servants shouldered much of the actual work) that critics of both sexes saw meals prepared in a cooperative housekeeping situation as evidence of a homemaker's negligence. Finally, cooking and eating dinner with family members in the privacy of an autonomous household had become a fundamental expression of American individualism, and cooperative housekeeping was simply incompatible with this ideal. Sometime in the nineteenth century, dinner had entwined itself with notions of what it meant to be American. It was no longer just about celebrating the nuclear family; it was also about celebrating the larger national family. At the dinner table, these two families overlapped.[37]

THE FRENCH FOOD craze of the mid-nineteenth and early twentieth centuries was more than a fad; it transformed the way we eat. Courses, particular types of dishes, such as soups and salad, and an abundance of French words, such as *sauté, hors d'oeuvre,* and *à la mode* have become so ingrained in American food culture that, for the most part, they have lost their Continental flair. But another force was also at work in the nineteenth century, a trend toward the informal and the plain. This Americanizing trend simplified dinner by lowering standards for entertaining and emphasizing less fussy, more traditional foods. The emblem of this trend was Thanksgiving, the late-November harvest feast that celebrates American heritage through a meal that, although prodigious, is ultimately ordinary. This exceedingly plain, if abundant, meal countered more flamboyant European ideas about dinner while simultaneously reconnecting Americans with their Pilgrim roots. It epitomized a new dinnertime ideal.[38]

The Thanksgiving dinner menu, as canonized in American literature during the Victorian era, was decidedly unfanciful, its lack of frills and decorum conspicuously un-French. Though French sauces and herbs were in vogue at the time, as were salad greens, exotic fruits, and delicate desserts, the holiday groaning board featured a simple, unadorned roast flanked by standard farm produce and followed by a homely pie. There were no courses and no servants. Frugality, simplicity, and thrift—Americans had embraced these values both to survive in a rugged new world and to ensure the success of their experiment in independence. They celebrated these ideals at the Thanksgiving dinner table when the New England holiday came into its own as a national celebration in the mid-nineteenth century.[39]

As early as the 1820s, Thanksgiving served as a subtle tool of protest against European superfluity. Squire Romilly, the protagonist of Sarah Josepha Hale's 1827 novel *Northwood,* defends the rusticity of his family's tastes in the presence of their English guest. On the table, vegetables and meats from the family farm substitute for fancier cuts from a butcher or imports from a grocer, and homemade currant wine is on offer instead of Madeira or Champagne. When the English guest jokingly asks whether the squire perceives a connection between the farm-raised goods on the table and the preservation of his liberties, the squire responds with a counterquestion: "If you had been in this country forty years ago, would you have imagined the article of *tea* could have had any influence in accelerating our independence?" The table is devoid of "foreign luxuries" for a reason. The plainer goods in their stead offer an object lesson in simplicity and self-sustenance. They are more than the mere fruits of the Romillies' labor; they are symbols of freedom.[40]

Although Thanksgiving had served as a bulwark against corrupting European influences, it was not entirely immune to the invasion of French fashion in the late nineteenth and early twentieth centuries. In 1897, elites could celebrate Thanksgiving at the Windemere Hotel in Chicago with a clam cocktail, cream of chicken *messinoise,* and croustade of goose livers to start. Magazines encouraged less affluent folks hoping to add nuance to inaugurate their dinners with an appetizer of oysters followed by a fine bisque or purée. Perusing Thanksgiving issues of newspapers and magazines, readers would have come across no small number of recipes for frenchified versions of standard American vegetable dishes: cauliflower au gratin, sweet potato croquettes, French peas, and green salads galore.[41]

To the delight of many, French culinary influence during the Victorian era had elevated American eating habits and dining ideals, but now it was encroaching on Thanksgiving dinner, and not everyone approved. The editors of the *New England Kitchen Magazine* were pleased to print recipes for French dishes such as chicken à la Marengo and to explain to readers the difference between a bouillabaisse and a consommé, but they insisted that Thanksgiving dinner include only "the very finest Native products of our own America." The editors thought it important to discourage other European traditions as well, German and English in particular. Turkey, as a native bird, was the ultimate choice for a roast. There was no cultural room for German pork or an English goose.[42]

The pushback against German pork and the proverbial English goose reflected concerns about a general supplanting of traditional American foods by European dishes. An unprecedented rise in immigration and a shift in the ethnicity of immigrants provided one impetus for this conservative response. During each decade between 1860 and 1880, about 2.5 million newcomers made the United States their home. Most were from western and northern Europe or the British Isles. But in the 1880s, that number rose to 5.6 million, more than double the previous decades' immigration, and in the succeeding decades it would continue to rise. Meanwhile, the foreign born were hailing from farther-away lands with more exotic cultures, languages, religions, and cuisines. There were Catholics from Sicily, Jews from Poland, a variety of Orthodox Christians and Jews from Russia. As the United States underwent drastic demographic changes, food provided one language through which those troubled by the changes voiced their anxieties.[43]

In 1877, the European musician Jacques Offenbach traveling in the United States complained that here "nothing is easier than to eat a meal in the French, Italian, Spanish, or German style. Nothing is more difficult . . . than to eat an American dinner in America." "Is there not a chance that we may be losing some of the choice cookery of ye olden time in our desire for new things?" wrote a concerned editor a year later in response to the growing popularity of teatime croquettes and salads at the expense of traditional biscuits and preserves. Here, "olden" is likely a euphemism for "American," and "new," a substitution for "French." In the context of the Continental onslaught, plain, old-fashioned American food was becoming invested with greater meaning, so much so that social workers would wield it as a tool of Americanization in their attempts to help immigrants assimilate through dietary reform. (If only they would stop eating garlic and take up Indian pudding.) During the war years, the meaning of plain, old-fashioned American food deepened further.[44]

The Great Depression and two world wars in the first half of the twentieth century sounded the death knell for formal dining and the lofty French fare that defined it. No longer were multicourse dinner parties, featuring lobster farci or *filet de boeuf aux champignons* and served by a liveried waitstaff, a standard for middle-class status. Prohibition contributed to the decline of Continental cuisine since fine restaurants, which by and large purveyed French fare, usually paired wine with food and could not survive without the sale of alcohol. But the revision of dinner expectations, precipitated by the instability and frugality of these years, did not make dinner any less important in daily life or in Americans' understanding of themselves as Americans.[45]

DURING THE WAR YEARS, especially during World War II, the sit-down family dinner became an anchor of stability and a symbol of what the nation was fighting for. No one meal of the year expressed these values better than Thanksgiving, and when Norman Rockwell painted his illustration "Freedom from Want" for the *Saturday Evening Post* in 1943, he seemed to have these values in mind. Informality is the rule in Rockwell's illustration. Despite the special occasion, plain white plates, not fine china, grace the table and reflect the afternoon light. Water-filled tumblers stand in for wine glasses, and the food, though appetizing, is both basic and familiar. The dishes are served simultaneously—no soup or oyster appetizer opens the meal, as in the French tradition of courses. Perhaps most tellingly, the family is relaxed; they lean forward casually, expressing anticipation and delight. This is no formal Victorian meal.

As in this picture, Thanksgiving had become a patriotic ritual, and, in a subtle way, so had the everyday American dinner. The middle class could no longer sustain French sensibilities, especially in the wake of the Depression and with the austerity necessitated by war. But perhaps it was just as well that a lifestyle contingent on servants was no longer viable since nationalistic pressures had made French sensibilities ideologically less compatible with American life. Of course, many French sensibilities remained—it is still standard to open meals with soup, salad, or other appetizer (at least in restaurants), and dessert shows no sign of going out of style. These customs have simply been naturalized, folded into American custom.

Americans continued to consume French foods, cook in French styles, and enjoy a modified tradition of courses after the French dining fad declined, but beginning in the early twentieth century, there was no longer room to think of these foods and customs as French. America was playing a new role in the world as a military power helping to dislodge the Third Reich from western Europe and repel Japan's forceful advances in Asia. At the same time, the country was suffering the anxieties and sacrifices characteristic of wartime. These two factors combined to create a climate in which the family meal took on new importance. Having simplified dinner by necessity, Americans now celebrated this meal's necessary simplicity as a virtue.

A family's dinnertime shift back to the basics was a patriotic expression of wartime republicanism. Dinner, once complicated, became ordinary. But now ordinary was more than ordinary; it was special. The newly ordinary meal was special not just because families ate it together but because it had become characteristically American. Lunch, on the other hand, never had to become American; it was native born.

5

WHY LUNCH IS COLD, CHEAP, AND QUICK

WHEN A FRENCH MAN traveling by train in the United States around 1890 could find no hotel or restaurant to dine in during a midday layover, he entered a small wooden building on the far side of the platform that bore a sign reading "Lunch Room." The patrons, he noticed, were eating pie. When the traveler inquired about the menu, an Irish waiter with a thick accent recited the options from behind the counter: "Peach poy, apricot poy, apple poy, and mince poy."

"Is that all?" asked the French traveler.

"What more do you want?" the waiter retorted.

The French man began to wonder whether instead of reading "Lunch Room," the sign on the wooden building should read "Beware," but it was too late now. To fill his stomach's noontime requirements, he ordered three slices—one each of the apricot, peach, and apple. Having anticipated a more substantial meal, perhaps like those he had enjoyed in England, he instead received the equivalent of a snack. "Lunch in America has not the meaning that it has in England," he remarked disappointedly. "In England lunch means something. In America, it does not."[1]

Perhaps the American lunch failed to mean something to the French traveler because it was no longer the hot, robust, English-style dinner he expected. It was lighter, colder, cheaper, and quicker; as such, it was something entirely new. Dinner, which of course was not new, had undergone a transformation, shifting from the afternoon to the evening and becoming a formal family affair in the process. Dinner had also taken on significance as a symbol of American freedom and prosperity. Lunch, on the other hand, followed an altogether different trajectory. It was not a traditional meal forced to adapt to the changing social and work patterns wrought by industrialization. In fact, it had not existed as a meal at all. It had to be invented.

The impetus for lunch was the vacuum that the newly shifted midday dinner left in its wake. A stand-in was necessary to tide the grumbling stomach over until evening, when one sat down to the main meal of the day. But there were obstacles to a midday meal, especially a traditional, dinnerly one, and the main obstacle was work. As discussed in the previous chapter, the Industrial Revolution shifted work from the home and workshop to the factory and the office, and these new sites of production made returning home for a meal in the middle of the day increasingly impractical.

Solutions to the lunch problem varied and included the restaurant, the saloon, the dining club, the cafeteria, and the brown bag. Each option solved the problem in its own way, but not without ramifications. What one ate for lunch, where, with whom, and how quickly revealed clues about social status, and this information could serve as an asset or a liability. Members of the working class were more likely to lunch in corner saloons, whereas businessmen dined in exclusive downtown clubs. Because people now ate lunch in public away from their families, it was easier than ever to pigeonhole an individual according to his or her particular approach to this meal.

Those seeking to boost social status and build a professional network capitalized on lunch, strategically choosing where (and where not) to eat, as well as with whom. They were not the only ones to make shrewd use of the new eating occasion. Companies, trade organizations, women's clubs, and public schools all discovered they had something to gain by opening their own lunch services, be it prestige, uplift, status, profit, or social reform. Each molded the emerging noontime meal to serve purposes larger than the mere filling of stomachs, and their imprint remains formidable today.

WHEN INVENTED in the mid- to late-nineteenth century, lunch as we know it borrowed heavily on the idea of the snack. Although the light midday meal was new, the word for it was not, originally referring to a between-meal pick-me-up. Samuel Johnson's 1755 dictionary relates "lunch" to "clunch" or "clutch," which meant "as much food as one's hand can hold." Whether or not Johnson's etymology is correct, clearly "lunch" originally signified something (usually food) both small and easy to hold in one's hand, as confirmed by the *Oxford English Dictionary,* which links "lunch" to "lump," as in a lump of cheese or bread. In short, lunch consisted of a ready-to-eat fare that required little or no immediate preparation, few if any utensils, and hardly any cleanup—in other words, whatever one could grab in a hurry and eat on the go.[2]

In the mid-nineteenth century, the word "lunch" meant an eating occasion that fell after morning breakfast but before midday dinner. Noah Webster defined it as "a slight repast" between those two meals. Health reformer William Andrus Alcott (a cousin of Louisa May Alcott, author of *Little Women*) did not much approve of eating between meals, but when it came to children and "laborers who perspire," he felt that a small quantity of fruit was appropriate as a ten or eleven o'clock "luncheon." New England worshippers, who typically attended two services on a Sunday during the seventeenth and much of the eighteenth centuries, were known to "lunch" in the pews between services, eating what they had brought from home in baskets—frequently doughnuts—to bridge the gap between breakfast and a later-than-usual dinner.[3]

Reference to Sabbath lunches as "snacks" reveals that the words "lunch" and "snack" were once interchangeable. "Snack" originally meant a dog's bite. Colloquial usage shifted to imply a verbal snap, as in a coarse remark or sharp jibe. Later the term came to mean a small portion of something larger (as in what might be bitten off). Beginning in the mid-eighteenth century, this small portion frequently referred to food, as in "a snack of bread," which literally meant a bite of bread. The snack that "lunch" originally referred to was a mid-morning stopgap, but the word eventually came to signify food taken apart from a meal during any time of day or night. In 1875, a Massachusetts longshoreman testified that he and his coworkers were afforded two short "lunch" breaks during the workday; in addition to their one-hour midday dinner, they were released for "lunch at ten and four o'clock, fifteen minutes each." In the mid- to late nineteenth century, and in some cases quite a bit later, to lunch was to snack, and to snack was to lunch. Practically speaking, they were one and the same.[4]

Not surprisingly, confusion surrounded the emergence of lunch as a noontime meal in the mid-nineteenth century. Meals, like society, were in flux, and many of the conventions we take for granted had yet to crystallize. In an 1877 acting charade published in the popular women's serial *Godey's Ladies Book,* a Miss Merrill cuts short her visit with a Mrs. Banks because she has to "get home to luncheon." "That is what they call a noon dinner now-a-days," the older woman explains. During this transitional period, when eating patterns were changing, what to serve at the midday meal would become a topic of debate, but deciding what to call the midday meal was the first order of business.[5]

Miss Merrill and Mrs. Banks were not the only fictional characters to employ different names for the midday meal. In the 1873 *Harper's New Monthly Magazine* short story "A Simpleton," a physician sees Lady Traherne for her "want of spirit." He suspects the cause to be gluttony and questions her on the topic of her meals:

"Dinner at two?" he asks.

"We call it luncheon," she responds.

"Are you a ventriloquist?" he replies with a hint of sarcasm. "It is only your lips [that] call it luncheon. Your poor stomach, could it speak, would call it dinner."[6]

Confusion about nomenclature mirrored confusion about the meal itself: Should it be more like the main meal of the day it was replacing or the glorified snack it was quickly becoming? For Lady Traherne, little besides time of day distinguished lunch from dinner; though she called it by a different name, her midday meal was essentially the same as her evening one. Finding herself in a pinch, one homemaker who embraced the notion of a dinnerly noontime meal justified the rather thin spread she served her guests through a strategic use of terms.

In the luncheon section of her 1875 cookbook *Breakfast, Luncheon, and Tea,* Marion Harland recounts the story of a friend whose widower brother unexpectedly brings three of his colleagues home for the midday meal. When the sister-turned-hostess inventories the pantry, she finds a paucity of ingredients, not even sufficient fixings for a humble soup. The brother consults with her, inquiring whether there is cake, pie, and fruit. "But it isn't a question of dessert," she replies. "There is literally nothing for *dinner*." The brother's solution is ingenious. "Set on sardines, cheese, pie, cake, claret, sauterne, and a dish or two of fruit. Make a royally strong cup of coffee to wind up with, and call it *luncheon*." In fifteen minutes the collation is ready, and none of the guests notices anything lacking. Thanks to a carefully chosen word, the meal is a success.[7]

The ad hoc nature of the meal Marion Harland describes was novel but increasingly acceptable, even fashionable, especially at ladies' luncheons, where women experimented with ways to reduce the workload of preparing and serving food, while cultivating a new kind of sophistication. "Ordinarily," notes the author of *Jennie June's American Cookery Book* (1870), "ladies' lunches are simple affairs—delicate, *recherché*, and more famous for the wit they evoke, and the enjoyment they create, than for the dishes." The food could be quite incongruous: chicken salad, a dish of poached eggs, sliced tomatoes, hot chocolate. The idea was to set forth a meal without undue scurrying. Of course, some ladies' lunches were more elegant and refined. One sample menu included pigeons served cold, oyster patties, blackberry jelly, pickled cauliflower, slices of red beetroot, blancmange, fruitcake, grapes, and wine. Whether elegant or simple, most of the dishes for a ladies' luncheon would have been prepared well prior to the meal, needing merely to be laid out. "Whatever the bill of fare," explained the cookbook author, "let it be such that the presence of the hostess will not be required in the kitchen, nor a large attendance of servants in removing dishes."[8]

The dishes typical of ladies' luncheons were not only cold and hors d'oeuvres–like, saving hosts more than a small amount of work, but they were also conspicuously light, reflecting current attitudes about how women should eat. In the latter decades of the nineteenth century, perhaps more than ever before, American middle- and upper-class women were defining themselves (and being defined) by their approach to the food on their plates. Ladies who indulged a robust appetite transgressed the celebrated virtue of restraint and risked appearing lower-class or morally weak. Since eating is a sensual act, it was especially incumbent upon women, considered the guardians of morality, to display their powers of self-control, and food presented a practical and immediate occasion for this display. As a result, the dishes at a ladies' luncheon were dainty preparations, often finger foods, characterized by style much more than substance.[9]

The style of these dishes embodied the femininity of the ladies' luncheon. In a world defined more and more by separate spheres, clothing fashions, mannerisms, leisure activities, and even the shape of the body (increasingly idealized as small waisted) became languages with which women defined themselves as middle-class, and food was one of those languages. Women's use of food as a language attained new heights in the early twentieth century when the cult of daintiness reached its zenith, epitomized by themed and color-coordinated luncheons as well as teas that featured sweet and jellied novelty dishes. Take, for instance, the "Daffodil and Pussy Willow Luncheon" outlined in a 1908 popular women's magazine, which featured cream of corn soup with whipped cream, followed by chicken in a molded aspic with layers of olives and hardboiled eggs and ornamented with early spring flowers. Table decorations included a bowl of "daffys" resting on a mat of ferns, paper doilies, pussy willows punctuated with homemade yellow crepe paper butterflies, yellow candlesticks (to match the daffodils and butterflies), and finally a collection of small, wax-paper-lined flowerpots, one for each setting. These doubled as party favors and dessert bowls to hold the macaroon-dusted pineapple sorbet, a flower stalk deftly inserted into each serving of the frozen dessert. The flower-themed ladies' luncheon was an aesthetically saturated event and serves as a fitting portrait of turn-of-the-century femininity, showing just how tightly notions of food and gender had become entwined.[10]

The emerging noontime meal combined simple elegance with modern convenience and evolving ideas about femininity to create an altogether new kind of meal. The new lunch, however, took time to gain a foothold, and many continued to consume the main meal of the day in the afternoon instead of the evening, especially in more rural areas. Inconsistency of habit caused complications for a host who, in planning her menu, had to consider whether her guests lunched at noon and dined in the evening, according to the new style, or dined at noon and supped in the evening, in the older tradition. In *The Correct Thing in Good Society* (1888), etiquette expert Florence Howe Hall advises readers to tailor meals they host to their acquaintances' varying dining times: "It is not the correct thing to invite people who are in the habit of dining in the middle of the day to take lunch with you unless you provide something substantial for them to eat." For this purpose, Hall suggests meat or fish. An invitation to a more formal lunch, however, would negate the concern because, as the author notes, "there is very little difference between a formal lunch and a dinner." Both were polite occasions marked by a carefully laid table featuring a multiplicity of finely prepared hot and cold dishes.[11]

Once the lighter midday meal took hold, middle-class women found themselves freed from the morning duties of preparing (or overseeing preparation of) a major meal to be served in the early afternoon. With their newfound time, they frequently spent part of the midday visiting neighbors and friends, attending luncheons, or hosting them. Meanwhile, their male companions, who no longer returned home for dinner, increasingly dined with colleagues. In cities across the country, ambitious businessmen passed their midday hours in the smoky, oak-paneled rooms of elite lunch clubs. As early as the 1870s, and especially around the turn of the century, such clubs proliferated, offering men arenas in which to escape the demands of the office while simultaneously pursuing business relations in a relaxed and sophisticated atmosphere. Lunch clubs frequently boasted professional affiliations: there was the Transportation Club for rail executives, the Underwriters' Club for insurance agents, the Merchants' Club for textile manufacturers, and the Press Club for newspaper and advertising men.[12]

Dining clubs provided an exclusivity and tranquility that restaurants could not offer. They became ideal places to hold official business meetings, connect with colleagues from other companies, and engineer deals with important clients. "The lunch table has taken the place of the office desk as the battleground of big business," reported a 1909 article in a business magazine. "To sell a piece of property to a magnate by appearing at his office as an unknown," pointed out the same article, "is quite a different matter from selling the same property to the same man as a result of a quiet and informal chat over the lunch table as guests of a mutual friend." It is hard to imagine a more elegant and esteemed place to entertain clients than under the oil portraits of famous authors at the Aldine Club or in the gothic interiors of the New York Lawyers' Club.[13]

ALTHOUGH AMBITIOUS men at elite professional clubs dined leisurely and well-bred women at ladies' luncheons picked daintily, the majority of Americans consumed prosaically: they ate prosaic food in prosaic settings with the help of prosaic utensils and containers. Dinner had become special, and, partly as a result, lunch did not have to. For the majority of Americans, the new midday meal was no sacred family ritual; it was a practical solution to problems associated with the new approach to business. Inherently flexible, it simultaneously accommodated the demands of the stomach and the increasingly regimented stipulations of work.

As early as the 1870s, when lunch was yet to become lunch and the midday meal was still called dinner, workers were bringing cold leftovers to the workplace in cylindrical metal buckets to satisfy their stomachs in the middle of the day. This was the routine of a mute, English-born mill worker in Massachusetts whose wife prepared and packed dinner for the two of them every evening because there was simply no time to do so in the morning. In the decades surrounding the turn of the twentieth century, southern cotton mill workers had their children ferry hot food from home to them in baskets. Until the passage of child labor laws, these young and often barefoot "dinner-toters" typically took over running the machinery while their parents broke for lunch. In 1910, the steel workers of Homestead, Pennsylvania, were still eating their main meal of the day in the mills and out of dinner pails. Thanks to wives and mothers who prepared and hand-delivered their midday sustenance, the workers were able to enjoy hot food—that is, until passes became necessary for entering the premises and made this practice impossible. Homestead women adapted, preparing cold meals each morning for their men to carry to work in buckets, often supplementing the unheated eatables with preserves as a small treat to compensate for the plainness (and less-than-ideal temperature) of the fare.[14]

During the late nineteenth century, the dinner pail became an icon of laboring America (though some folks used coffee tins, cigar boxes, and baskets). Eating dinner away from home and not in a club—a meal that looked increasingly like lunch—was a sure sign that one belonged to the working class, as attested to by the fact that carrying this humble bucket to work invited embarrassment for those who did not perform industrial labor. One prominent gentleman who found it necessary to take his main meal of the day to the office deliberated between the practicality and the stigma of doing so, ultimately deciding that "the common dinner pail . . . was not the thing for a professor to be seen carrying through the streets." (As a solution, his wife hired a tinsmith to fashion a pail commensurate with her husband's rank, but the effort failed, as the craftsman simply made a facsimile of the original, only twice the size.)[15]

For those who sweated in mills, the image of the tin dinner pail became a source of pride and a symbol of solidarity. It was "the mark of honest labor," according to a writer in *American Machinist,* who characterized its bearer as competent, proud, and reliably knowledgeable of his trade. One writer dubbed Fall River, Massachusetts, "the city of the dinner pail" because of the city's high number of mills and mill workers. Debates on labor issues increasingly referred to laborers collectively as the "dinner pail army" or the "tin pail brigade." In campaigning for the 1900 presidential election, William McKinley courted the labor constituency with the promise of a full dinner bucket.[16]

Factory workers were not the only ones toting their dinners around in buckets. Starting around the turn of the century, most schoolchildren were doing so as well. Before about 1900, schoolchildren typically returned home for the midday meal. They attended separate morning and afternoon sessions divided by a roughly two-hour break during which they walked home to their families for a hot, homemade afternoon dinner. Catharine Beecher observed in 1869 that children who didn't have to work in factories "spen[t] three hours in school, stimulating brains and nerves. Then home to a hearty dinner, and then again to school." Some did not go home; nor did they have a hearty or hot dinner. The mute spinner who labored with his wife at a Massachusetts mill in the 1870s left a portion of his dinner in his tin pail for his school-age daughter, who came to the factory during her midday recess, relying on her father's leftovers for her sustenance, then returning to school. Children who walked long distances to a schoolhouse sometimes stayed for the extended hiatus and ate a meal carried from home in a tin box or pail (often a recycled commercial food container). The contents might include potatoes, bread, cheese, or pie. But until around 1900, the norm was to return home to one's family at about noon for a full midday meal.[17]

The transition to a shorter break during which schoolchildren remained at school and ate their provisions on the premises did not unfold without criticism. When the Westerly, Rhode Island, school district changed its schedule at the turn of the century from separate morning and afternoon sessions divided by a substantial intermission for dinner to a single extended session with a short, half-hour break around noon, a principal in the district objected. Envisioning schoolchildren applying the old ways of eating to the new schedule, he predicted an impairment of both students' digestion and intellectual engagement. "To go home, eat dinner, and return, all in one half hour," he argued in the annual report, "makes it necessary for those who live any distance to rush to such a degree that it must sooner or later affect the health and must unfit such pupils for proper work in the afternoon periods." Dinner as he knew it was simply not compatible with a mere half-hour pause. An alternative schedule would have to be implemented—or else an alternative meal.[18]

The Westerly principal's preferred solution was a single-session school day that adjourned at one o'clock with no break for lunch. Children would go home for their midday dinner at the end of an abbreviated school day rather than for a shortened break in the middle of it, thereby avoiding the dangers of hurried eating and preserving the tradition of a large midday meal. But such a solution failed to take into account that fewer families were eating midday dinners in the first place. Fathers tended not to return home from work until evening, and mothers, freed from morning cooking responsibilities, had grown accustomed to using this time for other social and occupational activities. By the turn of the century, especially in urban areas, the traditional dinner recess had fallen out of step with a changing society.[19]

Now that schoolchildren's schedules incorporated the new, quicker, lighter midday meal without an extended break during which to return home, the lunch tin was more necessary than ever, and it contained especially convenient and practical foods. A common lunchbox feature was leftovers from breakfast. Homemakers, it turns out, often prepared the morning meal with leftovers for lunch in mind. A rural Kentucky man remembered eating six homemade breakfast biscuits every day for his lunch: "Two had pork on 'em, and two had blackberry jam or some other jelly, and the other two provided the variety." In summer, a tomato supplemented the biscuits; in winter, a boiled potato. Country children frequently brought potatoes to school and warmed them during morning lessons. A former pupil of a one-room schoolhouse recalled her typical midday meal: "We'd come in the morning and throw our potato on a shelf on the inside of the stove, and we'd have baked potatoes for lunch." When canned soup was available, they could heat it on the stove right in the metal can.[20]

The contents of adults' dinner pails overlapped with those of schoolchildren. The mute, English-born spinner in Massachusetts enjoyed "bread and meat and a little pie." In 1906, the wife of an Ohio steel mill worker reported that she packed her husband bread with meat, cheese or eggs, pie, cake, and some fruit. These offerings were typical: leftover meat when available, supplemented by the kinds of commonplace goods, often baked, that were easy to pack in a tin and carry over a distance.[21]

Dinner pail contents often reflected ethnic and racial differences. Polish factory workers were known to enjoy *bizos,* a combination of red and white sausage, sauerkraut, beef, pork, and barley boiled into a pudding that, when cold, could be sliced. In Poland, *bizos* was a hunting food; in America it was a lunch meat. Mexicans in the Southwest fancied tacos rolled in cornhusks. A fascinating variation of the dinner pail was the "shoe box lunch," an African American tradition in which railroad travelers carried boxed staples such as fried chicken, pie, and biscuits because dining cars and trackside restaurants were typically segregated in the South. As early as the 1870s, when the mute English mill worker toted bread and pie to the factory, African American women known as waiter-carriers peddled chicken and biscuits to

African American passengers as a restaurant alternative, exchanging food and cash through the train's open windows.[22]

Bizos and cornhusk tacos spiced up the American lunch as ethnic specialties with regional followings, but pie, that old-fashioned standby and perhaps the original convenience food, became a popular tin-pail standard for the majority of workers and schoolchildren. In some peoples' opinion, it was too standard. Cookbook author Marion Harland condemned its overuse as a meal replacement when time or appetite prohibited other options. One late-nineteenth-century factory worker testified that in place of cold meat, he sometimes brought a quarter of a medium-sized pie supplemented by cake and doughnuts, enough to fill out the container, for his midday meal. Our French traveler's unfortunate experience of pie as a typical lunch-counter staple (apparently at times the only staple) and Marion Harland's criticism of its unhealthy nature and ubiquitous, indiscriminate overconsumption by Americans (a phenomenon she called "pie-olotry") illustrate just how iconic a lunch item the fruit-filled pastry was.[23]

There were other predictable lunchtime items—apples, pickles, cookies—but bread was unquestionably the common element of the new midday meal in America. No lunch lacked some portion of a loaf. Bread was already a universal snack, perhaps the quintessential snack. Once baked or bought, it required no preparation except for slicing and, if desired, buttering. More than one influential nineteenth-century author prescribed it as a suitable pick-me-up for little ones: "Children who are growing fast need a luncheon [read "snack"] of simple bread between meals," wrote Catharine Beecher. The transformation of bread from the ideal snack into the foundation of the modern lunch mirrors the transformation of the midday meal itself. When lunch-the-snack grew into lunch-the-midday-meal, it carried along what had always defined it: the staff of life.[24]

Bread often appeared autonomously in the lunch pail, as a roll or muffin, say, likely accompanied by butter and jam, an egg, some cheese, or a piece of cold meat. But bread's most famous lunch pail iteration would quickly become a noontime sensation: the sandwich. The sandwich was nothing new when lunch was coming into its own. People had tucked meat, cheese, and condiments into bread since ancient times. Many have attributed the sandwich's invention to John

Montague, who, as the story goes, could not pull himself away from a riveting gambling streak and requested a supper he could eat without leaving the gaming table. An alternate explanation holds that the tireless politician, known for working long hours, desired a one-handed meal he could eat at his desk. Contrary to popular belief, Montague, the Fourth Earl of Sandwich, did not actually invent the sandwich, but his well-known affinity for it, combined with his prestige as a member of the nobility, did make the sandwich famous, and the trendy new bread-based phenomenon took its name from his title.[25]

When sandwiches grew in popularity in England in the 1760s, they typically showed up at late-night drinking parties among the gentry, and men were their primary consumers. By the end of the century, they appeared as refreshment at late-night balls, eventually making their way to the tea and supper tables of the English upper and middle classes. Simple recipes for basic sandwiches appeared in American cookbooks as early as the 1830s, but as the century progressed, their preparation became increasingly complex. Eliza Leslie's 1840 recipe for a bare-bones ham sandwich called for slices of cold boiled ham between thin pieces of buttered loaf served rolled up or flat. (If boiled ham didn't suit, she suggested grated tongue.) By contrast, an 1887 recipe of the same title in the *White House Cook Book* called for a dressing of butter, mustard, salad oil, red and white pepper, and egg yolks into which the preparer would mix chopped ham, originating a new concoction: the salad sandwich.[26]

Although fancy salad sandwiches were all the rage in cookbooks and would become a staple of upscale women's luncheons, simpler sandwiches became an anchor for the midday meal of schoolchildren and factory workers. Cookbooks provided instructions to homemakers about the kinds of sandwiches with which to fill children's lunch boxes. One book differentiated among sandwiches as appropriate for children of varying ages. Boiled eggs "finely chopped" and "mildly seasoned" between two slices of buttered bread or bread with a nut paste such as peanut butter "softened with milk or cream" were ideal for younger children. For older children there were the additional options of chopped cheese or meat, jam or jelly. Often fruit, both fresh and preserved, sweets such as cookies, custard, or cake, and juice or milk rounded out the schoolchild's lunchbox meal.[27]

Peanut butter sandwiches, jam sandwiches, and eventually the marriage of the two—peanut butter and jelly sandwiches—became particularly popular with children, especially in the second and third decades of the twentieth century. But these concoctions did not start out as children's fare. Invented in the nineteenth century by John Harvey Kellogg and initially popularized as a health food and meat substitute for vegetarians, peanut butter became a delicacy around the turn of the twentieth century. Upscale tearooms featured it as a novelty sandwich ingredient, and jam was just one of the pairing options. A 1928 recipe book for cold sandwiches features over thirty peanut butter combinations, including peanut butter and apricot; peanut butter and tomato; peanut butter, cheese, and lettuce; peanut butter and egg; peanut butter and ham; and peanut butter and pickle. Later in the century, Elvis Presley would popularize the peanut butter and bacon sandwich, to which he often added slices of banana.[28]

Perhaps not surprisingly, the double-sweet peanut butter and jelly sandwich survived its savory and arguably more esoteric cousins, and its sweetness was no small factor in its success. The advent of sliced bread in the 1920s only cemented the appeal as children could now assemble the sandwich without the aid or supervision of an adult because the loaf no longer required cutting with a sharp knife. In the same decade, manufacturers began proffering inexpensive nut butter to school cafeterias, institutionalizing peanut butter and jelly as the taste of mainstream American childhood for decades to come.[29]

Sandwiches became central to children's lunches for many reasons, such as taste, economy, and simplicity, but the clincher was their ease of preparation. In her 1924 cookbook, Ida C. Bailey touted the sandwich's nutritional value, noting that the bread and butter provided the necessary starch and fat, whereas a meat, cheese, egg, or nut-butter filling supplied the requisite protein. Designed properly, a sandwich could serve as a vehicle for good health. In the end, though, she declared it "undoubtedly the easiest way to combine a variety of foods for the school luncheon." "Sandwiches," wrote another cookbook author, "furnish the most convenient way of carrying foods that are to be eaten with bread," and bread, she remarked, "is the basis of almost all boxed lunches." That some cookbook authors attempted to justify the sandwich on the basis of nutritional value may indirectly betray concerns that two pieces of bread slapped together lacked the seal of love associated with a mother's time and effort in the kitchen. Whether or not the simple meal needed justification, its ubiquitous appeal hardly needed explanation: its convenience was irresistible.[30]

Although cardinal in schoolchildren's midday meal, sandwiches were also central to working men's lunches. The image of the cigar-chomping tycoon was giving way to that of the slim businessman—young, energetic, fit to compete in the new milieu of corporate capitalism—and the sandwich dovetailed aptly with this ideal. Tired of heavy restaurant fare that left him foggy and fatigued, one early-twentieth-century businessman reported that he asked his wife to prepare him two buttered slices of bread with meat or cheese and nothing else. She wrapped the pedestrian fare in oil paper and slipped it into an envelope, which he carried to work in his coat pocket. Sometimes she surprised him with raisins, almonds, or another "little dainty" on the side, which added variety and became an object of anticipation. The sandwich solution saved him time as well as energy. No longer did the businessman have to leave his office to seek out a restaurant; he simply ate what his wife packed him at his desk. With newfound time to work and less fogginess and fatigue to contend with, the sandwich eater was a more productive and profitable employee. White-collar professionals such as this man appreciated lighter sandwiches, but those who performed manual labor often opted for bulkier versions, which they could easily acquire at cafeterias and saloons if they didn't bring them from home.[31]

WITH THE TEMPERANCE movement in full swing in the late nineteenth and early twentieth centuries, sandwiches made an appearance in saloons, where they often formed part of the celebrated free lunch that kept patrons, who might otherwise be swayed by anti-alcohol rhetoric, coming back to the bar. Many saloons—about half in the city of Chicago at the close of the nineteenth century—set up a buffet between eleven and three o'clock, and some offered a veritable feast. One Chicago saloon served "frankfurters, clams, egg sandwiches, potatoes, vegetables, cheeses, bread, and several varieties of hot and cold meats"—all for the price of a beer or two. Less elaborate spreads might feature sandwich fixings such as bread, bologna, pickles, sliced tomatoes, onions, and radishes, perhaps with a soup option as a side. Most saloon menus also offered a "businessman's lunch," which, for the cost of some soup and a slice of pie at a regular restaurant, furnished the patron with a hearty midday dinner. Certain cities, including Boston, required saloons to serve food, though eventually laws passed there and elsewhere made the enticing free lunch illegal. Following such legislation, and especially with the emergence of Prohibition, business at saloons dried up, and new kinds of informal lunch restaurants took their place, many based on the emerging self-serve concept of the cafeteria.[32]

"Quick-lunch" restaurants sprang up in cities across the country around the turn of the century, and they generally lived up to their name. Here workers and businessmen could grab a bite of something simple and even hot without investing significant time or money. In order for the quick lunch to be genuinely quick, these establishments did away with many long-held restaurant traditions. There were no waiters, for example, and because patrons customarily served themselves, no tips. Although quick lunchers may have saved time and pennies, they had to navigate throngs of hungry workers. One commentator explained the method while alluding to the madness: "A tray is handed to you. . . . It is a struggle to get to the counter. . . . You join the press at the counter and seize whatever you may see." After the meal, lunch patrons paid a cashier based on the honor system, though some restaurants instituted a ticketing arrangement to keep track of purchases.[33]

Because so many of the quick-lunching clerks, stenographers, and other city workers ate their meals alone, proprietors often furnished their venues exclusively with single-customer tables. One fresh-off-the-boat immigrant looking for a place where he and his companions could eat their first meal in America rightly called this design an "unsociable arrangement." "We would have sat together," he explained, "but in this shop one table accommodated one customer only." Because the restaurant's layout required the companions each to sit separately, they communicated by way of glances and smiles rather than words. Other quick-lunch restaurants, known as "one-arm lunchrooms" or "one-arm joints," did away with tables altogether, replacing them with rows of specially designed chairs with broad arms offering surfaces for plates and a small round depression for the usual cup of coffee. Customers lunching in these broad-armed chairs sat side by side and did not face each other; they interacted with their food rather than with their fellow eaters.[34]

In 1902, a new kind of quick-lunch venue emerged that further eliminated sociality from the equation: the automat (see Figure 14). This "mechanical lunchroom," as Works Progress Administration writer Edward O'Brian dubbed it in the 1940s, was a glorified vending machine, a wall-length display with windowed compartments featuring pies, fishcakes, cinnamon buns, coffee—each available for a few nickels, which the customer slid into the appropriate slot. "Here, the man in a hurry is worried by no middle-men," noted O'Brian. "His relationship with his fodder, over which he may gloat, ruminate, or despair, is strictly private." No need to worry that ordering would take up excess time or that the weary luncher would have to assume an air of cheerfulness and engage in small talk with a restaurant employee: acquiring one's lunch had become an entirely automated affair.[35]

Drug stores, where the sale of carbonated medicines evolved into the sale of carbonated beverages, took a thick slice of the quick-lunch business starting around the turn of the century. "Practically all the low-priced quick noon luncheons are served from soda fountains," noted a business magazine in 1913 with regard to cities in the Southwest. At these venues, counters and stools eliminated the tray system as well as the social awkwardness of eating alone at a table. Special machines, such as an electric toaster that accommodated sixteen slices of bread on a revolving wheel, streamlined the food-preparation process. As a result, service was brisk. Servers, often working behind the counter within arm's reach of patrons, had little distance to cover when delivering menu items, and they became known for their quirky jargon: they called butter "axle grease"; soup, "bellywash"; milk, "cow juice"; and a cup of coffee, a "cup of mud." Though some of these amusing terms were longer than what they substituted for—ham and eggs was "two cackles in oink in the Southern way"—the jargon didn't seem to slow the pace. Whether delivered across the counter or to customers seated at a table, orders were usually "hot-footed."[36]

For the exceptionally hurried, some quick-lunch restaurants featured high counters in place of tables and lacked seating options altogether. Such restaurants catered to the "stand-uppers," eaters who considered sitting while munching an unnecessary expenditure of time. "You waste a minute sitting down and getting up again," explained a turn-of-the-century article. At such a venue, "not one fraction of a second is lost in the hunt for a seat." Here, the diner scarfed down soup, sandwiches, and pie while standing at a high counter before rushing back to the office with a toothpick in his mouth. If there was no room at the counter for him to set down his meal, he simply held his plate in one hand while poking food into his mouth with the other.[37]

The businessman, for whom time was money, considered speedy meals necessary. Consequently, in addition to ready-made food and rapid service, quick lunches featured breakneck consumption. Frequently referred to as "hustlers," quick-lunch patrons tended to "bolt" their food in a matter of minutes—often within fifteen or twenty, but sometimes in as few as five. One critic jokingly likened the lightening pace to that of a first-rate Ford automobile. Other commentators measured the "bolting" in terms of mouthfuls or chews; one estimated that the typical stand-upper spared no more than a dozen bites for a meal that consisted of a bowl of soup, a plate of beans, sandwiches, pie, and coffee. Another suspected that such a luncher averaged three chews per mouthful rather than the ideal thirty-three. Whatever his number of chews or mouthfuls, the quick-lunch patron was a creature of indubitable haste.[38]

URBAN LABORERS also felt the time crunch that drove white-collar workers to inhale sandwiches and coffee at quick-lunch venues, but factory working conditions that made lunch both hurried and frequently dangerous compounded their rush. In the 1870s, laborers in the Massachusetts textile mill where the mute spinner worked were allotted a half hour to eat. Equipment demands, however, could eat into this typical break period. Workers often spent part of their lunchtime cleaning and oiling machinery, a necessary task they could not perform during paid hours while the looms were in motion. All too often, time off awarded to workers on paper proved far from what they received in reality.

When investigators in the early twentieth century began to probe factory conditions, they discovered that while some laborers got more than the standard half hour for lunch, many felt compelled to work through their designated breaks. An inspector of the laundries in Troy, New York, reported that while launderers took a full hour for their meal, pieceworkers regularly skipped lunch entirely or else broke only for a brief ten minutes to swallow what they had brought from home in order to ensure maximum output at the end of the day. One writer only half-jokingly suggested renaming the lunch hour in sweatshops the "luncheon minute." Many sweatshop hands did not stop work for meals. One observer described the typical textile worker as snatching a bite from a link of sausage and a piece of bread resting on his sewing machine each time he finished a seam.[39]

In most factories, lack of sufficient washing facilities made eating a less than hygienic endeavor. At the Globe Malleable Iron Works in Syracuse, New York, fourteen female employees shared a single sink, which produced no hot water. The foundry section of the factory, staffed by 120 men, had, in addition to cold-water taps, eleven faucets that released live steam, but the workers did not use them for fear of burning their hands. These workers were the fortunate ones: many factories had no washrooms at all. In 1912, nearly three-quarters of New York foundries lacked washrooms, and over half lacked indoor toilets. Buckets of water stood in for sinks in many facilities, and outdoor pits—often unsheltered—substituted for water closets. In the few factories that had them, washing facilities were of little help because the time permitted to use them was usually insufficient to the task they were designed to accommodate. One metal worker explained that he did not wash before his meal because it would have taken him five to ten minutes—up to a third of his half-hour lunch break—just to remove the lead dust from his hands.[40]

In most factories, workers had nowhere to eat except in the workspace itself. In 1912, only 1 in 324 manufacturing establishments on New York City's West Side provided a separate lunchroom, which was particularly worrisome in facilities processing dangerous substances. When the New York Factory Investigating Commission asked a foreman in the lead-hardening department of a metal works what arrangements the establishment had made for its employees, he responded, "No arrangements; [employees] just simply sit down on a stool and put their lunch on a bench." The stools and benches, he confirmed, were in the same room where the men labored. An errand girl for a flower and feather factory, who ran out for the other girls' lunches, testified that they ate at a separate table from the one at which they worked. This was the exception rather than the norm. An inspector reporting on the occupational conditions of women and children in the shoe-polish industry noted that "the girls sit and eat wherever their work happens to be. If they are filling the cans with shoe polish, they sit right down where they are working."[41]

In 1913, less than 4 percent of New York factories offered employees separate lunchrooms, but thanks to reform efforts that exposed the dangers of poor factory conditions, the work climate began to change. Within a few years, lunchrooms had become fixtures in factories and shops, though sometimes these eating spaces were far from appealing. They were frequently located in cramped, unventilated basements or on upper floors of buildings where employees had no access to an elevator. One department store worker complained about crowding. She preferred to pay the extra money required to lunch in the customers' dining room, which was, in her mind, "the only way to get any rest or quiet at noon." There, she explained, she could "sit comfortably and feel a little less tired afterwards." The setting gave her a needed break from the commotion and renewed her vigor for the afternoon.[42]

Manufacturing companies eventually began to realize that comfortable and well-outfitted employee lunchrooms were more than a charity; they were a sound business investment. The new eating arrangement paid: it saved workers valuable energy and time and increased their productivity as a result. Workers who did not have to cram their lunch while standing at a machine, seated at an unclean worktable, propped up on a drafty windowsill, or hunkered on a pile of rags were more likely to return to their afternoon tasks revitalized and less prone to fall ill and miss work. Those who had regularly eaten out no longer had to squander precious minutes and energy hustling to sandwich counters and pushing through cafeteria lines. "The day will come," prophesied investigative journalist and muckraker

Ida Tarbell in 1916, "when the failure to furnish proper lunching places for a working force will be looked upon as one of the most uneconomical practices of . . . industry." This was, she explained, because "people who eat cold meals from the corner of their desks or machines do it at the expense of their afternoon efficiency."[43]

The new arrangement saved time and energy, and it was also better for digestion. Quick-lunch venues were gaining a reputation as "dyspepsia factories" responsible for chronic indigestion that threatened to reduce workers' output. By eating on the premises, workers were more likely to digest their meals properly and preserve their energy for the afternoon shift. Free hot beverages—coffee and tea, sometimes hot chocolate—were a central aspect of companies' efforts to improve their workers' digestion and, by extension, their yield. One foreman had complained that cold meals without the benefit of some hot drink lay heavily on his stomach. He noted that his peers frequently tried to warm food or drinks on stovepipes, adding that unheated meals were not only injurious to health but resulted in poor workmanship. By serving coffee, employers gave workers a way of transforming their cold provisions from home into the semblance of a hot meal. Company coffee also allowed workers to conclude their noon meals with something other than cold water, a practice popularly believed to wreak havoc on the stomach, resulting in headaches and "that awful tired feeling" that invariably hampered performance.[44]

Although company lunchrooms started out as just that, rooms set aside for lunching, many eventually offered food service. Early lunchroom menus commonly sported a single item, which workers supplemented with food brought from home. One Ohio factory girl appreciated that her employer furnished soup and hot drinks; they made her lunch-pail bread, cake, or pie more palatable, as it tended to stale by noon. A few lunchrooms offered three-course meals. More typical was the happy medium represented by the Dayton, Ohio, National Cash Register Company, a lunchroom pioneer that offered employees tea, coffee, or milk and a choice of two hot dishes. Employees supplemented the hot dish and accompanying beverage with bread and butter from home. Menu items at lunchrooms ranged from bacon and eggs to porterhouse steak, usually priced at or under cost.[45]

Lunchrooms provided a place for employees to rejuvenate over a hot, nourishing meal, but when workers sat down to eat, they were not free to sit anywhere they liked in the mostly segregated lunchrooms of the time. African Americans either sat at designated tables in their own section of the room or ate in a different room altogether. If the lunchroom offered hot food, black employees might have to carry their helpings to a remote space while whites ate in the room where the hot food was served. One study of 140 factories found inequitable working conditions in 101 of them, where segregated facilities disproportionately impaired African American laborers' ability to eat food and drink hygienically. Typically, white employees benefited from a modern cafeteria and adjacent restroom, whereas blacks suffered through midday meals in lunchrooms located in older, sometimes dilapidated, often dark and cramped sections of the building, which one reporter called "dingy." Additionally, their restrooms were not necessarily adjacent. Whereas whites had access to drinking water supplied by a bubble fountain with an automatic refrigeration system, blacks typically had to hydrate themselves from a common metal drinking cup that dangled from a barrel.[46]

Factories also segregated lunchrooms by gender and social class. As early as 1905, the Gorham Manufacturing Company's plant near Providence, Rhode Island, featured a large lunchroom for men, a smaller one for women, and a private dining room for the president, officers, and their guests. The Cleveland Bag Factory established a lunchroom for the office force, whereas "workpeople" ate at folding tables temporarily set up in passageways. The Heinz factory in Pittsburgh featured separate lunchrooms for "men and girls," with employees of both genders benefiting equally from the one lunchtime frill Heinz workers could count on: pickles. A 1921 advertisement for the Des Moines Hosiery Mills titled "Why Our Workers Stay with Us" pictured two separate lunchrooms for male and female employees. The caption under the photo of the men's dining room read, "These workmen didn't feel at home eating with the girl employees shown at left, so this room was equipped with a serving window for them."[47]

More than merely the norm, separation of the sexes also had its benefits. Thanks to parallel facilities, men did not have to hold to a standard of polished manners expected in the company of ladies, and ladies avoided the dubious prospect of eating with unknown men. Although the advertisement for the Des Moines Hosiery Mills suggests that the company instituted separate dining rooms for men and women primarily for the comfort of male employees, in reality they did so just as much (if not more) out of consideration for the female workforce. Factories were primarily masculine spaces owned and run by men. In entering the industrial world largely populated by male workers, most women likely stepped outside their comfort zone, and in this context, ladies' lounges and lunchrooms, often decorated like a living room, functioned as a welcome, homelike refuges.

The midday division of social spheres did not end in factory and department store lunchrooms; it flourished in the turn-of-the-century proliferation of lunch clubs. For females who worked outside the home, women's clubs provided an answer to the ever-gnawing "lunch question": where to eat. As one fictional character explained in "A Luncheon Plan," a story in a 1901 book for entrepreneurial women on how to make money, "Since I commenced business, I simply hate these cheap lunch places where food is jabbed out to you, . . . and I can't afford to go to places where I can be comfortable." For women in business and those who simply found themselves downtown at midday, lunch clubs offered an alternative to the male-dominated restaurant scene, where an unaccompanied woman might receive suspicious looks or, worse, be refused service altogether.[48]

By the turn of the twentieth century, women's lunch clubs were popping up in cities like New York and Chicago. These were not the bastions of wealth and tradition for which elite male lunch clubs would become famous; rather, they were cozy, modest, often homelike settings in which women could find supportive female companions during their midday break from a masculine working world. The first in the windy city was the Ogontz Club, opened as a charity by women of the Ogontz Seminary and consisting of a lunchroom and a reading room where factory girls without the benefit of a workplace cafeteria could come to eat and relax in a clean, quiet, and comfortable atmosphere. In the same city, the Wildwood Club served working women of a slightly higher class, providing members the opportunity to socialize with other self-supporting women in similar professions. For a small monthly or annual fee, members of these organizations could purchase warm food at cost, read the newspaper, borrow a book, relax on a couch, play the club piano, and even listen to a lecture or attend a class.[49]

Women's lunch clubs enjoyed a wide reputation for serving "good and cheap" food. The Women's Lunch Club of Denver took pride in preparing simple, home-cooked fare, whereas others relied on sandwiches, canned soups, and desserts. The menu at the Ogontz Club included salmon salad, potato salad, cold meat, baked beans, canned vegetables, soup, rolls, fruit, pie, cake, and ice cream. Unlike some of the more prestigious men's clubs, women's lunch clubs did not attempt to offer culinary perfection, but many improved on the quality of quick-lunch venues, and all offered a more restful atmosphere, which women found particularly appealing.[50]

Fanciful dishes mattered little largely because women's clubs were more about uplift than prestige. These organizations leant dignity to professional females while providing a place to eat and cultural enrichment to boot. Women's lunch clubs furnished sustenance for working women and afforded homemakers a midday place to rest when downtown, but they accomplished much more as well. "Women's clubs," estimated French countess Madeleine de Bryas during her post–World War I speaking tour in the United States, "[are] probably the origin of the feminine movement in this country." Many clubs engaged in civic causes that impacted society in ways we still benefit from today. They lobbied for women's rights—from the right to vote to the right to dine in an upscale restaurant unescorted by a man. They also pioneered a venture that shaped the midday meal for millions of children for a century and will continue to do so for many more years to come: school lunch.[51]

WHEN A QUICK LUNCH at their desks during a short recess at school replaced children's dinner with the family at home, more than the place of eating changed. So did the temperature of the food. Children who brought their midday meal to school generally had no choice but to consume their fare cold—a roll with jam, a slice of pie, cold leftovers from supper the night before. According to understandings of health emerging at the time, this practice was far from ideal. Cold food for lunch garnered increasing criticism on the grounds that heat stimulates digestive juices, whereas cold inhibits them. "Cold food is not palatable and requires too much time for digestion," summarized a 1921 article in an educators' bulletin. A cold lunch diverted blood to the stomach and away from the brain, resulting in a sleepy, listless pupil ill equipped for the intellectual demands of the afternoon. Chilly, rainy conditions heightened this effect. There were other arguments against cold lunches brought from home. Some claimed that they frequently "lacked bulk," others that they were prone to deterioration during morning lessons, becoming soggy and unappetizing by noon.[52]

If digestibility was an argument for hot lunch, even more compelling were the twin problems of malnourishment and hunger. Boston home economist Ellen Swallow Richards expressed concern about the penny lunches sweet-toothed and pickle-loving schoolchildren bought for themselves from delis, candy shops, pushcarts, and even goodie stands set up by school janitors seeking a little extra cash. She found the ignorance of impoverished mothers even more disturbing than children's poor eating and spending choices. "The thoughtful mother puts up a luncheon, usually of the things her child likes best: cake, pies, cookies," she pointed out in an 1894 issue of the *New England Kitchen Magazine*. Worse, "the careless mother may or may not fill the luncheon basket." Indeed, many children arrived at school without having eaten breakfast and sometimes with no provisions for lunch. A study of Chicago schoolchildren found that 8 percent of pupils in 1904 were chronically underfed. In New York City, an estimated 60,000 to 70,000 youths arrived at school daily with empty stomachs. Sadly, the greatest numbers of hungry children were among the youngest.[53]

Women's lunch clubs organized the first lunch programs in many schools, taking upon themselves the philanthropic task of providing warm, nutritious meals to pupils in their districts. In 1922, twenty mothers in Old Saybrook, Connecticut, formed a club called the School Lunch Association, and each mother took her turn preparing sandwiches and either soup or hot cocoa for 100 to 125 children one day a month. The same year in Suanico, Wisconsin, families threw a kitchen shower for their new lunch program that, rather than depending on mothers, relied on female students who participated in the Girl's Hot

Lunch Club and took turns cooking, cleaning, and serving. The menu here was somewhat more elaborate than in Old Saybrook, featuring nineteen hot dishes rotated throughout the month, including chili, macaroni and tomatoes, mashed potatoes, and corn soup.[54]

Club women typically saw their school lunch work as charitable. One self-professed lunch lady compared her efforts to missionary work, but not every woman pioneering school lunch programs saw herself as a missionary or her work as mere relief. Ellen Swallow Richards, proprietor of Boston's New England Kitchen and the first woman to graduate from MIT, experimented with ways to feed the poor economically, and the New England Kitchen, branches of which she established in working-class, immigrant neighborhoods, was her laboratory. Here, she and her collaborators concocted soups and stews with basic ingredients using low-fuel appliances and sold them at cost. As early as 1895, schools as well as hospitals were receiving hot meals from the outfit. Although the New England Kitchen ultimately failed, its school lunch work continued under the auspices of the Women's Educational and Industrial Union, which, in 1910, was serving lunch to 4,000 students in fifteen schools daily. Through their efforts these women had collectively laid the foundation for a municipal school lunch system.[55]

Although early-twentieth-century home economists and the members of various women's clubs understood the need for municipal school lunch systems, such programs would not become a reality until sufficient evidence demonstrated the dire need for them. Such evidence was not hard to find. A teacher in New York's Public School No. 1 discovered that the boys in her class, unable to access their houses during the lunch hour because their mothers worked, bought ginger beer and ice cream sandwiches with the pennies their parents had given them to spend at the noon hour. Such provisions were not only cold but laden with sugar and nutritionally unbalanced. Physicians were beginning to report that "lunches of the dill pickle-and-bag-of-candy variety" compromised children's stomachs, at least according to the club women who drew on doctors' rhetoric to garner credibility for their enterprise.[56]

Studies, books, reports, and lectures brought the issue of malnourishment to the public's attention, but public sympathy was not enough. In order to garner support for their ideas, proponents of school lunch justified their cause on the basis of education. Their argument was two-fold. Undernourished children, they claimed, were necessarily undereducated because lack of sufficient nutrition stunted capacity to learn. Good food, it turned out, was critical to good education. To sharpen their argument, they highlighted the economic implications of their cause: "It is costly to educate a child," argued Caroline Hunt in her 1909 US Bureau of Education report, "and the cost may become wasted if educational advantages are offered to those who are dull because of improper feeding." School lunch programs, not unlike factory lunchrooms, were looking more and more like a sound business investment.[57]

The second part of the proponents' argument for school lunch held that an organized midday meal furnished an opportunity for valuable social and nutritional instruction. "The paper-bag lunch, eaten without the reinforcement of dishes, tables, or other symbols of civilization," warned an *American Cookery* article, "[is] fast bringing the average high school student within three jumps of savagery." If a hot-food program were to replace the contents of paper bags, manners could be taught; so could proper hygiene. "We are beginning to see cultural possibilities in the noontime intermission," wrote Hunt. To get a sense of the possibilities, one needed only to look at the results of an experiment at the Speyer School, the New York City primary school associated with Columbia University's Teacher's College. Here, Hunt reported, one teacher gave children a cup of milk and graham crackers at half past ten every morning. As part of the morning ritual, they received two napkins, one to place on the desk and one for their personal use. "Children who begin by scattering crumbs quite recklessly end by eating in very orderly fashion," commented the proud teacher whose snack-time lesson was a success.[58]

Manners-minded supporters of school lunch programs assumed that instruction would not end with schoolchildren. There was a distinct possibility, perhaps even a likelihood, that children would instruct their parents in the basics of mealtime propriety acquired through municipal lunch programs. The New York City teacher whose pupils bought ginger beer and ice cream sandwiches found that only one of them sat down regularly at a table with his family, and he himself had introduced the practice to his parents, having acquired the habit at a convalescent home. When she made an arrangement with the school's cooking class to prepare meals for her pupils, the teacher was not only feeding the children's stomachs and nourishing their brains but imparting to them the virtues of proper mealtime habits, which might bubble up to their parents and perhaps even spread outward, to benefit the broader society.[59]

The first municipal lunch system in New York City opened in 1908 at Public School No. 51, a mostly Irish school at the time. The menu featured Irish stew with baked currant pudding on Mondays, pea soup on Tuesdays, rice pudding and milk on Wednesdays, cracked wheat with raisins on Thursdays, and a cheese sandwich with cocoa on Fridays. The lunch program that opened the following year at a mostly Italian school on the Lower East Side hired an Italian cook and provided largely Italian dishes: macaroni, minestrone with oil and garlic, and, with every meal, two slices of Italian bread. Although most school lunches were designed to provide one-third of a day's nourishment, those at the Italian school represented a half day's because Italian tradition placed a heavier emphasis on lunch than did contemporary American culture.[60]

Not until World War I, when 30 percent of military recruits were turned away because of malnourishment-related conditions, did Americans recognize fully the need for school lunch programs. States stepped up their efforts, and during the Depression, when they struggled to provide, the federal government chipped in, employing men and women through the Works Progress Administration to run cafeterias and can fruits and vegetables provided by the surplus program for school food services. By 1940, millions of children benefitted from federally subsidized school lunch programs.[61]

WHEN LUNCH EMERGED from the vacuum dinner left behind, it represented a new, particularly pragmatic and American way of eating. School cafeterias and their workplace counterparts fostered this idiom, which, at its most basic, was about work. Foreigners had long commented on Americans' hasty and informal approach to meals. Lunch legitimized and institutionalized these attributes. Lunch was hasty and informal because it catered to a growing emphasis on profitability—it shored up more time for business, and both individuals and institutions harnessed it to further economic purposes. Companies invested in lunchrooms to increase workers' output; school cafeterias nourished children's chances of becoming productive members of society; and dining clubs and ladies' luncheons helped businessmen and middle-class women bolster status and broaden professional connections. Lunch also advanced social causes as organizations transformed it into a platform for reform: activists waged and won battles for women's rights, laborers' working conditions, and children's welfare, in part, over the midday meal. But lunch served an even broader ideological function.

As America became an increasingly prosperous country that offered refuge to the immigrant and the promise of success to the person of ambition, a number of its cultural ways—including its lunch foods—gained worldwide recognition as icons of the land of the free and the home of the brave. The utensil-less sandwich proved a curiosity (some would say a barbarity) that has fascinated and repulsed propriety-loving Europeans and many others abroad; white bread has alternately served as an emblem of all that is good about America and all that is flawed; and quick-lunch restaurants laid the foundation for perhaps America's most famous and controversial cultural export: fast food. But lunch was not the only meal Americans could consume at lightening pace; nor was it the only one sculpted by the twin forces of American business and ideology. So was breakfast.

6

REINVENTING BREAKFAST

WHEN ENGLISHMAN J. Richard Beste and his family lodged at a hotel on a Midwestern prairie in the 1850s during their trip through the US interior, they enjoyed a particularly decadent breakfast, especially considering this was no major metropolitan area but rather, as Beste referred to it, "the backwoods." The meal featured "hot and cold bread of different sorts, including corn bread (a little of which was rather nice with plenty of molasses and butter), little seed cakes, pancakes and fritters, milk, butter buried in large lumps of ice, molasses, preserves and blackberry syrup in large soup tureens . . . hot beef steaks, roast and boiled chickens, and various sorts of cold meat. To drink, we had tea and coffee, and, occasionally chocolate, with hot, cold and iced milk, and white and brown sugar."[1]

The American breakfast's sheer profusion impressed nineteenth-century travelers, who enthusiastically noted the meal's details in journals, letters, and travelogues. It had come a long way from a simple steaming bowl of hasty pudding or a slice of toast with cheese and beer. At the hotel, Beste and his family could choose from a wide variety of dishes, and the meal incorporated both the old and the new. It included the proverbial corn bread typical of morning meals in earlier times, as well as hot beefsteak, a dish without which a proper nineteenth-century middle-class breakfast was increasingly considered incomplete. Breakfast in this era had become an accumulation of various types of breakfast foods, few of which seemed to have fallen out of fashion. But this elaborate compounding of dishes was more than a luxury; it was also a burden, and the prodigious, meat-centered breakfast ideal attracted no small amount of criticism.

Nineteenth-century health advocates recognized heavy breakfasts as one reason for the dyspepsia that was wreaking havoc on middle- and upper-class American stomachs, and they wrestled with this pandemic in part by reforming the morning meal. Initially using the patrons of their health resorts as guinea pigs for their at times outlandish panaceas, some enterprising wellness enthusiasts developed grain-based alternatives to the meat-centric breakfast and packaged them for sale by grocers across the nation. Thanks to their efforts, breakfast became a tool for improving physical well-being. Happily for them, it also became a lucrative business.

It is hard to say which came first: the new breakfast ideal or the products that helped Americans live up to it. Whatever the case, breakfast would never be the same after business-minded salubrity seekers got a hold of it. They made the once decadent morning meal more compatible with the increasingly sedentary late-nineteenth and early-twentieth-century lifestyle, and because their products required little or no preparation and were virtually ready to eat, these entrepreneurs also found themselves developing a new kind of commodity: convenience. Convenience accommodated a faster-paced society; it was good for the busy, career-driven consumer because it meant less time cooking and eating and more time working and earning. Much like lunch, breakfast ultimately owes its shape to the powerful forces of business. Business incentives drove entrepreneurs to create new products, grain producers to seek more profitable outlets than livestock agriculture for their goods, and middle-class Americans to simplify their morning routine in order to get to work.

J. RICHARD BESTE's morning meal at his prairie hotel was more a dinner than a breakfast, and many other travelers picked up on the correlation. In April 1861, the day after he toured Fort Sumter in South Carolina, journalist William Howard Russell wrote in his diary that he could not easily distinguish between the meals he was offered: "We dined or breakfasted, as the meals are alike save in point of time and drinks." After describing a substantial morning meal that included "more than you can think of," Morris Birkbeck, an English Quaker who immigrated to the United States and settled in Illinois, similarly observed an uncanny resemblance between the meals: "Dinner is much like breakfast, omitting the tea and coffee, and supper is breakfast repeated."[2]

The quantity of food served at breakfast was considerable, and so was the quantity consumed. At taverns and hotels, this may have had something to do with the mode of service. These establishments served breakfast on what Birkbeck called "the gregarious plan," riffing on what was known as the "English plan," a system wherein lodgers paid for individual meals and were free to eat at a restaurant rather than the hotel or even to skip a meal altogether, and the "American plan," wherein boarders paid for meals and lodging as a package and partook of three family-style meals in the dining room each day. The American plan, as its name implies, was the standard mode of service in the United States, and Europeans sometimes complained about the lack of freedom and privacy it afforded. In addition to not being able to choose when they ate, visitors staying at American-plan establishments could not pass up a meal or opt for a lighter one without losing out on their financial investment: they had paid for the food, so it only made sense to eat it. If they wanted their money's worth, it was expedient to consume as much as their stomachs could hold.[3]

When the English traveler William Blane breakfasted at a Philadelphia tavern in the early 1820s, he was stunned by the variety of dishes gracing the board. This meal was not the "ghost of a breakfast" he had subsisted on in England—"your curs'd tea and toast." It was ampler, more flavorful, and far more varied. In describing the spread, he divided it into two categories of dishes, those he expected to encounter as part of a standard tavern breakfast and those that exceeded his expectations: "Besides tea, coffee, eggs, cold ham, beef, and such like ordinary accompaniments, we always had hot fish, sausages, beefsteaks, broiled fowls, fried and stewed oysters, preserved fruits, &c. &c. &c." The et ceteras that close Blane's commentary accentuate the meal's quantity and variety. This was a repast to write home about.[4]

Americans were consuming substantial amounts of food for breakfast outside taverns as well. Private homes were also sites of copious morning repasts. Englishman John Lambert observed that in genteel urban households, families were eating the same way as patrons at city hotels; there was a similarly astonishing quantity and variety. For the Greenmans, a prospering middle-class family in Rhode Island during the mid-nineteenth century, breakfast, which included a combination of cold and hot meat as well as baked goods and porridge, was the second-largest meal of the day.[5]

Many big-breakfast eaters were earning the energy their morning meals provided by working up an appetite worthy of the meal prior to indulging in it. Farmers typically completed laborious chores before sitting down to their morning meals. Travelers covered as much as fifteen or twenty miles in carriages on bumpy roads over the course of several hours before the first refreshment of the day. Aristocratic gentleman embarked on lengthy horseback rides or long walks, surveying their property and subjecting themselves to the elements before taking a seat at the table. At Sing Sing, the infamous upstate New York prison, inmates chiseled and hauled rock in a stone quarry starting at five-thirty daily and only later took their morning nourishment: meat, potatoes, rye bread, and coffee.[6]

Some saw danger in Americans' big-breakfast routine. The English journalist and farmer William Cobbett called the meal "multifarious" and "discordant." Lambert elaborated on the theme: "Their meals, I think, are composed of too great a variety, and of too many things, to be conducive to health; and I have little doubt but that many of their diseases are engendered by gross diet, and the use of animal food at every meal." Breakfast, he pointed out, had once consisted of pies, puddings, and cider, but in the early nineteenth century, when he was writing, such simplicity characterized small farms and country taverns.[7]

Cobbett and Lambert, who wondered about the limits of human digestion, found the variety presented at American breakfasts unfathomable. Others saw digestion as a problem as much of inferior ingredients and sorry preparation. Charles Dickens's description of a "deformed beefsteak . . . swimming in butter" is all the commentary needed to understand that he found the morning fare in a Boston hotel in 1842 not only unpleasant but virtually inedible. If Dickens hinted that he took offense at his morning meal, the Frenchman Constantin-Francois Chasseboeuf, the Comte de Volney, downright indicted the American breakfast. It consisted, in his words, of "hot bread, half-baked, toast soaked in butter, cheese of the fattest kind, slices of salt or hung beef, ham, etc.," and he declared the mix "nearly insoluble."[8]

Such a breakfast was likely "insoluble" because of both the state of the food and the fashion in which it was eaten. Scotsman John Duncan complained that when he arrived in America in 1818, he was unable to match the speed with which his neighbors "dispatched" their meals. The morning meal, he explained, "rarely exceeds five minutes; they empty two half boiled eggs into a wine glass, and drink rather than eat them, swallow two cups of coffee, with a piece of toast and a sausage, and are off from table before you feel yourself comfortably seated in the chair." Volney noted that at the breakfast table, Americans "swallow, almost without chewing." One boardinghouse patron complained that when he arrived at breakfast fifteen minutes late, the table was entirely empty, the rest of the patrons having downed their meals and left the room.[9]

Not surprisingly, at some point during the nineteenth century the American stomach began to respond to its breakfast—with protest. The complaint most often voiced was dyspepsia. A so-called disease of civilization, dyspepsia was a fancy name for chronic indigestion. The term came into use in 1830, and its symptoms, according to Dr. William Whitty Hall, author of *Dyspepsia and Its Kindred Diseases* (1877), were as variable as "headache, heartburn, heaviness, palpitation, belching, hot skin, nightmares, sharp pains, nausea, nervousness, despondency, wakefulness, and cold feet." The tremendous size and complexity of meals, including breakfast, contributed greatly to the dyspepsia pandemic, but these factors were not the sole culprits. Shifting work patterns in an urbanizing and mechanizing nation were as much to blame.[10]

For many people, rigorous agricultural work was giving way to the less demanding dictates of offices and desks; a sedentary lifestyle was becoming one element of the march of progress. The problem: while Americans adapted their schedules to the new urban, clock-driven world of trade, they failed to adapt their eating habits. The traditional farmer's breakfast was simply no longer appropriate to a modern urban lifestyle, at least not for the majority of the middle class. As one doctor noted, "Ham and eggs, bacon and eggs, or a beef-steak or underdone chop with eggs to follow, and then a cup of nice tea, is a sensible break-fast for a man who is going away out into the fresh air to walk, or ride, or work till noon; but not for a person who has to sit all day." Habits proved difficult to change, however, and many people continued to indulge liberally, as strangers to restraint. As a result, their discomforts increased. So too did the rhetoric of big-breakfast critics.[11]

Dr. A. W. Chase was appalled by the quantity of food some of his patients consumed in the morning. In his 1864 household medicine guide, he described one gentleman's breakfast as consisting of "two large potatoes, two pieces of steak, two slices of bread, or from four to six hot pancakes, or two to four hot biscuits . . . all these eaten with butter, honey, or molasses too large in amount to be mentioned." No wonder his patients suffered from indigestion. Dr. Chase admonished the reader who saw him- or herself in this description to "stop [eating] this morning on one half of one potato, two inches square of steak, and half of one slice of cold wheat bread." He also instructed these unfortunate readers to "eat very slowly" and "chew perfectly fine." His instructions on mastication anticipated the slow-chewing movement that swept the nation in the early twentieth century.[12]

Theories about curing and preventing dyspepsia varied greatly. When it came to breakfast, everyone seemed to have a different idea about what to consume and what to forego in order to treat or avert the malady. The dangers of dessert-like breakfast dishes were not lost on the dyspepsia minded of the nineteenth century. An 1898 parent-ing manual lambasts pancakes as part of a "graveyard diet" and derides them as "one of the worst things that a child can put in its stomach under the pretense of food." The author warns that the child who eats pancakes for breakfast will prove unable to work or study. "Eat no bread or cakes of any kind soaked, fried, or baked in grease," warned a popular magazine in 1870. Such food was sure to cause headaches, flatulence, and bilious attacks. In the opinion of the author, fried bread was fit only for the iron bowels of an ostrich.[13]

Mid- to late-nineteenth-century Americans widely believed that underbaked bread caused dyspepsia. "Our people do not realize what miserable, sour, heavy, half-baked stuff under the name of bread is served and devoured at the family table in this country," chided a lecturer at the Plymouth Agricultural Society in 1870. Catharine

Beecher lamented the common practice of eating "newly baked" bread that was necessarily "clammy and indigestible when chewed." Some believed breakfasters should avoid coffee, which overstimulated the nervous system and ruined the appetite. In its place, one popular magazine writer suggested "slops," or warm water, milk, and sugar. Saturating meats in fat was another no-no, according to one doctor, as was "warming over" meats to eat as leftovers, a common nineteenth-century breakfast practice.[14]

Meat had become so central to breakfast in America that many physicians considered it essential even to the morning meal of a dyspeptic. Dr. Chase, as we have seen, did not ask his suffering reader to forgo steak, only to decrease the amount eaten. Medical writers differed as to which meats were appropriate for weak stomachs. One advocated "short-fibered" flesh such as chicken and beef. Veal, pork, turkey, goose, and duck were to be avoided. Another condemned breakfast bacon as "decidedly injurious," while upholding the virtues of mutton as a more easily digested alternative. A primary reason for including meat in the dyspeptic's breakfast, or anyone's for that matter, was the belief that it was a necessary stimulant to the digestive tract, functioning to carry the rest of the meal through the intestines. Without it, bread, butter, tea, and sugar would surely sit in the stomach and ferment.[15]

Some people were beginning to question the necessity of eating meat in the morning and turned their focus to grain as a lighter alternative. What is more, some saw eating grain as biblically sanctioned. After all, Adam and Eve had subsisted on plant food in the Garden of Eden. Starchy foodstuffs presented a logical alternative to the fatty, flesh-based breakfast dishes of the mid-nineteenth century, but the heavy, half-baked, and often fried starches Americans were increasingly heaping on their breakfast tables, drowning in butter and molasses or syrup, and gorging with gusto hardly proved an ideal substitute.[16]

WILLIAM ANDRUS ALCOTT had unusual notions about diet. He embraced vegetarianism and held fruit in high regard, although most Americans and their European ancestors had perceived it with some suspicion for centuries. Breakfast at Alcott's home was nothing short of a countercultural event. It might consist of beans and bread, hominy, or simply a large bowl of fresh-picked strawberries. Once, while giving a lecture, he announced that he had composed the words for his talk while breakfasting on cucumbers. The key to energy and vigor, he believed, was simple meals. "No healthy man will suffer for want of strength to labor simply because he ate nothing for breakfast but apples."[17]

Although Alcott preached vegetarianism, he did make allowance for young children and invalids to eat meat as long as they took it in the morning for breakfast rather than later in the day. He further stipulated that it be on the lean side, prepared with as little cooking as possible, and served without condiments or gravy. But Alcott generally eschewed meat as debilitating, inducing disease and a muddled mind. He himself had experienced the positive effect of embracing the "vegetable system," to which he attributed noteworthy strides in his personal health: eliminated respiratory complaints, reduced rheumatism, and a newfound clarity of mind. Whereas others believed meat's stimulating qualities to be redemptive, Alcott and his progressive-minded comrades saw them as degenerative. Like coffee, tobacco, liquor, and spices, meat drew on vital energies and caused slow but inevitable physical breakdown.[18]

Alcott proposed that Americans purge the breakfast table of meat dishes and, ideally, replace them with grain-based options. "I hope to see the time when farinaceous food will come to be universally regarded as the staff of life," he declared. For one ailing young gentleman, he recommended a breakfast of bread, crackers, and water. This would stand in for the "coffee, sugar, cream, butter, cheese, hot bread, toast, crackers, bread, pies, [and] hash" that his wife felt duty bound to serve him daily. Boiled rice, plain bread pudding, rye toast, parched corn, Indian cakes—all of these won Alcott's high praise. But his highest praise went to brown bread, which he ate daily for breakfast and considered a veritable panacea. "There are few things on which I could live exclusively from day to day and from month to month with as much pleasure as brown bread," he announced with confidence.[19]

The brown bread Alcott self-prescribed as a cure for dyspepsia, and as a rule for general health, became famous as graham bread and a widespread answer to the dyspeptic's dietary dilemma. An alternative to white bread, graham bread featured unbolted flour, which still contained the fiber- and nutrient-rich "middlings," or bran, that modern processing methods eliminated. A failed itinerant preacher and vociferous health fanatic with a similarly coarse personality, Sylvester Graham, with whom Alcott would join forces, also championed this coarse bread, which had come to bear his name.[20]

Like Alcott, Graham believed that diet was the key to health. Also like Alcott, he preached a meatless diet, condemned spices, alcohol, caffeine, and flesh as stimulating, and emphasized consumption of fruit and vegetables. Graham distinguished himself from other early reformers by calling for a return to old-fashioned homemade bread and, in particular, by praising the virtues of unbolted flour. His *Treatise on Bread and Bread-Making* (1837) was the first book published in America devoted entirely to the subject of bread, and in it he not only philosophized about the importance of bran but also warned against the dangers of contamination and adulteration in commercially baked loaves. He argued that large flour mills were not thoroughly removing impurities from wheat, that traces of fertilizer in the processed flour were perceptible to the tongue, and, worst of all, that commercial bakers were adding artificial whiteners, such as chalk and plaster of Paris, to boost their products' bulk and appearance.[21]

Graham ruffled many feathers with his revolutionary message, and his lectures often met with angry protest (frequently organized by disgruntled butchers and bakers). But individuals who experienced improved health based on his teachings spoke up, and before long the word was out. Graham's gospel became institutionalized in Graham boarding houses established by his followers, and certain college campuses—including Oberlin, Wesleyan, and Williams—designed student meal plans in accordance with the reformers' strict dietary principles. A number of famous American personalities embraced Grahamism, including Horace Greeley, and Graham cookbooks emerged as well as a periodical, *The Graham Journal of Health and Longevity*. Ironically, commercial millers even started producing processed graham flour. With this development, the word "graham" entered the lexicon and referred to whole wheat itself rather than to the person who made it famous. Recipes for graham bread, graham gems, graham muffins, graham pudding, graham porridge, graham biscuits, and graham griddle cakes proliferated in popular cookery literature. Bakeries advertised graham wafers and, eventually, the well-known graham cracker, though the nineteenth-century version bore little resemblance to the sugary, highly refined, white-flour children's snack that bears its name today.[22]

Though not broadly accepted in his time, Sylvester Graham's ideas had a resounding impact on American eating habits, especially on breakfast. Reformers, physicians, hydrotherapists, and even businessmen came to see the merit (and the money-making potential) of Graham's teachings and passed them on to an increasingly health-conscious public. One such individual, a physician named James Caleb Jackson, built on Graham's ideas and invented a breakfast food that would revolutionize the morning meal.

Jackson ran Our Home on the Hillside in Danville, New York, a spa where, beginning in the 1850s, people could come to renew their health through alternatives to traditional medicine. Jackson's *How to Treat the Sick Without Medicine*, published a decade later in 1868, outlined his approach to healing through therapeutic application of water and a grain-based, vegetarian diet. Given the horrors of mercury purging, the stinging of mustard plasters, and the pain and weakness resulting from bleedings—all standard medical procedures of the time—one can understand the power of this book's title and the appeal of its alternative approach. At his sanitarium, Jackson prescribed customized bathing regimens for his patients, along with two simple daily meals based on whole wheat. Breakfast consisted of graham pudding with unleavened bread, fresh fruit, and water. Dinner was the same. "I have never found so good food as wheat meal, or what we term Graham flour," he declared. Like Graham, Jackson treated whole wheat as nature's panacea.[23]

Jackson experimented with various graham flour preparations, including a bran and fruit juice drink and several grain-based coffee substitutes. Not all of his concoctions were successful, but one, which he devised in 1863, proved particularly promising. The new product emerged when Jackson baked a mixture of whole wheat and water in a slow oven until it became brittle and wafer-like. He broke up the mass, returned it to the oven, then ground the hard, twice-baked wheat

Figure 1. Two Native Americans sitting on a straw mat help themselves to a mess of food, likely maize, a New World staple colonists came to rely on heavily. Natives did not adhere to set meal times, and Europeans judged them as uncivilized for it, but settlers' approach to food was hardly more refined: colonists' meals were also informal, and like the natives pictured here, many partook of one-pot meals without the luxury of tables, chairs, or utensils.

Figure 2. Pots, a skillet, and a Dutch oven with its concave lid hang from hooks over a cooking fire in an 1840s stone hearth at Hart Square, a museum of pioneer life in Hickory, North Carolina. Early American cooks adjusted temperatures by lowering and elevating vessels as well as rearranging the fire, sometimes propping logs against the andirons, such as the two seen here, to increase ventilation.

Tin Kitchen.

Figure 3. Tin kitchens became prominent in the late eighteenth century when colonists more fully embraced the English ideal of roasted meat. For roasting fowl, the three-sided reflector oven had advantages over traditional spits: basting was easier, as was the collection of drippings, and because the contraption produced a more even heat, cooks had to rotate the roast less frequently. In wealthy households, mechanical jacks automated rotation, a task once performed by children or slaves.

Figure 4. The cookstove replaced the hearth in American households starting in the 1830s, presenting a challenge to homemakers familiar with open fireplaces but un-acquainted with closed fireboxes. Once they mastered the new kitchen installation, homemakers found it produced a high heat amenable to baking, ushering in the era of quick breads. Recipes for gems, muffins, popovers, and other breakfast cakes were everywhere, many disseminated through promotional pamphlets printed by cook-stove manufacturers.

Figure 5. In the mid- to late nineteenth century, dinner shifted to evening and became a formal family affair. Dining rooms like this one in Moorestown, New Jersey, emerged in middle-class homes and featured elegant sideboards, matching chairs, and elaborate table settings. Essential to any respectable evening meal was etiquette, and even without the company of guests, children were expected to practice polite conversation and follow social rules strictly. For them, dinnertime served as a rehearsal for adult membership in middle-class society.

Correct position for holding a knife and fork.

Incorrect position for holding a knife and fork.

Figures 6(a–b). Injunctions riddled nineteenth-century dining, and authors of etiquette manuals filled hundreds of pages with them. These 1897 illustrations demonstrate proper and improper ways to hold a knife and fork. For the middle-class recipient of a formal dinner-party invitation, studying up on dining decorum helped ensure the appearance of gentility—crucial when a faux pas at the table might compromise one's reputation and any business prospects dependent on it.

Figure 7. Popping corn in wire-mesh poppers over the coals of a hearth or in the firebox of a cookstove was a favorite children's pastime in the nineteenth and early twentieth centuries, as depicted in this 1906 illustration. While snacks were a popular pastime for children during the Victorian era, they were also criticized as meal spoilers sure to ruin children's appetites and weaken their characters. Even so, popcorn remained a national favorite and could be purchased at ballparks, from street vendors, and later in picture houses.

Figure 8. Some snack foods acquired a seedy reputation during the nineteenth and early twentieth centuries because of their association with indigent peddlers, many of whom were immigrants and African Americans. Of particular concern was lack of hygiene. In this 1896 photograph, a robust pretzel vendor displays her wares (in perhaps unwashed hands), while additional goods perch precariously close to the sidewalk in open-air baskets. The vendor's association with the unkempt, pipe-wielding foreigner to her right invited further wariness about the cleanliness of her merchandise.

Figure 9. Chocolate, a genteel breakfast and afternoon drink in the eighteenth century, became associated with women in the nineteenth century, especially in the form of bonbons, the quintessential gift from a bachelor to his love interest. This somewhat risqué 1896 advertisement for Owl Brand chocolate creams showcases a saleswoman in the act of indulging. The busty owls mirror her own full figure.

Figure 10. Two young immigrant boys arrive for their shift at a Pittsburgh, Pennsylvania, glass-manufacturing plant, dinner pails in hand. Like the weavers pictured in Figure 11, they likely ate their provisions in the spaces where they labored, as did many of their day who lunched in the same rooms in which shoe polished was mixed and paint pigments were ground. Reforms led to company lunchrooms, where employees could bring cold provisions or buy hot foods at cost and consume them without fear of contamination.

Figure 11. When returning home for the midday meal became unfeasible for factory laborers beginning in the mid-nineteenth century, they toted bread, cheese, leftovers, and pie in baskets (above) or dinner pails (Figure 10). Schoolchildren who lived far from their schoolhouses also carried provisions, though they often relied on a metal tobacco box or a cookie tin instead. These young weavers in Salisbury, North Carolina, are taking their meal seated on the factory floor between two looms.

Figure 12. Women's lounges, lunchrooms, and lunch clubs offered female employees a respite from the masculine world of business. Here they could read, chat with companions over tea, or partake of a hot meal. These women at the Treasury Department in Washington, DC, appear to be enjoying their provisions and each other's company. During an era when ladies without a male escort might be refused a table at a restaurant or viewed with suspicion if eating alone at a quick-lunch venue, exclusively female spaces were welcome refuges.

Figure 13 (top). Quick-lunch venues such as this Harlem delicatessen pictured in 1942 enabled urban employees to consume hot meals in convenient, downtown locations with little investment of time or money. As this photograph suggests, a quick lunch, often taken at a counter, was not usually a very peaceful one, and many complained about the pressing crowds as well as the indigestion necessarily caused by "bolting" the midday meal. *Figure 14 (above).* Automats, emerging in the early 1900s, eliminated wait staff from the lunch equation, at least from the perspective of the patron, who simply inserted a coin into a slot, turned a knob, opened a glass door, and pulled out a bowl of chowder, dish of beans, roll, or cup of coffee. Of course, behind the scenes employees busily cooked, cleaned, and replenished empty compartments. Above, a man retrieves a slice of pie at an Eighth Avenue automat in Manhattan in 1936.

Figure 15. This frame from a 1942 Farm Security slide film depicts a model farm family enjoying a satisfying spread of appetizing but ultimately ordinary dishes: ham, home-canned green beans, potatoes, mixed vegetables, salad, biscuits with butter, custard, and milk. The American dinner-time ideal simplified in the early twentieth century due to the decline in servants and the economic hardships of two wars and a depression. Here, abundance trumps elegance.

Figure 16. The Crouch family of Ledyard, Connecticut, is about to conclude its 1940 Thanksgiving dinner with that customary, all-American dessert: pie. No wine glasses, candlesticks, or fancy table arrangements grace this groaning board—only tumblers, pitchers, plain dishware, and a cluster of grapes. With Thanksgiving as its model, dinner shed its French associations and became a patriotic expression of freedom, middle-class prosperity, the nuclear family, and ultimately that larger family—the nation.

Figure 17. Early electric toasters, such as the one with unenclosed wire filaments pictured above, heated single sides of bread and required vigilance on the part of the toast maker, who flipped the slice (hopefully) at just the right moment. This 1908 General Electric advertisement presents toast as a genteel breakfast food, but its striking convenience appealed widely to the middle and working classes, especially once the pop-up toaster (Figure 19) appeared on the scene in the 1920s along with commercially sliced bread.

Figure 18 (top). Cold breakfast cereal, developed by health-minded entrepreneurs beginning in the 1860s, was one of the first commercial food products to be sold in individual boxes with brand logos. After a half century of indigestion from heavy, meat-centered breakfasts combined with sedentary lifestyles, Americans embraced the lighter, grain-based breakfast with enthusiasm. *Figure 19 (above)*. Because her husband leaves the house early, Lynn Massman of Washington, DC, breakfasts alone, their son, Joey, asleep on the table. Her morning fare is typical for her time: toast, milk, and possibly fruit or cereal. A second glass suggests orange juice. Whereas dinner in the mid-twentieth century was generally a family event, people frequently breakfasted on their own (or, in this case, in a baby's company).

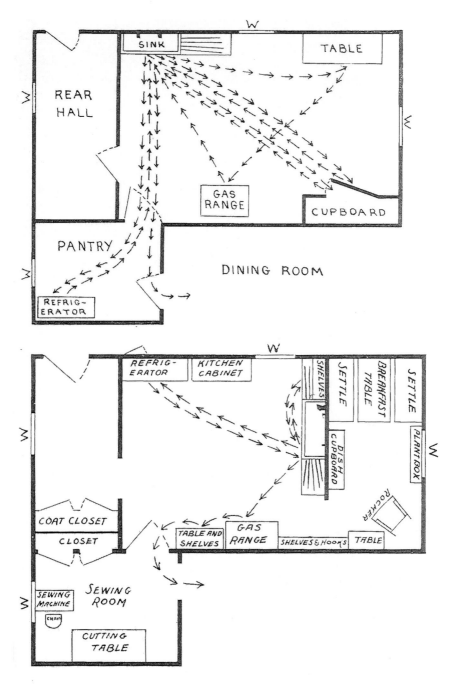

Figures 20(a–b). In the 1910s, efficiency experts consolidated production processes in factories to save time and boost profit, and home economists took a cue, applying the concept to domestic duties, especially those in the kitchen. Step-saving advice appeared in women's magazines and housekeeping manuals, and architects began designing kitchens with efficiency in mind. These 1923 diagrams compare the distances covered by a homemaker making the same dish in the context of two different kitchen layouts.

Figure 21 (below). A cooking class instructor in Daytona, Florida, inspires her pupils at Bethune-Cookman College to see domestic tasks as an opportunity for creative self-expression, a message promoted by leading home economists as well as, eventually, the food industry, which framed certain products as useful in glamorizing frugal dishes and, later, doctoring up meals comprised of processed foods. The cook-as-artist theme was one of uplift, but it also perpetuated traditional gender roles and, for African American women, was all the more fraught. *Figure 22 (bottom).* With the decline of domestic service, appliance manufacturers advertised their products as time-saving servant substitutes, though these devices hardly saved time. Instead, they simply raised household standards. Here, a woman demonstrates an electric mixer in a model kitchen at the 1939–1940 New York World's Fair. Her casual air of command suggests that, thanks to the appliance industry, housewives could perform with dignity and ease kitchen tasks once assumed by servants.

Figure 23. Two Chinese sailors on leave from a British freighter in New York City in 1942 get their first taste of American food: a hot dog and a soda. By World War II, fast foods—largely handheld novelties one could consume casually as a snack or a meal—were international symbols of American culture, and foreign visitors, from athletes to diplomats, partook of them with relish. Eventually, these Americanisms came to symbolize the nation's flaws as well as its freedoms.

nuggets until they were the size of small peas. He baptized the invention Granula, Latin for "little grains."[24]

Granula appealed in part because homemakers didn't have to cook or reheat the nuggets in the morning, as with porridge; rather, as an advertisement for the product would later claim, Granula was "ready for immediate table use." In reality, it was only ready for immediate table use if the "wheat rocks," as critics liked to call the granules, were submersed in milk prior to consumption. The minimum soaking time was twenty minutes, but it became standard practice to let the nuggets slowly absorb milk overnight. In addition to serving Granula at the sanitarium, Jackson established a company and peddled his product to grocers in a number of major US cities, boldly charging ten times the cost of flour for the fancified wheat. Although his Granula did not sell as widely as he would have liked, the margin of profit was considerable. The first cold breakfast cereal was a success.[25]

Generally acknowledged as the inventor of cold breakfast cereal, Jackson did not make it famous. Credit for that belongs to others, including Charles W. Post and the Kellogg brothers. John Harvey Kellogg was a young doctor and vegetarian recruited in the 1870s to direct the health services of the new Western Health Reform Institute in Battle Creek, Michigan, founded by Seventh-Day Adventist visionary Ellen G. White and later called the Battle Creek Sanitarium, or simply the "San." Kellogg supervised a menu of bland, vegetarian, grain-based meals that embodied Graham's and other reformers' notions of health and Christian moralism. Here, he taught his patients the virtues of masticating, or "fletcherizing," a special chewing technique developed at the turn of the twentieth century by digestion guru Horace Fletcher. Fletcherizing proved difficult for patients with dental problems, and in the nineteenth century a broad swath of the population fell into this category. As a result, soft and mushy foods were in demand. So too were novelty foods.[26]

As at Jackson's institution, monotony plagued patients' diets at the San, and Kellogg risked losing their business to competing therapeutic establishments if their palates revolted against the predictably drab daily fare. If that weren't enough, at least one other reason provided the impetus for experimentation. Kellogg regretted the inconvenience of cooking cold cereal and believed he was not the only one.

During medical school he had rented a room in New York City with severely limited kitchen amenities. There, in the doctor's own words, "the breakfast food idea first made its appearance." If others cared about economy of time and energy as much as he did, then a promising business opportunity had presented itself.[27]

At the San, where Kellogg had access to kitchens, he put his breakfast food ideas (and eventually his wife) to work. Kellogg ground and mixed the hard zwieback served to patients for breakfast with oats and cornmeal to create a cold cereal similar to toasted breadcrumbs. He also called the concoction Granula but later renamed it Granola, following a lawsuit by the former term's coiner, Our Home on the Hillside's James Caleb Jackson. Kellogg's other innovations included a steamrolled wheat cereal called Granose, a spinoff of Shredded Wheat, invented by Henry Drushel Perky, who established the Cereal Machine Company and promoted his product through a Denver restaurant where every dish on the menu included some form of the cereal. Kellogg's wife, Ella, had a hand in the forging of new Battle Creek breakfast cereals. In her husband's words, she served as an "incubator of ideas," and when it came to testing the first batches of Granose, she hand-cranked the rollers. Just after the turn of the twentieth century, Kellogg improvised on Granose and created his most famous product: a corn-based flaked cereal that would one day outstrip all others in popularity.[28]

Cornflakes initially created a quarrel. John Harvey Kellogg, an idealist, viewed his cereals as therapeutic foods for sale exclusively to sanitariums, which would use them to improve patients' health. His brother, Will Keith Kellogg, an entrepreneur, valued cornflakes less for their health-promoting qualities than for their profit-making potential. This divergence of views came to a head when the brothers found themselves with a problem on their hands. It turned out that their newly invented cereal was prone to spoilage because of the corn's high oil content. Sugar stabilized the product and solved the problem, but John believed that sugar compromised the cereal's nutritional purity; sugar, in his opinion, was more damaging than meat. Will, on the other hand, argued that sugar not only stabilized the product but improved its taste, promising greater sales. Will won the argument, and Kellogg's Corn Flakes went on to become a resounding commercial success (although the Seventh-Day Adventists ex-communicated Will for dietary violations). In the wake of this triumph, the Kellogg brothers' differences deepened. So too did the contentious relationship between business motives and health claims that would characterize the breakfast cereal business for years to come.[29]

If Will Kellogg was an unabashed entrepreneur, Charles W. Post was even more unapologetic about his business goals. Through fiercely innovative marketing methods, Post pioneered the modern advertising of processed foods and helped transform breakfast cereal from a fringe phenomenon into a mainstay of the morning meal. As a former patient at the San, Post was familiar with Kellogg and his products. Upon recovering from chronic illness in the early 1890s, he opened his own health institute in Battle Creek, Michigan, La Vita Inn, to which he attempted to divert some of Kellogg's business by charging lower prices. He also wrote an autobiography, *I Am Well!* (1893). At the inn and in his book, Post touted what he called the "mind-cure," the idea that right thinking could heal disease. When his first product—the molasses and wheat bran coffee substitute called Postum (an imitation of the coffee substitutes served at Kellogg's sanitarium)—proved a success, he abandoned his clinic and replaced his old ideas with a new belief: rather than positive thinking alone, positive thinking washed down with a generous draught of Postum, cured sick people. As one advertisement claimed, "You can recover from any ordinary disease by discontinuing coffee and poor food, and using Postum Food Coffee." Before long, Post was making similar claims about his other breakfast inventions, Grape Nuts and Elijah's Manna.[30]

Newspaper and magazine advertisements promoted Grape Nuts with sensational testimonies by patrons whose medical conditions the cereal had allegedly improved or even cured. In one, a sickly woman unable to hold down any sustenance discovers she can miraculously tolerate, even thrive on, Grape Nuts. The cereal saves her life. In another, a "careworn" man suffering from nervous exhaustion finds that Grape Nuts make him "lively and happy": "All my troubles have disappeared." There was no end to the medical advantages this product promised, and the detailed, first-person narratives of individuals' experiences presented in advertisements designed to look like news articles anchored and legitimized these assurances.[31]

The inventor named what he called the cereal's "digestibility" as the source of the apparent miracles outlined in Grape Nuts advertisements. The secret lay in the product's special processing, which Post cryptically called "mechanical digestion." His advertisements laid out the (pseudo)science of this technique and reinforced his claims with tables, quotations, and plenty of jargon. Because of this special manufacturing technique, Grape Nuts came to the table ready for assimilation by even the weakest of stomachs. Post claimed the cereal was "more soluble than any other food" and that it did not "tax" the gastrointestinal organs. At a time when dyspepsia was on the rise (as was the print media's sensational attention to it), the superior digestibility of Grape Nuts would have appealed to Americans broadly. He made similar health claims about Elijah's Manna (which he later renamed Post Toasties to appease outraged ministers).[32]

Post folded much of his profits back into publicity and crudely pointed out the power of ads over the American palate: "It's not enough just to make and sell cereal. After that you get it halfway down the customer's throat through the use of advertising. Then they've got to swallow it." Post raised food advertising to an unprecedented level, and through it, he brought breakfast cereal to a newfound prominence. Advertising itself came to play an important role in changing American eating habits.[33]

Because of his innovative promotional techniques, Post's influence on the morning meal, as well as on the art of selling processed food, was profound. The story of breakfast and of food advertising would not be complete, however, without a nod to at least one other innovative marketer: Henry Crowell, founder of Quaker Oats. Breakfast cereals have long sported colorful cardboard packages, and Crowell was the first to put them to work.

In 1877, Henry Crowell bought a mill in Ravenna, Ohio, equipped with the latest technology to process oats for quicker cooking than was possible with whole or steel-cut varieties. He sold the oats in round, mass-manufactured cardboard containers, a form of packaging invented only the previous year. For Crowell, these boxes served two strategic purposes. First, they protected the product from contaminants in grocers' bins and disease-producing germs. Purity was an important selling point at a time when contaminants and adulterants were widespread, as Graham had pointed out in his criticism of store-bought bread, and individual packaging reassured the consumer that the product was indeed free of unwanted particles accumulated in transit from mill to grocer to kitchen. Germ theory, developed in the 1870s and 1880s, provided scientific grounds for popular associations between unsanitary conditions and disease and further reinforced the logic of selling food in packages.[34]

As its second strategic function, cardboard packaging supplied surface area for advertising a brand name. The previous owner of Crowell's mill had designed a picture of a Quaker as a trademark, and when Crowell took over, he bought it. He printed the image in four colors on the cardboard containers, which now were no longer merely practical but also promotional. Here, the makers of Quaker Oats could emphasize their message of purity through the image of a virtuous, morally pure American man. To emphasize the theme, they printed the word "pure" onto the Quaker's scroll. A colonial, Ben Franklin–type figure, the Quaker also offered a sense of continuity with the past, building trust in the new approach to consumption, which asked the consumer to put faith in the integrity of a brand and its packaging rather than a farmer, miller, or grocer. Both the container and the image it bore set Crowell's product apart, making it recognizable and trustworthy, and the public responded. In 1898, an article in *The Living Age* called Quaker Oats "the form of porridge most in vogue." Quaker Oats had become fashionable.[35]

Americans saw oatmeal, like cold breakfast cereals, as a health food in the late nineteenth and early twentieth centuries, and Quaker Oats capitalized on these curative associations. Advertisements focused less on the product's ability to correct ailments than on its capacity to bestow energy and strength, and some even promised improvements in appearance: ads claimed that the cereal "tire[s] not the digestion," gives children "strong bones [and] sound teeth," and for women, produces a "lovely" complexion. What is more, oats presented a more nourishing and economical alternative to meat: an 1892 promotion claimed that the cereal delivered three times the nutrition of the best beef at one-third the cost.[36]

Although many nutritional and beauty claims about Quaker Oats may have been dubious, one ad linking cereal consumption with the waning presence of meat at breakfast was amusingly prophetic. In it, the Quaker assures a cow jumping over the moon (to escape his fate at the slaughterhouse?) that "the butcher's occupation is gone. Even he eats Quaker Oats." Such a message assured old-fashioned breakfasters that even the most stalwart of meat eaters were softening their grip on tradition and embracing a grain-based breakfast. If butchers could eat oatmeal for breakfast, so could they.[37]

This ad was prophetic because it pointed to an actual decline in demand for meat. Preference for a lighter, grain-based, vegetarian breakfast had become widespread, and by the 1910s, cold cereal had displaced beefsteak and lamb chops on many breakfast tables. To accommodate these consumption patterns, farmers shifted their efforts from cattle to corn, many of them "firing their old four-foot companions," according to a *New York Times* article titled "How the Breakfast Foods Are Absorbing the Cattle Ranges of the West." Breakfast cereal manufacturers facilitated this shift by building railroad spurs to farms and offering growers ready cash for grain. For many western farmers, the deal was a no-brainer. Feeding the maize they grew to their cattle meant waiting for a return on the investment and gambling on its profitability. By selling it directly to companies like Kellogg's, they could avert this risk and immediately pocket the income. When more than a few farmers embraced the logic that "a bird in hand is worth two in the bush," a meat shortage ensued, triggering price hikes at the butcher. Ironically, surges in the cost of meat furnished extra incentive to start the day with a bowl of puffed grains, toasted flakes, or quick oats.[38]

By the turn of the twentieth century, entrepreneurs such as James Caleb Jackson, John Harvey Kellogg, Will Keith Kellogg, Charles Post, and Henry Crowell had married the ideas of health reformers, such as William Andrus Alcott, Catharine Beecher, and Sylvester Graham, with their own business savvy and reinvented the American breakfast. They had responded to a need for lighter, healthier, and faster fare that would accommodate a modern, busy, and increasingly sedentary lifestyle. In the process, they mastered a rhetoric that cast their products as the answer to nearly every physical affliction. The public bought both the rhetoric and the products. And they liked these new foods, especially with milk.

ALTHOUGH IT HAS long been a part of the American diet, milk has not always been central to it. Prior to the twentieth century, Americans consumed it primarily in the form of butter and cheese, which were far less perishable. Those who depended on liquid milk most were children and the elderly. Invalids and those with weak constitutions drank it therapeutically as a kind of medicine. Milk, as well as cream, was a common accompaniment to cornmeal mush and other grain-based porridges and a basic ingredient in baked and boiled dishes such as pudding and custard, but it was less likely to appear on its own as an autonomous component of breakfast or any other meal. For most of American history, it played a supporting rather than a starring role in the American diet—and for good reason.

Prior to refrigeration and pasteurization, drinking milk could be dangerous. Outbreaks of contagious diseases such as diphtheria, typhoid, cholera, and scarlet fever were often traced to contaminated milk. The most scrutinized of the milk-borne diseases was tuberculosis, or consumption, which one could acquire from drinking the milk of tuberculosis-infected cows or milk infected by consumptive dairy workers. As this dreaded lung condition was a leading cause of death in the early twentieth century, Americans thought twice about drinking milk or offering it to their infants and children. Starting in the 1820s, swill milk—produced by urban distillery dairies, where sickly bovines living in squalor were fed "swill," or fermented grain, a by-product of whisky making—posed a threat to health. The milk, if one could still call it that, was inferior; it sometimes carried disease and was typically diluted with water to increase bulk, then thickened with chalk or other, more harmful additives. Journalists such as Frank Leslie brought the public's attention to swill milk through sensational illustrations in popular newspapers of emaciated cows and conniving dairymen, and reformers published lengthy articles and books blaming swill milk and consumptive cows for the high infant-mortality rates that plagued American cities. These campaigns resulted in protective legislation that in turn set the stage for municipal pasteurization.[39]

Pasteurization made milk drinking significantly safer, but developments in nutrition, combined with two national war efforts, brought milk to the forefront of the American diet and made it central to breakfast. During the malnutrition scares of the early twentieth century, which emerged out of rising awareness of under-nourishment among poor and working-class Americans, researchers discovered that certain foods cured such dreaded deficiency diseases as scurvy, pellagra, and rickets, and they christened the unknown disease-preventing factors of these foods "vital amines." Nutritionist Elmer McCollum, father of the vitamin movement, isolated what he called vitamin A in 1918, an essential element prevalent in milk. McCollum publicized the discovery and persuasively illustrated its implications through well-circulated photographs of two laboratory rats, one fed an inferior diet and the other fed the same inferior diet supplemented with milk. The contrast was astonishing. The first rat was thin haired, bony, and weak, whereas the second was furry, vigorous, and robust. The images made a convincing connection between milk and the absence of disease, but they also took the message further, promising the avid milk drinker strength, vitality, and, by extension, success.[40]

These sensational graphics pointed to milk as a miracle food, but no one knew just how much of it was necessary to prevent disease or obtain optimum health, so McCollum advocated liberal quantities. He recommended that children drink a quart each day. His sample breakfast menus frequently featured milk as a beverage as well as an accompaniment for cereal, and the cover of his book, *The American Home Diet: An Answer to the Ever Present Question: "What Shall We Have for Dinner"* (1920), which displays a mother holding a glass of milk in her right hand while pouring a glass of milk from a pitcher for her child with the left, serves as a pictorial prescription for the white, vitamin-rich, drinkable food from cows. By the end of the 1920s, one-fourth of all restaurant patrons ordered milk with their meals.[41]

Around the time some Americans were becoming aware of vitamins, they were also becoming aware that poor health pervaded their society more broadly and deeply than they could have imagined. Public health officials began to systematically measure school children's height and weight and found their stature lacking. The armed services rejected one-third of recruits during World War I due to inadequate health. Harvey D. Wiley, US Department of Agriculture food chemist and the chief crusader for the Pure Food and Drug Act, claimed that over half those found unfit when called to the colors failed to qualify specifically because of a "deficiency of milk in their diet as young children." Drinking milk was no longer just a matter of personal health; it was a matter of national importance. By World War II, Americans viewed milk as a weapon that could help win the war. "White ammunition" would strengthen fighting men and help ensure victory, according to a propaganda film of that title, which juxtaposed scenes of milk bottles being filled in bottling plants with American bombers flying over the ocean on their way to help liberate occupied Europe.[42]

Drinking milk had become patriotic. It helped strengthen the nation one citizen at a time. And for citizens making sacrifices in the kitchen to help feed the troops and Allies overseas, milk came in handy. When, as a domestic expression of patriotism, families across the country pledged to observe regular meatless and wheat-less days, they found themselves searching for adequate substitutes. Cookbooks and circulars, including *Victory Meal Planner* (1942), a pamphlet published by the New York State Bureau of Milk Publicity, touted milk as a meat substitute and supplied basic recipes for milk- and cream-heavy preparations. *Food and Victory* (1918), a World War I–era cookbook, claimed that a quart of milk contained as much "food value" as a pound of steak and advised housewives, or "soldiers of the kitchen," to buy fresh milk for their families daily. Milk consumption in the United States peaked in 1945, the culminating year of World War II.[43]

If there were two nutritional musts when it came to eating breakfast in the early twentieth century, the first was milk, and the second was orange juice. Americans had formerly associated citrus, long an expensive import, with special occasions like Christmas. When railroad lines connected Florida and California to major US cities, the domestic citrus industry burgeoned, and oranges and grapefruit became more available and affordable to American consumers. Not until the vitamin mania of the 1920s, though, did orange juice hit the American breakfast table, and when it hit, it hit hard.[44]

Fruit growers' associations touted the often exaggerated benefits of vitamin C, but as it turned out, the public did not need much convincing. Many had read about and seen pictures of the benefits of drinking milk (or at least the dangers of not drinking it), and they were more than ready to embrace another protective food with a similar ability to ward off disease while affording generous measures of energy and health. At the start of its popularity, mothers gave orange juice to infants to prevent scurvy and to young children to cure gum problems and ward off tooth decay. With rising fears about "acidosis," Sunkist promoted the alkaline-forming qualities of citrus as the perfect antidote to an overly acidic stomach. These uses were peripheral, but by 1933, orange juice had become such a standard part of the American breakfast for children and adults alike that Mary Meade, a food writer for the *Chicago Daily Tribune,* called it "routine." In fact, it had become so routine by then that she suggested occasionally replacing it with alternative juices to break up the morning monotony. Rarely have so many taken up a food habit so quickly.[45]

Like milk, orange juice served patriotic purposes during wartime. The military saw citrus groves as veritable vitamin factories and hired scientists to develop ways of preserving the processed crop and transporting it to the troops. Canning created too much bulk, and the government could not spare the metal anyway. Early concentrates were more portable but tended to brown when reconstituted, and the taste was so off-putting that soldiers compared it to battery acid. Powdered citrus seemed the natural choice: light, easy to package, and readily reconstituted overseas, it merely required mixing two tablespoons of powder in a single glass of water. The lackluster beverage that resulted, however, was hardly a winning solution.

Powdered orange juice sufficed for the army, but when it went on the market after the war, it flopped—its taste simply did not appeal. So John M. Fox, vice president of the National Research Corporation, applied a processing method used during the war to preserve penicillin: vacuum dehydration. Instead of evaporating all the moisture from the juice, however, he evaporated only 80 percent, creating a dense, orange sludge that, when properly diluted with water, tasted more like fresh squeezed than the early concentrates. He founded the Boston-based Minute Maid Corporation (which took its name from the word "minuteman," simultaneously anchoring the product in America's heritage while highlighting its modern convenience) and successfully sold his invention to the public. Within a decade of going on sale, orange juice concentrate accounted for 20 percent of the frozen-food market.[46]

IN 1933, when food writer Mary Meade encouraged her *Chicago Daily Tribune* readers to take a break from their regular dose of orange juice to break up the morning monotony, she also hoped to displace another item in the breakfast canon, at least on occasion: toast. Though it had always been a popular snack and breakfast accompaniment, in the early decades of the twentieth century, toast took its place front and center as one of the morning meal's main attractions. Two logistical factors paved the way for this phenomenon. The first was the electric pop-up toaster.

Toasters were originally long-handled, two-pronged forks, which a person held over hot embers for a time and at a carefully practiced distance. The art of toasting bread doubled as a pastime for children, who would later reminisce in memoirs and novels about the pleasures of browning the crust to perfection (as well as the frustrations of burning it beyond repair). When cookstoves replaced hearths, smaller toaster forks (simply called "toasters"), which looked like miniature wire rug beaters, appeared for heating a single slice of bread. One could heat multiple slices on pyramid toasters, tin-and-wire cages that sat over an opening in the stove and held four pieces of bread slanted slightly inward. Heat rose up the center of the cage, warming the interiors of the bread slices, and at just the right moment, one flipped the bread to heat the exteriors as well. Flipping bread slices by hand was also necessary when making toast with such early electrical toasters as the Edison General Electric Company's 1909 model D-12, with its single vertical heating element flanked by two wire racks. There was no external casement.[47]

Whoever manned the toaster in the company cafeteria that Minnesota mechanic Charles Strite frequented during World War I apparently lacked the knack for judging the right moment to flip bread. Tired of burned toast day in and day out, Strite set to work on a contraption that would heat both sides of the bread equally and mechanically terminate the process before burning ensued. In 1919, he added springs and a timer to the stove-top toaster oven, inventing the pop-up toaster, which restaurants began to employ almost immediately. In 1926, the Toastmaster went on the market, the first electronic pop-up toaster manufactured for home use. No longer was it necessary to fire up the stove in order to enjoy a crisp slice of wheat or rye in the morning; nor was it necessary to settle for charred bread when you or the person overseeing the toasting operation succumbed to distraction.[48]

Shortly after the creation of the electronic pop-up toaster, a second invention helped make toast an indelible part of the morning routine: the bread slicer. Sliced bread first appeared on the market in 1928, but the mechanism for slicing it had been in the making for over sixteen years. Iowa native Otto Frederick Rohwedder had been experimenting with the idea since 1912. Bread had not been sold in precut slices prior to Rohwedder's invention primarily because individual pieces staled quickly. But Rohwedder believed that holding the slices together in the shape of the original loaf would keep the bread fresh longer. The challenge he faced in creating a bread-slicing machine was less the cutting action than the means of keeping the pieces together. His first solution, hat pins, failed. Eventually, he decided to wrap the slivered portions together in the shape of the original loaf with wax paper as the final step in the slicing process, and the machine he designed to do this was a success. Continental Bakeries became the first major food-processing company to put Rohwedder's invention to use, and in 1930, the company inaugurated what would become a veritable American food phenomenon, Wonder Bread, the "wonder" being that the loaves were presliced. Within five years, Americans were eating more sliced bread than unsliced, and toast had become easier to make and eat than ever before.[49]

The enormous popularity of toast in the early twentieth century and beyond relied on the products of Strite's and Rohwedder's ingenuity, but their clever inventions cannot explain the toast-for-breakfast phenomenon entirely. The world was moving fast. Mary Meade called it a "hurrying, scurrying age." There were always buses to catch, meetings to attend, bills to pay, homework assignments to complete, appointments to keep, clothes to wash, phone calls to make. Business and institutions had gained an unprecedented grip on middle-class Americans' lives, and for homemakers, new cleaning apparatuses such as vacuums and washing machines raised the standard of cleanliness for the average household, eating up the time the apparatuses saved and keeping housewives chained to a long list of domestic chores. Meade understood the relationship between the morning diet and the modern lifestyle: "Some morning just try serving a good old pioneer breakfast of beefsteak, boiled potatoes, bread and butter, sausages, cake, and apple pie to a hurrying husband or a bustling assortment of runabouts, and watch yourself get royally run down," she warned. If ever time was at a premium, it was now. Eating habits proved more malleable than work schedules and business obligations, and meals— including breakfast—changed in order to adapt.[50]

The breakneck pace of weekday breakfasts all but ensured a slowing down on weekends, and for many, Sunday morning became a time for leisurely, old-fashioned spreads. Meat made its appearance in the form of bacon and sausages but was no longer the morning anchor it had been, upstaged by griddle cakes and quick breads that various mixes made newly convenient. In 1889, Aunt Jemima Self-Rising Flour appeared on the market, the first commercial ready-mix food, and it was a big hit at the 1893 Columbian Exposition in Chicago where former Kentucky slave Nancy Green played the part of the bandana-wearing mammy and flipped griddle cakes in front of a twenty-four-foot-high flour barrel. A few years earlier, Log Cabin Syrup, a combination of maple syrup (45 percent) and cane sugar, had come on the market (Postum, when it acquired the product in 1927, reduced the maple syrup content to 3 percent). Mixes made pancakes—which once required yeast, not to mention careful combination of various ingredients—easier to prepare than ever, and inexpensive syrups added extra appeal.[51]

Mixes also catered to Americans' preference for fluffier, lighter flapjacks, pushing those made with darker grains such as buckwheat and rye further to the sidelines. Since breakfasters traditionally associated dark-grain pancakes with winter (a nineteenth-century cookbook warns readers for health reasons not even to attempt them in summer), their displacement by mixes may have helped sever the pancake's seasonal associations. By the 1910s, homemakers were whipping boxes of preblended ingredients into hearty hotcakes redolent of the rugged frontier but with a lightness more conducive to modern lifestyles, and they did so especially on weekend mornings (and sometimes at noon or in the evening) not only during the colder seasons but on Saturdays and Sundays throughout the year.[52]

Mixes really took off in the 1930s. At the beginning of the decade, the Chelsea Milling Company of Chelsea, Michigan, introduced the first biscuit mix, Jiffy, issuing recipes for muffins, waffles, and biscuits along with its packaged mixture of flour, salt, and shortening. The following year, General Mills introduced Bisquick, the brainchild of company salesman Carl Smith, who, after boarding a late-night train to San Francisco, was impressed that dinner was still being served, and with piping-hot biscuits fresh out of the oven to boot. The railroad chef explained to Smith that he kept a preblended mix in the icebox, which he combined with the wet ingredients at the last minute for late-night orders. Smith brought the idea and the basic recipe back to his company. Bisquick was such a hit that within six months of its debut, it had ninety-five imitators, though most would fall by the wayside within a few years, leaving Jiffy as Bisquick's main competitor. Thanks to the increasingly snack-like weekday breakfast and the emergence of commercial bread and cake mixes, once ambitious and time-consuming treats like biscuits, waffles, pancakes, muffins, and later coffee cakes, cinnamon rolls, and other breakfast breads and pastries became a regularly anticipated weekend staple for many middle-class families.[53]

NOT EVERYONE embraced the quick workweek breakfast balanced by brunch-like weekend specials. Adam Clayton Powell Jr., the first African American member of Congress from New York, recalled nostalgically a different hot bread every morning during his childhood in the 1910s and 1920s—muffins, biscuits, corn bread, oatmeal bread, popovers—plus pancakes, salted mackerel, eggs, codfish cakes, and baked beans. Kentucky native Lina E. Wells reported of her family's routine in the 1950s, "I'd always get up and get a big breakfast. We fried meat, made biscuits, made gravy, fried eggs. And I always had something sweet on the table." But while bacon and eggs, potatoes and pancakes were also part of the new breakfast equation—holdovers from the meat-heavy farmer's breakfast—in the majority of households, they took a backseat to the lighter repast of toasted bread, cereal, fruit juice, and milk. By the early twentieth century, the dinner-like breakfast of a generation before had largely yielded to a lighter, more urban way of eating.[54]

The new American breakfast accommodated the demands of a fast-paced, business-driven society and reflected changing understandings about health. But digestibility and a faster-paced society were not the only ingredients in the transformation of the morning meal. Entrepreneurs designed special products that met consumers' needs for convenience and nutrition, and they promoted them with relentless creativity until these items came to redefine the day's opening meal. Perhaps the most iconic of these products, now practically synonymous with breakfast, is cold cereal. Breakfast from a box was surely a novelty, but it was really only a new twist on a long established American theme. For all its bells and whistles, mass-produced cereal was merely a cold, prepackaged, ready-to-eat version of cornmeal mush, that old-time American staple and pioneer standby. Entrepreneurs had managed to commercialize cornmeal mush and, by extension, the meal with which Americans associated it. It would not be long before they commercialized snacking too.

7

SNACKING REDEEMED

IN HORATIO ALGER'S 1868 novel *Ragged Dick,* the protagonist, a twice-orphaned street boy, is all "rags and dirt." He sleeps in a straw-filled cardboard box, dons hole-riddled trousers, and bears grimy streaks across his face. His appearance says much about his lot in life, but equally telling is the food he subsists on: dry bread and apples. When he has a few pennies, he goes to the Old Bowery, a theater frequented by immigrants, and eats peanuts in one of the cheap galleries. One step above living on peanuts and apples is selling them, and Dick dreams of trading his boot blacking for a more "genteel" occupation, such as keeping an apple stand or "disseminatin' peanuts among the people." But even Dick knows that such a business is hardly more genteel. He recounts to a friend the sad decline of a beautiful young lady who, having lost her husband to a Broadway carriage accident, has been forced to open an apple and peanut stand. "There she is now"—Dick points her out—"a hideous old woman."[1]

Details such as these in Horatio Alger's novel provide today's readers a glimpse of nineteenth-century public perceptions, including prevalent attitudes toward snacks. Although peddlers and vendors furnished the opportunity to procure snacks (or, as in Dick's case, meals) and selling snacks opened up avenues for the impoverished to make a few pennies, such foods bore a certain stigma. They were inextricably linked with the street and those forced to live on it and make it their business. Two additional factors compounded this stigma. First, many of the poor who sold street food were foreigners. Their accents and unusual garb announced a deep cultural difference that prevented many Americans from trusting these foods. Second, when it came to hawking their wares off the streets, vendors favored rowdy, working-class places of entertainment—fairs, sports games, vaudeville theaters—and these lowbrow sites left their imprint on American perceptions of the kinds of food associated with eating between meals.

Although marred by its associations with unclean, impoverished, foreign vendors and rowdy, working-class entertainment, snack food—food products designed and sold primarily for between-meal consumption—was eventually redeemed, and the story of its salvation hinges on commercialization. When entrepreneurs began manufacturing snack food on a larger, more industrial scale, they cleaned up snacking's image, and their key tactic was developing enticing boxes, cartons, and bags. Sealing products in packages, a strategy breakfast cereal makers also came to rely on, removed the huckster and the dusty cracker barrel from the once iffy munching equation, while, at the same time, opening up a world of possibilities for advertising. Packaging also escorted snacks into a new realm: the home. No longer were munchies merely extensions of ballparks, circuses, sidewalk carts, and, later, cinemas; nor was their consumption limited to special occasions such as outings and holidays. Now people could buy them at the grocery store, stash them in the cupboard, and enjoy them at leisure on the patio or in the living room at any time of day, on any day of the year.

Packaged snacks accompanied television watching superbly, and manufacturers planted them even more deeply into domestic experience when they engineered ways to use them as ingredients in meals. Nothing exemplified the domestication of snack food better than the integration of packaged snacks into casseroles and piecrusts. But snack food had a long way to travel from its dubious origins to its triumphant redemption. Its trajectory from a less than civilized street food to a standard feature of domestic pastimes and even a basic ingredient in the American dinner is colorful and at times surprising, and it starts with popcorn and peanuts.

NATIVE TO SOUTH AMERICA, peanuts (which are not actually nuts but legumes) came to the United States primarily through the slave trade, having first been introduced to Africa by European explorers. Slave cooks in the antebellum South incorporated peanuts into the dishes they prepared on plantations, and some southern cookbooks, such as Sarah Rutledge's *The Carolina Housewife* (1847), featured recipes for African-influenced peanut dishes, including groundnut soup. Growing and selling peanuts was one of the few ways that some slaves and free blacks could generate income during this time, and for many years after, peanut vendors were largely African American. When Union soldiers entered the Confederate states during the Civil War, they too developed a taste for peanuts, as the famous Civil War ditty "Eating Goober Peas" attests. Following the war, peanuts migrated north and quickly became a fad food. Street vendors peddled them, mostly roasted in their shells, outside candy stores and on train cars or touted their wares at fairgrounds. As early as the 1840s, peanuts had become a staple at circuses, thanks in part to the fictitious notion that elephants are particularly fond of them.[2]

Because peanuts were largely sold in their shells, eating them was an untidy business, and the peanut lover frequently left behind an unsightly mess. An 1866 *New York Times* editorial titled "Peanuts and Politeness" lamented the "crackling carpet" that trailed munchers in public streetcars, on sidewalks, and in the cheap upper balconies of theaters, dubbed "peanut galleries." The writer further bemoaned the perpetual "scrunching" of the shells and found the habit particularly unbecoming in women. The untidiness and the noise pollution revealed a shameful relaxation of manners, which the commentary sought to rectify. The author of those words was not alone in disdaining popular peanut-consumption practices.[3]

Although welcome attractions at circuses and fairgrounds, peanut vendors could be a nuisance elsewhere. Some people complained that, along with the many other sidewalk vendors "squatting" in urban corridors, they impeded the natural flow of pedestrian traffic and got in the way of carriages and streetcars. Others found annoying the regular blast of the peanut cart's steam-pipe whistle, which one city dweller called "nerve-shattering" and "never ending." At least one person took offense that vendors, including peanut "hucksters," had set up stalls in the US Capitol in Washington, DC, turning the historic house of democracy into a commercial marketplace and the white marble halls into veritable paths of trodden goober jackets. As the proverbial "peanut trail" image persisted, peanuts garnered a reputation as unsophisticated and even crude, and the person who ate them risked acquiring the stigma of the lowly legume.[4]

Popcorn proved somewhat less controversial, though it too could make a mess. American Indians in the Southwest ate popcorn (*zea mays everta*, also native to South America), which arrived in New England in the early nineteenth century, probably via traders and whalers. By the 1840s, Americans were popping it in larded skillets (from which individual kernels frequently and amusingly went flying) as well as in newly invented wire-mesh corn poppers, which, with their long handles, even children could hold over the glowing embers (see Figure 7). Small backyard popcorn plots were common among households with youngsters for whom popping corn served as traditional holiday fun. Away at boarding school, Richard Tucker of Wiscasset, Maine, anticipated popping corn with his siblings, who harvested what he had planted and tended over the summer: "I hope we will have a good time with it when I come home," he wrote to them.[5]

With the invention of the steam-driven popcorn machine in the 1890s, the fluffed maize took to the streets. Popcorn carts emerged as a regular sidewalk institution, and popcorn, like peanuts, became strongly associated with fairs, circuses, picnics, camp meetings, and political events. Despite its seeming ubiquity, popcorn had to overcome substantial obstacles before making its way into the public venue with which it would become most famously associated: the cinema.[6]

In the 1920s, movie theaters did not sell popcorn. Though not as untidy as peanuts, it was still likely to leave evidence of itself on theater carpets and seats, especially when used as a projectile. The mess would be not only unsightly but also expensive to clean up. Although popcorn was not for sale at downtown picture houses (nor were any other concessions, for that matter), many appetizing edibles were available from the small food businesses that strategically established themselves close to cinemas, and it was not unusual for patrons to arrive early for a movie and avail themselves of snacks and drinks or a meal at one of these venues before attending a show. Manufacturers of steam corn poppers went out of their way to court these particular clusters of businesses, and before long, cinema patrons were entering theaters with a bag or two of the buttery snack to munch on in the flickering light of the illuminated screen.[7]

The popcorn business was astonishingly profitable, as hesitant cinema owners would eventually find out. When one legendary failed Oklahoma banker invested in a steam popper, set up shop at the entrance to a cinema, and earned enough money to buy three farms, theater owners took note. Theaters, hit hard during the Depression, began to rent space to peddlers to sell their wares at cinema entrances and later in cinema lobbies, but they did not see a significant rise in their bottom lines until they established and operated their own popcorn concessions. Growers also saw a difference. The prevalence of popcorn consumption at movies caused a sharp escalation in popcorn production. In 1934, farmers harvested 5 million pounds of popcorn in the United States; by 1940, the harvest totaled 100 million pounds.[8]

DURING ITS EARLY history, snacking entailed eating in public, and until commercialization transformed snack food into a more domestic product, people associated peanuts, popcorn, and their compatriots with the frolicking and often rowdy contexts in which Americans typically ate them. At circuses, fairs, organized picnics, theaters, and amusement parks, you could smell the aroma of roasting goobers. Snack food was also prevalent at political rallies, camp meetings, and holiday celebrations, such as the Fourth of July. Vendors worked the sidewalks of busy urban streets and hopped aboard trains, selling their wares from car to car. So many vendors clamored for business at some tourist sites that visitors and journalists criticized them for upstaging the main attraction. Sports events in particular were hotspots for snacking, especially baseball games.

Ball games frequently took place at fairs, where fans could purchase goodies from fairground concessions to munch on while rooting for their favorite team. In 1888, the Long Island Livestock Fair Exhibition hosted a game between the Long Island Suffolks and the Connecticut Norwalks, and one fairgoer reported that the air "vibrated" with "the incessant crack of the double-jointed peanut." Informal ball games also punctuated organized picnics. In the late nineteenth century, the New York Letter Carriers' Mutual Benefit Association held its annual "picnic and games" to raise money for a funeral fund. In 1908, the American ambassador to Germany hosted a Fourth of July celebration for diplomats that featured lunch under the trees, a scrub baseball game, and plenty of peanuts and pink lemonade.[9]

The picnic, a French fad exported to the American middle and upper classes as early as 1810, became popular around the same time that baseball was gaining traction as a national phenomenon in the late nineteenth century, and the two amusements share a host of overlapping qualities. Characterized by a suspension of mealtime formality, picnicking gave diners an opportunity to relax strict standards of etiquette, do without the usual paraphernalia of tables, chairs, and utensils, and ignore taboos about gluttony—all under the open sky and in the fresh, appetite-provoking air. Though usually involving an amount of food equivalent to a meal, picnicking, because of these informalities, was not at all unlike snacking. In an era of industrialization, urbanization, and increasing social dislocation, the picnic served as a welcome retreat into the pastoral; a reminder of the simple life, it provided a therapeutic antidote for overcivilization. To a certain extent, the ballpark did the same: it provided similar opportunities to enjoy fresh air, sunshine, and a green, parklike environment, while offering a break from the drab, hard surfaces of the city and the wearing stresses of urban life. Here, too, the tyranny of rules that defined proper dining yielded refreshingly to a more relaxed way of eating.[10]

Like a picnic spread, baseball parks offered a variety of concessions, and no visit to a game was complete without enjoying at least one. Peanuts were the earliest food associated with the game, perhaps because they naturally accompanied beer, the main ballpark refreshment of the nineteenth and early twentieth centuries. Another typical accompaniment to beer was sausages, and they began showing up in buns on city streets as early as the 1860s and in baseball parks not long after.

Some attribute the sausage innovation to German immigrant Charles Feltman, who sold "red hots," as he first called them, from his pie wagon at Coney Island. Others have located its birth within the baseball park. German beer garden proprietor Chris von der Ahe, owner of the St. Louis Brown Stockings (the Cardinals today), first introduced the steaming sausages in buns to hungry fans, according to one version of the story. Another credits Harry Mosley Stevens, who legendarily sent his vendors out into New York neighborhoods on a chilly April day to bring back hot sausages and bread for wrapping them in so that shivering Polo Grounds fans wouldn't have to subsist on chilly ham sandwiches and lemonade. Whoever invented the torpedo-shaped sausage sandwich, it became a baseball phenomenon, a hot and meaty snack that could support a variety of condiments and, most importantly of all, be consumed entirely by hand.[11]

At ballparks, as at picnics and fairs, snacking was more than tolerable; it was fun, it was rebellious, it was indulgent, and it was encouraged. The setting, with its vendors, peanut shells, and picnic-like atmosphere served as a kind of prescription to munch, and not to snack bordered on unsociable. To punctuate one's cheers with ballpark snacks while taking in an array of appetizing aromas was to engage in the full ballpark experience. And an experience it was, as fans indulged freely in a manner refreshingly diametric to life beyond the green. Here, they handled a variety of festive foods in a particularly tactile way: cracking and shelling peanuts, plunging greasy fingers into a bag of buttery popcorn, artfully balancing a mustard-slathered hot dog in the right hand while gripping an ice-cold beer in the left. At the ballpark, one was free from rigid moral strictures and stiff social decorum. One could toss away scruples about breaking mealtime protocol. One could simply eat whenever and however one liked.

Associations with ballparks and other amusement venues both fostered and tainted interest in snack food during the late nineteenth and early twentieth centuries. Relaxed manners, sensational entertainment, indulging the appetite at whim—these behaviors starkly contrasted with the Victorian ideal, and snack food epitomized them. But as snack food underwent a process of commercialization, these associations waned. Layer by layer, industry peeled away what were becoming old-school perceptions of the American snack and remade munching into something widely acceptable, appealing, and even trendy. It refashioned snack food from a lowbrow, at times transgressive, public indulgence into a clean, innocent, and even quaintly domestic one. Consider the case of the pretzel.

The Dutch likely introduced the pretzel to the colonies. In the 1650s, New Netherlanders were selling them to Native Americans despite an ordinance that, as a scarcity measure, prohibited selling white-flour goods—especially cakes and pretzels—to indigenous people. Julius Sturgis of Lititz, Pennsylvania, first produced the knotted dough commercially in the United States in 1861, and it remained a regional treat throughout the nineteenth and early twentieth centuries. Immigrant pretzel vendors were a common sight in New York City streets and parks during this time. They sold large hard pretzels either from handheld baskets or stacked vertically on poles that rested on the sidewalk. *Harper's Weekly* described the proverbial pretzel vendor as carrying "a long staff" on which he "slipped" his wares.[12]

Often dirt poor, pretzel vendors were widely perceived as lax in the way of hygiene. An 1896 photograph (see Figure 8) reveals just how laid-back they could be. In the image, a robust vendor hawks her wares with bare, perhaps unwashed hands. Bread loaves behind her teeter in the open air, while a newspaper sheet, probably meant to protect the edibles, dangles over the side of the table. Baskets perched on crates and considerably close to the littered sidewalk cradle more uncovered goods. Although the vendor herself does not betray any overt uncleanness, an unkempt, pipe-wielding man standing at her side adds a new layer of grit to the image. Their amicable rapport associates them as possibly hailing from the same immigrant background and, by extension, adhering to the same hygienic standards.

Late nineteenth- and early-twentieth-century commentators regularly complained of vendors' lack of concern for cleanliness, and they accused pretzel vendors in particular of this sin. A 1923 article comparing the proverbial New York City apple vendor with her pretzel-peddling counterpart reveals popular perceptions of those who sold the twisted dough. The article pictured "Apple Mary" as a lively, entrepreneurial woman of Irish descent who was intelligent and always abreast of local news. An umbrella marked her spot, and from under it she sold fine crisp fruit that "snapped" when you bit into it. The "Pretzel Woman," on the other hand, was a rover, mostly marketing her wares to newsboys and messengers who snacked between rounds among brokers' offices and rowdy matches of penny pitching. An immigrant of Slavic or Latin birth, she was, according to the article, "stolid, dull witted, and short of speech and temper." Friendless, cold, and aloof, the pretzel seller was, in the popular mind, notoriously unassimilated and hopelessly ignorant.[13]

Readers of the article comparing apple and pretzel vendors would have found some basis for its stereotypes in various news features. When New York City police investigated the death of an elderly German pretzel woman on Stanton Street, they described her lodging as a "miserably furnished garret." She had collapsed while chasing after young boys who had stolen her pretzel basket. (Pretzel-basket theft by children, especially among elderly hucksters, was not uncommon.) A different immigrant woman was summoned to court for selling wares she left unprotected and exposed to the elements. So moved by testimony about her tragic, impoverished life as a widowed mother who had lost ten of her eleven children, watched her savings disappear in a bank failure, and struggled to eke out a living by peddling pretzels in the Bowery, the judge not only acquitted her but handed her $10 out of his own pocket. The judge declared the case the saddest he had ever heard, but most people perceived pretzel hawkers with suspicion, not pity, and pretzels came to symbolize their poverty and squalor.[14]

Pretzels bore at least one more negative association during this era: they were the choice snack of drinkers. When no longer permitted by law to offer free lunches to beer-buying patrons, bars could still put out complimentary bowls of thirst-provoking pretzels, and pretzels became so central to the American bar experience that with the enforcement of Prohibition, pretzel sales dropped. The marriage of pretzels and alcohol is amusingly depicted in an early-twentieth-century short story about pretzel painters on strike. In support of the fictitious laborers who varnished pretzels with a salt brine to make them shiny when baked, the beer-drinking population systematically boycotts saloons serving "dull pretzels." Thanks to the guzzlers' devotion to the pretzel as they know and like it, the pretzel painters are victorious, winning both a raise and more reasonable hours. The bond between alcohol and pretzels has been tested but not broken.[15]

The growth of pretzel sales slowed in the second and third decades of the twentieth century. Numerous cracker bakers cut back on pretzel production during World War I to focus on more essential products, and many consumers, who associated pretzels with Germany, patriotically refused to eat them. The advent of Prohibition a few years after the war threatened to seal the pretzel's fate: bar owners no longer needed the salted snack to put an edge on patrons' thirst. As one journalist explained, "The old merry-go-round of pretzels to follow beer and more beer to wash down the pretzels came to an end." But the pretzel's downfall was actually its salvation.[16]

When the country went dry in 1920, pretzel manufacturers had to come up with new ways to entice Americans to buy their product. They curried favor with housewives by advertising the twisted dough as a healthful children's snack rich in minerals. A Columbia University professor leant dignity to the snack by publishing the results of a study finding pretzels to be a "valuable concentrated food," and by 1938, infants could even teeth on a specially designed "teething" pretzel. Manufacturers fashioned pretzels into new shapes—sticks, half-moons, letters of the alphabet—and marketed them as perfect for brunches and bridge parties. With the temporary death of the corner bar, pretzels found a new niche in the home. Thanks to Prohibition, and innovative promotional campaigns, pretzels shed their old married associations and embarked on a new career.[17]

Although pretzels' new career began during Prohibition—pretzel consumption doubled during Americans' fourteen-year hiatus from drinking—it really took off in 1933 when the government lifted its ban on the bottle. Pretzel factories that had laid dormant for over a decade went back on line, sometimes to the consternation of neighbors who had grown used to the quiet. Factories that were still running, such as the National Biscuit Company in St. Louis, stepped up production but often could not keep up with demand even after hiring hundreds of new employees. The same year, the National Pretzel Manufacturers Association held its first meeting in Harrisburg, Pennsylvania, to establish standards for the major pretzel producers. The biggest boon to the industry appeared when the Reading Pretzel Machinery Company of Reading, Pennsylvania, unveiled the first automatic pretzel-twisting machine. No longer did workers have to coil each knot by hand. The pretzel was on the rise, and there was at least one more reason for its commercial success.[18]

Pretzel makers finished cleaning up pretzels' sordid reputation by packaging their products. In the early 1930s, laws began requiring pretzel peddlers to cover their baskets with cloths or to sell their wares in paper bags. The Milwaukee Health Department declared bowls of pretzels on saloon counters unsanitary and required that the edibles be "wrapped in something." Envelopes constituted the initial solution. Manufacturers were used to selling their wares by the barrel, box, or pound, but with the invention of cellophane in 1927, new possibilities emerged. Individual packages of pretzels began appearing in food shops and at soda fountains, ensuring that the contents remained fresh and untouched. And homemakers could rely on them not to go stale when stashed in a cupboard or pantry. The peddler and the saloon had finally been removed from the equation, and both the middle-class housewife concerned about her family's health and the urban businessman concerned about his reputation could buy the brittle twists without so much as a second thought.[19]

Between the 1930s and 1950s, pretzel consumption became increasingly domesticated. Promotional material paired pretzels with a variety of foods and drinks, grafting the snack onto the afternoon and evening meals. A natural accompaniment for beer, it now also went well with coffee or lemonade. As a side, it paired nicely with soup or fish. "Pretzels are the ONLY thing to eat with tuna-fish salad," claimed a 1947 article in *Kiplinger Magazine,* and when it came to dessert, nothing beat pretzels and ice cream, a "delicious combination," according to Ruth Rutenberg, who relished the sweet and savory contrast as a child in Philadelphia during the 1930s. In addition, pretzels were versatile and lent themselves well as an ingredient in appetizers, main dishes, and desserts. There was pretzel soup (which, the industry pointed out, was actually a long-standing Pennsylvania Dutch tradition), pretzel lollipops (made by inserting pretzel sticks into small cubes of American cheese), and pretzel piecrust (one option for containing lemon meringue filling). According to manufacturers, there was hardly a dinner or dessert dish this handy snack food would not improve.[20]

By the mid-twentieth century, pretzels had become so benign and so well loved that public figures willingly associated themselves with them, including Pennsylvanian Arthur T. McGonigle, who ran for governor on the Republican ticket in 1958 using a giant pretzel as his campaign symbol. Earlier that decade, Republican representative Paul Dague spoke to the Pennsylvania House on behalf of the salted twist in honor of commercial pretzel manufacturing's ninetieth birthday. He proudly traced the pretzel's history and declared that, with Americans consuming approximately 1 million pounds every year (more than the total displacement of the nation's largest battleship, he pointed out), the pretzel had become a "national institution." He entreated those clinging to old-fashioned attitudes toward the snack not to disregard it entirely. It was no longer appropriate to "sneer" at the lowly pretzel now that it had clearly earned Americans' respect. The once seedy, uncouth, and low-class salted twist now sported a squeaky-clean image. Commercialization had redeemed the pretzel—and other snacks too.[21]

WHEN ENTREPRENEURS pioneered the large-scale manufacture of snack food, new possibilities emerged for framing the public's perception of the once distrusted eatables, and those possibilities pivoted on a strategic element that producers had not yet fully exploited: the package. Packaging gave manufacturers a way to control the patron's consumption experience by ensuring the product's freshness. It suited the product for grocery store shelves, helping retailers to use their sales space more efficiently, and quickly became preferable to selling air-exposed bulk goods out of jars, crates, and barrels. Most of all, packaging created an opportunity to set the product apart visually by providing a blank canvas on which the manufacturer could apply a colorful logo as well as enticing imagery and persuasive rhetoric. The first snack food entrepreneur to draw on the promise of the package was German immigrant Frederick Rueckheim. When he went to work with some peanuts, a corn popper, and a kettle of molasses, Cracker Jack—not to mention a new snacking era—was born.

Frederick Rueckheim came to Chicago in 1871 to help rebuild after the Great Fire and decided to invest his earnings as a farm laborer in the popcorn business. He sold popcorn on city sidewalks, along with marshmallows, taffy, and other tasty treats, but he also devoted himself to culinary experimentation, applying various sweeteners and nuts to the fluffed kernels to create innovative concoctions he called "popcorn specialties." His brother Louis joined him from Germany, and in 1893 they took a particularly promising combination of peanuts, popcorn, and molasses to the Columbian World's Exposition, where they promoted it, appropriately, as "candied popcorn and peanuts." No one knows for sure how Cracker Jack got its name, but an apocryphal story tells of an enthusiastic salesman tasting the snack and declaring it "crackerjack," meaning top-notch or first-rate. The title became official in 1896, the same year that Cracker Jack went on tour—literally. A promotional train carrying multiple cars of the product wound its way from Chicago to New York, providing free samples to lucky bystanders along the way.[22]

The first major commercial snack food based on a patented recipe and bearing an official trademark, Cracker Jack was also the first snack food sold exclusively in packages. Until the early twentieth century, many goods in grocery stores were sold in bulk from bins, boxes, jars, and barrels. When a customer wanted some quantity of a dry item, the grocer wrapped it in paper or scooped it directly into the customer's personal tin or glass vessel. Most of these goods, exposed to the air day after day, were not particularly fresh; nor were they necessarily clean. Dampness and dust contaminated flour, sugar, and milk, as did a host of odors. One advertisement for an early packaged-food product illustrated the liabilities of this approach by recounting the off taste of crackers sold from a barrel that the grocer's helper had covered with a codfish crate when the lid went missing. With less than ideal conditions at the grocery store and increasing demand for ready-to-eat goods, the market was ripe for entrepreneurs willing to sell their products in individual, sealed packages.[23]

Cracker Jack followed in the path forged by Quaker Oats, the first commercial food product sold in folded paperboard boxes, which Robert Gair had invented in 1879. The Rueckheim brothers, who first sold Cracker Jack in barrels and tins, found that boxes did not keep their product as crisp as they had hoped. So they hired Henry Eckstein, who created the wax paper lining that would keep Cracker Jack fresh (Eckstein actually paid a German scientist to teach him how to wax paper, then improved on the process). The new packaging strategy, which included waxing the interior of the box as well as sealing the contents in a waxed-paper liner, enabled the Rueckheim brothers, with Henry Eckstein as their partner, to advertise their product as "put up in triple-proof airtight packages which keep it as fresh, snappy, and crisp as when newly made." The ads assured crispness as much for grocers' as for snackers' benefit since stale Cracker Jack, like stale crackers, not only tasted inferior but were bad for business. Soon others were picking up on the idea.[24]

The National Biscuit Company (Nabisco) set its wildly popular Uneeda Biscuit apart from other crackers by building on the freshness strategies pioneered by the Rueckheim brothers. The company was so sure of the efficacy of its packaging that it centered its 1899 advertising campaign on it. At the heart of the campaign was the charming, chubby-cheeked "Nabisco Boy" dressed in a yellow slicker and toting an enormous box of the biscuits through a downpour. The image implied that because of its packaging, which served as a kind of raincoat, the product would not become damp or soggy but would arrive at its destination fresh and crisp. The company knew this to be the case because it had tested its packaging's moisture-proof qualities by suspending the sealed product for three days in damp, closed barrels with pools of water at the bottom. Advertisements for Uneeda praised the company's packaging more than its product, and this emphasis not only garnered respect for Uneeda but created a demand for a new way of selling and buying food.[25]

Like Nabisco, manufacturers of breakfast cereal picked up on emerging packaging innovations, imitating Cracker Jack's freshness strategy. By 1914, Kellogg's had patented "waxtite," a wax paper lining around the exterior of the box. (The lining would eventually migrate to the interior, but not for nearly fifty years.) In an ad titled, "The Most Important Announcement I Ever Made," Will Keith Kellogg confessed that there had always been a difference between cornflakes as "we make them" and cornflakes as "you buy them." But now the difference was gone. In the ad, a consumer's hands remove the exterior wax paper and crumple it for disposal as if the outer lining were transparent gift wrap. Packaging technology, the image suggests, ensures the product will arrive at the consumer's home new as a gift and in the same state in which it left the factory, unsullied by dampness, dust, or a middleman's hands.[26]

Cracker Jack shared much in common with breakfast cereals. Both Cracker Jack and Kellogg's Corn Flakes emerged at the turn of the twentieth century just as the food industry and modern advertising were emerging. Both benefited from novel paperboard container technology that distinguished them as safe, fresh, and uncontaminated, as well as from sealed, wax paper linings that extended shelf life. Both became highly recognizable and visually appealing products, thanks to the strategic use of enticing, color-rich packaging that worked as a kind of silent salesman. Both revolutionized particular modes of eating: cornflakes functioned as the flagship of the new cereal-and-toast-based breakfast, and Cracker Jack legitimized snack food as a popular new category of eatables and helped make indulging between meals respectable. And while only one was associated with breakfast, both served as snack foods: "Kellogg's makes a fine snack between meals or at bedtime too," suggested a 1930s advertisement in *Boy's Life*. In short, both exemplified the commercialization of food in America.[27]

SNACK FOOD manufacturers used packaging not only to clean up snack food's image but also to dress it up. Snack food had suffered from a distinct lack of glamour, and the package countered this by giving snacks an aura of novelty and modernity. Manufacturers hired graphic design firms to develop snazzy looks for their products, and marketing campaigns engineered occasions for munching (house parties) and dreamed up new uses for snack foods (extra energy for soldiers). Candy and chocolate became glamorized, as did the peanut.

To garner demand for the humble peanut from a more sophisticated middle-class market, Amedo Obici put a new face on the legume—along with a new set of clothes. An Italian immigrant who sold peanuts from a horse-drawn cart in Wilkes-Barre, Pennsylvania, Obici joined forces with Mario Peruzzi, also from Italy, and established the Planters company in 1906. The partners experimented with the sale of preshelled nuts in individual bags, eliminating a good deal of the messiness associated with the snack. In 1916, they held a contest for the design of a logo. The winner was a fourteen-year-old boy whose image of a peanut man, polished off by a Chicago graphic design firm, would appear on Planters packages for a century to come. Mr. Peanut, the company's new mascot, was a tall, smart, and urbane anthropomorphized goober. Sporting a top hat, white gloves, a monocle, and a cane, Mr. Peanut was a gentleman who helped give peanuts a new, polished, more mannerly look.[28]

Candy also received a makeover around this time. Invention of the candy press in 1847 enabled confectioners to mass-produce hardened, colored sugar in various shapes at little cost. Although upper-class Americans enjoyed fine, hand-crafted confections, the main consumers of penny candy were working-class children who learned how to spend money responsibly—or not—at the corner store. Danger lurked under the surface of the sweets, as candies were notoriously subject to adulteration. A 1911 exposé in *Pearson's Magazine* reported that unscrupulous manufacturers frequently bulked their candies up with cheap materials that had no food value at best and at worst were injurious to health. Paraffin, iron oxide, and furniture glue were a few of the fillers the exposé uncovered.[29]

Costlier, more sophisticated candies were also suspect, but for different reasons. Enjoyed by the middle and upper classes and especially associated with women, chocolates and bonbons were a typical gift from bachelors to their romantic interests. But during the Victorian era, when Americans viewed eating, particularly eating sweets, as a sensual act to be suppressed—not unlike sex—indulging in sugary orbs and melt-in-your-mouth chocolates was decidedly frowned upon. Even children's penny candy came under moral scrutiny, and many reformers condemned it as character weakening and sure to lead to more deviant vices.[30]

Packaging helped change popular perceptions of candy. Developed by Austrian immigrant Leo Hirschfield in 1896 and named after his daughter, Tootsie Rolls were the first individually wrapped penny candies. A brand name meant accountability, an individual wrapper suggested purity, and buying candies "dressed up" in colored papers and foils was certainly more elegant than selecting them from a jar on the grocery store shelf. By the 1930s, grocers still sold some penny candies in bulk, but more and more were appearing in glossy, transparent cellophane that, in addition to being more hygienic, made them appear fresher and more appetizing and kept them, as one advertiser put it, "sticky-free."[31]

Packaging, whether for brand-name products or grocer-wrapped bulk items, was not the only factor in candy's second career. In the early twentieth century, a new use for sweets emerged, particularly for chocolate, one that entrepreneurs were more than happy to exploit. The high energy density of the processed cocoa bean meant that marketers could frame it as nutritious. Milton Hershey, a caramel maker based in Pennsylvania, recognized this when he noticed a customer cutting caramels into small pieces and dipping them in chocolate. Caramels, he concluded, were a fad, but chocolate was not: it was a food. When chocolate went to war in 1917 as a ration for the troops, it took on a new identity as a kind of fighting fuel. The Walter Baker Company stamped its bars "W. T. W.," which stood for "Win the War." No longer merely a sumptuous indulgence, chocolate had become a patriotic essential, a weapon powerful enough to help overcome the Central Powers.[32]

Not surprisingly, veterans came home from World War I with a sweet tooth that confectionary companies were delighted to satiate, and they did so with more than mere plain chocolate. Peanuts, raisins, caramel, almonds, marshmallows, nougat, and other sweet and crunchy additions gave chocolates novelty and distinction, glamorizing them and turning them into a new genre of snack food: the candy bar. Candy bars came into their own between the wars when more than 30,000 different varieties were introduced. Some of the more popular ones included Butterfinger (1923), Mounds (1932), 3 Musketeers (1932), Baby Ruth (1933), Kit Kat (1935; originally Chocolate Crisp), Chunky (1936), Mars Bar (1936; originally Mars Almond Bar), Fifth Avenue Bar (1936), and Nestle Crunch (1938). Other popular candies—such as Twizzlers (1929), Sugar Daddy (1934; originally Papa Sucker), Rolo (1937), and M&Ms (1941; originally M&M's Plain Chocolate Candies)—emerged during this period as well. Sweets were decidedly on the rise. Between 1914 and 1935, candy consumption more than doubled in the United States.[33]

During World War II, the War Food Administration limited sugar and chocolate for civilian candy and soft drink production in order to supply soldiers and war workers with sufficient fighting fuel, and it also reserved half the candy industry's output for use by the military. The Association for the Advancement of Science had declared sugar in candy bars a "useful brain food for workers in war plants," and Coca-Cola touted the "pause that refreshes" as a vital booster of military morale. American GIs came to rely heavily on this redirection of sugary essentials. Candy bars constituted 40 percent of all food consumed by servicemen outside mess halls at home and abroad, and a study found that soldiers tended to avoid fats during meals so as to take full advantage of the liberal amounts of chocolate and soda at hand. During World War II, as during the war that preceded it, sweets, particularly chocolate in the form of candy bars, took on the status of superfoods: they doubled as ammunition.[34]

While the GIs enjoyed their generous allotments of chocolate, American civilians made up for scarcity of sugar and cocoa by shifting to salty snacks. The War Food Administration sloganeered on behalf of unsweetened, cocoa-less nosh, namely popcorn, which became a patriotic snack. Ever since the war Americans' predilection for savory, crunchy between-meal nibbles has rivaled their sweet tooth, but the shift did not occur merely because of a government campaign. It occurred in part because, like their more sugary counterparts, salted snacks underwent their own process of glamorization as part and parcel of another important snack food trend: domestication. Incorporating packaged munchies into ordinary dishes glamorized those dishes, making them more modern, tastier, and chic.[35]

As early as the 1930s, marketers looked for ways to integrate commercial snack foods into meals, thereby weaving them into the very fabric of American everyday eating, and they started with crackers. Crackers would come into their own as a necessary element of hors d'oeuvre spreads at informal house parties, but, a versatile product, they could do more than serve as a delivery mechanism for cheese. They could accompany a soup or salad nicely and, more inventively, even function as a filler. During the Depression, cooks used crushed crackers to extend a meatloaf and fill out an omelet: with a handful of coarsely crumbled wafers, four eggs could do the work of six. According to one *Chicago Daily Tribune* food contributor, crackers added not only "body" but "a spark of life" to such all-too-familiar staples as white sauce, vegetable casserole, and leftover fish. Of course, they were not as cheap as using one's own stale bread crumbs, but the industry was quick to remind consumers that crackers cost less than eggs or meat. Indeed, they provided a distinct economic benefit by offering the thrifty housewife a practical way to save a few pennies.[36]

As cracker manufacturing took off—some would say exploded—in the 1930s, marketers found fancier ways for housewives to incorporate these products into daily meals. The soda cracker piecrust, and later the ubiquitous graham cracker piecrust, serve as two examples; graham cracker pudding and salt cracker fondue are two others. Ritz claimed that its crushed crackers mixed with butter, sugar, and lemon juice made a tasty filling for mock apple pie. Cracker variety had expanded formidably, and food writers for newspapers and magazines helped the housewife make sense of the new lexicon of possibilities. They suggested particular pairings for specific dishes and drinks. Tomato soup, for example, combined best with cheese crackers, egg salad with caraway seed crackers, fish chowder with oyster crackers, tuna fish with soda crackers, grapefruit juice with pretzels, milk and cocoa with graham crackers, and cider with ginger snaps. And then there was cheese: Muenster was a natural companion for pretzels, whereas caraway crackers went best with Swiss. As both accompaniment and ingredient, crackers wound their way deeply into American meals.[37]

Before long, potato chips took over where crackers had left off. First appearing at Moon's Lake House in Saratoga Springs, New York, in the mid-nineteenth century, the deep-fried potato shavings, eventually known as "Saratoga crisps," became popular at a number of area restaurants. Many small, home-based chip businesses emerged, but potato chips did not sell commercially until the late nineteenth century, when factories began to mass-produce them, and no one knows which factory was the first. The most celebrated belonged to William Tappenden of Cleveland, Ohio, who in 1895 converted the barn behind his house into a chipping facility in order to expand his kitchen production. In 1925, the automatic potato-peeling machine was invented, and the following year Laura Scudder of Monterey Park, California, developed a wax paper package that could be sealed with an iron rather than stapled or paper-clipped. With these developments, the potato chip business went big time, but only after Herman W. Lay of Nashville, Tennessee, arrived on the scene could potato chips be associated with a national brand name. Lay opened his business in 1938 and, in 1945, joined forces with Elmer Doolin, the inventor of Fritos, a corn chip based on tortilla chips, which Doolin had seen Mexicans selling at Texas gas stations. From this team emerged Frito-Lay, which in the 1960s became the nation's largest snack food company.[38]

Initially, Americans primarily nibbled on potato chips with hot meals, then between meals, including at fairs and festive occasions. Starting in the 1940s, however, the salted sensations entered American cuisine, especially in the form of breading, fillers, and garnishes. A 1949 advertisement for Tasty Chips suggested breading hamburgers and cutlets with the crisps as well as using them to stuff roasts and fowl. The product, the ad claimed, furnished a new "taste-thrill." During this decade, the Potato Chip Institute International hired a home economist to develop recipes incorporating potato chips. The institute published a thirty-two-page pamphlet including recipes for Welsh rarebit and apple pie, and it held baking contests for one of its more outlandish ideas: the potato chip cookie. Although not all of these potato chip combinations resonated with the American cook, at least one did overwhelmingly: the tuna-noodle casserole.[39]

Tuna-noodle casserole was quintessential can-opener cookery, touted as an especially quick and convenient dish to prepare and thus the perfect dinner for female "careerists" with minimal time to cook. A 1945 *Good Housekeeping* recipe for "Holiday Tuna Loaf" boasted that the dish, which homemakers could prepare twenty-four hours in advance, was "quickly put together," calling for ingredients "you are likely to have on hand." Marketers did not see a conflict between convenience and class. Being quick to prepare did not make it unsophisticated. With this logic in mind, advertisers touted the holiday tuna-noodle loaf as gourmet. What made it special was the inclusion of store-bought condiments: pickle relish, bottled sauce, and, of course, potato chips. The salted crisps, layered inside the dish and sprinkled on top, gave the casserole its finishing visual touch, its subtle crunch, and, by extension, its glamour. They also helped cover up the almost embarrassing ease of preparation, the bland taste and nebulous texture of the dish's highly processed ingredients, and the lackluster of its one-pot-hits-the-spot substitution for what might have otherwise been a more dynamic holiday meal.[40]

Potato chips were one of the early snack foods, perhaps the first, to be glamorized through tie-in advertising with other commercial food products. Companies were looking for ways to sell more munchies, and they found success by cooperating with one another to engineer strategic product pairings. In the mid-1940s, Royal Crown Cola combined forces with potato chip manufacturers and motion picture studios to produce ads such as "Neat Treats," featuring Maria Montez, star of the Universal picture *Sudan* (1945). Here, Montez holds a tray of Royal Crown bottles and proffers several tips for how best to enjoy the cola: "Serve potato chips for a tasty between-meal snack. You'll find they're even tastier with best-selling Royal Crown Cola." Another, more glamorous option: "Top potato chips with anchovy paste or cream cheese and serve with Royal Crown Soda."[41]

As early as 1932, when the Snackmaster's Guild was formed, snack food manufacturers came together to pool resources and collaborate on advertising campaigns. The idea was that if they paired products, "one would sell the other." By mid-century, companies had inaugurated a number of tantalizing and sometimes far-fetched combinations. Quinlan butter pretzels were advertised alongside Gulden's mustard, and Bachman's joined forced with Pennsylvania Dairies to promote pretzels and ice cream as a "Dutch treat." Pretzels, advertisers claimed, made a perfect crunchy topping for a vanilla sundae or banana float. Merchandisers in stores caught on, placing pretzels near the dairy freezers. In many stores, merchandisers also began displaying sour cream in close proximity to potato chips. The dip era had begun.[42]

Dip glamorized commercial snack foods by legitimating them as trendy hors d'oeuvres. Snack food now not only formed part of Americans' cooking repertoire but had become fashionable enough to put out at a party. Strategically serving one snack food in combination with another could augment its fashion status. Dips made chips more glamorous, just as chips added interest to a salad or casserole. Pretzels, Chex, and salted nuts were far more tantalizing when mixed together than on their own. Such combinations required little to no preparation. The act of assemblage, or simply of creating harmonious proximity so that a guest could marry one snack with another, was more than sufficient to meet the newly informal standards for household entertaining.[43]

In her *Chicago Daily Tribune* food columns, Mary Meade highlighted snack-food-based hors d'oeuvres as central to the "modern approach to informal entertaining." It was simple: just set out a few "dunks" (guacamole and cottage cheese dip) alongside a few "dippers" (potato chips, pretzels, and crackers), and you were well on your way to pleasing your guests. This style of entertaining was more than a convenience for the modern housewife; it also charmed partygoers, who were beginning to favor the "select-your-favorite-appetizer" type of gathering. Social critics had lauded this informal, snack-based approach to entertaining as early as the 1930s. "Help-Yourself Parties Best of All," announced the headline for a *Daily Boston Globe* column, which suggested that an ideal spread would include pretzels—"glorified and beautified, they now appear in polite society"—cheese and crackers, and a variety of ingredients for sandwiches that guests could happily collate for themselves in the host's kitchen.[44]

In a reversal of history, meals were, in a sense, becoming snacks again, at least at parties where hors d'oeuvres substituted for a more formal and ordered intake of food. In their *Guide to Easier Living* (1950), designers Mary and Russel Wright called it "the new hospitality." If serving lunch or dinner, a hostess was no longer expected to have servants deliver it steaming hot to guests at a carefully set table. Instead, guests helped themselves, at whim, to a smorgasbord of cold delectables, many of which, such as olives, cheese, and crackers, the hostess simply poured out of the jar or package into bowls or sliced and arranged on platters. The Wrights called this type of affair a "snack-meal" and used the prototype of the picnic to legitimize it. Like a picnic, at which participants may sit where they please and serve themselves as they like, a "snack-meal" enables guests to eat their food where they fancy—installed on the living room couch, conversing over the kitchen counter, or surveying the backyard patio. They are always free to go back for more, and as at a picnic, guests at "snack-meals" are free, perhaps even expected, to pitch in and help clean up, though paper plates and napkins, a novelty the Wrights approved and encouraged, lessened the task considerably.[45]

The partnership between the snack and the meal was a new standard for house parties, although it could come in handy for families at lunch- or dinnertime as well. It typically took the form of a spread of snacks that, when guests nibbled in sufficient quantity and variety, stood in for a meal. Certain foods that did not fall squarely into the snack or meal category and often functioned as both epitomized this partnership. The most iconic of these foods is the hot dog, that ballpark and backyard grill favorite.

Whereas we tend to think of the hot dog today as the mainstay of a meal, Americans in the first half of the twentieth century considered it a snack, even if it sufficed for lunch. Perhaps this is because informal lunches taken on the go and consisting of handheld foods were still a novelty, very different from a traditional, sit-down, utensil-laden dinner. Calling such casual foods snacks reflected the food's informal nature as much as its relationship to meals. In the first several decades of the twentieth century, Americans referred to sandwiches as snacks, even those eaten as a midday meal. At the same time, people sometimes ate hot dogs and other sandwiches, substantial as they were, between meals as bona fide snacks.

A variety of types beyond ravenous baseball players (Babe Ruth was credited with eating ten a day) and their spirited fans enjoyed hot dogs; the motorist, the college student, the marine, and even the diplomat relished them. As early as the 1920s, roadside stands sold hot dogs to motorists and hikers requiring substantial food they could eat in transit. Other roadside "snacks" included hamburgers and barbeque. In 1938, Radcliffe students opened a late-night snack bar on campus, serving coffee, chocolate bars, sandwiches, and hot dogs between ten and ten-thirty in the evening. During World War II, the Red Cross furnished hot dogs and "real American coffee" for doughboys stationed in Ireland who might desire a snack "over and above the ordinary meals." Hot dogs, in this case, were more than between-meal nourishment; they served as comfort food that, like "real American coffee," gave the fighting men at least a fleeting taste of home.[46]

Frankfurters, along with the idea of a snack-like lunch, had become so symbolic of America that many foreigners made a point to indulge in them during visits from abroad. For non-American celebrities and political figures, dispatching a hot dog in front of the camera-clicking media could even serve as a form of international diplomacy. In 1951, Japanese tennis players from the Davis Cup team indulged in hot dogs and soft drinks in Louisville, Kentucky. The Associated Press's snapshot of the event, titled "Enjoying an American Snack," features two players in tennis gear with rackets pressed under their elbows. Each holds a soda bottle in one hand while devouring a frank-filled bun in the other. Two years later, Japan's Crown Prince Akihito, approaching San Francisco at the conclusion of a monthlong ocean crossing, radioed an order for a "snack luncheon." The snack-like meal (or meal-like snack) consisted of a hot dog, a hamburger, and potato salad, and it served a dual purpose: first, to celebrate the prince's arrival with an iconic American food, and second, to expedite his trip—he was on his way to London for Queen Elizabeth II's coronation, and he had a plane to catch posthaste. A photo of the event reveals that the dignitary ignored royal dining formalities, consuming the sandwiches by hand from a plate balanced on his lap.[47]

By the 1950s, hot dogs had moved from the baseball park, roadside stand, and college snack bar into the American home, where homemakers regularly prepared them as part of the family dinner. "Everyone knows that the frankfurter is America's favorite snack," wrote one journalist who called the sausage sandwich "ubiquitous," whether served from vendors' steamers at baseball parks or hot off the backyard grill. A contraption called the L'il Frankie might come in handy for parties where hostesses served hors d'oeuvres. It was a grill-like cast-aluminum mold designed to make eight finger-sized sandwiches. Although fillings could include tuna, chopped egg, or cheese, the favorite, as the appliance's name implies, was the frankfurter—in this case miniature, or cocktail, frankfurters, meant to be dipped in batter and grilled into what became known as "pigs in blankets."[48]

As a snack food folded into the American meal, the hot dog followed in the footsteps of the cracker and the potato chip. Thanks to recipes for baked frankfurter casseroles, such as "Frankfurters St. Germaine" and "Franks Mexicana," hot dogs became a viable family dinner option. Franks and beans, a twist on the traditional New England pork and beans, was a favorite at working-class diners in the 1950s, and the homemaker could purchase the dish ready-made in cans and serve it to her family for the evening meal. A dinner that incorporated hot dogs, whether hot off the grill or baked in a casserole, bore a certain novelty as playfully inventive and uniquely American, and it perfectly accompanied a ball game—not for a spectator in the stands but for a family in its living room captivated by the nation's new favorite domestic pleasure: the television.[49]

TELEVISION HAD (and continues to have) a dual impact on snacking. It simultaneously provided an occasion for between-meal munching while also serving as a venue for snack food promotion. Television's partnership with snacking arose as Americans shifted their leisure time from the public sphere to the suburban home. In the first half of the twentieth century, people increasingly spent their leisure time at home, rather than at theaters, circuses, sporting parks, and fairs, as in the past. Young Americans found themselves more than ready to start families and settle down following the lean and tumultuous years of the Depression and the world wars. Beginning in 1945, marriage rates reached record highs, and, shortly afterward, a baby boom thundered its way across the nation. Thanks to postwar affluence, luxuries that most Americans could not afford before finally came within reach: a house in the suburbs, a station wagon in the garage, a washing machine in the pantry, a dishwasher in the kitchen, and a lawnmower in the shed. They sought no appliance more, however, than the television. It was perhaps the ultimate form of domestic entertainment: it brought the world into the home, occasioned family togetherness, and delivered hours of relaxing entertainment—all at the flip of a switch. Not surprisingly, the rise of television prompted a rise in home snacking.[50]

Popcorn provides a fitting picture of snack food's migration from the public arena to the private home and of television's key role in this migration. Once a highlight of amusement parks and country fairs, and later the delight of theater and cinema patrons, popcorn was rapidly becoming a living room phenomenon. At mid-century, popcorn production surged: between 1936 and 1947, it averaged 170 million pounds, but by 1950, it had reached 242 million, and within another decade it climbed to 332 million. At the heart of declines in moviegoing and the rise in kernel sales was the new broadcasting technology;

popcorn, cinemagoers' favorite snack, naturally became the television watcher's nibble of choice. Although film fans might have attended the cinema once a week, they now viewed sitcoms, westerns, and variety shows in their living rooms on multiple nights. By the mid-1950s, almost two-thirds (63 percent) of the nation consumed popcorn in front of the TV set four evenings out of seven. With Americans devoting more hours to their RCAs than they ever had to the big screen, popcorn flew off grocery store shelves and landed squarely in the suburban kitchen cupboard.[51]

Although perhaps the obvious choice for television watchers, popcorn was not the most convenient one. Someone still had to pop the kernels on the stovetop using a pan greased with a generous helping of oil. This kitchen operation generated dishes to clean and errant kernels to sweep up. Entrepreneurs, including Chicago theater owner Benjamin Banowitz, saw the writing on the wall and began to repackage popcorn for home consumption. Banowitz developed an all-in-one hermetically sealed bag that compartmentalized kernels on one side and oil and salt on the other. The cleverly designed cellophane package, which offered the consumer a framed window onto the product, resembled a television, and the product was fittingly called "TV-Time Popcorn." Jiffy Pop would expand on Banowitz's contribution by designing an aluminum foil pan with a paperboard handle later replaced by wire. The pan served as both package and preparation utensil and was a novel approach to stove-top popping that saved the homemaker several tasks at once. Whether these packaging innovations significantly increased popcorn sales or simply catered to the greater demand generated by television is hard to say, but they definitely contributed to American snacking culture and strengthened the bond between snacking and watching TV.[52]

Popcorn was not the only between-meal refreshment enjoyed in front of the TV in the 1950s. Television had generated the perfect conditions for a proliferation of commercial snacks. Some of the products emerging during the early television era include Korn Kurls (advertised as the "Aristocrat of snacks"), Chex Party Mix (also known as TV Mix), Ruffles (featuring a novel, rippled texture), and Lipton dried onion soup mix (which combined with sour cream to make a popular dip). Advertisers presented many of the new products as if manufacturers had designed them exclusively for the television viewer. One breakfast cereal ad promoted Kellogg's Rice Krispies as "good for TV snacks." "If you could peek into TV rooms across the nation," read an ad in *Life* magazine, "you'd find potato chips, popcorn, sandwiches—and 7-Up," the carbonated beverage that "makes whatever you eat taste better." Television watching could also transform non-snack foods, such as canned fish and sliced bread, into snacking staples, according to ads for Maine Sardines and Gentle Raisin Bread.[53]

Some snack food manufacturers underwrote television programs and used costumed stars to promote their products at the opening and closing of broadcasts. TV-Time Popcorn sponsored *Annie Oakley*, and Kellogg's, *The Adventures of Wild Bill Hickok*. In a commercial for Kellogg's Sugar Corn Pops, Guy Madison (Hickok) and Andy Devine (Jingles) proclaim the virtues of the presweetened cereal, which eaters can enjoy "out of the bowl or out of the box." This clever ditty suggested that Corn Pops was not merely a breakfast cereal but a snack food as well, and it was not just for morning but for any time of day. The comforting familiarity of these entertaining characters merged with the celebrity appeal of the actors to pitch a product that promised not only to please the palate but also to make the snacker more like his or her television idols.[54]

With the advent of television and the accompanying increase in snacking, use of domestic space changed: the living room became a secondary dining room. Capitalizing on this change, furniture and appliance manufacturers designed items that facilitated munching in front of the television, of which the fold-up tray table was perhaps the most successful. The tray table meant that one could eat where one pleased, including in front of the TV. It was perfect for playing canasta or entertaining at holiday parties, it catered to the television-watching family wishing to munch or even dine while taking in a favorite show, and the decorative tray could be mounted on the wall when not otherwise in use. Special "Thermo-Trays" could keep food piping hot at any location, including on a tray table in the living room. And for the hostess who wished to offer guests snacks or a light meal in the company of the TV, Toastmaster advertised "television's twin": a hospitality set featuring a toaster, a tray, and square glass plates designed to fit the tray without sliding. With the help of this "smart snack service,"

the hostess could set out some spreads or sandwich fixings on tray tables and make toast right in the midst of the conversation (which was
sure, at some point, to touch on the trendy, mobile contraption). This
way she did not have to retreat from her guests to the kitchen in order
to serve them, nor did she have to risk missing a crucial moment of
the broadcast.[55]

Tray tables and hospitality sets anticipated another innovation
closely associated with television, though not originally intended for
consumption in front of a TV. In 1953, Swanson, a frozen-food company that built on the pioneering work of Clarence Birdseye, the father of the frozen-food industry, transformed the reheated airplane
meal, served in an aluminum tray and designed for servicemen during
World War II, into a wildly successful household novelty: the TV Dinner. The name and the crafty package, which mimicked a television
set—knobs, wooden frame, and all—linked the wonder of the frozen
dinner with the wonder of the living room television screen.[56]

Early manufacturers had often associated commercial food with
nature and the pastoral life—a milk bottle might display the image
of a cow, or a can of pumpkin puree might feature a farmer wearing
overalls and a straw hat. But Swanson chose to link its popular innovation with cutting-edge technology. After all, the TV Dinner was the
fruit of a prospering new science: flash freezing. As a meal cooked in
a factory, portioned into three compartments, sealed in a paperboard
box, and stored at subzero temperatures, the TV Dinner was decidedly distanced from nature—as were most snacking products, assembled
in large manufacturing facilities and sporting fantastical shapes and
textures that bore little or no resemblance to their constituent foods.
It turns out that TV Dinners shared another intriguing characteristic
with snack foods too: package appeal.

Like commercial munchies, the TV Dinner was a discrete eating
occasion tucked into a fancy package. In the 1950s, dinner usually involved a variety of foods either mixed together in a casserole dish and
baked in the oven or cooked separately and delivered from pots or
serving dishes to a bowl or plate. The TV Dinner, on the other hand,
was an all-in-one affair. As with a bag of chips or a box of Cracker Jack,
the preparer didn't have to do any washing, chopping, mixing of ingredients, cooking, or supplementing with additional dishes. He or

she simply opened the box and heated its contents. Of course there was no confusing the TV Dinner with a snack: it required a heating appliance and utensils and was best consumed at a table (though a tray table would certainly do). But the simple direct-from-the-package convenience of Swanson's invention, along with the colorful box's visual appeal, subtly connected the TV Dinner with the snack foods of the 1950s. Although it provided serious sustenance, the TV Dinner was something more than a traditional dinner: it was a self-contained eating experience, and like snack foods, it was at the same time whimsical, novel, trendy, and fun.

Television helped transform snacking into a household activity, and, as the success of TV Dinners makes clear, it also left its mark on family dining. Nibbling in front of the television—whether on popcorn, pretzels, cereal, or toast—epitomized snacking's new identity as a respectable middle-class norm. As snacking joined the TV in the living room, eating dinner while taking in the news or an episode of *I Love Lucy* became increasingly acceptable. The furniture and appliances that facilitated living room consumption, and the products designed specifically with such furniture and appliances in mind, eased the transition of snacks into the home, and both snacks and, to a certain extent, dinner into the armchair-furnished territory of the television. Tray tables, TV-Time Popcorn, hospitality sets, and of course TV Dinners underscore just how much of a norm the new, more casual eating habits had become.

SINCE THE MID-NINETEENTH century, when eating between meals was first strongly discouraged, snacking had come a long way. Once seen as a moral weakness, an affront to the family dinner, and a lowbrow indulgence that went hand in hand with boisterous crowds and sketchy immigrant vendors, snacking had become a regular household leisure activity by the 1950s. The public no longer associated it primarily with working-class revelry, unwashed vendors, and vagrant street children such as Dick, the dirt-streaked bootblack, in Horatio Alger's novel *Ragged Dick*. Like Dick, who would one day rise to respectability, snacking had come up in the world. Commercialization was the key ingredient in snacking's makeover, and at the heart of commercialization were packaging innovations and advertising campaigns that transformed snack food into a proper, store-bought staple with a sleek, winning, modern look.

Snack-food companies benefited from the new focus on domestic life, especially with the advent of TV; they shrewdly piggybacked on the population's heightened interest in family and home, presenting their products as solutions to a variety of domestic challenges. When popcorn migrated from movie houses to the living room, the food industry sealed the association by designing products that made stove-top popping more manageable and pitching them as television-watching accessories. It also framed various snack foods as servant stand-ins: as an alternative to the fancy fare of formal dinner parties, packaged snacks provided a refreshingly modern spread that freed the hostess to enjoy her company with sophistication and ease. When hard times hit, forcing households to skimp, manufacturers promoted snack foods as fillers that helped a housewife feed her family frugally. And when business picked up and more women left the home to work, certain snack foods, combined with a can of soup and a few basic ingredients, made quick, stick-to-the-ribs casseroles that proved so tasty and convenient they remain classics today.

As snacking became subject to the forces of commercialization and domestication, it also underwent a kind of Americanization. Wares hawked by immigrant vendors whose accents betrayed their foreign backgrounds gave way to packaged goods sold on grocery store shelves. The frankfurter, that German sausage in a bun, was rechristened the hot dog, and pretzels, also of German descent, became more symbolic of Pennsylvania than the German Fatherland. Commercial snack foods also subsumed regional, racial, and gender associations. Corn chips, initially associated with the Hispanic Southwest, became a national munching standard; peanuts shed their distinct affiliation with the South and the African Americans who had once been their predominant peddlers; and chocolate's reputation as a feminine indulgence made room for new ways of looking at the processed cocoa bean: first as a manly source of wartime power and then as a sugary pleasure congenial for both sexes.

Freed from the grip of these cultural associations, snack foods themselves became expressions of American freedom. If he rolled up his sleeves, an immigrant-entrepreneur could scrape by in the New

World by entering the business of twisting and salting dough or peddling popcorn, and if he dreamed up a tantalizing new product, he stood a chance of great success. Snack food also embodied the freedom to indulge. Though it went against Victorian notions of propriety, eating whenever one pleased had an inherently American quality. If immigrants could now afford to eat cake for breakfast, white bread on weekdays, and dessert on any ordinary evening, it seems only natural that having the freedom to snack at whim was also part of being American. Dispatching nuts or candies between meals subtly laid claim to the nation's heritage of abundance and constituted a simple exercise of liberty.

Advertising dished out plenty of excuses for crossing once sacred consumption boundaries, and the proliferation of commercially packaged goods made crossing them remarkably easy. But as Americans began to suffer from more chronic health problems, especially in the second half of the twentieth century, worries surfaced that they had taken the widely embraced license to snack too far. Yesterday's special treat had become a culprit contributing to today's escalating ailments. The snack now not only compromised Americans' health but worse, it also threatened to infringe on the family dinner. With the exaltation of the snack, dinner, the meal by which Americans had come to understand themselves as members of a family and a nation, began to teeter on the threshold of decline.

8

THE STATE OF THE
AMERICAN MEAL

WHEN SHARON comes home from college to Port Jefferson, New
York, she usually eats dinner seated at the table with her family, just
as she did when growing up. Although the weekday morning meal,
generally consisting of breakfast cereal, is self-service and she takes
lunch at school (a packed lunch in elementary school, cafeteria food
in middle and high school, dining hall fare when away at college),
the family almost always enjoys dinner together, usually between six
and seven—that is, with the exception of her father, a truck driver
who does not return home until nine or ten at night. Sharon's mother
cooks meals from scratch two or three times a week, and on the days
after she has cooked, she serves leftovers. Sharon calls Friday "leftovers of leftovers day." On this last day of the workweek, her mother takes a break, and dinner is usually "on your own," though the
fridge contains plenty of options to choose from. Sharon's parents
were born in Barbados, and the family's cuisine reflects this. Favorites
include *cou-cou* (a polenta-like cornmeal dish), provision soup, and
macaroni and cheese pie. On weekends, the family eats the morning
and evening meals together, with Sharon's father at the table. A south-
ern-influenced Saturday morning breakfast might include some combination of scrambled eggs with green peppers and orange peel, hash
browns, grits with sardines, pancakes, bacon, and tea, hot chocolate,

or orange juice. At Sunday dinner, Sharon's father has been known to engage his family in a discussion of the message delivered at church or to relate an instructive story from his own life experience. When I asked about convenience food, Sharon explained that the family patronizes fast-food restaurants about three times a year.[1]

Sharon's roommate, Edna, from Santa Clara, California, shares a similar experience of family meals growing up, though the food her family eats is significantly different. Edna's parents are from Taiwan and Hong Kong, and they maintain their Chinese food traditions at dinner, which typically features rice flanked by tofu and two or three vegetable dishes. "To my mother, it's very important that at dinner everyone's together," she shares. But as she and her brother grew older, the family dinner tradition became more lenient, especially when her brother discovered he made quite a good cook and began to use his newfound talent to prepare his own meals, taking them whenever he pleased. Although Sharon's family never watches television or movies during a meal, Edna's family occasionally views a public television special or a movie on DVD. When they decide to watch a movie, they set up a laptop on the kitchen counter and seat themselves all on one side of the kitchen table so that each can comfortably view the screen. If they decide to view a TV show, they relocate to the living room. As long as everyone is watching and eating together, Edna's mother is happy. News, however, does not qualify as acceptable dinnertime viewing. "There is a sense that it interferes with family life," Edna explains, hinting that the frequently disturbing content would undermine the dinnertime harmony her mother tries so hard to cultivate.

Sharon and Edna's friend Kyle, from Brooklyn, New York, shares a very different experience of meals. Kyle is African American but does not identify with the soul food that his extended southern family loves. His idea of a good meal is whatever he can order at the local diner or, alternatively, a fresh Brooklyn bagel with a generous dose of butter. His mother, a single parent, worked at a school during his childhood and adolescence, so their schedules synchronized, and the two usually ate together. Kyle would do the shopping, which he says "is very fun, actually." He took pride in knowing where specific products were shelved, felt a sense of power in determining what went into the fridge, and got a good workout carrying the groceries eight blocks from the store back to the apartment. Kyle's mother would cook about half their dinners from scratch—fried chicken one night, pasta with meat sauce another. She assembled the rest of their meals from packaged convenience foods, such as frozen fish sticks or ready-to-bake pizzas. Kyle and his mother relied on fast-food restaurants for dinner about once a week.

"Mealtime was more central then," explains Kyle, whose mother no longer works in a school but drives a subway train and comes home around ten o'clock at night. There is no longer a table in the kitchen, and when Kyle is at home during vacation or over the summer, he usually takes his food in the living room. "Eating most of my meals alone is something I have become used to," he says. He sees eating as purely functional—a survival activity that he considers boring. For this reason he tends to distract himself at mealtimes by surfing the Internet, watching television, writing, or playing video games. When on campus, he rarely heads to the dining hall without a set of head-phones around his neck, which he wears partly in case he finds himself without a dining companion. Kyle does enjoy munching though. "I probably snack more than any human being," he confesses. Oreos are perhaps his favorite nibble. "I could eat a bag in a few hours."

Sharon, Edna, and Kyle's stories illuminate fascinating meal and snacking patterns that tie into larger national trends. Americans' relationship with home-cooked family dinners has changed significantly over the past half century. The Victorian family dinner ideal reached its zenith in the 1950s and has declined gradually ever since. We are dining together less frequently, and whether we eat with others or alone, we are more prone than ever to rely on food prepared out-side our kitchens. These choices have many implications: to start, they affect nutritional intake, family cohesion, and children's intellectual and social maturity.

AMERICANS HAVE been losing their grip on the tradition of family dinner in no small part because societal factors have made coming together in the evening over hot, homemade food more and more difficult. The demands of work, social, and television schedules have proved major obstacles, as has the proliferation of prepared-food venues and affordable packaged conveniences that make grabbing a bite—often away from the company of others—a characteristic of modern American life. A broad swath of the goods we find particularly suitable for grabbing on the go and bolting or savoring as we please count as snack food, and they have developed an unhealthy reputation. Several decades ago, snack food acquired the nickname "junk food" as Americans began to perceive high-calorie munchies nibbled between (and sometimes instead of) meals as health liabilities. But this did not faze the food industry or the majority of consumers, whose taste buds continued to demand fast food and packaged snacks, whatever the impact on health or the fallout for the traditional family meal.

The term "junk food" first came into common parlance in the 1950s, but the dangers of too much snacking were not yet a hot topic in popular culture. Only in the 1970s did a serious critique of snack and fast foods enter public discourse. In the early part of the decade, that critique tied in almost exclusively with the rising problem of overweight among teenagers. Speaking to a 1972 meeting sponsored by the American Heart Association in Washington, DC, nutritionist Mary Goodwin warned that many adolescents had become trapped in a cycle of eating snack foods at the expense of balanced meals, only to compensate for the increased calories with crash diets, which led to nutritional deficiencies. By the end of the decade, however, junk food was taking the blame not just for weight gain but for chronic disease.[2]

In 1967, the CBS special *Hunger in America* raised popular awareness of poverty and malnutrition in the United States, which led to a public outcry and the formation of a Senate Committee on Nutrition and Human Need, headed by democrat George McGovern of South Dakota. The committee developed legislation that expanded food assistance to the poor, but it also studied the diets of the more affluent and found their habits riddled with health risks. The result was a 1977 report, *Dietary Goals for the United States.* This benchmark government publication held a mirror up to American eating habits and revolutionized the way Americans looked at food.[3]

Until the late 1970s, Americans had consistently heard one message: "Eat more." The malnutrition scares of the turn of the century and the failure of countless young male recruits to qualify physically for service during World War I had given rise to this mantra. So did the discovery of vitamins in the 1910s, which prompted Americans to consume large quantities of such vitamin-rich foods as citrus and milk in order to prevent feared deficiency diseases like rickets, pellagra, and scurvy. Eating more was not only a health practice but a cultural imperative. In a land of plenty, it was appropriate to eat abundantly. Doing so celebrated economic success and expressed notions of American freedom. For formerly famished immigrants, it was a figurative and literal partaking of the American dream.[4]

Beginning in 1977 with the McGovern committee's report on dietary goals, Americans started to receive a different and much more controversial message: "Eat less." The nation's diet had changed over the century, and not entirely for the better. In 1909, Americans had derived 40 percent of their calories from fruit, vegetables, and grains, but by 1976, these foods represented only 20 percent of their caloric intake. During this span, consumption of sugars rose 31 percent, and between 1921 and 1976, Americans' intake of dietary fats climbed by a stunning 56 percent. In the course of only one year, US residents took in 125 pounds of fat and 100 pounds of sugar. Of particular concern was the rising consumption of soft drinks. According to the report, the average American downed 295 twelve-ounce cans of soda in 365 days. Soft drinks had eclipsed not only coffee but milk. Not surprisingly, a host of health problems accompanied these dietary changes. In 1909, infectious diseases like tuberculosis and pneumonia had been the leading causes of death, but by 1976, chronic conditions, including coronary heart disease, cancer, and diabetes, topped the list. The obvious solution was to revamp the way Americans ate.[5]

To help reduce rates of chronic illness, the committee's report prescribed certain dietary modifications. Reduction was the name of the game, as only one of the suggested modifications fell under the "eat more" category; the rest urged Americans to "eat less." Intake of carbohydrates could afford to go up, but consumption of pitfalls like fats, sugar, cholesterol, and sodium required significant reining in. The guidelines were asking Americans to avoid precisely what gave processed foods and most restaurant fare their tantalizing appeal. If Americans valued health, they would have to seriously curb their hankering for greasy dishes, snack foods, soda, and dessert, but their strong affinity for these temptations (perhaps even addiction to them) would make breaking this habit difficult. Here, industry intervened.

Instead of Americans revising their habits, manufacturers adjusted their products. After all, if the food industry could tailor its goods to help Americans meet the new mandate to eat healthily, companies would find themselves with an extraordinary business opportunity on their hands. Enter the low-fat ideology.[6]

With industry's help, Americans could have their cake and eat it too. They could follow the governmental guidelines—or at least a popular interpretation of them—and still indulge when they pleased. In the 1980s and 1990s, companies offered numerous low-fat alternatives to conventional products, now reviled as fat packing and artery clogging. There were low-fat versions of salad dressings, pasta sauces, crackers, cheese, muffins, pretzels, ice cream, potato chips, dips, cookies, pastries, yogurt, and cake. The demonization of fat made the new alternatives look angelic, but as it turned out, they were hardly as innocent as they first appeared. Many products contained higher sugar content to make up for the reduced fat and maintain the product's taste appeal. With the added sugar, low-fat products were often just as caloric as their higher-fat counterparts.[7]

Not surprisingly, those who adjusted their diets according to the new health trends did not always fare better than those who maintained the old ways. Not only did the high sugar content of low-fat options make these options less healthy than they appeared, but so did the license to indulge they conveyed. When consumers substituted products they perceived as healthier for those now deemed less healthy, they typically rewarded themselves with greater quantities. They quickly made up for the initial benefits of reducing the targeted ingredient and often surpassed the calorie and fat values of the original food. This consumption pattern became known as the "Snackwell phenomenon," named for a popular line of nonfat cookies that flew off grocery store shelves during these decades. The Snackwell phenomenon goes a long way in explaining why Americans gained weight in the 1980s and 1990s even though the percentage of dietary fat they consumed dropped from 40 to 34 percent. The food industry had found a way to whitewash its products, eradicating the tarnish of junk food rhetoric by catering to new understandings of health.[8]

Finding processed low-fat alternatives everywhere they turned, consumers were less likely to choose naturally low-fat goods. Fresh fruit and vegetables missed out on all the attention. Because only packaged products were labeled as "low-fat," produce fell below the radar of many consumers looking to root out sources of fat in their diets and replace them with more slimming alternatives. In such a commercial climate, a reduced-fat box of crackers seemed more in line with reigning dietary advice than half a dozen carrots bunched with a yellow rubber band. Even when shoppers did consider fruit and vegetables as low-fat snack alternatives, carrots, celery, oranges, and apples held less sway because they lacked a certain taste appeal (no salt or sugar made up for their absence of fat) and required prep work, such as washing, peeling, and chopping. In the end, processed snacks tantalized the taste buds and offered a detour around the kitchen, but more immediately, they showed up in cartons and bags emblazoned with health-related buzz words the public was all too eager to embrace.

Although the government and health professionals cautioned Americans to eat less, industry supplied them with a way to follow that advice by actually eating more. It was simply a different approach to the math. Perhaps this explains why, despite an abundance of rhetoric that condemned overconsumption and a high-fat diet, snacking in America did not actually decline. Surprisingly, it increased—dramatically. Between the mid-1980s and mid-1990s, snack consumption doubled, and between the late 1970s and the early 1990s, so did obesity among children and adolescents. Since then, both snacking and obesity rates have only continued to rise. Americans buy more snack food today than they did two or three decades ago—more even than they did just a few years ago. According to the consumer research group Packaged Facts, Americans spent $68.1 billion on snack foods in 2008, up from $60 billion in 2004. That's an increase of over $8 billion, or nearly 9 percent, in just four years. A veritable snacking explosion has rocked the nation.[9]

Society's quickened pace and increasingly harried lifestyle helped generate this snacking explosion. Beginning in the 1980s, parents began to shoulder more professional responsibilities than in previous generations (with both often holding down jobs), and they actually began encouraging their children to snack: it was one way to ensure that the kids ate over the course of the day. During this same decade, the grazing fad, which glorified snacking as a healthier and more natural alternative to standard scheduled meals, took hold. Americans' growing snacking habit emerged out of disruptions in American life such as these. Ironically, their growing snacking habit also helped them cope with and accommodate the disruptions. But jarring changes in work schedules and family life were not the only impetus for an increase in snacking. In the closing decades of the twentieth century, manufacturers flooded the country with an unprecedented array of scrumptious munching options. The snack food industry had become more robust, more fecund—a veritable cultural force in American society—and it was turning out new and more tempting products faster than ever.[10]

Snack food aisles and checkout counters in grocery stores looked much different twenty or thirty years ago than they do today. Back then, there were far fewer options to choose from. The number of different high-calorie snack foods marketed in the 1960s and 1970s remained stable at about 250 per year, but that number leaped to about 1,000 per year in the mid-1980s and then doubled to about 2,000 by the end of the decade. In the 1980s and 1990s, the profusion of tantalizing new flavors, shapes, colors, and ingredient combinations proved irresistible.[11]

Growth in the diversity of snack foods available to American consumers is significant because humans respond psychologically to variety. Confronted with multiple choices, people will generally consume more than when presented with only a single option. In a recent study, consumer psychologist Brian Wansink and his colleagues at the Cornell Food and Brand Lab found that participants offered an assortment of three hundred M&Ms in ten colors ate 43 percent more of the candies than those given the same number in only seven colors, even though the various colors tasted identical. Precisely this behavior has prompted companies to create additional versions of standard favorites, especially around holidays, and sometimes with only a cosmetic modification to distinguish them.[12]

As greater and more seductive variety sparked the snack food explosion of the past few decades, the increasing presence of television in Americans' lives fanned the flames. Leading snack food companies know that frequent exposure to ads for tempting, high-calorie foods subliminally influences what television watchers purchase for their pantries and reach for during commercial breaks. Companies spend staggering amounts of money advertising their products—especially on television—because it works. For an advertising investment of $8 million in 2003, General Mills made a return of $147 million on its Nature Valley Bars alone. The same year, Pepperidge Farm/Campbell's Soup spent $16 million promoting its goldfish crackers and raked in $258 million. Kraft/Altria spent $17 million enticing consumers to buy Ritz Crackers; in response, consumers, influenced no doubt by catchy TV messages broadcast into their living rooms, shelled out $329 million for the salty wafers in the fire-engine-red box.[13]

Television not only gets us to buy snack food but influences what we snack on, and one of the more vulnerable segments of the population in particular falls under its sway: children. Young people's snacking choices correlate predictably with what they watch on television, which in turn corresponds with the foods they nag their parents, often at great length, to buy for them at the store. In addition to influencing the kinds of snacks children prefer, television commercials prime them for automatic consumption. In other words, snack food ads motivate us not just to want what they are advertising but to start eating, whether we have access to the precise product featured in the commercial or not. In one study, children watching a cartoon interrupted by food advertising ate 45 percent more snacks than children watching the same cartoon with nonfood advertising. Although the implications of these findings are particularly worrisome with regard to youngsters, this experiment determined that television advertising had a similar priming effect on adults.[14]

Commercials hold sway over our eating habits—this is a well-established fact. "If you do not respond to food marketing," claims New York University nutritionist Marion Nestle, "you would be highly unusual." But factors other than commercials—including the act of watching television itself—influence how much consumers snack. Even if a viewer does not encounter a single reference to food that acts as a cue to eat (a highly unlikely scenario), caloric consumption will remain consistently higher in both children and adults while they are sitting in front of a television. Viewers who reach for a snack while watching TV prefer more caloric foods. A bag of barbeque-flavored corn chips is a more likely candidate for a television snack than an apple, and a bowl of cookie-dough ice cream is harder to resist when sitting down to the finale of a network drama than a container of blueberry yogurt. But the main reason for the calorie hike is probably that screens disrupt the body's habituation process—that is, they interfere with the biological response generated by the nervous system when the body has consumed its fill. When viewers munch in front of a screen, they simply do not and cannot know when they have had enough.[15]

Today, snacking is more embedded in the American diet than ever. On any given day, 90 percent of American adults snack (up from 59 percent in the 1970s), and most American adults snack two to three times a day. The average number of snacks we consume per day has doubled in the last three decades. Statistically speaking, Americans are more likely to snack in a given day than they are to eat breakfast. In other words, Americans may skip breakfast, and they may even skip lunch, but they will snack.[16]

As the content of snack foods has changed, so have Americans' snacking habits. Americans not only eat more snacks more frequently than they used to, but they also consume them differently. In the 1980s, a commitment to healthier snacking options, including milk, fruit, fruit juices, and bread, balanced nibblers' predilection for baked goods, dairy desserts, and salty snacks. Today, such healthier options are less popular, and as Marion Nestle has put it, snacking has become "more junky." Current top sources of snacking calories include desserts, sweetened beverages, alcoholic drinks, and salty snack foods. These "junkier" snacks are also more caloric. The caloric intake of the average snacking occasion increased by 26 percent between 1977 and the mid-1990s.[17]

New York Times blogger Tara Parker-Pope calls today's children "Generation Snack." On average, kids snack three times every day, consuming about 600 calories from between-meal indulgences, a jump of 168 calories since the mid-1970s. Children's daily snack calories represent 27 percent of their overall daily energy intake. Cookies, cakes, and other desserts are their favorites and the biggest sources of snack food energy, with salty snacks running a close second. Juice drinks are now more likely to replace fruit, a traditional standby. Snacks have become an expected part of children's extracurricular activities, be they sports practices, play rehearsals, scout meetings, or tutoring sessions, and of course social gatherings would be incomplete without them.[18]

With so much snacking, it is surprising that children have any room left in their stomachs for dinner. In fact, they do not, or at least not much. Whereas children's snack calories have risen steadily, their meal calories have failed to keep pace. Today's children derive fewer calories from breakfast, lunch, and dinner than they once did, and their caloric intake from between-meal indulgences has risen considerably. Statistically speaking, snacking has started to eclipse the American meal.

ALTHOUGH MODERN snacking habits have put a dent in the traditional sit-down family dinner, other factors have also shaped the way we approach the evening meal. At the top of the list is the appeal that processed, prepared foods hold for our taste buds and the way these foods have transformed (some would say undermined) our relationship with our kitchens. In his 2009 *New York Times Magazine* article "Out of the Kitchen, onto the Couch," journalist and author Michael Pollan points out an intriguing irony: Americans' enthusiasm for television food shows parallels a considerable decline in actual cooking. "A great many Americans are spending considerably more time watching images of cooking on television than they are cooking themselves," he explained. We seem to have an increasing affinity for the kitchen and the many activities associated with it but prefer to watch others perform those activities rather than engage in them personally, a pattern proved by significant decreases in our cooking load over the past half century. In 1965, married women who did not work outside the home spent over two hours every day cooking and cleaning up after meals. In 1995, the same tasks occupied less than half that time. Today, the average number of minutes spent preparing food in American households has bottomed out at a mere thirty. This would seem a boon for housewives, but some regard it as a likely culprit in the rise of obesity, observing that the less time we spend cooking, the more likely we are to be overweight. Studies have found that the more involved we are in the process of preparing our food, the healthier the choices we make about what we put in our mouths.[19]

Logically, one reason for the decline in cooking may be a lack of time. Some have argued that the number of minutes or hours spent cooking reflects a household's time resources. In other words, how much Americans cook depends on the demands of their jobs and responsibilities outside the home. Americans work more hours than the citizens of any other industrialized nation, and their cooking habits seem to reflect acute time constraints. Women who work generally spend less time cooking than women who do not work, and women who work full-time spend less time cooking than women who work part-time. But women who do not work at all today still cook less than women who did not work in the 1960s, so the mere reduction in a household's time resources fails to explain fully why we spend so little time cooking (especially when we seem to have plenty of time to watch cooking shows on TV). Certainly time constraints play a role in shaping Americans' relationships with their kitchens, but another factor holds significant sway: food processing.[20]

Americans consume no small amount of food prepared away from home, whether at restaurants, as takeout, as packaged snack foods, or as frozen meals designed to be popped into a microwave oven, and we have come to rely on these foods more heavily than ever. In the 1970s, Americans forked over 25 percent of their food dollars on these conveniences, and by the mid-1990s, that number had risen to 40 percent. Today, the cost of meals and snacks prepared away from home represents half the total amount Americans spend on what they eat. Not surprisingly, we source a greater proportion of our calories and fat from these foods than we did in the past. In the 1970s, foods prepared away from home represented 18 percent of daily caloric intake, but by the mid-1990s, they accounted for 34 percent. If the saying is true that you are what you eat, then Americans are less what they cook for themselves in their kitchens and more what the food industry processes for them.[21]

When we enjoy food prepared outside the home, we eat differently, consuming more calories, salt, and unhealthy fats than when dining on what we prepare for ourselves in our kitchens. The reason is (at least) threefold. First, processed food simply contains more calories, salt, and unhealthy fats. This is not by accident. The food industry is in the business of palatability, a quality that David Kessler, former commissioner of the US Food and Drug Administration, defines as a food's "capacity to stimulate the appetite and prompt us to eat more." Because the body is wired to respond to fat, sugar, and salt, limiting oneself to a single salted French fry or a lone forkful of chocolate-chip brownie cake is exceptionally difficult. More than a matter of mere psychology, the salty or sweet food's appeal is also a matter of biology. When the tongue encounters these particular tastes, the brain releases endorphins, activating the body's primary pleasure system and encoding neurons to recognize these tastes. When the encoded neurons detect the same foods at a later time, they respond more vigorously, increasing the pleasure associated with the item and prompting the eater to take in more.[22]

Not surprisingly, the food industry has capitalized on these biological processes. Some of the larger manufacturers have designed their products in light of research using brain scans to measure neurological responses to various foods, particularly sugar. Restaurants have likewise exploited this phenomenon, especially in their "layering" approach to menu items. Combining certain food characteristics—adding sugar to fat, salt to fat, or fat to fat or even mixing all three—elicits an even stronger biological response because it engages a higher number of encoded neurons. When nachos are blanketed with melted cheese and served with sour cream; when buffalo wings are deep-fried, then covered with a sweet sauce and served with a creamy, salted dip; or when peanut butter cheesecake is encased in a salted, buttery graham cracker crust—these foods become hyperpalatable, and people presented with hyperpalatable food at a bistro, grill, or fast-food joint invariably eat more.[23]

A second reason why Americans eat differently when relying on foods prepared away from home is portion size. Processed foods are typically plated or packaged in much larger portions than Americans serve themselves at home. Over the century, portion sizes have increased steadily for restaurant items as well as packaged foods. In 1916, Coca-Cola came in 6.5-ounce bottles; by the 1950s, 10- and 12-ounce bottles had become the norm, and today the drink sells in 20- and 30-ounce bottles, the 20-ounce constituting the adult standard. In general, items on fast-food menus are two-to-five times larger than they were two decades ago. Commercial bakers' muffin tins are larger than they used to be, and pizza makers' pie pans are broader. It is hardly surprising that the diameter of the average American restaurant plate has also increased in the space of only a few years.[24]

Just because restaurants serve larger portion sizes than are likely to appear in private dining rooms does not mean we have to swallow more than we would at home, yet time and again we do. The larger the portion size, the more an eater will inevitably consume. When a customer has a choice of sizes, the larger often wins out because of its perceived higher value. When, on the other hand, the customer does not have a choice—the restaurant serving is already overly generous or all the candy bars at the movie theater are king-size—he or she will still eat more. Statistically speaking, when presented with a larger portion, restaurant patrons consume 30 to 50 percent more (and when snackers find themselves with a larger package, they eat 20 to 40 percent more). Consumption norms increase with portion size, and it makes no difference whether the eater is wealthy or disadvantaged, degree toting or uneducated. Strangely, it makes little difference whether the eater is even hungry. Everyone is susceptible to what has been called "portion distortion." But the reason we consume differently when eating out is more than a matter of environmental influence (i.e., the size of the plate or package, the palatability of the food); when we eat out, we seem to want to eat differently.[25]

Enjoying food prepared away from home is one of Americans' favorite ways to self-gift, and this is the third reason we eat differently when eating out. Whether it's fettuccine Alfredo garnished with a sprig of rosemary and accompanied by a glass of Chardonnay or a thrown-together, foil-wrapped burrito washed down with a bottle of soda or lemonade, prepared food sooths and comforts. It helps mitigate the stress of a fast-paced, highly demanding world, and in a culture of entitlement, it fulfills a need for reward. When we treat ourselves to a meal at a restaurant, we do not skimp because skimping would defeat the purpose. An executive of a major restaurant chain characterized Americans' attitude in restaurants as "When I go out to eat, I want what I want." Perhaps calorie counts on menus have proved of little help in reducing restaurant patrons' orders precisely because we see ourselves as entitled to a treat when we walk into a food venue. As consumers keep up with the hectic pace of modern life, they see themselves as deserving a break. McDonalds's "You deserve a break to-day" advertising campaign, which infiltrated pop culture in the 1980s and has been called the top jingle of the twentieth century, is as much a reflection of Americans' attitudes toward eating foods prepared away from home as it is a prescription to indulge in them.[26]

A concept that behavioral psychologists call the "halo effect" reveals just how far hungry Americans will go to treat themselves when eating out. Glancing at a menu, a patron is attracted to the deluxe burger but instead decides on a salad because his conscience obliges him to choose the healthier option. Chances are, he will reward himself for his healthy choice, using it as permission to order complementary dishes and drinks—a caloric beverage, a deep-fried side dish, perhaps a decadent dessert. In the end, he still indulges, and the salad conveniently launders his guilt. Unbeknownst to the patron, he has actually consumed more calories than if he had merely ordered the deluxe burger in the first place.[27]

The halo effect also operates on a larger scale. The mere presence of a salad on the menu, for instance, can make all the other menu items seem healthier by association (just as inversely, a pricier item can make the others seem more reasonable). This phenomenon encourages "vicarious goal fulfillment," a subtle behavior by which the restaurant goer successfully satisfies both his conscience and his cravings. Surveying the menu, the patron is attracted to the deluxe burger but begins to consider the salad option because he perceives it to be better for his body. When it comes time to place the order, he opts for the deluxe burger. If you ask a consumer researcher why, she will explain that the patron's ultimate choice of a burger is a reward, albeit subconscious, for considering the salad. Vicarious goal fulfillment and the halo effect help explain why restaurants such as McDonald's have seen rises in sales of their more indulgent items since they added fruit, salad, and other healthier options to their menus.[28]

Americans love to eat food prepared away from home because it is convenient, tastes good (sometimes too good), and acts as a comforting, well-deserved treat after a wearing and monotonous workday. But we must consider at least one more important factor: price. The cost of eating food prepared away from home has, for many, become comparable to that of cooking dinner from scratch. Foods prepared away from home have not become cheaper, but the difference has become more negligible, especially when we factor cost in time, not just money, into the equation. Time is money, and an hour or two not spent shopping at the grocery store, chopping vegetables, and washing dishes opens up an extra hour or two for getting ahead at work. "When I add my hourly rate [to] the time to cook at home, I can instead take my family out to dinner, and it comes out pretty even," explains Pennsylvania managerial instructor Paul Howard. Even with the recent recession, dining out is becoming a more popular option and currently represents about 4.4 percent of Americans' paychecks, a slightly higher percentage than before the economic dip in 2008. As the price of industrially prepared foods has approached the cost of cooking from scratch, and as devoting free time to paid work has evolved into an economic imperative, restaurants have functioned as extensions of family dining rooms. Eating out has become the new eating in.[29]

AMERICANS DO still eat in. We make casseroles and salads from scratch, join our families around the dinner table in the evening, and catch up between bites—just not as much as we used to. Fewer families regularly dine together today than did during the mid-twentieth century. Only about half of American households with children eat together four to six nights a week, and about a quarter of American families with children sit down together at the table no more than three nights a week. Although the majority of young adults eat with others, many do not. Over a third of the participants in a study of young-adult eating patterns claimed they consistently lacked time to take a proper meal with others and, as a result, consumed their sustenance alone and often on the run.[30]

Changes in family eating habits may seem innocuous, but they do have repercussions, one being a decline in nutritional intake. Studies show that eating with others has a direct impact on nutrition. Having mealtime companions modifies both what people consume and how much. Just as Americans eat differently when consuming food prepared away from home, they also eat differently when consuming food with others. Young adults who sit down for meals with friends generally have a higher intake of fruits and vegetables (especially dark green and orange vegetables), whereas those who do not eat with friends have a lower intake of those foods and a higher intake of soft drinks, fast foods, and saturated fat. Children and teenagers who eat regularly with their families consume more fruits, vegetables, grains, and calcium-rich goods and tend to incorporate these into their diets as young adults; they also take in less fried food and guzzle fewer soft drinks. When the family dinner unfolds at a restaurant instead of at home, many of these patterns remain intact.[31]

Eating in company exerts a positive effect on nutrition—people generally eat better when they eat together—but it also exerts a positive impact on intellect, especially when it comes to children. Children who grow up eating with their families develop a wider vocabulary, on average, than those who grow up without a family dinner routine. Family meals, it turns out, are more beneficial to children's word banks than play or having adults read to them, and because these children benefit from a wider and richer vocabulary, their reading skills develop earlier and more quickly. Teenagers' educational success also correlates to participation in family meals. Those who join their parents and siblings at the table fewer than three times a week are one and a half times more likely to earn mostly Cs or lower grades in school than their counterparts who sit down to family dinner five to seven evenings per week.[32]

Family dinners are good for the brain, but they also promote healthy bodies and sound behavior. Researchers from the National Center on Addiction and Substance Abuse at Columbia University found that children who eat family meals regularly have lower body mass indexes and are less likely to smoke, use drugs, abuse alcohol, develop depression, and struggle with eating disorders. In short, family meals have a surprisingly protective quality—some have even called them a kind of vaccine. Of course, no one knows conclusively that family dinners cause all these boons; perhaps in some instances they are the effect. In either case, studies associate the simple act of eating together as a family with numerous nutritional, social, and educational benefits—except when it happens in front of the television.[33]

As evidenced by the popularity of products such as TV-Time Popcorn, TV Mix, and Swanson's TV Dinner (even if, as mentioned previously, TV dinners were not actually designed for consumption in front of a TV), the idea of eating in front of a television has never been far from people's minds. On average, Americans consume 20 to 25 percent of their daily energy intake with their eyes fixed to the screen. Perhaps those who watch television the most while eating meals are kids: about a third of American children age six and under regularly take their snacks and meals in the tube's company. A study of preschoolers and their parents revealed that in those families where a television was on during dinner, children's nutrient intake was lower, especially when it came to fruits and vegetables. The family meal has a potentially powerful influence on health, education, and quality of life, but it is susceptible to screens, which has been shown to compromise, or "undo," the positive effects of eating together.[34]

IN TWO PARTICULAR households where family dinner is the nightly norm, there is little danger of television stealing the meal's beneficial effects.

David and Amy live in rural northern Michigan, where he works as an electrician and she homeschools their seven- and eleven-year-old daughters. The family eats dinner together almost every night, loosely following a weekly schedule. Monday is pasta night, and on Wednesdays, when David cooks and Amy takes the night off, they enjoy a "breakfast dinner": eggs, potatoes, pancakes, French toast—all the staples David used to cook when he worked in the kitchen of a breakfast chain restaurant. In this family's household, about 75 percent of lunches are dinner-like—hot meals cooked from scratch—and the girls regularly participate in the preparation. "As they watch me enjoy myself cooking, I believe they will eventually enjoy cooking as well," explains Amy about her approach to incorporating her children into making the midday meal. Her strategy appears to be working: the girls have developed such kitchen skills as peeling vegetables and whisking together sauces—and they seem to like putting these skills to use.

Although cooking is not part of the family's official homeschooling curriculum, meals under their roof have become an opportunity for instruction, and the children have learned not just how to cook but also how to appreciate the quality and taste of fresh ingredients. "If it isn't a real egg, they won't eat it," Amy professes with a humble sense of accomplishment. The girls have also learned about making their own eating choices, and this lesson comes into play during breakfast and snacking. "I try to get the girls to self-motivate," she explains with regard to the morning meal, when options such as toast, yogurt, oatmeal, and eggs are available. (You will find no breakfast cereal in this family's cupboards.) Between meals, the girls are invited to satiate their cravings with healthy items like nuts, fruit, and vegetables. The family budget is limited, which is one reason why they do not purchase much processed food. When the kids were younger, they sometimes ordered takeout or made dinner from frozen prepared foods, but Amy and her husband eventually eliminated these convenience items from their routine because they were too expensive and ultimately unsatisfying.

For a welcome change and a break from cooking, David and Amy's budget does permit them the weekly indulgence of a local Mexican restaurant's wintertime Wednesday night special: $1.50 tacos. This has become a family tradition. From time to time they opt for a more elegant meal at one of the town's upscale restaurants. Ordinarily, the families' finances would preclude them from eating at this pricy venue, but David trades his services as an electrician for credit at the restaurant, enabling them to enjoy a fine meal away from home periodically. As their youngest daughter puts it, "We can't afford to go to McDonald's, but we can eat at the most expensive restaurant in town." Even when they eat out, David, Amy, and their children preserve their tradition of eating together. "Something magical happens at a dinner table," explains Amy, who believes that eating together deepens friendships and that good food can heal.

John and Diane live in Burlington, Vermont, where he is a mechanic for a local Jeep dealer and she is an administrative assistant at a small four-year college. They do not have children, but when they married, they envisioned making their home a community. Now they rent rooms at cost to other community-minded folks. Every night around six, the household comes together for the evening meal. When I visited, four tenants made themselves at home around the plainly set table: a medical student, two undergraduates, and a hospital intern from Peru. And because it was Monday night, Sarah, Mark, and their two-year-old son joined us. Sarah, a former tenant, enjoyed living in John and Diane's household so much, she has maintained a tradition of returning for dinner on Monday nights for the better part of the past eight years, even after she married Mark and started a family. On this night, the menu featured chicken sausage; green beans from Sarah's garden; braised cabbage with apples, onions, and raisins; roasted potatoes; salad with store-bought dressing; and a watermelon fresh from the garden for dessert. Sarah's husband, Mark, did the cooking.

In John and Diane's home, each member of the household cooks once a week. "Gourmet is not required," explains John. "There's always cereal," he jokes. Some tenants go all out: relying on the household food fund to cover expenses, they shop for special ingredients and prepare carefully planned meals. Others whip up an ad hoc meal from whatever happens to be in the fridge. When a tenant prepares a dinner, he or she also sets the table and washes the dishes, and it has become a household custom for the cook to say grace as well.

For Diane, slowing down at mealtime is important, and she intentionally cultivates a relaxed atmosphere. A candle flickers at the center of the table, and classical music from a local radio station plays softly in the background. The two undergraduate tenants appreciate that John and Diane's home is a calming place (and having a dog around, they add, is nice). One of them likens the household to a second family. "It can get lonely living in the dorms," she adds.

During my visit, the dinnertime conversation touched on a variety of topics—gardening, a tenant's recent kayaking trip, Peruvian food—and when I asked my fellow diners to elucidate how dining together nightly has influenced their individual eating patterns, each volunteered an insight. The medical student confessed that, for the sake of time and expense, he would likely have resorted to one-week batches of peanut butter and jelly stockpiled in his freezer had he not taken up residence in a community with shared meals. "Yitzak always eats better when others are around," Sarah told me as she balanced her blond toddler on her lap while cutting up food for him on her plate. One of the undergraduates explained that when she was on the college meal plan, she would carry dinner to her dorm room three to four nights a week in order to study while eating. The other student commented that she no longer snacks like she used to now that she is living with John and Diane—occasionally she will have some crackers or an apple, but with a hot, sit-down, family-style dinner to look forward to every evening, between-meal nibbling no longer holds much appeal. Diane shares a deeper confession: in the past she struggled with an eating disorder. Through an intentional return to a traditional family dinner, she overcame her compulsive tendencies and regained a healthy, more satisfying relationship with food.

The stories of these two households demonstrate that for all the inroads snacking has made, it has not entirely crowded out breakfast, lunch, and dinner; nor has home cooking vanished or the sit-down evening meal become obsolete. These households are adapting the construct of the family dinner in a modern, on-the-go world and reaping an abundance of benefits, which they strive to pass on to younger generations. These two families represent an approach to eating that is at once old-fashioned and innovative, conservative and progressive, and through their daily routines, they are helping to position the American meal to flourish in an uncertain future.

Conclusion

THE FUTURE OF
THE AMERICAN MEAL

IF WE WANT TO glimpse the future of the American meal, and perhaps even have a hand in shaping the meal's future, we can take some cues from history. Looking at the past helps us understand why we eat the way we do. Sometimes we eat in a particular way because of conscious decisions, but, more often than not, our eating choices are hardly choices at all: they are reflections of our culture, and our culture is largely a product of our history.

The story of the American meal is, in large part, the story of our becoming American. Colonists adapted to New World flora and fauna and borrowed Native American foodways, going, to a certain extent, native themselves. Later, they capitalized on the identity-forging potential of food to strengthen their ties with Great Britain, then, in the decades surrounding the American Revolution, to break away from Great Britain and express their confidence in the experiment of forging a new nation. When French delicacies were all the rage in the late nineteenth century, some Americans called for a return to traditional foods and native ingredients, especially on Thanksgiving, and when fancy French foodways proved unsustainable, especially during wartime and economic depression, simpler, plainer dishes became patriotic.

Immigrants have long adopted eating as a symbol of the American dream, and many have successfully capitalized on the wealth of business opportunities that meals and snacks have presented in order to achieve it. Inversely, foreigners abroad have embraced American food images as icons of American culture: the soft drink, the hot dog, sweetened breakfast cereal, the packaged snack. America exported not only these foods and their iconic images but also some of the country's meal (and nonmeal) conventions. The modern quick lunch is an American invention, and snacking—that slightly rebellious and indulgent, childlike behavior—is widely emulated abroad as an idiom of American prosperity and freedom.

The quest for American identity has left its imprint on the American meal. So have other threads of history, such as industrialization, new understandings of family, and the emergence of a middle class. When we take time to reconnect with our families in the evening over dinner at the kitchen table (or regret that we do not), we are unlikely to think of this custom as a nineteenth-century innovation that emerged as a result of America's shift from an agrarian to an industrial society. The traditional family dinner is an artifact of an era when new ways of manufacturing, along with new understandings of class status and gender roles, fragmented households and assigned men, women, and children to different tasks and separate spheres. Dinner brought family members together in the evening and gave them a chance to bond as a group—that is why it became special.

The pattern and content of the contemporary dinner also bears the stamp of history. When we open the evening meal with salad and finish it with dessert, French influences on American dining in the Victorian era are probably far from our minds: we have long forgotten salad's continental origins and long since folded once fancy French desserts neatly into American food culture. But these taken-for-granted foods and the standard sequence in which we eat them are imports that, at one time, were novel, genteel, and an esteemed marker of class identity. Americans' approach to dinner today also reflects the country's eventual shift away from French sensibilities and incorporates the necessary simplicity that servantless households came to embrace, the kitchen techniques the home economics movement instilled, and the patriotic republicanism that undergirded the American Revolution and, later, World Wars I and II.

The assumption that we eat the way we do because we always have is inherently false; it was never true for dinner, lunch, or breakfast. In fact, it cannot be true for lunch because at one time lunch did not even exist. The modern noontime meal was invented in the mid- to late nineteenth century as a mechanism for keeping the working body productive in a world where business took place at a distance from home and home-cooked midday dinners were no longer compatible with emerging patterns of vocation and commerce. Lunch has not changed much since its debut, at least not compared to dinner and breakfast. Light, cheap, and frequently cold fare consumed with an eye on the clock and often away from home continues to characterize the midday bite. We dispatch sandwiches from brown paper bags or hot soup from cafeteria steamers because they are practical and convenient, but we also do so because a century ago and more, these foods best accommodated the changing lifestyles of a modernizing society.

Breakfast, unlike lunch, had been around for a long time, but in the eighteenth and especially the nineteenth centuries it underwent significant change that laid the foundation for what many of us look forward to when we wake up in the morning. Simple, often meatless morning meals featuring toast, cheese, and beer or milk and mush gave way to heavy, meat-centric repasts when Americans graduated from mere subsistence living to moderate prosperity. But with the shift away from agrarian lifestyles spurred by the Industrial Revolution, an alternative breakfast was in order, especially for the middle-class, which found itself tied to offices and desks to an unprecedented degree. The light, grain-based breakfast we enjoy in the twenty-first century is the offspring of a historical moment when a nearly national case of indigestion revealed the incompatibility of Americans' diet and lifestyle. Zealous reformers, many of whom turned breakfast into a spectacular business opportunity, came to the rescue, introducing the kinds of products that have come to define the opening nourishment of the day.

With regard to snacking, our habits are also products of historical developments. Certainly, taste plays a part in our attitudes toward snacks, as do concerns about health and weight, but the past continues to exert a significant sway on our between-meal eating habits. Contemporary ambivalence toward munching bears the indelible mark of Victorian notions of propriety, which, borrowing from Puritan values, framed indulgence as sinful and vulgar and restraint as virtuous and genteel. The idea that snacking is categorically bad because it spoils the appetite is a nineteenth-century cultural relic. So too is the perceived need to justify a mid-morning pick-me-up or late-afternoon bite, as if these indulgences revealed some shameful moral weakness or character flaw.

Historical tensions about snacking continue to shape our attitudes today, but so do historical triumphs over these tensions, especially those engineered by snack food manufacturers. Through packaging and advertising, manufacturers reframed what people once considered seedy and even crass as novel and glamorous. They also created new uses for snack foods, transforming them from street food and ballpark fare into a welcome accompaniment to television watching, a fashionable offering at house parties, a novel garnish for casseroles and salads, and even a money-saving filler for economizing cooks. Because manufacturers cleaned up snack food in the first half of the twentieth century, winning widespread cultural approval for their products, we are not prone to worry that consuming them will sully our reputation. Now hot dogs and pretzels are for bankers and ball fans alike.

If one historical element has shaped the way we eat more than any other, it is business. The Industrial Revolution reorganized Americans' approach to business in the nineteenth century and, with it, their approach to life. Meals evolved to accommodate, and the new characteristics they assumed represented these changes both functionally and ideologically. Rigid work schedules streamlined breakfast and lunch, and the largely no-frills foods that came to characterize these meals reflected pragmatic purposes. But there was meaning behind the pragmatism. The health minded embraced functional simplicity as beneficial to the body, whereas the profit minded adopted it as a vehicle of efficiency and productivity. Business also molded dinner, but rather than accommodating business, dinner provided a needed counterweight to it. It became what business was not: relaxed, domestic, familial. It was about kin and home, and the cold, harsh, profit-driven world of industry and corporations made the coming to-gether of loved ones around the dinner table nothing less than sacred.

Business also shaped meals (and nonmeals) by innovating new ways of thinking about food and eating. Companies have exerted for-midable influence over the way Americans perceive food, all for the sake of selling products. The food industry reinvented breakfast with cereal and toast at its center, and ever since, cereal and toast have been synonymous with the morning meal. Thanks to the discovery of vitamins, milk and orange juice processors managed to position their products as nutritional essentials and thus as logical cereal-and-toast accompaniments. Business also revolutionized the way Americans think about between-meal foods, and it welded the distinct categories of snacking (eating between meals) and snack food (goods primarily consumed between meals) so seamlessly that people came to think of them as one and the same. Business even found its way into the most domestic of American meals, dinner, by framing particular products as practical ingredients that delivered taste, texture, convenience, and style.

Following its historical trajectory, business continues to play a central role in American food culture today. Both the business we do and the businesses that surround us exert pressures on how we eat. Our jobs and daily responsibilities dictate our lifestyles, and we contour our meals (and mealtimes) to accommodate these priori-ties. The food industry has picked up on the pressures of meeting modern priorities and is committed to helping us along the way. It furnishes us with products promoted not only as irresistible but also as solutions to our overcrowded schedules, soothers of our tensions, and antidotes for our problems. Business has carved out a need for processed food in American life and in turn provided the solution to this need. And this complicated dance between demand and supply, consumer and manufacturer unfolds in our environment.

We live in a food environment shaped by culture and history, but as history makes clear, it is also shaped by business. If business is the key to understanding why we ate as we did in the past, it is even more cru-cial to our understanding of how we eat today and will likely eat in the future. To see evidence of this, all we have to do is look around. Bill-boards, television commercials, convenience stores, vending machines, drive-throughs, magazine advertisements, fast-food restaurants, even automobile cup holders—all of these visual and material elements of the world in which we live make food easily available and serve as messages encouraging us to consume. When we enter a cinema, drive to the mall, arrive at a party, or board an airplane, we enter particular food environments. Our offices, homes, and schools are also food environments, and when we go to a supermarket, restaurant, or coffee shop, we penetrate food environments strategically designed (often with the help of consumer psychologists) to court our taste buds and influence us to buy and eat. Americans have always inhabited a food environment, but ours is more commercialized than ever, and never have we been so bombarded with powerful cues to eat.

Our food environment increasingly influences our consumption patterns, yet we generally fail to discern its sway on our choices. The story of history's influence is similar—despite its deep, indelible mark on our everyday habits, we fall short of recognizing its critical role in shaping the way we eat. When we do recognize the role of history, though, we have a valuable tool at our disposable. History uncovers patterns at work through time, and once we understand them, we can choose to reject or embrace, encourage or revise them. When it comes to facing the influence of business on our food choices today and in the future, history can help because it opens our eyes to the possibility of choice. By exposing the various trajectories of food conventions such as meals through time, history proves that none of these paths is inevitable.

When we sit down to dinner (or swallow it standing up), we are helping ourselves not only to meat and mashed potatoes—or tofu and broccoli, as the case may be—but also to a generous serving of history. And since today is tomorrow's past, when we eat, we are also making history. We cannot know the future of the American meal, but we are currently, if imperceptibly, charting its direction when we buy pork chops and potatoes at the farmer's market, teach a child how to peel carrots, choose to support the new corner bakery, or invite the neighbors over for pie. We are charting it when we adopt a new recipe, plant an herb garden in an abandoned lot, chaperone a field trip to a dairy farm, or can the last of the summer's tomatoes.

Why chart the future of the American meal? Why not let it determine its own course? Because the shape of a meal is also the shape of society. If Jean Anthelme Brillat-Savarin's aphorism "We are what we eat" is true, then it must also hold true that we are how we eat. How we eat in the future will reflect who we are today, and how we eat today will determine in part who we will become tomorrow. Whether we know it or not, the state of the American meal is in our hands. Our knives and forks may prove to be cultural tools more powerful than we have yet dared to dream.

ACKNOWLEDGMENTS

Solitude—hours and hours of it—is crucial to the stringing together of words and ideas that eventually become a book, this one notwithstanding. But just as crucial is conversation, and penning these pages has furnished a welcome opportunity to connect (or reconnect) with cultural historians and food studies scholars whose work I admire and whose insights have enriched this project. Anne Fishel (Co-founder, The Family Dinner Project), Karin Goldstein (Plimoth Plantation), Harvey Green (Northeastern University), Sandra Oliver (*Food History News*), Andrew F. Smith (The New School for Social Research), Jan Whitaker (independent scholar), and Susan Williams (Fitchburg State University) generously reviewed chapters at various stages of completion, each offering apt feedback that has added depth and texture. I am honored that this monograph should benefit from their knowledge.

In addition to conversing with scholars, I engaged ordinary Americans on their personal experiences of meals. Weaving the perspectives of contemporary diners into my discussion of the American meal today would not have been possible without the willing interviewees who graciously shared their stories with me and, in one case, their dinner table. Thanks to John and Diane Byrnes of Vermont and their tenants, including former tenants Sarah and Mark Jennings; Amy Daniels Moehle of Michigan; and Middlebury College students (now graduates) Edna Tang, Kyle Williams, and Sharon-Rose Broome for lending their voices to this project.

Equally rewarding as my conversations with scholars and friends have been those with editors; their expertise with words has at times left me breathless. First and foremost, I would like to recognize Lara Heimert of Basic Books, who, with her keen sense of narrative, helped me sharpen my concept, shape my chapters, and tell the story of the American meal as just that: a story. Roger L'Abrie, Jen Kelland Fagan, Melissa Veronesi, and Renee Caputo each offered careful and perceptive edits, as did Katy O'Donnell. If the prose gracing these pages is clear and cogent, it is due in no small part to this superlative team.

In addition to her edits, Katy O'Donnell patiently coached me through the art and tedium of curating an image gallery. I am thankful to her for this, as well as to the librarians and archivists who contributed to the gallery: Steve Burks at the Durick Library, St. Michael's College; Stephanie Herz at the Historical Society of Moorestown, New Jersey; Thomas Lisant at the New York Public Library; Leslie Tobias-Nelson at the John Carter Brown Library, Brown University; and John Shaw at Michigan State University Libraries. In addition, I am indebted to Barbara Swell for use of an image from her blog "Log Cabin Cooking," to Cynthia Young for her judicious composition, to Betsy DeJesu for her publicity wizardry, and to Nicole Caputo for a cover design that could not have pleased me more.

Before conversations with scholars and editors could unfold, conversations about publishers and agents first needed to take place. Warren Belasco gave me helpful advice in securing an agent, and putting his advice to work resulted in a happy collaboration with the Gernert Company, where Erika Storella has championed my work skillfully. I am grateful to Erika for helping me revise my proposal from one for a book on the American snack into one for a book on the American meal, but most of all, I am grateful for her confidence in my idea.

Finally, I would like to thank family and friends with whom I've been conversing about food history for years: Cozette and Julian Russell, who offered astute insights on an early draft of the introduction and generously furnished the author's photograph, respectively; Harvey Green, who introduced me to cultural history in the first place; Margery Milne, who believed in my writing from a young age; and my parents, John and Diana Carroll, who gave me one of the greatest gifts parents can give: a heritage of homemade family meals at which the supply of food never dwindled and intelligent conversation never lacked. Their enthusiasm has been unwavering.

NOTES

Introduction: We Are *How* We Eat

1. Wansink, *Mindless Eating*.

Chapter 1: Why Colonial Meals Were Messy

1. Williams and Williams, *The Redeemed Captive*, 33.

2. Williams and Williams, *The Redeemed Captive*, 33. Another captivity narrative rich with food-related details of New England Native Americans is Rowlandson, *A Narrative*.

3. Smith, *An Account of the Remarkable Occurrences*, 45. For an overview of Native American meal structure, see Berzok, *American Indian Food*, 129–130.

4. Kalm, quoted in Russell, *Indian New England*, 90. See also Douglas, "Deciphering a Meal." On *nocake*, see Wood, *New England's Prospect*, 8; Stavely and Fitzgerald, *America's Founding Food*, 30–31. On *pemmican*, see Speth, *The Paleoanthropology*, 72–75.

5. LeClercq, *New Relation of Gaspesia*, 110. On hunger and fasting as a Native American subsistence strategy and on explorers' and settlers' responses, see Cronon, *Changes*, 40–41.

6. Catlin, *Illustrations*, 123; Parker, *Parker on the Iroquois*, 132.

7. On European and colonial American attitudes toward gluttony, see Eden, *The Early American Table*, 117–120.

8. Smith, *An Account of the Remarkable Occurrences*, 45.

9. Wood, *New England's Prospect*, 87; Catlin, *Illustrations*, 103.

10. Parker, *Parker on the Iroquois*, 65.

11. Hamilton, *Itinerarium*, quoted in McWilliams, *Revolution at the Table*, 179–180.

12. Washington, *Up from Slavery*, 9. On the irregularity of eating and lack of decorum, see Gillis, *A World of Their Own Making*, 89.

13. Freeman, *Reminiscence*, quoted in Nylander, *Our Own Snug Fireside*, 192. On colonial- and federal-era meal times, see Oliver, *Food in Colonial and Federal America*, 157. On dinner as the larger and main meal of the day, with breakfast and supper as smaller satellite meals, see Pillsbury, *No Foreign Food*, 33–34. On Lizzie Borden's breakfast, see Stavely and Fitzgerald, *America's Founding Food*, 326n82.

14. McWilliams, *A Revolution in Eating*, 202.

15. On domestic tasks in colonial America, see Mays, *Women in Early America*, 26–28.

16. Thanks to Sandra Oliver for her insight about the impracticality of preparing an evening dinner during the preindustrial era due to light limitations.

17. Kalm, quoted in Dunn, "Understanding the Mabee House Fireplace." On the placement of bake ovens in or adjacent to hearths, see Cromley, *The Food Axis*, 27–28. On raised hearths in Pennsylvania, see McWilliams, *A Revolution in Eating*, 186. On Dutch hearths in New Netherlands, see Dunn, "Understanding the Mabee House Fireplace." On outdoor ovens, see Cromley, *The Food Axis*, 21–22; Kniffen, "The Outdoor Oven in Louisiana." On *hornos*, see Roberts and Roberts, *New Mexico*, 77–78.

18. On "Big House" kitchens, see Rice and Katz-Hyman, *The World of a Slave*, 299–300; Carlisle, Nasardinov, and Pustz, *America's Kitchens*, 50–51.

19. Goodrich, *Recollections*, 67; Stowe, *Oldtown Folks*, 61. On building hearth fires, see Alice Ross, "Hearth Cookery," in Smith, *The Oxford Encyclopedia of Food and Drink in America*, 1:596–600; Nylander, *Our Own Snug Fireside*, 87–88.

20. Lee, *The Cook's Own Book*, 143; Howland, *The New England Economical Housekeeper*, 45; Emerson, *The New England Cookery*, 24. For more on the hearth and hearth cooking, see Oliver, *Food in Colonial and Federal America*, 106–107; Schenone, *A Thousand Years*, 64–67; Nylander, *Our Own Snug Fireside*, 185–187; Cromley, *The Food Axis*, 25–29; Carlisle, Nasardinov, and Pustz, *America's Kitchens*, 30–45.

21. On different woods' heat-producing qualities, see Carter, *The Frugal Housewife*, 83.

22. Thomas Hazard, quoted in Stavely and Fitzgerald, *America's Founding Food*, 53. On ash cooking, see Alice Ross, "Hearth Cookery," in Smith, *The Oxford Encyclopedia of Food and Drink in America*, 1:598. On Dutch ovens, see Nylander, *Our Own Snug Fireside*, 198; Alice Ross, "Dutch Ovens," in Smith, *The Oxford Companion to American Food and Drink*, 1:202.

23. Beecher, *Miss Beecher's Domestic Receipt Book*, 84. On colonial bake ovens, see Cromley, *The Food Axis*, 21, 27–28; Plante, *The American Kitchen*, 7. On testing the temperature of ovens, see Stavely and Fitzgerald, *America's Founding Food*, 55–56; Nylander, *Our Own Snug Fireside*, 198.

24. Emerson, *New England Cookery*, 27; Lee, *The Cook's Own Book*, 143. On the amount of time women spent cooking, see Volo and Volo, *Daily Life on the Old Colonial Frontier*, 148.

25. Quoted in Richard Bushman, "Bodies and Minds," in Fischer and Hinderaker, *Colonial American History*, 293. On women's eating habits, see Earle, *Home Life in Colonial Days*, 101–102; Gottlieb, *The Family in the West-*

ern World, 43–44; Gillis, *A World of Their Own Making,* 88–89. On furniture in seventeenth-century rural Virginia, see Isaac, *The Transformation of Virginia,* 72.

26. Isaac, *The Transformation of Virginia,* 72; Volo and Volo, *Daily Life on the Old Colonial Frontier,* 129, 146.

27. On trenchers, see Wilson, *Food and Drink in Britain,* 243; Toussaint-Samat, *A History of Food,* 206–207; Visser, *The Rituals of Dinner,* 190–191; Earle, *Home Life in Colonial Days,* 81–83.

28. On having trencher mates, see Earle, *Home Life in Colonial Days,* 80–81; Mays, *Women in Early America,* 86. On carrying one's own knife, see Oliver, *Food in Colonial and Federal America,* 112; Cromley, *The Food Axis,* 29–30. On eating with one's fingers and using the knife to spear food, see Oliver, *Food in Colonial and Federal America,* 24–25; Deetz, *In Small Things Forgotten,* 76, 81, 168; Kasson, *Rudeness and Civility,* 189.

29. Eliza Ware Farrar, *The Young Lady's Friend* (1837), 346–377, quoted in Visser, *The Rituals of Dinner,* 190; Trollope, *Domestic Manners,* 37. On the rounding of the knife in response to after-meal teeth picking with the point, see Petroski, *The Evolution of Useful Things,* 11–12; Visser, *The Rituals of Dinner,* 186–187. On the early history of the fork, see Petroski, *The Evolution of Useful Things,* 3–21; Wilson, *Consider the Fork,* 189–195.

30. Erasmus quoted in Visser, *The Rituals of Dinner,* 163. For more on napkins, see Cathy Kaufman, "Napkins," in Smith, *The Oxford Encyclopedia of Food and Drink in America,* 2:194.

31. Duncan, *Travels,* 319; Alexander, *Transatlantic Sketches,* 102–103. On Americans' rapid eating, see Kasson, *Rudeness and Civility,* 186.

32. Morton, *Cupboard Love,* 195.

33. Morton et al., *New-England's Memorial,* 47.

34. On the etymology of "pottage," see Morton, *Cupboard Love,* 236. On frumenty, see Hess, *Martha Washington's Booke of Cookery,* 123–124.

35. Markham, *The English Housewife,* 74. On sippets, see Ruth Tobias, "Toast," in Smith, *The Oxford Encyclopedia of Food and Drink in America,* 1:122.

36. Josselyn, *New England's Rarities Discovered;* Kalm, *The America of 1750,* 607. On cooking apples like pumpkins, see Earle, *Home Life in Colonial Days,* 145–146; Oliver, *Food in Colonial and Federal America,* 23. The first cookbook printed in America was Smith, *The Complete Housewife.* Oliver, *Food in Colonial and Federal America,* xiv. For more on English cookbooks reprinted in America, see McWilliams, *A Revolution in Eating,* 227–229. For more on Amelia Simmons's *American Cookery,* see Ridley, "The First American Cookbook"; Theophano, *Eat My Words,* 233–241. For more on preparing food without cookbooks, or "vernacular cookery," see Oliver, *Food in Colonial and Federal America,* 21ff. For more on hired help in the colonial era, especially in New England, see Nylander, *Our Own Snug Fireside,* 41–53.

37. Carver, quoted in Ott, *Pumpkin,* 50; Conforti, *Saints and Strangers,* 11. On Moravian pioneers' use of pumpkins, see *The Moravian Indian Mission,* 458.

38. On vegetables in the colonial diet, see McMahon, "A Comfortable Subsistence," 39–41; Harbury, *Colonial Virginia's Cooking Dynasty,* 104–107. On vegetables and the prevention of scurvy, see Volo and Volo, *Family Life in 17th- and 18th-Century America,* 35–36; Oliver, *Food in Colonial and Federal America,* 201ff.

39. McMahon, "A Comfortable Subsistence," 39; Oliver, *Food in Colonial and Federal America,* 55.

40. On fresh fruit in the colonial diet, see Harbury, *Colonial Virginia's Cooking Dynasty,* 108–111; Stavely and Fitzgerald, *America's Founding Food,* 207–208. On food and the humoral system, see Laudan, "Birth of the Modern Diet," 4–11.

41. Gardiner, Hepburn, and Randloph, *American Gardener,* 239. On the European poor eating onions, see Henisch, *Fast and Feast,* 107–108. On perceptions of fresh fruit as causing flatulence and indigestion, see Adamson, *Food in Medieval Times,* 8–9; Dyer, "Did Peasants Really Starve in Medieval England?" in Carlin and Rosenthal, *Food and Eating in Medieval Europe,* 69. On associations between fresh fruit and dysentery and other illnesses, see Stavely and Fitzgerald, *America's Founding Food,* 207.

42. McMahon, "A Comfortable Subsistence," 41, 47.

43. Andrew Coe, "Lamb and Mutton," in Smith, *The Oxford Encyclopedia of Food and Drink in America,* 2:25–26; Cronon, *Changes,* 129; Russell, *A Long, Deep Furrow,* 95, 154–158, 290; Stavely and Fitzgerald, *Northern Hospitality,* 217–218.

44. Cronon, *Changes,* 129; Roger Horowitz, "Meat," in Smith, *The Oxford Encyclopedia of Food and Drink in America,* 2:70–78; McMahon, "A Comfortable Subsistence," 34–38; McWilliams, *A Revolution in Eating,* 81; Russell, *A Long, Deep Furrow,* 94–95, 152; Stavely and Fitzgerald, *Northern Hospitality,* 222–223. On pigs in the South, see Taylor, *Eating, Drinking, and Visiting,* 21–24.

45. On salt pork, see McDaniel, *An Irresistible History,* 42; Browne and Kreiser, *Civil War and Reconstruction,* 76, 79.

46. Markham, *The English Housewife,* 74; Josselyn, *New England's Rarities Discovered,* 88. On silpee, see Earle, *Customs and Fashions in Old New England,* 150. On sowens, see Katz and Pollan, *The Art of Fermentation,* 221; Hope, *A Caledonian Feast,* 111–112. On grain exports from the Mid-Atlantic colonies, see McWilliams, *A Revolution in Eating,* 269.

47. DeVries, quoted in Jameson, *Narratives,* 219. On white bread as a Sabbath luxury, see Weaver, *America Eats,* 76. On banning the sale of white bread to Native Americans in the New Netherlands, see Jacobs, *The Colony of New Netherland,* 134–135; Rose, *Food, Drink, and Celebrations of the Hudson Valley,* 55–56. On the early difficulties of growing wheat in certain regions, see

McMahon, "A Comfortable Subsistence," 30–33; McWilliams, *A Revolution in Eating*, 63–64, 151; Cronon, *Changes*, 153–155.

48. On associations between grains and class, see Braudel, *The Structures of Everyday Life*, 136–138; Stavely and Fitzgerald, *America's Founding Food*, 8–12, 234–239. On the use of peas, beans, and acorns as grain substitutes for bread in England, see Stavely and Fitzgerald, *America's Founding Food*, 16–17, 235. On peas porridge, see Davidson, *Oxford Companion to Food*, 591; Wilson, *Food and Drink in Britain*, 216–217.

49. McMahon, "A Comfortable Subsistence," 39–40.

50. On meanings and uses of the word "corn," see Morton, *Cupboard Love*, 92; Curtin, Oliver, and Plimoth Plantation, *Giving Thanks*, 19–20.

51. William Bradford and Edward Winslow, "Mourt's Relation," in Philbrick, *The Mayflower Papers*, 127. On beer in the early American diet, see McWilliams, *A Revolution in Eating*, 246–255.

52. Thomas Harriot, quoted in Smith, *Drinking History*, 8. John Winthrop Jr., quoted in DeWitt, *Founding Foodies*, 12–13. On brewing maize beer in Jamestown and New England, see Dick Cantwell, "Brewing in Colonial America" in Oliver, *The Oxford Companion to Beer*, 163–164. On brewing pumpkin and other grain alternatives, see Ott, *Pumpkin*, 50–51; McWilliams, *A Revolution in Eating*, 250; Smith, *Drinking History*, 11–14.

53. John Gerard, *The Herball or Generall Historie of Plants* (1597; repr., London, 1636), 83, quoted in Mood, "John Winthrop, Jr.," 123. On European and colonial American perceptions of maize, see Eden, *The Early American Table*, 60, 73–77, 80–81. On settlers' hesitation to consume corn, see McWilliams, *A Revolution in Eating*, 82–84; Stavely and Fitzgerald, *America's Founding Food*, 11–12.

54. Gabaccia, *We Are What We Eat*, 25; Roger Williams and Howard M. Chapin, *Key into the Language of America* (1643; repr., Bedford, MA: Applewood Books, n.d.), 11, quoted in Mood, "John Winthrop, Jr.," 130; Stavely and Fitzgerald, *America's Founding Food*, 35. On samp/hominy, see Stavely and Fitzgerald, *America's Founding Food*, 22–23; Fussell, *The Story of Corn*, 195–200; Zanger, *The American History Cookbook*, 9–10. On Johnny cakes, see Stavely and Fitzgerald, *America's Founding Food*, 29–33; Zanger, *The American Ethnic Cookbook*, 13–14; McWilliams, *Story Behind the Dish*, 57–58; Oliver, *Saltwater Foodways*, 45–46; Fussell, *The Story of Corn*, 222–223. On Rye and Indian, see Stavely and Fitzgerald, *America's Founding Food*, 23–29; McWilliams, *Story Behind the Dish*, 57–58. On brown bread, see Stavely and Fitzgerald, *America's Founding Food*, 23–29; Weaver, *America Eats*, 77–78; Oliver, *Saltwater Foodways*, 78.

55. Josselyn, *New England's Rarities Discovered*, 53. On mush, see Fussell, *The Story of Corn*, 229–238. On mush's regional names, see Yoder, *Discovering American Folklife*, 131; Yoder, "Pennsylvanians Call It Mush," 44–53. On oat/bread stirabout, see Stavely and Fitzgerald, *America's Founding Food*, 19–22.

56. Quoted in Barth, *Travels*, 434. On cornmeal mush as an African staple, see Holloway, *Africanisms*, 48; Fussell, *The Story of Corn*, 236–237. On hoe cakes and ash cakes, see Zanger, *The American History Cookbook*, 122–123; McWilliams, *Story Behind the Dish*, 58–59; Weaver, *America Eats*, 78; Stavely and Fitzgerald, *America's Founding Food*, 29–38; Fussell, *The Story of Corn*, 222–223.

57. On Barlow's "Hasty Pudding," see Zafar, "The Proof of the Pudding." On hasty pudding (the dish), see Stavely and Fitzgerald, *America's Founding Food*, 19–22; Zanger, *The American History Cookbook*, 51–53; Quinzio, *Pudding*, ch. 6.

58. Franklin, *The Writings*, 395.

59. Franklin, *The Writings*, 395. On Franklin's writings on corn, see De-Witt, *The Founding Foodies*, 14–19.

60. On food and republican simplicity, see Zafar, "The Proof of the Pudding," 133–135; McWilliams, *Food and the Novel*, 5–9. On corn as symbolic of American character, see M. McWilliams, *Food and the Novel*, 8–9.

Chapter 2: The British Invasion

1. Lesley, *Recollections*, 418.

2. On increased meat consumption during the eighteenth century, see Stavely and Fitzgerald, *Northern Hospitality*, 206–208.

3. On the influence of colonists' increased prosperity on their food in the eighteenth and early nineteenth centuries, see McMahon, "A Comfortable Subsistence."

4. On the re-anglicization of colonial America, see Deetz, *In Small Things Forgotten*, 61. James E. McWilliams subtitles Chapter 6 of *A Revolution in Eating* "The British Invasion."

5. On the re-anglicization of the colonial kitchen, see McWilliams, *A Revolution in Eating*, 201–210. On lean-tos and ells, see Cromley, *The Food Axis*, 18–19, 82, 84–85.

6. On regional preferences for boiling, roasting, frying, and simmering, see Fischer, *Albion's Seed*, 134–139, 349–354, 538–544, 727–731. On fricassees, see McWilliams, *A Revolution in Eating*, 223–224.

7. On boiling, see Volo and Volo, *Family Life in 17th- and 18th-Century America*, 209; Oliver, *Food in Colonial and Federal America*, 107–108.

8. On roasting, see Oliver, *Food in Colonial and Federal America*, 109–110; Volo and Volo, *Family Life in 17th- and 18th-Century America*, 209; Wilson, *Consider the Fork*, 85–89. On clockjacks, see Schinto, "The Clockwork Roasting Jack"; Rogers, *Beef and Liberty*, 19–23; Wilson, *Consider the Fork*, 87–89.

9. Carter, *The Frugal Housewife*, n.p. On roasted meat as a British culinary ideal and patriotic symbol, see Rogers, *Beef and Liberty*, 7–18. On the use of British cookbooks in colonial America, see McWilliams, *A Revolution in Eating*, 227–229; Janice Bluestein Longone, "Cookbooks and Manuscripts: From the

Beginnings to 1860," in Smith, *The Encyclopedia of Food and Drink in America,* 1:285–291.

10. Mennell, *All Manners of Food,* 59; Woodforde, *The Diary,* 111.

11. Carter, *The Frugal Housewife,* n.p.; Woodforde, *The Diary,* 390.

12. Quoted in Harbury, *Colonial Virginia's Cooking Dynasty,* 78; Chastellux, *Travels,* 67; Andrews, *Colonial Folkways,* 103; Fithian, *Journal and Letters,* 143, 271.

13. On eating multiple meats at meals as intentional separation from a past marked by scarcity, see Harbury, *Colonial Virginia's Cooking Dynasty,* 74–75. On the multiplicity of meats served at eighteenth- and early-nineteenth-century New England Thanksgiving feasts, see Nylander, *Our Own Snug Fireside,* 274–276; Curtin, Oliver, and Plimoth Plantation, *Giving Thanks,* 30–32; Appelbaum, *Thanksgiving,* 265–279.

14. Dwight, *New-England and New-York,* 352; Rose, *The Sensible Cook,* 27–28; Richard Tucker III's letter to Molly Tucker (mother), January 17, 1875, Tucker Family Papers, Historic New England, Boston, Massachusetts.

15. King, *When I Lived in Salem,* 99. On baked beans and pie as New England Sabbath foods, see Lee, *Taste of the States,* 18–21; Oliver, *Saltwater Foodways,* 18; Stavely and Fitzgerald, *America's Founding Food,* 59–65. On fish for breakfast, see Oliver, *Saltwater Foodways,* 68. On Protestant New England attitudes toward eating fish, see Oliver, *Saltwater Foodways,* 349–351. On rockfish and oysters for breakfast, see Lea, *Domestic Cookery,* 139–140, 175.

16. Hodgson, *Letters,* 108–109; Ashe, *Travels,* 143–144.

17. Beste, *The Wabash,* 68; Hulme, *Hulme's Journal,* 337.

18. Burnaby, *Burnaby's Travels,* 63. On scrapple, see Weaver, *Country Scrapple.* On Pennsylvania Germans' affinity for beefsteak for breakfast, see Weaver, *Sauerkraut Yankees,* 29. On ham (as well as other meats) for breakfast in the South, see Taylor, *Eating, Drinking, and Visiting,* 54–55. On Irving's encounter with buffalo for breakfast on the frontier, see Irving, *The Journals of Washington Irving,* 162. On horse meat on the frontier, see Farnham, *Farnham's Travels,* 136.

19. Lesley, *Recollections,* 418; Fithian, *Journal and Letters,* 271.

20. Wilson, "Americans Learn to Grow the Irish Potato," 334; Morgan, *Slave Counterpoint,* 360. On George Washington's cultivation of potatoes, see Zuckerman, *The Potato,* 88; Wilson, "Americans Learn to Grow the Irish Potato," 344.

21. Rice and Katz-Hyman, *World of a Slave,* 402. On Africans' cultivation of vegetables in eighteenth- and early-nineteenth-century America, see Covey and Eisnach, *What the Slaves Ate,* 73–94; McWilliams, *A Revolution in Eating,* 43, 46, 117–118.

22. McMahon, "A Comfortable Subsistence," 41. On colonial kitchen gardens, see Mays, *Women in Early America,* 158–159; McMahon, "A Comfortable Subsistence," 39–41, 47; McWilliams, *A Revolution in Eating,* 66–73.

23. Harbury, *Colonial Virginia's Cooking Dynasty*, 106. On asparagus, see Oliver, *Food in Colonial and Federal America*, 56; Harbury, *Colonial Virginia's Cooking Dynasty*, 105–106.

24. On the practical advantages of pudding, see Fussell, *The Story of Corn*, 231; Stavely and Fitzgerald, *America's Founding Food*, 13–14. On pudding as a food-preservation technique, see Quinzio, *Pudding*, 16. On pie as a food-preservation technique, see Stavely and Fitzgerald, *America's Founding Food*, 220, 226–228; Clarkson, *Pie*, 35, 44–45.

25. Davidson, *Oxford Companion to Food*, 82. On the use of "boudin" in Cajun Louisiana, see Sokolov, *Fading Feast*, 125–133. On pudding, see Joseph Carlin, "Pudding," in Smith, *The Oxford Encyclopedia of Food and Drink in America*, 2:325–327; Stavely and Fitzgerald, *Northern Hospitality*, 325–328; Colquhoun, *Taste*, 123–126; Weaver, *The Christmas Cook*, 155–181; Quinzio, *Pudding*.

26. Winthrop and Winthrop, *Some Puritan Love-Letters*, 163–165.

27. Davidson, *Oxford Companion to Food*, 184–185, 638–639; Harbury, *Colonial Virginia's Cooking Dynasty*, 242, 245. On "plum" as a generic term for fruit in pies and puddings, see Weaver, *The Christmas Cook*, 155–157.

28. Sweet potato pudding and chicken pudding are frequently celebrated as "Southern" in nineteenth-century cookbooks such as Lafcadio Hearn's *La Cuisine Creole* (1885) and Anna Maria Collins's *The Great Western Cook Book* (1857). Mary Randolph calls chicken pudding "an old Virginia dish." Rice puddings appear in greater abundance in Southern cookbooks, paralleling the emphasis on other baked rice dishes appearing in them, like rice waffles and rice bread. On Indian pudding, see Stavely and Fitzgerald, *America's Founding Food*, 15–19; Mark H. Zanger, "Indian Pudding," in Smith, *The Oxford Companion to American Food and Drink*, 317–318; Curtin, Oliver, and Plimoth Plantation, *Giving Thanks*, 162–163. On benne and benne pudding, see Bedigian, "African Origins"; Rice and Katz-Hyman, *World of a Slave*, 416–417. On persimmon pudding, see Weaver, *America Eats*, 77–78, 89; Sokolov, *Fading Feast*, 30. On dumpling puddings, including *brod-pudding*, see Weaver, *Sauerkraut Yankees*, 105–108.

29. Richards, *Abigail Adams*, 263. On "pudding" as a synonym for "dinner," and on pudding as served with and/or before the meal, see Stavely and Fitzgerald, *America's Founding Food*, 14; Zanger, *The American History Cookbook*, 68–69; Mary Sanker, "Desserts," in Smith, *Oxford Companion to American Food and Drink*, 187–188.

30. For an instructive nineteenth-century recipe for battalia pie, see Carter, *The Frugal Housewife*, 138. On battalia pies, see Stavely and Fitzgerald, *America's Founding Food*, 220–221. On pie in the colonial and federal eras, see Stavely and Fitzgerald, *America's Founding Food*, 218–226; McWilliams, *A Revolution in Eating*, 224–225. On mincemeat pie, see Weaver, *The Christmas Cook*, 157–162, 178–179; Stavely and Fitzgerald, *America's Founding Food*, 220–221.

31. Israel Acrelius, *A History of New Sweden* (1759), quoted in Stavely and Fitzgerald, *America's Founding Food,* 221. On hard piecrusts and the use of pie as a means of food preservation, see Stavely and Fitzgerald, *America's Founding Food,* 84, 219–222; Shephard, *Pickled,* 188–189; Weaver, *Christmas Cook,* 160; Clarkson, *Pie,* 18–20.

32. McWilliams, *Story Behind the Dish,* 49–52; Pat Willard, "Pies and Tarts," in Smith, *The Oxford Encyclopedia of Food and Drink in America,* 2:272–275. For definitions of "cobbler," "grunt," and other potpie terms, see Kipfer, *The Culinarian.*

33. Christopher Sauer, quoted in Weaver, *Sauer's Herbal Cures,* 101; William Byrd, quoted in Harbury, *Colonial Virginia's Cooking Dynasty,* 121. On historic uses of chocolate as a medicine in America, see Wilson and Hurst, *Chocolate as Medicine,* 78–81. On chocolate as a medicinal, a drink (rather than a solid food), and a breakfast provision, see Schivelbusch and Jacobson, *Tastes of Paradise,* ch. 3. On coffee, tea, and chocolate in New Netherland, see Rose, *Food, Drink, and Celebrations of the Hudson Valley,* ch. 9.

34. Grivetti and Shapiro, *Chocolate,* 63; Wickman, "Breakfast on Chocolate," 487. On Aztec consumption of chocolate, see Coe, *America's First Cuisines,* 101–107. On chocolate consumption by Revolutionary War soldiers, see John U. Rees, "Historical Overview: Revolutionary War Food," in Smith, *The Oxford Companion to American Food and Drink,* 283.

35. Kalm, quoted in Roth, "Tea-Drinking," 442. On the emergence of tea in colonial America, see Roth, "Tea-Drinking," 439–440.

36. On afternoon tea and tea parties in colonial and federal America, see Roth, "Tea-Drinking," 444–447; Nylander, *Our Own Snug Fireside,* 240–246. On specialized tea furnishings, see Roth, "Tea-Drinking," 447–458.

37. On tea-drinking times, see Roth, "Tea-Drinking," 442.

38. On the sequence of a proper tea ritual, see Roth, "Tea-Drinking," 457–458. Tea gowns were popular from 1875 through the 1920s. Moffat, *Afternoon Tea,* 28–29.

39. On tea parties as a site for courtship, see Roth, "Tea-Drinking," 445.

40. On the tea boycott and tea alternatives, see Kerber, *Women of the Republic,* 39–44; Roth, "Tea-Drinking," 442–444; Unger, *American Tempest,* 121–123.

41. Fithian, *Journal and Letters,* 194, 110. On coffee in Europe, see Schivelbusch and Jacobson, *Tastes of Paradise,* ch. 2. On the emergence of coffee in colonial America, see Ukers, *All About Coffee,* 105–112. On coffee as a more public beverage than tea, see Roth, "Tea-Drinking," 440. On the Green Dragon, the Boston Tea Party, and the relationship between coffee and tea consumption before and after the American Revolution, see Wild, *Coffee,* 128–138. On the origins and early spread of coffee, see Pendergrast, *Coffee,* ch. 1.

42. Stavely and Fitzgerald, *America's Founding Food,* 86. For another description of eel for breakfast in the nineteenth century, see Schweid, *Consider the Eel,* 118–119.

43. Weaver, *A Quaker Women's Cookbook,* 320–321. For a nineteenth-century recipe for "common pancakes," see Croly, *Jennie June's American Cookery Book,* 242. For more on pancakes, see Albala, *Pancake.*

44. On the historical consumption of waffles and pancakes in the United States, see van der Sijs, *Cookies, Cole Slaw, and Stoops,* 144; Weaver, *Sauerkraut Yankees,* 132–134. On pancakes, waffles, and other foods in seventeenth-century Dutch art, see Barnes and Rose, *Matters of Taste.* On chicken and waffles, see Weaver, *Sauerkraut Yankees,* 132; Whitaker, *Tea,* 12, 71–72, 131–132; Edge, *Fried Chicken,* 51–62.

45. Irving, *Washington Irving's Works,* 257; Carter, *The Frugal Housewife,* 206. On the early history of doughnuts in America, see Mullins, *Glazed America,* 37–44; Stavely and Fitzgerald, *America's Founding Food,* 256–259; Rose, *Food, Drink, and Celebrations of the Hudson Valley,* 76–77. Oliver, *Saltwater Foodways,* 117–118; Zanger, *The American History Cookbook,* 44–45; Alice Ross, "Doughnuts," in Smith, *The Oxford Encyclopedia of Food and Drink in America,* 1:408–409; Linda Campbell Franklin, "Doughnut-Making Tools," in Smith, *The Oxford Encyclopedia of Food and Drink in America,* 1:408. Thanks to Sandra Oliver for bringing my attention to early doughnut-cutting techniques. For a doughnut recipe with instructions for using tumbler rims, see Corson, *Miss Corson's Practical American Cookery,* 503–504. For examples of doughnut recipes calling for diamond shapes, see Leslie, *Directions for Cookery,* 358–359; Beecher, *Miss Beecher's Domestic Receipt Book,* 140.

46. Abel, *Practical Sanitary and Economic Cooking,* 105. On the etymology and ethnic origins of French toast, see Lipkowitz, *Words to Eat By,* 233–237. For a recipe for Mennonite toast, see Wilcox, *The Original Buckeye Cook Book,* 52. On Queen Esther's bread, see Zanger, *The American History Cookbook,* 185.

47. On the Erie Canal and the rise of Midwestern grain production, see Smith, *Eating History,* 13–17. On wheat consumption eclipsing that of meat, see Trager, *The Food Chronology,* 218, 245.

48. On leavening agents, see Sandra L. Oliver, "Chemical Leavening," in Smith, *The Oxford Encyclopedia of Food and Drink in America,* 1:217–219; Weaver, *America Eats,* 133–135; Stavely and Fitzgerald, *America's Founding Food,* 240–243.

49. Carter, *The Frugal Housewife,* 85. For examples of recipes requiring the cook to whip eggs "to a snow" and beat ingredients for fifteen minutes or more, see Lee, *The Cook's Own Book,* 20–22, 32–34, 36–39. Some recipes called for more than an hour of mixing: Lee's recipe for nun's cakes called for two hours of beating, and Eliza Leslie's recipe for Maryland biscuit required the baker to alternately knead then pound the dough with a rolling pin for two

to three hours. Lee, *The Cook's Own Book,* 37; Kreidberg, *Food on the Frontier,* 56–57. For more on Maryland biscuit, see Weaver, *America Eats,* 32.

50. Zanger, *The American History Cookbook,* 140. For more on the early history of muffins and cupcakes, see Davidson, *Oxford Companion to Food,* 234, 517; Stephen Schmidt, "Cakes," in Smith, *The Oxford Encyclopedia of Food and Drink in America,* 1:160; Sylvia Lovegren, "Breakfast Foods," in Smith, *The Oxford Companion to American Food and Drink,* 68–70. On the etymology of "muffin," see Morton, *Cupboard Love,* 200–201. On the cupcake craze beginning in the 1990s, see Humble, *Cake,* 109–114; Krondl, *Sweet Invention,* 369–371.

51. Rorer, *Mrs. Rorer's Philadelphia Cook Book,* 331, 326. On the first White House cookstove, see McWilliams, *Food and the Novel,* 55; Brewer, *Fireplace to Cookstove,* 138.

52. On the advantages of cookstoves for baking with saleratus as well as cookstove manufacturing companies' sale of baking ware and their circulation of recipes, see Weaver, *America Eats,* 134–141.

53. The emergence of cookstoves is not the only factor in women's rising dependence on cookery literature, simply one factor. Simmons, *American Cookery,* 37. On the transition from hearth to cookstove, see Cromley, *The Food Axis,* 83–89, 123–125; Weaver, *America Eats,* 134; Carlisle, Nasardinov, and Pustz, *America's Kitchens,* 71–74, 83; Gideon, *Mechanization Takes Command,* 527–536. Ierley, *The Comforts of Home,* 161–164. On the shift toward dependence on recipes, see Plante, *American Kitchen,* 128.

Chapter 3: How Dinner Became Special

1. Croly, *Jennie June's American Cookery Book,* 225.

2. Hiatt, *Diary of William Owen,* 60, 10; Franklin, *Autobiography,* 156. On colonial mealtimes, see Oliver, *Food in Colonial and Federal America,* 157; Williams, *Savory Suppers,* 144.

3. Aubertin, *A Fight with Distances,* 310; T. D. L. *Peep at the Western World,* 99; "Life in the White House."

4. On the new opportunities and dangers young rural folk faced when relocating to cities, see Ryan, *Cradle of the Middle Class,* 223; Halttunen, *Confidence Men,* 1, 12–13, ch. 2; Kasson, *Rudeness and Civility,* 69.

5. "Duties and Rights of Mill Girls," 79; Farley, "Letters from Susan," 170. On mealtimes in the mills, see English, *A Common Thread,* 26, 32; Robinson, *Loom and Spindle,* 31.

6. Editorial, *Lowell Offering,* 69.

7. Woodward and Woodward, *Country Homes,* 38. On early suburbs, see Warner, *Streetcar Suburbs;* Marsh, "Suburban Men."

8. "The Proper Hour for Dinner," 345; "Times of Taking Food," 344.

9. "The Proper Hour for Dinner," 345.

10. Herrick, *What to Eat*, 166; T. W. H., "Women and Men," 330; Roberts, *The Collected Contributions*, 169.

11. "Household Department"; T. W. H., "Women and Men," 330.

12. Devereux, "The Philosophy of Eating," 5; Hale, "The Bruntons' Family Problem," 10.

13. Childs, "The Etiquette of Dining," 193; Devereux, "The Philosophy of Eating," 5.

14. Ayers, "Co-operative Housekeeping," 171.

15. Mintz and Kellogg, *Domestic Revolutions*, 53. Although working-class gender roles also diverged, with husbands tending to leave home for work and women tending to concentrate on domestic tasks, traditional notions of economic cooperation persisted; each member of the family was expected to contribute to the family's income. Mintz and Kellogg, *Domestic Revolutions*, 88.

16. Devereux, "The Philosophy of Eating," 5. On the transition from the corporate family economy to the conjugal family, see Ryan, *Cradle of the Middle Class*.

17. On the colonial hall, see Carlisle, Nasardinov, and Pustz, *America's Kitchens*, 30; Wright, *Building the Dream*, 15. On nineteenth-century dining rooms, see Ames, *Death in the Dining Room;* Williams, *Savory Suppers*, esp. ch. 3; Clifford Clark Jr., "Vision of the Dining Room," in Grover, *Dining in America*, 142–172.

18. On nineteenth-century sideboards, see Williams, *Savory Suppers*, 53–55, 63–69; Ames, *Death in the Dining Room*, ch. 2.

19. On trestle tables, see Lockwood, *Colonial Furniture*, 76–77; Volo and Volo, *Daily Life on the Old Colonial Frontier*, 156n15. On forms, see Lockwood, *Colonial Furniture*, 124–125; Earle, *Home Life in Colonial Days*, 100. On women serving and eating meals, see Mintz and Kellogg, *Domestic Revolutions*, 267n64. On children at the table, see Nylander, *Our Own Snug Fireside*, 247; Earle, *Home Life in Colonial Days*, 88. On sharing trenchers and vessels, see Earle, *Home Life in Colonial Days*, 80, 93–94; Kasson, *Rudeness and Civility*, 183; Deetz, *In Small Things*, 76. On the idiom "room and board," see Morton, *Cupboard Love*, 47.

20. Trollope, *Domestic Manners*, 25; Dickens, *American Notes*, 2:76; *A Pretty Little Pocket Book*, quoted in Earle, *Home Life in Colonial Days*, 102. On sparse colonial furnishing and on chairs as the prerogative of a family's male head, see Mintz and Kellogg, *Domestic Revolutions*, 24. On extended family at dinner and everyone sitting on the same side of the table, see Gottlieb, *The Family in the Western World*, 44.

21. Hooker, "A Few Homely Words."

22. Hooker, "A Few Homely Words," 162. On conversation at the dinner table, see Williams, *Savory Suppers*, 46–47.

23. Hooker, "A Few Homely Words," 162.

24. Childs, "The Etiquette of Dining," 193; Herrick, *What to Eat*, 172.

25. Herrick, "The Art of Dining," 19. On dining room formality as a dress rehearsal for children's anticipated entrance into society, see Gillis, *A World of Their Own Making*, 92.

26. Leslie, *The Behaviour Book*, 99. On reading strangers' appearances in urbanizing America, see Halttunen, *Confidence Men*, ch. 2.

27. Devereux, "The Philosophy of Eating," 5.

28. Phelps, *The Educator*, 314; Gow, *Good Morals*, 230.

29. Hale, "The Bruntons' Family Problem," 10.

30. Phelps, *Educator*, 314. According to Steven Mintz and Susan Kellogg, "Each family member had a proper 'place' that was appropriate to his or her age and gender and contributed in his or her way to the family's effective functioning." Mintz and Kellogg, *Domestic Revolutions*, 53.

31. Perkins, "Childhood," 388.

32. Beecher and Stowe, *American Woman's Home*, 130, 129. On Catharine Beecher's domestic moralism, see McWilliams, *Food and the Novel*, 64–70.

33. On the relationship between food and sexual self-restraint in the nineteenth century, especially concerning women, see Brumberg, "The Appetite as Voice."

34. Gow, *Good Morals*, 229. For Gow's table rules, see Gow, *Good Morals*, 229–237. On the internalization of prohibitions in Victorian child rearing, see Mintz and Kellogg, *Domestic Revolutions*, 58. On teaching restraint through family snacking prohibitions, see Smith, "She Moves the Hand," 210. On training children's appetites as a safeguard against darker appetites, see University Society, *The Child Welfare Manual*, 367; Alcott, *The Young Mother*, 202.

35. Beecher and Stowe, *American Woman's Home*, 129.

36. Chase, *Dr. Chase's Recipes*, 91; Hall, *Dyspepsia*, 30.

37. Beecher and Stowe, *American Woman's Home*, 129; Chase, *Dr. Chase's Recipes*, 2–3.

38. Chase, *Dr. Chase's Recipes*, 63; Leslie, *The Behaviour Book*, 293.

39. Beecher and Stowe, *American Woman's Home*, 137; Mary Scharlieb, "Adolescent Girls in University Society," *The Child Welfare Manual*, 367; Alcott, *The Young Mother*, 203.

40. Chase, *Dr. Chase's Recipes*, 3.

Chapter 4: How Dinner Became American

1. Marjoribanks, *Travels*, 165.

2. Marjoribanks, *Travels*, 165; Dickens's term "Dirty Feeders" appears in *Martin Chuzzlewit*.

3. Menu, annual banquet held by the Ohio Society of New York at Delmonico's, New York, New York, May 7, 1886; Buttolph Collection of Menus, New York Public Library, 1886–0022, http://digitalgallery.nypl.org/nypldigital/dgkeysearchdetail.cfm?trg=1&strucID=269598&imageID

=4000000594&total=9258&num=140&word=col_id%3A159&s=1&notword
=&d=&c=&f=&k=0&lWord=&lField=&sScope=images&sLevel=&sLabel
=Miss%20Frank%20E.%20Buttolph%20American%20Menu%20Collect . . .
&imgs=20&pos=146&e=w&cdonum=0 (accessed January 5, 2012). On *service à
la russe* in France, see Symons, *A History*, 288–289. On *service à la russe* in Britain,
see Colquhoun, *Taste*, 251–256. On *service à la russe* in the United States, see
Williams, *Savory Suppers*, 152–153; Farmer, *The Boston Cook School*, 520–524. In
2009, Chris Kimball, host of *America's Test Kitchen*, recreated Fannie Farmer's
1896 "full course dinner" and wrote about it in Kimball, *Fannie's Last Supper*.

4. On middle-class Americans' adoption of French foods and foodways,
see Levenstein, *Revolution at the Table*, ch. 1; Williams, *Savory Suppers*, 112;
Smith, *Eating History*, 20–24.

5. Herrick, "The Art of Dining," 19.

6. On oysters as appetizers, see Kurlansky, *The Big Oyster*, 109; Conlin, *Bacon, Beans, and Galantines*, 119. On the history of soup in America, see Andrew
F. Smith, "Soups and Stews," in Smith, *The Oxford Encyclopedia of Food and Drink
in America*, 2:461–467. On Brillat-Savarin's Boston "restorateur," see Trager,
The Food Chronology, 189.

7. On soup as a patriotic food during wartime, see Bentley, *Eating for Victory*, 66; Andrew F. Smith, "Soups and Stews," in Smith, *The Oxford Encyclopedia
of Food and Drink in America*, 2:461–467.

8. Henderson, *Practical Cooking*, 86, 359.

9. On salad during the nineteenth century, see Williams, *Savory Suppers*,
113–114; Oliver, *Saltwater Foodways*, 47.

10. Dallas, *Kettner's Book of the Table*, 293; Henderson, *Practical Cooking*,
219. On the origins of mayonnaise, see Morton, *Cupboard Love*, 191; Barnette,
Ladyfingers, 93; Dallas, *Kettner's Book of the Table*, 295–300. On the tradition of
women tossing salad with bare hands and the feminine connotations of salad,
see Visser, *Much Depends*, 216, 222; Dallas, *Kettner's Book of the Table*, 300, 401.
For red mayonnaise sauce, see Henderson, *Practical Cooking*, 222. On salads at
the turn of the twentieth century, see Shapiro, *Perfection Salad*, 90–96.

11. See note 10.

12. On the etymology of the word "dessert," see Morton, *Cupboard Love*,
110.

13. On mincemeat and mincemeat pies, see Weaver, *Christmas Cook*, 158–
161; Curtin, Oliver, and Plimoth Plantation, *Giving Thanks*, 38, 176; Stavely
and Fitzgerald, *America's Founding Food*, 220–225. On sugar as a flavoring and
on fruit preserves, see Stavely and Fitzgerald, *America's Founding Food*, 207–218.

14. Hale, *A New England Boyhood*, 118. Not all French influence on the
American table arrived via England. Much came directly from the Continent, for example, through the numerous French chefs who fled to North

America during the French Revolution. On banquets as precursors to dessert, see Thong, "Performances," 107–108; Mason, *Food Culture,* 32.

15. On French desserts in the United States, including the charlotte russe, see Williams, *Savory Suppers,* 115; Mariani, *The Encyclopedia,* 64. On the Charlie Roosh, see Scarcella, *Made in Sicily,* 55; Bellin, *The Jewish Cook Book,* 324; Nathan, *Jewish Cooking in America,* 322.

16. On the European origins of etiquette, see Williams, *Savory Suppers,* 5–7. On etiquette books, see Kasson, *Rudeness and Civility,* ch. 2.

17. Hall, *The Correct Thing,* 74, 105, 90, 86; Beecher, *Miss Beecher's Domestic Receipt Book,* 239.

18. Hall, *The Correct Thing,* 130, 144, 118, 147, 131, 130; Andrews, "Around the Dinner Table," 110.

19. Anonymous, *As a Chinaman Saw Us,* 46. On the proliferation of specialized dining utensils, see Williams, *Savory Suppers,* 86–89; Rainwater, "Victorian Dining Silver," 177–182; Kasson, *Rudeness and Civility,* 188–193.

20. Hall, *The Correct Thing,* 137; anonymous, *As a Chinaman Saw Us,* 46–47. It is unknown whether this anonymous work was written by a Chinese traveler or an American in the voice of a Chinese traveler. Most suspect it was written by an American. Either way, it offers a valuable glimpse into the eating fashions of the elite at the turn of the twentieth century. On correct and incorrect usage of silverware, see also Hall, *The Correct Thing,* esp. chs. "At A Dinner," "At Table," and "At Luncheon."

21. Anonymous, *As a Chinaman Saw Us,* 45.

22. Howells, *The Rise of Silas Lapham,* ch. 19.

23. Williams, *Savory Suppers,* 20. For a succinct list of dinner table dos and don'ts, see Andrews, "Around the Dinner Table," 109–110. See also Florence Howe Hall's *The Correct Thing in Good Society.*

24. Beecher, *Miss Beecher's Domestic Receipt Book,* 240. On servants in middle-class American households, see Levenstein, *Revolution at the Table,* 18, 60–71.

25. Schwartz, *More Work for Mother,* 122–123.

26. On domestic service as a stopgap, see Schwartz, *More Work for Mother,* 123–126; Strasser, *Never Done,* 169–173. On the changing ethnicity of servants, see Levenstein, *Revolution at the Table,* 63.

27. Marryat, *Second Series,* 51; Beecher, *Miss Beecher's Domestic Receipt Book,* 240; Harland, *Breakfast,* 12–13. On training servants, see Schwartz, *More Work for Mother,* 122, 126. For an example of nineteenth-century advice for managing servants, see Beecher and Stowe, *American Woman's Home,* ch. 25.

28. Collier, *America,* 49; Ward, "The Homelike House," 337.

29. Kelvinator Home Economics Department, *New Delights,* 5. On the Home Economics Association's plan to establish schools for training servants, see Levenstein, *Revolution at the Table,* 64. On electric appliances as servant

replacements, see Strasser, *Never Done,* 76–82; Forty, *Objects,* 209–215; Sutherland, "Modernizing Domestic Service," 243–251.

30. On formal dinners yielding to everyday household demands in the newly servant-less household, see Forty, *Objects,* 210–211; Levenstein, *Revolution at the Table,* 71.

31. Frederick, *Household Engineering.* On Christine Frederick's step-saving approach to the kitchen, see Lupton and Miller, *The Bathroom,* 44–47; Carlisle, Nasardinov, and Pustz, *America's Kitchens,* 140–141; Freeman, *The Making of the Modern Kitchen,* 29–32. On the pragmatic food aesthetic of the home economists, see Shapiro, *Perfection Salad,* 5, 74.

32. On the rise of processed foods and the emergence of can-opener cooking, see Shapiro, *Something from the Oven,* chs. 1–2; Endrijonas, "Processed Foods." On home economists' collaboration with the food industry, see Shapiro, *Perfection Salad,* esp. ch. 8. On Frederick's endorsements of commercial products, see Matthews, *Just a Housewife,* 70.

33. On cooking and domestic duties as opportunities for artistic self-expression from the 1860s to the 1950s, see Carlisle, Nasardinov, and Pustz, *America's Kitchens,* 82; Endrijonas, "Processed Foods," 159–164; Inness, *Dinner Roles,* ch. 6; Schenone, *A Thousand Years over a Hot Stove,* 254.

34. Hayden, *The Grand Domestic Revolution,* 207. On Melusina Fay Pierce, see Hayden, *The Grand Domestic Revolution,* ch. 4. On the Carthage, Missouri, dining club, see Hayden, *The Grand Domestic Revolution,* ch. 10.

35. Gilman, *What Diantha Did,* 26–27. On the Twentieth Century Food Company in New Haven, see Hayden, *The Grand Domestic Revolution,* ch. 10.

36. On cooperative housekeeping articles in women's service magazines, see Levenstein, *Revolution at the Table,* 65–67; Hayden, *The Grand Domestic Revolution,* 269–270, 224–226; Scanlon, "Old Housekeeping."

37. On critiques of cooperative housekeeping and reasons for its failure, see Levenstein, *Revolution at the Table,* 65–71; Miller, "Technology and the Ideal."

38. For more on the history of Thanksgiving dinner as a patriotic and nationalistic American meal, see Carroll, "Colonial Custard," ch. 5.

39. On the culinary history of Thanksgiving, see Appelbaum, *Thanksgiving,* 265–279; Stavely and Fitzgerald, *America's Founding Food,* 226–231; Oliver, *Saltwater Foodways,* 242–245; Curtin, Oliver, and Plimoth Plantation, *Giving Thanks.*

40. Hale, *Northwood,* 94, 93.

41. Menu, Windemere Hotel, Chicago, November 25, 1897, New York Public Library, http://menus.nypl.org/menu_pages/41930 (accessed November 28, 2012).

42. "The American Thanksgiving," 99.

43. Martin, *A Nation of Immigrants,* 105.

44. Offenbach, *Offenbach in America,* 86; editorial, *New England Kitchen Magazine.* On the revival of traditional American foods in the late nineteenth and early twentieth centuries, and on the uses of traditional American foods as Americanization tools in the hands of social reformers, see Carroll, "Colonial Custard."

45. On Prohibition's role in the decline of formal dining, see Levenstein, *Revolution at the Table,* 183–193; Levenstein, *Paradox of Plenty,* 45.

Chapter 5: Why Lunch Is Cold, Cheap, and Quick

1. O'Rell, *A Frenchman,* 297–298.

2. Johnson, quoted in Visser, *The Rituals of Dinner,* 159; Morton, *Cupboard Love,* 184.

3. Webster, quoted in Williams, *Savory Suppers,* 145; Alcott, *The Young House-Keeper,* 225; "Editor's Chair," *Harper's New Monthly Magazine,* 559.

4. State of Massachusetts, *Report on the Statistics of Labor,* 56. On uses of the word "lunch," see "Editor's Chair," *Harper's New Monthly Magazine,* 559. On the etymology of "snack," see Morton, *Cupboard Love,* 282–283.

5. "Acting Charade," 67.

6. Reade, "A Simpleton," 562.

7. Harland, *Breakfast,* 170–171.

8. Croly, *Jennie June's American Cookery Book,* 307. On ladies' luncheons, see Williams, *Savory Suppers,* 147–148, 164–166.

9. On women and eating during the Victorian era and early twentieth century, see Shapiro, *Perfection Salad,* 68–69, 94–95; Levenstein, *Paradox of Plenty,* 34–35; Inness, *Dinner Roles,* ch. 3.

10. Lee, "A Flower Luncheon," 155–156. On themed luncheons, see Gordon, *The Saturated World,* 5–7, 65. On women's restraint in eating, see Brumberg, "The Appetite As Voice."

11. Hall, *The Correct Thing,* 132–133.

12. For period descriptions of men's dining clubs, see University Club, *The University Club of New York.*

13. Banning, "Deals," 133. For a description of the Aldine Club, see Ellsworth, "The Aldine Club," 159–161.

14. State of Massachusetts, *Report on the Statistics of Labor,* 29; Byington, *Homestead,* 64.

15. Sweet, "Machine Designing," 110.

16. Entropy, "The Tin Dinner Pail," 778; Lincoln, "The City." On William McKinley's full dinner pail promise, see Lautenschlager, *Food Fight,* 26–29, 34, 42–43.

17. Beecher and Stowe, *American Woman's Home,* 437; State of Massachusetts, *Report on the Statistics of Labor,* 30.

18. Rhode Island Board of Education, *Thirty-Second Annual Report*, 109.

19. In some areas, children continued to return home for lunch through the first half of the twentieth century. See Levine, *School Lunch Politics*, 101–102; Mullen, *An Arkansas Childhood*, 82–84.

20. Willigen and Willigen, *Food and Everyday Life*, 35; Leight and Rinehart, *Country School Memories*, 56. See also Oliver, *Saltwater Foodways*, 70–71.

21. State of Massachusetts, *Report on the Statistics of Labor*, 29; Edington, "Six Hundred a Year," 35.

22. On *bizos*, see Wood, *Foods*, 51. On cornhusk tacos, see Gabaccia, *We Are What We Eat*, 43. On shoebox lunches, see Williams-Forson, *Building Houses*, 116; Opie, *Hog and Hominy*, 56–57. On waiter-carriers, see Williams-Forson, *Building Houses*, 125–126.

23. Harland, *Breakfast*, 207; State of Massachusetts, *Report on the Statistics of Labor*, 203. The Beecher sisters also criticized pie, and piecrust in particular, as one of the "most unhealthful kinds of foods" (Beecher and Stowe, *American Woman's Home*, 133, 137, 169).

24. Beecher, *Miss Beecher's Domestic Receipt Book*, 25.

25. On the origins and early development of the sandwich, see Wilson, *Sandwich*, ch. 1; Morton, *Cupboard Love*, 266; Trager, *The Food Chronology*, 165–166; Andrew F. Smith, "Sandwiches," in Smith, *The Oxford Encyclopedia of Food and Drink in America*, 2:397–400.

26. Leslie, *Directions*, 123; Gillette, *White House*, 14.

27. Burdick, *What Shall We Have to Eat?* 50.

28. Cowles, *Seven Hundred Sandwiches*, ch. 6. On peanut butter as a vegetarian meat substitute, see Schwarz, *John Harvey Kellogg*, 118–119; Smith, *Peanuts*, 31–34. On the origins and early history of the peanut butter (and jelly) sandwich, see Smith, *Peanuts*, 34–35; McWilliams, *The Story Behind the Dish*, 163–166. On Elvis's affinity for peanut butter and bacon sandwiches (which sometimes included jelly as well as bananas), see Krampner, *Creamy and Crunchy*, 163; Lauer, *Bacon*, 91–92.

29. Smith, *Peanuts*, 35; "Peanut Butter," in Katz and Weaver, *Encyclopedia of Food and Culture*, 3:56–57.

30. Allen, *Mrs. Allen on Cooking*, 45–46; Greer, *A Text-Book of Cooking*, 328.

31. "Discoveries by Our Observers and Experimenters," 334.

32. Kingsdale, "The Poor Man's Club," 477–478. On saloon lunches, see also Duis, *The Saloon*, 52, 56, 157–158; Powers, *Faces Along the Bar*, ch. 10.

33. Sudley, "Luncheon for a Million," 842.

34. Graham, *With Poor Immigrants*, 49. On one-arm joints, see Allen, *The City in Slang*, 97; Duis, *Challenging Chicago*, 159; Grimes, *Appetite City*, 184.

35. O'Brian, quoted in Kurlansky, *The Food of a Younger Land*, 42–43. On the automat, see Elias, *Food*, 82–83; Duis, *Challenging Chicago*, 161; Grimes, *Appetite*

City, 187–193; Allen, *The City in Slang,* 100; Haley, *Turning the Tables,* 184–185. On pie as a popular quick lunch food in New York, see Grimes, *Appetite City,* 118.

36. Hunt, "How a Druggist," 432–433; O'Brian, quoted in Kurlansky, *The Food of a Younger Land,* 58. On drug store and soda fountain jargon, see also Grimes, *Appetite City,* 117.

37. Pennell, "Eats," 857; see also Cowan, "How Busy People Eat," 656.

38. Bose, *Fifteen Years,* 14; Cowan, "How Busy People Eat," 656.

39. Sudley, "Luncheon for a Million," 837; State of New York, *Preliminary Report of the New York Factory Investigating Commission,* 3:1395.

40. State of New York, *Preliminary Report of the New York Factory Investigating Commission,* 3:1212–1213, 1278, 784. Factories that did provide washrooms frequently discriminated against African American employees. Separate facilities were the norm, and they were not generally equal. The Bureau of Labor reported that one lead factory (which was typical of many others) supplied black workers with a small, dirty building in the back lot. Unlike in the white workers' cleaner and more centrally located lavatory, there were no baths. Blacks often had no choice but to approach their meals less hygienically than whites because factories that did not accommodate them with separate facilities generally barred them from using the sinks at all.

41. State of New York, *Preliminary Report of the New York Factory Investigating Commission,* 2:1636, 1710, 1778, 830.

42. State of New York, *Preliminary Report of the New York Factory Investigating Commission,* 2:1210.

43. Tarbell, *New Business Deals,* 42–43.

44. Bombo, *Reflections,* 55; State of Massachusetts, *Report on the Statistics of Labor,* 103; Meakin, *Model Factories,* 178.

45. Meakin, *Model Factories,* 177–178.

46. US Department of Labor, US Women's Bureau, "Negro Women," 30.

47. Meakin, *Model Factories,* 170, 166; Des Moines Hosiery Mills advertisement, *Factory,* 191; US Bureau of Labor, *Employers' Welfare Work,* 43.

48. Birdsall, "A Luncheon Plan," 47.

49. Head, "Lunch Clubs," 284–286.

50. Sudley, "Luncheon for a Million," 844. See also Shuey, *Factory People,* 191.

51. De Bryas and De Bryas, *A Frenchwoman's Impressions,* 242; Nicola, "Lunch."

52. Hopkins, "A Girl's Hot Lunch Club," 9; Calvin, "Warm Lunches," 11.

53. Richards, "The Food of Children," 147. See also Hunt, "The Daily Meals of School Children," 45–47.

54. Bennett, "The Hot Lunch," 418–419; Hopkins, "A Girl's Hot Lunch Club," 419–422.

55. Hartman, "Driving Out the High School Pickle," 23; Levenstein, *Revolution at the Table*, ch. 4; Moran, "Boston High School Lunches," 181–184; "A Larger Work," 45.

56. Hartman, "Driving Out the High School Pickle," 23; Hunt, "The Daily Meals of School Children," 10.

57. Hunt, "The Daily Meals of School Children," 7.

58. Hunt, "The Daily Meals of School Children," 9; Hartman, "Driving Out the High School Pickle," 23.

59. Hunt, "The Daily Meals of School Children," 10.

60. Kittredge, "Experiments," 174–177. On typical foods served in early municipal school lunch programs, see Bryant, *School Feeding*, 149–153.

61. Cooper and Holmes, *Lunch Lessons*, 33–35.

Chapter 6: Reinventing Breakfast

1. Beste, *The Wabash*, 68–69.

2. Russell, *My Diary*, 39; Birkbeck, *Notes*, 38–39.

3. Birkbeck, *Notes*, 38.

4. Blane, *An Excursion*, 27.

5. Lambert, *Travels*, 40; Oliver, *Saltwater Foodways*, 17, 44–45, 68, 70.

6. On breakfast at Sing Sing, see Sturge, *A Visit*, 165.

7. Cobbett, *A Year's Residence*, 67–68; Lambert, *Travels*, 40.

8. Dickens, *American Notes*, 1:142; Volney, *View*, 324.

9. Duncan, *Travels*, 319; Volney, *View*, 324; Buckingham, *America*, 349.

10. Hall, *Dyspepsia*, 11–12. For more on dyspepsia, see Green, *Fit for America*, 104.

11. "Food in Its Relation to Health," 159. On the slowness of the American diet to change, see Oliver, *Saltwater Foodways*, 44–45.

12. Chase, *Dr. Chase's Recipes*, 89.

13. "Hygienic Rules," 326; Shaftsbury, *Child Life*, 178.

14. Davis, "Agriculture," 99; Beecher, *Miss Beecher's Domestic Receipt Book*, 13; Kirk, "Common Sense," 626; Hawxhurst, "Food in Indigestion," 148.

15. Hawxhurst, "Food in Indigestion," 148; "Cookery," 251.

16. On Christian influence on nineteenth- and early-twentieth-century vegetarian reformers, see Iacobbo and Iacobbo, *Vegetarian America*, chs. 2 and 3.

17. Alcott, *The Young House-Keeper*, 198; Alcott, *Lectures*, 348. For more on William Andrus Alcott, see Iacobbo and Iacobbo, *Vegetarian America*, 34–44.

18. Alcott, *Vegetable Diet*, 13–14. On meat as a stimulant, see Iacobbo and Iacobbo, *Vegetarian America*, 21–22. On coffee, spices, tobacco, and so forth, as stimulants, see Beecher and Stowe, *American Woman's Home*, 138–147; Green, *Fit for America*, ch. 2; Smith, *Eating History*, 34.

19. Alcott, *Boy's Guide*, 265, 367; Alcott, *The Young House-Keeper*, 130.

20. On the collaboration between Alcott and Graham, see Iacobbo and Iacobbo, *Vegetarian America*, 34–35.

21. On Sylvester Graham, graham bread, Graham boarding houses, and Graham publications, see Iacobbo and Iacobbo, *Vegetarian America*, 13–70; Carson, *Cornflake Crusade*, esp. ch. 4; Green, *Fit for America*, esp. 45–53; Smith, *Eating History*, ch. 4; Riely, "Sylvester Graham," 198–201.

22. On anti-Graham protests, see Carson, *Cornflake Crusade*, 52–53. On Graham Crackers, see Smith, *Encyclopedia of Junk Food and Fast Food*, 120.

23. Jackson, *How to Treat*, 395. On James Caleb Jackson and Our Home on the Hillside, see Smith, *Eating History*, 34–35, 142–144; Green, *Fit for America*, 65–66; Carson, *Cornflake Crusade*, 59–70. Thanks to Harvey Green for pointing out the widespread appeal of homeopathic therapies in an era when many allopathic treatments were painful and dangerous.

24. On the naming of Jackson's cereal, see Davidson, *Penguin Companion to Food*, 124.

25. Jackson, quoted in Smith, *Eating History*, 142.

26. On Fletcherizing, see Green, *Fit for America*, 295–301; Levenstein, *Revolution at the Table*, 87–92. On the Christian underpinnings of breakfast cereals, see Grummett and Muers, *Theology on the Menu*, 67–68; Green, "Tricksters and the Marketing of Breakfast Cereal," 54–56.

27. Kellogg, quoted in Carson, *Cornflake Crusade*, 93.

28. On John Harvey Kellogg's breakfast cereal innovations, see Smith, *Eating History*, ch. 16; Carson, *Cornflake Crusade*, esp. chs. 7–10; Levenstein, *Revolution at the Table*, 33–35; McWilliams, *Story Behind the Dish*, 63–68. On Henry D. Perky and the invention of Shredded Wheat, see Carson, *Cornflake Crusade*, 119–124; Smith, *Eating History*, 145–146. On Ella Kellogg, see Carson, *Cornflake Crusade*, 111–112, 116–128.

29. On the sweetening of cornflakes, see Smith, *Eating History*, 149. On William Keith Kellogg's excommunication, see Sander L. Gilman, "Charles William Post," in Gilman, *Diets and Dieting: A Cultural Encyclopedia*, 216–217. On the advertising and business history of breakfast cereals, see Joy Santofler, "Breakfast Cereals," in Allen and Albala, *The Business of Food*, 61–64.

30. Quoted in Pendergrast, *Uncommon Grounds*, 93. On Charles W. Post and his breakfast cereal innovations, see Smith, *Eating History*, ch. 16; Carson, *Cornflake Crusade*, ch. 11; Green, *Fit for America*, 305–311; Levenstein, *Revolution at the Table*, 33–35.

31. Advertisement, *New York Times*, October 9, 1903, 5.

32. Advertisement, *New York Times*, October 9, 1903, 5. On the Elijah's Manna controversy, see Rubin, *American Empress*, 76–77.

33. Post quoted in Carson, *Cornflake Crusade*, 163.

34. On Henry Crowell and Quaker Oats, see Smith, *Eating History,* ch. 12; Trager, *The Food Chronology,* 319, 336, 368; Hine, *The Total Package,* 77–80. On germ theory and food, see Tomes, *The Gospel of Germs,* 100–103, 168–171.

35. Lucas, "Concerning Breakfast," 713. On Quaker Oats' packaging and advertising, see Hine, *The Total Package,* 77–80; Joy Santofler, "Breakfast Cereals," in Allen and Albala, *The Business of Food,* 61–64.

36. Quaker Oats advertisements, *New York Times,* February 13, 1892, 3; *New York Times,* December 9, 1891, 3; *Washington Post,* October 5, 1893, 7.

37. Quaker Oats advertisement, *Chicago Daily Tribune,* April 13, 1894, 5.

38. "How the Breakfast Foods Are Absorbing the Cattle Ranges of the West."

39. On milk sickness, see Dary, *Frontier Medicine,* 63–64. On the perceived dangers of milk, see Levenstein, *Fear,* ch. 2. On swill milk, see Wilson, *Swindled,* 154–167; DuPuis, *Nature's Perfect Food,* 18–22; Meckel, *Save the Babies,* 63–65. An additional factor in the decline of swill milk was the invention of refrigerated railroad cars, which made transporting country milk into cities more feasible and decreased city dwellers' dependence on urban dairies. Meckel, *Save the Babies,* 65.

40. McCollum and Simmonds, *The American Home Diet,* 15–16, 104. On pasteurization, see Levenstein, *Revolution at the Table,* 130–131, 134; DuPuis, *Nature's Perfect Food,* 82–89. On McCollum, vitamins, and milk as a protective food, see Levenstein, *Revolution at the Table,* ch. 12; Green, *The Uncertainty of Everyday Life,* 172–173.

41. McCollum and Simmonds, *The American Home Diet,* 104; Green, *The Uncertainty of Everyday Life,* 177; Levenstein, *Revolution at the Table,* 113–114.

42. Keene, *World War I,* 39; Wiley, "Milk," 50.

43. Greer, *Food and Victory,* 48. See also Rose, *Everyday Foods,* ch. 1.

44. On the early history of Florida's orange juice industry, see Hamilton, *Squeezed,* ch. 1.

45. Meade, "Variety." On orange juice and scurvy, acidosis, and tooth decay, see Levenstein, *Paradox of Plenty,* 12–13. On orange juice as an overnight fad, see Andrew F. Smith, "Orange Juice," in Smith, *The Oxford Encyclopedia of Food and Drink in America,* 2:215.

46. On John M. Fox, Minute Maid, and processed orange juice, see Liberman, *American Food,* 104–105; Wyman, *Better Than Homemade,* 75–77; Smith, *Drinking History,* 151–153.

47. "A Convenient Small Toaster," 25. On toasters (iron and electric), see Weaver, *America Eats,* 36–38; Wilson, *Consider the Fork,* 109–110; Linda Campbell Franklin and Alice Ross, "Toasters," in Smith, *The Oxford Encyclopedia of Food and Drink in America,* 2:544; Sobey, *The Way Kitchens Work,* 165–170; Plante, *American Kitchen,* 217, 254–255; Thwaites, *The Toaster Project.*

48. Panati, *Panati's Extraordinary Origins of Everyday Things,* 117–118; Liberman, *American Food,* 42.

49. On Rohwedder's invention of the bread slicer, see Gref, *The Rise and Fall*, 97; Bobrow-Strain, *White Bread*, ch. 2. On Wonder Bread, see Wyman, *Better Than Homemade*, 72–74.

50. Meade, "Cereal," 17. On higher expectations for household cleanliness, see Strasser, *Never Done*, 251.

51. On Aunt Jemima, Nancy Green, and the World's Fair, see Manring, *Slave*, 72–78; Albala, *Pancake*, 46–48. On Log Cabin Maple Syrup, see Trager, *The Food Chronology*, 342. On buckwheat in the mid-Atlantic, and on pancakes as a winter food, see Weaver, *A Quaker Woman's Cookbook*, 320–321.

52. Colbrath, *What to Get for Breakfast*, 217–218. Peter Kalm noted that buckwheat pancakes were the favorite winter breakfast of Philadelphia residents in the mid-eighteenth century. Weaver, *A Quaker Woman's Cookbook*, 320–321.

53. On Jiffy-Biscuit, see Trager, *The Food Chronology*, 463, 467. On Bisquick, see Trager, *The Food Chronology*, 467; Patrick and Thompson, *Uncommon History*, 32.

54. Willigen and Willigen, *Food and Everyday Life*, 14; Powell, *Adam by Adam*, 16–17.

Chapter 7: Snacking Redeemed

1. Alger, *Ragged Dick*, 42–43.

2. Rutledge, *The Carolina Housewife*, 45; Michael W. Twitty, "Peanuts," in Rice and Katz-Hyman, *The World of a Slave*, 365–366; Smith, *Peanuts*, 25.

3. *New York Times*, January 21, 1866, 4.

4. *New York Times*, September 17, 1869, 4; letter to the editor, "Wants Peanut Cart Whistles Stopped," 6; "General Gossip: Peanuts and Doughnuts," 2.

5. Letter, Richard Tucker III to Mollie Tucker, Maine, October 27, 1872, Tucker Family Papers, Historic New England, Boston, Massachusetts. On Native American consumption of popcorn, see Berzok, *American Indian Food*, 114; Smith, *Popped Culture*, 18–23. On handheld poppers, see Fussell, *The Story of Corn*, 12.

6. On the steam-driven popcorn machine, see Fussell, *The Story of Corn*, 11; Smith, *Popped Culture*, 90–96.

7. On theaters' hesitation to sell popcorn, see Smith, *Popped Culture*, 100–101.

8. Smith, *Popped Culture*, 101. "Samuel M. Rubin, 85, Vendor," B8.

9. "Huntington's Stock Fair," 2; "Letter Carriers' Picnics," 13; "Picnic for Dr. Hill," C2.

10. On the picnic, see Hern, "Picknicking"; Miller, "Nature's Transformations"; Walter Levy, "Picnics," in Smith, *The Oxford Encyclopedia of Food and Drink in America*, 2:268–271.

11. On peanuts as an early baseball park concession, see Smith, *Peanuts*. On Charles Feltman, see Kraig, "American Hot Dog," 34–35; Immerso, *Coney*

Island, 23. On Chris von der Ahe, see Hetrick, *Chris von der Ahe,* 10–11; Popik, "Hot Dogs at Baseball Games." On Harry Mosley Stevens, see Kraig, "American Hot Dog," 24–25, 29–32. See also McWilliams, *Story Behind the Dish,* 133–138; Kraig, "American Hot Dog," 108–111; Popik, "Hot Dog (Polo Grounds Myth)."

12. "East Side Street Merchants," 50. For a brief historical overview of the pretzel, see Petroski, *Uncommon History,* 36; Mimi Martin, "Pretzel," in Smith, *Oxford Companion to American Food and Drink,* 477–478. On prohibitions against selling pretzels to Native Americans, see Venema, *Beverwijck,* 287. See also Rose, *Food, Drink, and Celebrations of the Hudson Valley,* 47–49.

13. Austin, "Thinning Ranks."

14. "An Old Pretzel Peddler's Death"; "Woman Vendor, 80, Wins Court's Mercy."

15. Bercovici, *The Dirt of New York,* 107.On pretzels' shine, see Voorhees, *Why Do Doughnuts Have Holes,* 117.

16. "Pretzel Minus Beer." On pretzel consumption during Prohibition, see "Pretzels in Upturn with Sales of Beer." On boycotting the pretzel, see Green, *The Uncertainty of Everyday Life,* 145.

17. "Science Gives Pretzel," 28. On innovative pretzel shapes, see Spielvogel, "Pretzels"; "Two Billion Pretzels." On teething pretzels, see Allen, "Let's Eat."

18. Lusas and Rooney, *Snack Foods Processing,* 32; "Pretzels in Upturn with Sales of Beer"; "Pretzel Makers Work on Code."

19. "Will Put Cases on Pretzels," N20; "Pretzel Vendors Fined."

20. "Pretzel's Progress," 36; Rutenberg, "M-m-m, Ice Cream and Pretzels"; "Tea Party Treats," *Woman's Home Companion,* 78; Spielvogel, "Pretzels Become Big Business Item"; "Pretzels in Upturn with Sales of Beer"; "Pretzel Minus Beer"; Weaver, *Pennsylvania Dutch Country Cooking,* 65.

21. "House Unbends to Learn History of the Pretzel," 33. On Arthur McGonigle, see Glueck, "New Twist." On Dague, see "Pretzel at Ninety"; "'Pretzel Town.'"

22. Egelhof, "Candy Makers Know Value of a Brand Name," 1. On the Rueckheim brothers and the invention of Cracker Jack, see Smith, *Eating History,* 14.

23. Twede, "Uneeda," 82–88.

24. Cracker Jack advertisement, *Chicago, the Great Central Market,* 139; Griffin, "Cracker Jack's Sweet Smell of Success," H42. On Robert Gair and package manufacturing, see Hine, *The Total Package,* 62. On the Rueckheim brothers' initial disappointment with cardboard packaging, see Griffin, "Cracker Jack's Sweet Smell of Success," H42. On Henry Eckstein, see Smith, *Eating History,* 125.

25. Cahn, *Out of the Cracker Barrel,* 73. On Uneeda Biscuit packaging and advertising, see Cahn, *Out of the Cracker Barrel,* esp. chs. 6–8; Laird, *Advertising*

Progress, 82–83; Hine, *The Total Package,* 81–83; Levenstein, *Revolution at the Table,* 35–36.

26. Kellogg's Toasted Corn Flake Company, *A Little Journey,* 22; Kellogg's Toasted Corn Flakes advertisement, *Saturday Evening Post,* n.p.

27. Kellogg's Corn Flakes advertisement, *Boy's Life,* 35.

28. Smith, *Peanuts,* 49–55.

29. Theiss and Theiss, "Fake Sweets and Soft Drinks to Be Dodged," 79–80. On the invention of the candy press and the early history of penny candies, see Krondl, *Sweet Invention,* 342–346; Woloson, *Refined Tastes,* ch. 2.

30. On associations of candy and chocolate with women and on candy as character compromising, see Dusselier, "Bonbons"; Cooper, "Love, War, and Chocolate"; Woloson, *Refined Tastes,* ch. 4.

31. Loft's advertisement, *New York Times,* 35. On Tootsie Rolls, see Kimmerle, *Candy,* 154; Wendy A. Woloson, "Candy and Candy Bars," in Smith, *The Oxford Encyclopedia of Food and Drink in America,* 179. On cellophane, see Hine, *The Total Package,* 124–128; Trager, *The Food Chronology,* 484.

32. Grivetti and Shapiro, *Chocolate,* 356. On Hershey's shift from caramel to chocolate, see Trager, *The Food Chronology,* 340; Cadbury, *Chocolate Wars,* 147–148. On chocolate as fighting fuel during wartime, see Dusselier, "Bonbons," 36–40; Moss and Badenoch, *Chocolate,* 64.

33. On the proliferation of new candy bars, see Rees, "Bite-Sized Marketing," 127; Dusselier, "Bonbons," 41. On increases in candy consumption, see Trager, *The Food Chronology,* 410, 484. On the invention of specific candy bars, see Trager, *The Food Chronology,* 471, 473, 485, 489, 496, 481, 493, 506; Batchelor, *American Pop,* 311; Liberman, *American Food,* 53–54, 111.

34. "Armed Forces to Get Fifty Pct. Candy by Govt Order"; "Editorial Bears Out Suggestions on Candy Future"; "Confectioners Plan Program"; Pendergrast, *For God, Country, and Coca-Cola,* 195–197.

35. On the proliferation of salty snacks, see "Snack Foods" in Smith, *Encyclopedia of Junk Food and Fast Food,* 246–247. On popcorn as a patriotic food during the world wars, see Eighmey, *Food Will Win the War,* 187; Smith, *Popped Culture,* 108–111. For an overview of glamorizing food in the mid-twentieth century, see Endrijonas, "Processed Foods."

36. Meade, "Crackers Far Cry," E1. On the early history of crackers, see Cahn, *Out of the Cracker Barrel,* 27–30; Andrew F. Smith, "Crackers," in Smith, *The Oxford Encyclopedia of Food and Drink in America,* 1:353–354.

37. Meade, "Crackers Far Cry," E1. On cracker cookery, see Thorne and Thorne, *Serious Pig,* 178–180. On Ritz Cracker mock apple pie, see McWilliams, *Story Behind the Dish,* 4.

38. Burhans, *Crunch!* 20, 23, 31–32, 44–46. See also McWilliams, *Story Behind the Dish,* 185–190; Smith, *Eating History,* 128–129; Liberman, *American Food,* 83–84; Lusas and Rooney, *Snack Foods Processing,* 30–31.

39. Tasty Chips advertisement, *New York Times,* 35; Lusas and Rooney, *Snack Foods Processing,* 11; Potato Chip Institute International, *Prize-Winning Recipes Starring Potato Chips.*

40. Fisher, "They'll Put Glamour in Your Meals," 92. On tuna noodle casserole, see McFeely, *Can She Bake,* ch. 6; Liberman, *American Food,* 140–141.

41. Neat Treats and Royal Crown Soda advertisement, *Good Housekeeping,* 234.

42. "Related Tie-Ins Boost Sales," 311; Warner, "Odd-Hour Munching in the Machine Age," SM14; Quinlan Butter Pretzels and Gulden's Mustard advertisement, *New York Times,* 34; "Two Pennsylvania Companies Join in Ice Cream, Pretzel Promotion," 99.

43. On Chex Mix, see Liberman, *American Food,* 129–130; Lovegren, *Fashionable Food,* 215. On dips, see Liberman, *American Food,* 136; Lovegren, *Fashionable Food,* 208–211; Smith, *Encyclopedia of Junk Food and Fast Food,* 75–76.

44. Meade, "Easy Snacks," I58; "Help-Yourself Parties Best of All," 41.

45. Wright and Wright, *Guide to Easier Living,* 164, 180; see also 165–190.

46. "Doughboy Boredom," 14; "Snack Shop," 54; "Topics of the Times: Snacks for Hikers," 18.

47. Davis, "Akihito Welcomed"; "Enjoying an American Snack," 30.

48. Owen, "Food: Frankfurters," 24; Beilenson, *ABC,* 43.

49. Owen, "Food: Frankfurters"; Hurley, *Diners, Bowling Alleys, and Trailer Parks,* 76.

50. On postwar domesticity and the rise of television, see Spigel, *Make Room,* 32–35; Young and Young, *The 1950s,* 26.

51. Smith, *Popped Culture,* 122–123. See also "Popcorn Production Up"; "Pop Pops—Popcorn Sales Net Farmers $9,000,000 in 1946." On snacking and television, see Young and Young, *The 1950s,* 102–105.

52. On TV-Time Popcorn and Jiffy Pop, see Smith, *Popped Culture,* 125–128.

53. Kellogg's Rice Krispies advertisement, *Life,* 127; 7-Up advertisement, *Life,* 6; Gentle Raisin Bread advertisement, *Daily Boston Globe,* 21; Maine Sardines advertisement, *Journal of Home Economics,* 607. On Party Mix and Lipton's Onion Soup mix, see Young and Young, *1950s,* 103; Lovegren, *Fashionable Food,* 14–15. On Korn Kurls, see Smith, *Encyclopedia of Junk Food and Fast Food,* 93.

54. Kellogg's Sugar Corn Pops television commercial. On television tie-ins for commercial products, see Spigel, *Make Room,* 158.

55. Thermo-Tray advertisement, *Daily Boston Globe,* 14; Toastmaster Hospitality Set advertisement, *Good Housekeeping,* 180. On tray tables and other television-influenced furniture, see "For the Home: Some New Serving Trays for Holiday Parties," 24; Marling, *As Seen on TV,* 188–193.

56. Smith, *Eating History,* ch. 18.

Chapter 8: The State of the American Meal

1. Quotations are taken from a group interview of three Middlebury College students, October 2011.

2. "Nutritionist: Snacking Leads to Poor Nutrition," N_A10. On the term "junk food," see Popik, "Junk Food," http://www.barrypopik.com/index.php/new_york_city/entry/junk_food (accessed February 24, 2013).

3. On the impact of *Hunger in America* and the development of *Dietary Goals*, see Mudry, *Measured Meals*, 80–85; Nestle, *Food Politics*, 38–42.

4. On the "eat more" message, see Nestle, *Food Politics*, 32–33.

5. On shifts in calorie sources, see Trager, *The Food Chronology*, 636. On rises in sugar and fat consumption, see *Dietary Goals for the United States*. On the rise of soft drink consumption, see Brewster and Jacobson, *The Changing American Diet*; Trager, *The Food Chronology*, 628. On the rise of diet-related chronic conditions, see Nestle, *Food Politics*, 20–31; Levenstein, *Paradox of Plenty*, 202–203.

6. *Dietary Goals for the United States*.

7. On the low-fat trend, see La Berge, "How the Ideology"; Pollan, *Defense of Food*, 50–51, 58–61.

8. On consumption patterns of low-fat products, see La Berge, "How the Ideology," 155, 161. On the Snackwell phenomenon, see Napoleoni, *Rogue Economics*, 136.

9. On the rise of snack food sales and obesity in the 1980s and 1990s, see Nestle, *Food Politics*, 7–8, 19; Critser, *Fat Land*, 3–4, 41. On the rise of snack food sales in the early twenty-first century, see Steinhauer, "Snack Time Never Ends."

10. "Nutritionist: Snacking Leads to Poor Nutrition," N_A10; Critser, *Fat Land*, 39.

11. Critser, *Fat Land*, 40.

12. Wansink, "Environmental Factors," 466. On variety's influence on consumption, see also Critser, *Fat Land*, 40.

13. Nestle, *What to Eat*, 360.

14. On TV commercials' influence on children, see Goldberg, Gorn, and Gibson, "TV Messages," 73; Galst and White, "Unhealthy Persuader." On automatic consumption, see Harris, Bargh, and Brownell, "Priming Effects," 404–413.

15. Nestle, *What to Eat*, 359. On high-calorie foods and TV watching, see Blass et al., "On the Road"; Elizabeth Levin, "Children's Television Programming," in Keller, *Encyclopedia of Obesity*, 1:143–145. On habituation, see Temple et al., "Television Watching."

16. Sebastian et al., "Snacking Patterns of US Adults."

17. Nestle, *What to Eat*, 360; Zizza, Siega-Riz, and Popkin, "Significant Increase in Young Adults' Snacking Between 1977–78 and 1994–96 Represents a Cause for Concern," 303–310.

18. Piernas and Popkin, "Trends in Snacking Among U.S. Children," 398–404; Steinhauer, "Snack Time Never Ends."

19. Pollan, "Out of the Kitchen, onto the Couch," *New York Times Magazine,* July 29, 2009; Cutler, Glaeser, and Shapiro, "Why Have Americans Become More Obese?" 93–118; OECD; Larson, Perry, et al., "Food Preparation by Young Adults."

20. Mancino and Newman, *Who Has Time to Cook?*

21. Critser, *Fat Land,* 32; US Department of Agriculture, *Agricultural Fact Book, 2001–2002,* 21; Critser, *Fat Land,* 32.

22. Kessler, *The End of Overeating,* 12–17.

23. Kessler, *The End of Overeating,* 35–36: Moss, *Salt, Sugar, Fat,* xxvii.

24. French, Story, and Jeffrey, "Environmental Influences on Eating and Physical Activity," 309–335, 314; Ledikwe, Ello-Martin, and Rolls, "Portion Sizes and the Obesity Epidemic," 905–909; Young and Nestle, "The Contribution of Expanding Portion Sizes to the U.S. Obesity Epidemic," 246–249.

25. Wansink and Van Ittersum, "Portion Size Me," 1103–1106, 1103.

26. Stewart, Blisard, and Jolliffe, "Let's Eat Out," 2; Harnack et al., "Effects of Calorie Labeling and Value Size Pricing on Fast Food Meal Choices"; Smith, *Encyclopedia of Junk Food and Fast Food,* 4.

27. Chandon and Wansink, "The Biasing Health Halos of Fast-Food Restaurant Health Claims," 301–314, 307–309.

28. Wilcox et al., "Vicarious Goal Fulfillment," 380–393.

29. Bhardwaj, "Why It's Cheaper to Dine Out Than Eat In"; Jonsson, "For Not That Much More, Americans Opting to Eat Out"; Cutler, Glaeser, and Shapiro, "Why Have Americans Become More Obese?"

30. Kiefer, "Empty Seats"; Larson, Neloson, et al., "Making Time for Meals," 72–79.

31. Larson, Neloson et al., "Making Time for Meals"; Larson, Neumark-Sztainer et al. "Family Meals During Adolescence." Weinstein, *The Surprising Power of Family Meals,* 137, 139.

32. Weinstein, *The Surprising Power of Family Meals,* 206; National Center on Addiction and Substance Abuse at Columbia University, *The Importance of Family Dinners III,* 2.

33. National Center on Addiction and Substance Abuse at Columbia University, *The Importance of Family Dinners III.*

34. Matheson et al., "Children's Food Consumption During Television Viewing"; Fitzpatrick, Edmunds, and Dennison, "Positive Effects of Family Dinner Undone by Television Viewing," 666–671.

BIBLIOGRAPHY

Collections

Buttolph Collection of Menus, New York Public Library

Feeding America: The Historic American Cookbook Project, Michigan State University Libraries

Tucker Family Papers, Historic New England, Boston, Massachusetts

Government Documents

Davis, Charles C. *Agriculture in Europe*. Annual Report of the Secretary of Massachusetts State Board of Agriculture. Boston: Wright & Potter, 1871.

Dietary Goals for the United States. Report of the Select Committee on Nutrition and Human Committee on Nutrition and Human Needs, US Senate. Washington, DC: Government Printing Office, 1977.

Hunt, Caroline Louisa. "The Daily Meals of School Children." US Bureau of Education Bulletin no. 3. Washington, DC: Government Printing Office, 1909.

Mancino, Lisa, and Constance Newman. *Who Has Time to Cook? How Family Resources Influence Food Preparation*. US Department of Agriculture Economic Research Report no. 40. May 2007.

Massachusetts, State of. *Report on the Statistics of Labor*. 6th ed. Boston: n.p., 1875.

New York, State of. *Preliminary Report of the Factory Investigating Commission*. Albany, NY: Argus, 1912.

New York, State of. *Report of the Factory Investigating Commission*. Vol. 2. Albany, NY: J. B. Lyon Company, 1913.

Sebastian, Rhonda S., Cecilia Wilkinson Enn, and Joseph D. Goldman. "Snacking Patterns of US Adults." Food Surveys Research Group Dietary Data Brief No. 4, June 2011. USDA Agricultural Research Group.

Stewart, Hayden, Noel Blisard, and Dean Joliffe. "Let's Eat Out: Americans Weigh Taste, Convenience, and Nutrition." USDA Economic Information Bulletin no. 19. October 2006.

US Bureau of Labor. *Employers' Welfare Work*. Washington, DC: Government Printing Office, 1913.

US Department of Agriculture. *Agricultural Fact Book, 2001–2002.* Washington, DC: US Government Printing Office, 2003.

US Department of Labor, US Women's Bureau. "Negro Women in Industry." Bulletin of the Women's Bureau no. 20. Washington, DC: Government Printing Office, 1922.

Books and Journal Articles

7-Up advertisement. *Life,* March 10, 1958, 6.

"A Chinese Critic." Review of *As a Chinaman Saw Us. New York Times,* July 30, 1904.

"A Convenient Small Toaster." *American Agriculturalist* 38, no. 1 (January 1879): 25.

Abel, Mary Hinman. *Practical Sanitary and Economical Cooking.* 1890. Reprint, Bedford, MA: Applewood Books, n.d.

"Acting Charade." *Godey's Lady's Book* 95 (July 1877): 67.

Adams, John. *The Works of John Adams,* edited by Charles Francis Adams. Vol. 3. Boston: Charles C. Little and James Brown, 1851.

Adams, John, and Abigail Adams. *The Letters of John and Abigail Adams,* edited by Frank Shuffelton. 1876. Reprint, New York: Penguin Classics, 2004.

Adamson, Melitta Weiss. *Food in Medieval Times.* Westport, CT: Greenwood, 2004.

Albala, Ken. *Pancake: A Global History.* London: Reaktion, 2008.

Alcott, William Andrus. *The Boy's Guide to Usefulness.* Boston: Waite, Pierce, 1844.

———. *Lectures on Life and Health.* Boston: Philips, Sampson, 1853.

———. *The Young House-Keeper, or, Thoughts on Food and Cookery.* Boston: George W. Light, 1838.

———. *The Young Mother.* Boston: C. D. Strong, 1851.

———. *Vegetable Diet.* Boston: Marsh, Capon & Lyon, 1838.

Alexander, James Edward. *Transatlantic Sketches.* London: Richard Bentley, 1833.

Alger, Horatio. *Ragged Dick, or, Street Life in New York with the Boot-Blacks.* 1868. Reprint, Philadelphia: John C. Winston, 1910.

Allen, Gary T., and Ken Albala, eds. *The Business of Food: Encyclopedia of the Food and Drink Industries.* Westport, CT: Greenwood, 2007.

Allen, Ida C. Bailey. "Let's Eat: Now Special Pretzels for Teething Babies." *Norwalk Hour,* November 15, 1938.

———. *Mrs. Allen on Cooking, Menus, Service.* Garden City, NY: Doubleday, Page, 1924.

Allen, Irving Lewis. *The City in Slang: New York Life and Popular Speech.* Oxford: Oxford University Press, 1993.

"American Thanksgiving, The." *New England Kitchen Magazine* 2, no. 2 (November 1894): 99.

Ames, Kenneth. *Death in the Dining Room and Other Tales of Victorian Culture.* Philadelphia: Temple University Press, 1992.

"An Old Pretzel Peddler's Death." *New York Times,* October 3, 1892.

Andrews, Charles McClean. *Colonial Folkways: A Chronicle of American Life in the Reign of the Georges.* New Haven, CT: Yale University Press, 1919.

Andrews, Mary Livingston. "Around the Dinner Table." *Good Housekeeping* 19, no. 3 (September 1894): 109–110.

Anonymous. *As a Chinaman Saw Us: Passages from His Letters to a Friend at Home.* New York: D. Appleton, 1904.

Appelbaum, Diana Karter. *Thanksgiving: An American Holiday, An American History.* New York: Facts on File, 1984.

"Armed Forces to Get Fifty Pct. Candy by Govt. Order." *Billboard* 56, no. 43 (October 21, 1944): 68.

Ashe, Thomas. *Travels in America Performed in 1806.* Newburyport, MA: Edmund M. Blunt, 1808.

Aubertin, J. J. *A Fight with Distances: The States, the Hawaiian Islands, Canada, British Columbia, Cuba, the Bahamas.* London: K. Paul, Trench, 1888.

Austin, F. A. "Thinning Ranks of Sidewalk Vendors." *New York Times,* August 19, 1923.

Ayers, William A. "Co-operative Housekeeping." *Good Housekeeping* 18, no. 4 (April 1894): 169–173.

Baker, T. Lindsay, and Julie Philips Baker. *The WPA Oklahoma Slave Narratives.* Norman: University of Oklahoma Press, 1996.

Banning, Kendall. "Deals Across the Table." *System: The Magazine of Business* 15, no. 2 (February 1909): 132–138.

Barnes, Donna, and Peter G. Rose. *Matters of Taste: Food and Drink in Seventeenth-Century Dutch Art and Life.* Syracuse, NY: Syracuse University Press, 2002.

Barnette, Martha. *Ladyfingers and Nun's Tummies: A Lighthearted Look at How Foods Got Their Names.* Lincoln, NE: ASJA Press, 2005.

Barr, Andrew. *Drink: A Social History of America.* New York: Carroll & Graf, 1999.

Barth, Henry. *Travels and Discoveries in North and Central Africa.* Vol. 1. New York: Harper & Brothers, 1857.

Batchelor, Bob. *American Pop: Popular Culture Decade by Decade.* Vol. 1. Westport, CT: Greenwood, 2009.

Bedigian, Dorothea. "African Origins of Sesame Cultivation in the Americas." In *African Ethnobotony in the Americas,* edited by Robert Voeks and John Rashford, 67–122. New York: Springer, 2013.

Beecher, Catharine. *Miss Beecher's Domestic Receipt Book.* New York: Harper, 1850.

Beecher, Catharine, and Harriet Beecher Stowe. *American Woman's Home.* New York: J. B. Ford, 1869.

Beilenson, Edna. *The ABC of Canapés.* N.p.: Peter Pauper Press, 1953.

Bellin, Mildred Grosberg. *The Jewish Cook Book.* New York: Tudor, 1958.

Bennett, H. Arnold. "The Hot Lunch: A Symposium: Hot Lunch Served by a Mother's Club." *Journal of Rural Education* 2, no. 9 (May 1922): 418–419.

Bentley, Amy. *Eating for Victory: Food Rationing and the Politics of Domesticity.* Urbana: University of Illinois Press, 1998.

Bercovici, Konrad. *The Dirt of New York.* New York: Boni & Liveright, 1919.

Berzok, Linda Murry. *American Indian Food.* Westport, CT: Greenwood, 2005.

Beste, J. Richard. *The Wabash: Or, Adventures of an English Gentleman's Family in the Interior of America.* London: Hurst & Blackett, 1855.

Beverley, Robert. *The History of Virginia.* 1705. Reprint, Richmond: J. W. Randolph, 1855.

Bhardwaj, Nick. "Why It's Cheaper to Dine Out Than Eat In." *Fiscal Times,* December 3, 2011.

Birdsall, Katharine Newbold, "A Luncheon Plan," In *How to Make Money: Eighty Novel and Practical Suggestions for Untrained Women's Work, Based on Actual Experience,* edited by Katharine Newbold Birdsall, 47–52. New York: Doubleday, Page, 1903.

Birkbeck, Morris. *Notes on a Journey in America.* 2nd ed. London: Severn, 1818.

Blane, William N. *An Excursion Through the United States and Canada During the Years 1822–23.* London: Baldwin, Cradock & Joy, 1824.

Blass, Elliott M., Daniel R. Anderson, Heather L. Kirkorian, Tiffany A. Pempek, Iris Price, and Melanie F. Koleini. "On the Road to Obesity: Television Viewing Increases Intake of High-Density Food." *Physiology and Behavior* 88, no. 4–5 (July 2006): 597–604.

Bobrow-Strain, Aaron. *White Bread: A Social History of the Store-Bought Loaf.* Boston: Beacon, 2012.

Bombo, Dr. *Reflections of a Bass-Drum Player: Or, Everything Worth Thinking About.* New York: Eastern, 1904.

Bose, Sudhindra. *Fifteen Years in America.* Calcutta: Kar, Majumder, 1920. Reprint, New York: Arno, 1974.

Braudel, Fernand. *The Structures of Everyday Life: The Limits of the Possible.* 1971. Reprint, Berkeley: University of California Press, 1992.

Brewer, Priscilla J. *From Fireplace to Cookstove: Technology and the Domestic Ideal in America.* Syracuse, NY: Syracuse University Press, 2000.

Brewster, Letitia, and Michael F. Jacobson. *The Changing American Diet.* Washington, DC: Center for Science in the Public Interest, 1978.

Browne, Ray B., and Lawrence A. Kreiser Jr. *The Civil War and Reconstruction.* Westport, CT: Greenwood, 2003.

Brownell, Kelly D. *Food Fight: The Inside Story of the Food Industry, America's Obesity Crisis, and What We Can Do About It.* New York: McGraw-Hill, 2004.

Brumberg, Joan Jacobs. "The Appetite as Voice." In *Food and Culture: A Reader*, edited by Carole M. Counihan and Penny van Esterik, 159–179. New York: Routledge, 1997.

Bryant, Louise Stevens. *School Feeding: Its History and Practice at Home and Abroad*. Philadelphia: J. B. Lippincott Company, 1913.

Buckingham, J. S. *America: Historical, Descriptive, Statistic*. London: Fisher, 1841.

Burdick, Jennie Ellis. *What Shall We Have to Eat?* New York: University Society, 1922.

Burhans, Dirk E. *Crunch! A History of the Great American Potato Chip*. Madison, WI: Terrace, 2008.

Burnaby, Andrew. *Burnaby's Travels Through North America*. 1798. Reprint, New York: A. Wessels, 1902.

Byington, Margaret Frances. *Homestead: The Households of a Mill Town*. New York: Charities Publication Committee, 1910.

Byrd, William. *The Secret Diary of William Byrd of Westover, 1709–1712*. Richmond, VA: Dietz, 1941.

Cadbury, Deborah. *Chocolate Wars: The 150-Year Rivalry Between the World's Greatest Chocolate Makers*. New York: PublicAffairs, 2010.

Cahn, William. *Out of the Cracker Barrel: From Animal Crackers to Zuzus*. New York: Simon & Shuster, 1969.

Calvin, Henrietta W. "Warm Lunches for Rural Schools." *School Life*, March 1, 1921, 11.

Carlin, Martha, and Joel Thomas Rosenthal, eds. *Food and Eating in Medieval Europe*. London: Hambledon, 1998.

Carlisle, Nancy, Melinda Talbot Nasardinov, and Jennifer Pustz. *America's Kitchens*. Gardiner, ME: Tilbury House, 2008.

Carroll, Abigail. "'Colonial Custard' and 'Pilgrim Soup': Culinary Nationalism and the Colonial Revival." PhD diss., Boston University, 2007.

Carson, Gerald. *Cornflake Crusade*. New York: Rinehart, 1957.

Carter, Susannah. *The Frugal Housewife*. 1765. Reprint, New York: G. & R. Waite, 1803.

Catlin, George. *Illustrations of the Manners, Customs, and Condition of the North American Indian*. Vol. 1. London: Henry G. Bohn, 1851.

Chandon, Pierre, and Brian Wansink. "The Biasing Health Halos of Fast-Food Restaurant Health Claims: Lower Calorie Estimates and Higher Side-Dish Consumption Intentions." *Journal of Consumer Research* 34, no. 3 (October 2007): 301–314.

Chase, A. W. *Dr. Chase's Recipes, or Information for Everybody*. Ann Arbor, MI: Author, 1864.

Chastellux, Francois Jean. *Travels in North America*. 1828. Reprint, Bedford, MA: Applewood, n.d.

Childs, George W. "The Etiquette of Dining and Dinner Giving." *Good House-keeping*, March 1, 1890, 193–196.

Clark, Clifford E., Jr. "The Vision of the Dining Room: Plan Books, Dreams and Middle-Class Realities." In *Dining in America, 1850–1900,* edited by Kathryn Grover, 142–172. Amherst: University of Massachusetts Press, 1987.

Clarkson, Janet. *Pie: A Global History.* London: Reaktion, 2009.

Cobbett, William. *A Year's Residence in the United States.* London: Sherwood, Needly & Jones, 1819.

Coe, Sophie D. *America's First Cuisines.* Austin: University of Texas Press, 1994.

Cohen, David Steven. *The Dutch-American Farm.* New York: New York University Press, 1992.

Colbrath, M. Tarbox. *What to Get for Breakfast.* Boston: James H. Earle, 1883.

Collier, Price. *America and the Americans from a French Point of View.* New York: Scribner's Sons, 1897.

Collins, Anna Maria. *The Great Western Cook Book.* New York: A. S. Barnes, 1857.

Colquhoun, Kate. *Taste: The Story of Britain Through Its Cooking.* New York: Bloomsbury, 2007.

"Confectioners Plan Program: War Restrictions Will Be Main Topic at National Convention." *Billboard* 55, no. 23 (June 5, 1943): 65, 71.

Conforti, Joseph A. *Saints and Strangers: New England in British North America.* Baltimore: Johns Hopkins University Press, 2006.

Conlin, Joseph, R. *Bacon, Beans, and Galantines: Food and Foodways on the Western Mining Frontier.* Las Vegas: University of Nevada Press, 1986.

"Cookery." *The Magazine of Domestic Economy* 1, no. 7 (January 1836): 213–216.

Cooper, Ann, and Lisa M. Holmes. *Lunch Lessons: Changing the Way We Feed Our Children.* New York: HarperCollins, 2006.

Cooper, Gail. "Love, War, and Chocolate: Gender and the American Candy Industry, 1890–1930." In *His and Hers: Gender, Consumption, and Technology,* edited by Roger Horowitz and Arwen Mohun, 67–94. Charlottesville: University Press of Virginia, 1998.

Corson, Juliet. *Miss Corson's Practical American Cookery.* New York: Dodd, Mead, and Co., 1886.

Covey, Herbert C., and Dwight Eisnach. *What the Slaves Ate: Recollections of African-American Food and Foodways.* Santa Barbara, CA: ABC-CLIO, 2009.

Cowan, John F. "How Busy People Eat." *Christian Work and the Evangelist,* May 7, 1904, 656.

Cowles, Florence A. *Seven Hundred Sandwiches.* New York: Little, Brown, 1928.

Cracker Jack advertisement. *Chicago, the Great Central Market: A Magazine of Business* 4, no. 3 (July 1907): 139.

Critser, Greg. *Fat Land: How Americans Became the Fattest People in the World.* New York: Houghton Mifflin, 2003.

Croly, Jane Cunningham. *Jennie June's American Cookery Book.* New York: American News Company, 1870.

Cromley, Elizabeth Collins. *The Food Axis: Cooking, Eating, and the Architecture of American Houses.* Charlottesville: University of Virginia Press, 2010.

Cronon, William. *Changes in the Land: Indians, Colonists, and the Ecology of New England.* New York: Hill & Wang, 1983.

Curtin, Kathleen, Sandra L. Oliver, and Plimoth Plantation. *Giving Thanks: Thanksgiving Recipes and History from Pilgrims to Pumpkin Pie.* New York: Clarkson Potter, 2005.

Cutler, David M., Edward L. Glaeser, and Jesse M. Shapiro. "Why Have Americans Become More Obese?" *Journal of Economic Perspectives* 1, no. 3 (2003): 93–118.

Dallas, Eneas Sweetland. *Kettner's Book of the Table.* London: DuLau, 1877.

Daniels, Roger. *Coming to America: A History of Immigration and Ethnicity in American Life.* 2nd ed. New York: HarperCollins, 2002.

Dary, David. *Frontier Medicine: From the Atlantic to the Pacific, 1492–1941.* New York: Knopf, 2008.

Davidson, Alan. *Oxford Companion to Food.* Oxford: Oxford University Press, 1999.

———. *Penguin Companion to Food.* New York: Penguin, 2002.

Davis, Lawrence E. "Akihito Welcomed in San Francisco: Japanese Prince Proves Good Mixer on Ship and Orders a Hot Dog Snack on Landing." *New York Times,* April 12, 1953.

De Bryas, Madeleine, and Jacqueline de Bryas. *A Frenchwoman's Impressions of America.* New York: Century, 1920.

Deetz, James. *In Small Things Forgotten: An Archaeology of Early American Life.* Rev. ed. New York: Anchor, 1996.

Des Moines Hosiery Mills advertisement. *Factory: The Magazine of Management* 26, no. 2 (August 1921): 191.

Devereux, Marian S. "The Philosophy of Eating: Dinner." *Good Housekeeping,* September 5, 1885, 5.

DeWitt, Dave. *The Founding Foodies: How Washington, Jefferson, and Franklin Revolutionized American Cuisine.* Naperville, IL: Source, 2010.

Dickens, Charles. *American Notes.* 1842. Reprint, New York: Viking Penguin, 1972.

Diner, Hasia R. *Hungering for America: Italian, Irish, and Jewish Foodways in the Age of Migration.* Cambridge, MA: Harvard University Press, 2001.

"Discoveries by Our Observers and Experimenters." *Good Housekeeping* 39, no. 3 (September 1904): 327–336.

"Doughboy Boredom Is Foe to Red Cross: Shows, Games, and Snacks Help to Keep Troops in Ireland Fit." *New York Times,* March 15, 1942.

Douglas, Mary. "Deciphering a Meal." *Daedalus* 101, no. 1 (1972): 61–81.

Dow, George Francis. *Every Day Life in the Massachusetts Bay Colony*. 1935. Reprint, Bowie, MD: Heritage Books, Inc., 2002.

Duis, Perry R. *Challenging Chicago: Coping with Everyday Life, 1837–1920*. Urbana: University of Illinois Press, 1998.

———. *The Saloon: Public Drinking in Chicago and Boston, 1880–1920*. Urbana: University of Illinois Press, 1999.

Dunaway, Wilma A. *The African-American Family in Slavery and Emancipation*. Cambridge: Cambridge University Press, 2003.

Duncan, John M. *Travels Through Part of the United States and Canada in 1818 and 1819*. Glasgow, Scotland: University Press, 1823.

Dunn, Shirley. "Understanding the Mabee House Fireplace." *Newsletter of the Dutch Barn Preservation Society* 11, no. 1 (spring 1998). http://dutchbarns. info/dbpsnewssp98.htm (accessed January 12, 2012).

DuPuis, E. Melanie. *Nature's Perfect Food: How Milk Became America's Drink*. New York: New York University Press, 2002.

Dusselier, Jane. "Bonbons, Lemon Drops, and Oh Henry! Bars: Candy, Consumer Culture, and the Construction of Gender, 1895–1920." In *Kitchen Culture in America: Popular Representations of Food, Gender, and Race*, edited by Sherrie A. Inness, 13–49. Philadelphia: University of Pennsylvania Press, 2001.

"Duties and Rights of Mill Girls." *New England Offering*, n.s., July 1848, 79–82.

Dwight, Timothy. *New-England and New-York*. New Haven, CT: Timothy Dwight, 1822.

Earle, Alice Morse. *Customs and Fashions in Old New England*. New York: C. Scribner's Sons, 1894.

———. *Home Life in Colonial Days*. New York: Macmillan, 1898.

"East Side Street Merchants." *Harper's Weekly*, January 7, 1891, 50.

Eden, Trudy. *The Early American Table: Food and Society in the New World*. DeKalb: Northern Illinois University Press, 2010.

Edge, John T. *Fried Chicken: An American Story*. New York: Putnam's, 2004.

Edington, D. J. "Six Hundred a Year." *Good Housekeeping* 47, no. 1 (July 1908): 35–36.

"Editor's Chair." *Harper's New Monthly Magazine* 22, no. 130 (March 1861): 556–560.

Editorial. *Lowell Offering and Magazine*, December 1842, 69.

———. *New England Kitchen Magazine* 4, no. 2 (November 1895): 99.

"Editorial Bears Out Suggestions on Candy Future." *Billboard* 55, no. 34 (August 21, 1943): 69.

Egelhof, Joseph. "Candy Makers Know Value of a Brand Name." *Chicago Daily Tribune*, November 9, 1951.

Eighmey, Katherine Rae. *Food Will Win the War: Minnesota Crops, Cooks, and Conservation During World War I*. St. Paul: Minnesota Historical Society, 2010.

Elias, Megan J. *Food in the United States, 1890–1945.* Westport, CT: Greenwood, 2009.

Ellis, Markman. *The Coffee House: A Cultural History.* London: Orion, 2004.

Ellsworth, William W. "The Aldine Club." *The Critic,* March 6, 1897, 159–161.

Emerson, Lucy. *The New-England Cookery.* Montpelier, VT: Printed for Josiah Parks, 1808.

Emery, Sarah Smith. *Reminiscences of a Newburyport Nonagenarian.* Newburyport, MA: William H. Huse, 1879.

Endrijonas, Erika. "Processed Foods from Scratch: Cooking for a Family in the 1950s." In *Kitchen Culture in America: Popular Representations of Food, Gender, and Race,* edited by Sherrie A. Inness, 157–173. Philadelphia: University of Pennsylvania Press, 2001.

English, Beth Anne. *A Common Thread: Labor, Politics, and Capital Mobility in the Textile Industry.* Athens: University of Georgia Press, 2006.

"Enjoying an American Snack." Associated Press wire photo. *New York Times,* July 23, 1951.

Entropy. "The Tin Dinner Pail Again?" *American Machinist,* October 21, 1920, 778.

Fales, Winnifred S. *The Easy Housekeeping Book.* Boston: Small, Maynard & Company, 1923.

Farley, Harriet. "Letters from Susan." *Lowell Offering* 4 (June 1844): 170.

Farmer, Fannie Merritt. *The Boston Cooking-School Cook Book.* Boston: Little, Brown, 1896.

Farnham, Thomas Jefferson. *Farnham's Travels in the Great Western Prairies.* 1843. Reprint, Carlisle, MA: Applewood, n.d.

Fischer, David Hackett. *Albion's Seed: Four British Folkways in America.* Oxford: Oxford University Press, 1989.

Fischer, Kirsten, and Eric Hinderaker. *Colonial American History.* Malden, MA: Blackwell, 2002.

Fish, Elmer Henry. *How to Manage Men: The Principles of Employing Labor.* New York: Engineering Magazine Company, 1920.

Fisher, John C. *Food in the American Military: A History.* Jefferson, NC: McFarland & Company, 2011.

Fisher, Katharine. "They'll Put Glamour in Your Meals." *Good Housekeeping* 120, no. 1 (January 1945): 79–81.

Fithian, Philip Vickers. *Journal and Letters, 1767–1774,* edited by John Williams. Princeton, NJ: The University Library, 1900.

Fitzpatrick, Eileen, Lynn S. Edmunds, and Barbara A. Dennison. "Positive Effects of Family Dinner Undone by Television Viewing." *Journal of the American Dietetic Association* 107, no. 4 (April 2007): 666–671.

Fitzpatrick, Joan, ed. *Renaissance Food from Rabelais to Shakespeare: Culinary Readings and Culinary Histories.* Surrey, UK: Ashgate, 1991.

"Food in Its Relation to Health." *Cassell's Family Magazine*. London: Cassel, 1886.

"For the Home: Some New Serving Trays for Holiday Parties." *New York Times*, October 31, 1950.

Forty, Adrian. *Objects of Desire: Design and Society Since 1750*. London: Thames & Hudson, 2000.

Franklin, Benjamin. *The Autobiography of Benjamin Franklin*. Philadelphia: Henry Altemus, 1895.

———. *The Writings of Benjamin Franklin*, edited by Albert Henry Smyth. New York: Macmillan, 1907.

Frederick, Christine. *Household Engineering: Scientific Management in the Kitchen*. Chicago: American School of Home Economics, 1919.

Freeman, June. *The Making of the Modern Kitchen: A Cultural History*. New York: Berg, 2004.

French, Simone A., Mary Story, and Robert W. Jeffrey. "Environmental Influences on Eating and Physical Activity." *Annual Review of Public Health* 22 (May 2001): 309–335.

Fussell, Betty Harper. *The Story of Corn*. 1992. Reprint, Albuquerque: University of New Mexico Press, 2004.

Gabaccia, Donna R. *We Are What We Eat: Ethnic Food and the Making of Americans*. Cambridge, MA: Harvard University Press, 1998.

Galst, Joann Paley, and Mary Alice White. "Unhealthy Persuader: The Reinforcing Value of Television and Children's Purchase-Influencing Attempts at the Supermarket." *Child Development* 47, no. 4 (December 1976): 1089–1096.

Gardiner, John, David Hepburn, and John Randolph. *The American Gardener*. 3rd ed. Washington, DC: William Cooper, 1826.

Gately, Iain. *Drink: A Cultural History of Alcohol*. New York: Gotham, 2009.

"General Gossip: Peanuts and Doughnuts." *Chicago Daily Tribune*, December 13, 1877, 2.

Gentle Raisin Bread advertisement. *Daily Boston Globe*, May 7, 1952.

Giedion, Siegfried. *Mechanization Takes Command: A Contribution to Anonymous History*. 1948. Reprint, New York: Norton, 1969.

Gillette, Fanny Lemira. *White House Cook Book*. Chicago: R. S. Peale, 1887.

Gillis, John R. *A World of Their Own Making: Myth, Ritual, and the Quest for Family Values*. Cambridge, MA: Harvard University Press, 1996.

Gilman, Charlotte Perkins. *What Diantha Did, 1909–1910*. Fairford, UK: Echo Library, 2009.

Gilman, Sander L., ed. *Diets and Dieting: A Cultural Encyclopedia*. New York: Routledge, 2008.

Gipson, Lawrence Henry, ed. *The Moravian Indian Mission on White River: Diaries and Letters, May 5, 1799, to November 12, 1806*. Indianapolis: Indiana Historical Bureau, 1938.

Glueck, Grace H. "New Twist in an Old Biscuit." *New York Times,* June 25, 1951, SM52.

Goldberg, Marvin E., Gerald J. Gorn, and Wendy Gibson. "TV Messages for Snack and Breakfast Foods: Do They Influence Children's Preferences?" *Journal of Consumer Research* 5, no. 2 (September 1978): 73–81.

Goodrich, Samuel. *Recollections of a Lifetime.* New York: Miller, Orton & Mulligan, 1856.

Gordon, Beverly. *The Saturated World: Aesthetic Meaning, Intimate Objects, Women's Lives, 1890–1940.* Knoxville: University of Tennessee Press, 2006.

Gottlieb, Elizabeth. *The Family in the Western World: From the Black Death to the Industrial Age.* New York: Oxford University Press, 1993.

Gow, Alexander Murdoch. *Good Morals and Gentle Manners: For Schools and Families.* Cincinnati, OH: Van Antwerp, Bragg, 1873.

Graham, Stephen. *With Poor Immigrants to America.* New York: Macmillan, 1914.

Grape Nuts advertisement. *New York Times,* October 9, 1903.

Gratton, Henry Pearson, ed. *As a Chinaman Saw Us: Passages from His Letters to a Friend at Home.* New York: D. Appleton, 1904.

Green, Harvey. *Fit for America: Health, Fitness, Sport, and American Society.* Baltimore: Johns Hopkins University Press, 1986.

———. *The Uncertainty of Everyday Life: 1915–1945.* Fayetteville: University of Arkansas Press, 2000.

Green, Thomas. "Tricksters and the Marketing of Breakfast Cereal." *Journal of Popular Culture* 40, no. 1 (January 2007): 49–68.

Greer, Carlotta C. *Food and Victory.* Norwood, MA: Norwood, 1918.

———. *A Text-Book of Cooking.* Boston: Allyn & Bacon, 1915.

Gref, Lynn G. *The Rise and Fall of American Technology.* New York: Algora, 2010.

Griffin, Dick. "Cracker Jack's Sweet Smell of Success." *Chicago Tribune,* November 20, 1983.

Grimes, William. *Appetite City: A Culinary History of New York.* New York: North Point Press, 2009.

Grivetti, Louis E., and Howard-Yana Shapiro. *Chocolate: History, Culture, and Heritage.* New York: Wiley, 2012.

Grover, Kathryn, ed. *Dining in America, 1850–1900.* Amherst: University of Massachusetts Press, 1987.

Grummet, David, and Rachel Muers. *Theology on the Menu: Asceticism, Meat and the Christian Diet.* New York: Routledge, 2010.

Hale, Edward Everett. *A New England Boyhood.* Boston: Little, Brown, 1910.

Hale, Lucretia P. "The Bruntons' Family Problem." *Good Housekeeping* 1, no. 4 (June 27, 1885): 10–11.

Hale, Sarah Josepha. *Northwood; or, Life North and South: Showing the True Character of Both.* 1827. Reprint, New York: H. Long & Brother, 1852.

Haley, Andrew P. *Turning the Tables: The Aristocratic Restaurant and the Rise of the American Middle Class, 1880–1920.* Chapel Hill: University of North Carolina Press, 2011.

Hall, Florence Howe. *The Correct Thing in Good Society.* 1888. Reprint, Boston: Estes & Lauriat, 1902.

Hall, William Whitty. *Dyspepsia and Its Kindred Diseases.* New York: R. Worthington, 1877.

Halttunen, Karen. *Confidence Men and Painted Women: A Study of Middle-Class Culture in America, 1830–1870.* New Haven, CT: Yale University Press, 1982.

Hamilton, Alexander. *The Itinerarium of Dr. Alexander Hamilton,* edited by Carl Bridenbaugh. Chapel Hill: University of North Carolina Press, 1948.

Hamilton, Alissa. *Squeezed: What You Don't Know About Orange Juice.* New Haven, CT: Yale University Press, 2009.

Harbury, Katharine E. *Colonial Virginia's Cooking Dynasty.* Columbia: University of South Carolina Press, 2004.

Harland, Marion. *Breakfast, Luncheon, Tea.* New York: Scribner, Armstrong, 1875.

Harnack, Lisa J., Simone A. French, J. Michael Oakes, Mary T. Story, Robert W. Jeffrey, and Sarah A. Rydell. "Effects of Calorie Labeling and Value Size Pricing on Fast Food Meal Choices: Results from an Experimental Trial." *International Journal of Behavioral Nutrition and Physical Activity* 5, no. 63 (December 2008): 63.

Harris, Jennifer L., John A. Bargh, and Kelly D. Brownell. "Priming Effects of Television Food Advertising on Eating Behavior." *Health Psychology* 28, no. 4 (2009): 404–413.

Hartman, Zoe. "Driving Out the High School Pickle." *American Cookery* 19, no. 1 (June–July 1914): 22–27.

Hawxhurst, H. H. "Food in Indigestion." *Table Talk* 10, no. 5 (May 1895): 146–148.

Hayden, Dolores. *The Grand Domestic Revolution: A History of Feminist Designs for American Homes, Neighborhoods, and Cities.* Cambridge, MA: MIT Press, 1991.

Head, Katharine. "A Lunch Club." *Outlook,* April 7, 1894, 628–629.

——. "Lunch Clubs." In *Christianity Practically Applied,* edited by *Evangelical Alliance for the United States of America,* 284–286. New York: Baker & Taylor, 1894.

Hearn, Lafcadio. *La Cuisine Creole.* New Orleans: F. F. Hansell, 1885.

"Help-Yourself Parties Best of All." *Daily Boston Globe,* April 8, 1932.

Henderson, Mary F. *Practical Cooking and Dinner Giving.* New York: Harper & Brothers, 1876.

Henisch, Bridget Ann. *Fast and Feast: Food in Medieval Society.* University Park: Pennsylvania State University Press, 1976.

Hern, Mary Ellen W. "Picnicking in the Northeastern United States, 1840–1900." *Winterthur Portfolio* 24, no. 2–3 (summer–autumn 1989): 139–152.

Herrick, Christine Terhune. "The Art of Dining: The Home Dinner Carefully Considered." *Good Housekeeping*, August 22, 1885, 19.

———. *What to Eat, How to Serve It.* New York: Harper & Brothers, 1891.

Hess, Karen, ed. *Martha Washington's Booke of Cookery.* New York: Columbia University Press, 1995.

Hetrick, J. Thomas. *Chris von der Ahe and the St. Louis Browns.* Lanham, MD: Scarecrow Press, 1990.

Hiatt, John, ed. *Diary of William Owen from November 10, 1824, to April 20, 1825.* 1906. Reprint, Carlisle, MA: Applewood Books, n.d.

Hine, Thomas. *The Total Package: The Secret History and Hidden Meanings of Boxes, Bottles, Cans, and Other Persuasive Containers.* Boston: Little, Brown, 1995.

Hodgson, Adam. *Letters from North America.* London: Hurst, Robinson, 1820.

Holloway, Joseph E., ed. *Africanisms in American Culture.* 2nd ed. Bloomington: Indiana University Press, 2005.

Hooker, Ellen Bliss. "A Few Homely Words on the Matter of Conversation." *Good Housekeeping*, February 4, 1888, 162–163.

Hope, Annette. *A Caledonian Feast.* Edinburgh, Scotland: Canongate, 2002.

Hopkins, Carrie Lieurence. "A Girl's Hot Lunch Club." *Journal of Rural Education* 2, no. 9 (May 1922): 419–422.

Hopkins, Muriel. "Hot Lunches at School." *Oklahoma Teacher* 2, no. 4 (December 1920): 9.

"House Unbends to Learn History of the Pretzel." *New York Times,* May 8, 1951.

"Household Department." *Pomoroy's Democrat,* November 25, 1876.

"How the Breakfast Foods Are Absorbing the Cattle Ranges of the West." *New York Times,* July 25, 1909.

Howells, William Dean. *The Rise of Silas Lapham.* 1884. Reprint, Boston: Houghton Mifflin Company, 1922.

Howland, Esther Allen. *The New England Economical Housekeeper.* Cincinnati, OH: H. W. Derby, 1845.

Hulme, Thomas. *Hulme's Journal, 1818–19.* Cleveland: A. H. Clark, 1904.

Humble, Nicole. *Cake: A Global History.* London: Reaktion, 2010.

Hunt, Carl. "How a Druggist Has Increased His Drug and Cigar Sales by Serving Lunches at His Soda Fountain." *Magazine of Business* 24, no. 4 (October 1913): 432–433.

"Huntington's Stock Fair: Long Island Farmer's Have a Day's Outing." *New York Times,* September 20, 1888.

Hurley, Andrew. *Diners, Bowling Alleys, and Trailer Parks: Chasing the American Dream in Postwar Consumer Culture.* New York: Basic Books, 2002.

"Hygienic Rules." *The Eclectic: A Monthly Magazine of Useful Knowledge* 2 (December 1870): 325–327.

Iacobbo, Karen, and Michael Iacobbo. *Vegetarian America: A History.* Westport, CT: Praeger, 2004.

Ierley, Merritt. *The Comforts of Home: The American House and the Evolution of Modern Convenience.* New York: Three Rivers, 1999.

Immerso, Michael. *Coney Island: The People's Playground.* New Brunswick, NJ: Rutgers University Press, 2002.

Inness, Sherrie A. *Dinner Roles: American Women and Culinary Culture.* Iowa City: University of Iowa Press, 2001.

———. *Kitchen Culture in America: Popular Representation of Food, Gender, and Race.* Philadelphia: University of Pennsylvania Press, 2001.

Irving, Washington. *The Journals of Washington Irving,* edited by William P. Trent and George S. Hellman. Boston: Bibliophile Society, 1919.

———. *Washington Irving's Works: Knickerbocker's History of New York.* New York: G. P. Putnam's Sons, 1895.

Isaac, Rhys. *The Transformation of Virginia, 1740–1790.* Chapel Hill: University of North Carolina Press, 1999.

Jackle, John A., and Keith A. Sculle. *Fast Food: Roadside Restaurants in the Automobile Age.* Baltimore, MD: Johns Hopkins University Press, 1999.

Jackson, James Caleb. *How to Treat the Sick Without Medicine.* Dansville, NY: Austin, Jackson, 1871.

Jacobs, Jaap. *The Colony of New Netherland: A Dutch Settlement in Seventeenth-Century America.* Ithaca, NY: Cornell University Press, 2009.

Jamison, John Franklin, ed. *Narratives of New Netherland, 1609–1644.* Vol. 6. New York: Charles Scribner's Sons, 1909.

Jonsson, Patrik. "For Not That Much More, Americans Opting to Eat Out." *Christian Science Monitor,* October 6, 2006.

Josselyn, John. *New England's Rarities Discovered.* 1672. Reprint, Bedford, MA: Applewood, 1986.

Kalm, Peter. *The America of 1750: Peter Kalm's Travels in North America: The English Version of 1770,* edited by Adolph B. Benson. New York: Dover, 1964.

Kasson, John F. "Rituals of Dining: Table Manners in Victorian America." In *Dining in America, 1850–1900,* edited by Kathryn Grover, 114–141. Amherst: University of Massachusetts Press, 1987.

———. *Rudeness and Civility: Manners in Nineteenth-Century Urban America.* New York: Hill & Wang, 1990.

Katz, Sandor Ellix, and Michael Pollan. *The Art of Fermentation: An In-Depth Look at Essential Concepts and Processes from Around the World.* White River Junction, VT: Chelsea Green, 2012.

Katz, Solomon H., and William Woys Weaver, eds. *Encyclopedia of Food and Culture.* New York: Charles Scribner's Sons, 2003.

Keene, Jennifer D. *World War I.* Westport, CT: Greenwood, 2006.

Keller, Kathleen. *Encyclopedia of Obesity.* Thousand Oaks, CA: Sage, 2008.

Kellogg's Corn Flakes advertisement. *Boy's Life* 26, no. 1 (January 1936): 35.

Kellogg's Rice Krispies advertisement. *Life,* November 9, 1953, 127.

Kellogg's Sugar Corn Pops television commercial featuring Guy Madison and AndyDevine,1950s.YouTube.http://www.youtube.com/watch?v=vZ5CPC vf6aA (accessed December 10, 2012).

Kellogg's Toasted Corn Flake Company. *A Little Journey to the Home of Kellogg's Toasted Corn Flakes.* Battle Creek, MI: Kellogg's Toasted Corn Flake Company, 1916.

Kellogg's Toasted Corn Flakes advertisement. *Saturday Evening Post,* May 25, 1914.

Kelvinator Home Economics Department. *New Delights from the Kitchen.* Dayton, OH: Reynolds and Reynolds, n.d.

Kerber, Linda K. *Women of the Republic: Intellect and Ideology in Revolutionary America.* Durham: University of North Carolina Press, 1997.

Kessler, David A. *The End of Overeating: Taking Control of the Insatiable American Appetite.* New York: Rodale, 2009.

Kiefer, Heather Mason. "Empty Seats: Fewer Families Eat Together." Gallup, January 20, 2004. http://www.gallup.com/poll/10336/empty-seats-fewer -families-eat-together.aspx (accessed October 18, 2011).

Kieran, John. "A Snack Isn't a Meal." *New York Times,* September 18, 1930.

Kimball, Chris. *Fannie's Last Supper: Re-Creating One Amazing Meal from Fannie Farmer's 1896 Cookbook.* New York: Hypernion, 2012.

Kimmerle, Beth. *Candy: The Sweet History.* Portland, OR: Collectors Press, 2003.

King, Caroline Howard. *When I Lived in Salem, 1822–1866.* Cambridge, MA: Stephen Daye, 1937.

Kingsdale, John M. "'The Poor Man's Club': Social Functions of the Urban Working-Class Saloon." *American Quarterly* 25, no. 4 (October 1973): 472–489.

Kipfer, Barbara Ann. *The Culinarian: A Kitchen Desk Reference.* Hoboken, NJ: Wiley, 2011.

Kirk, Eleanor. "Common Sense." *Arthur's Illustrated Home Magazine* 44, no. 11 (November 1876): 626.

Kittredge, Mabel. "Experiments with School Lunches in New York City." *Journal of Home Economics* 2, no. 2 (April 1910): 174–177.

Kniffen, Fred. "The Outdoor Oven in Louisiana." *Louisiana History: The Journal of the Louisiana Historical Association* 1, no. 1 (winter 1960): 25–35.

Kraig, Bruce. "American Hot Dog: Standardised Taste and Regional Variations." In *Oxford Symposium on Food and Cookery 1987: Taste,* edited by Tom Jaine, 108–113. London: Prospect, 1988.

————. *Hot Dog: A Global History.* London: Reaktion, 2009.

Krampner, Jon. *Creamy and Crunchy: An Informal History of Peanut Butter, the All-American Food.* New York: Columbia University Press, 2013.

Kreidberg, Marjorie. *Food on the Frontier: Minnesota Cooking from 1850 to 1900 with Selected Recipes.* St. Paul: Minnesota Historical Society, 1975.

Krondl, Michael. *Sweet Invention: A History of Dessert.* Chicago: Chicago Review Press, 2011.

Kurlansky, Mark. *The Big Oyster: History on the Half Shell.* New York: Random House, 2006.

————. *The Food of a Younger Land.* New York: Riverhead, 2009.

La Berge, Ann F. "How the Ideology of Low Fat Conquered America." *Journal of the History of Medicine* 63, no. 2 (April 2008): 137–177.

Laird, Pamela Walker. *Advertising Progress: American Business and the Rise of Consumer Culture.* Baltimore: Johns Hopkins University Press, 1998.

Lambert, John. *Travels Through Canada and the United States of North America in the Years 1806, 1807, and 1808.* 2nd ed. London: C. Cradock and W. Joy, 1814.

"Larger Work, A." *New England Kitchen Magazine* 3, no. 1 (April 1895): 45.

Larson, Nicole I., Melissa C. Neloson, Dianne Neumark-Sztainer, Mary Story, and Peter J. Hannan. "Making Time for Meals: Meal Structure and Associations with Dietary Intake in Young Adults." *Journal of the American Dietetic Association* 109, no. 1 (January 2009): 72–79.

Larson, Nicole I., Dianne Neumark-Sztainer, Peter J. Hannon, Mary Story. "Family Meals during Adolescence Are Associated with Higher Diet Quality and Healthful Meal Patterns during Young Adulthood." *Journal of the American Dietetic Association 107,* no. 9 (September 2007): 1502–1510.

Larson, Nicole I., Cheryl L. Perry, Mary Story, and Dianne Neumark-Sztainer. "Food Preparation by Young Adults Is Associated with Better Diet Quality." *Journal of the American Dietetic Association* 106, no.12 (December 2006): 2001–2007.

Laudan, Rachel. "Birth of the Modern Diet." *Scientific American* 238 (2000): 80–85.

Lauer, Heather. *Bacon: A Love Story.* New York: HarperCollins, 2009.

Lautenschlager, Julie L. *Food Fight! The Battle over the American Lunch in Schools and the Workplace.* Jefferson, NC: McFarland, 2006.

Lea, Elizabeth. *Domestic Cookery.* Baltimore: Cushings & Bailey, 1859.

LeClercq, Christian. *New Relation of Gaspesia: With the Customs and Religion of the Gaspesian Indians.* Translated by William F. Ganong. Toronto: Champlain Society, 1910.

Ledikwe, Jenny H., Julia A. Ello-Martin, and Barbara J. Rolls. "Portion Sizes and the Obesity Epidemic." *Journal of Nutrition* 135, no. 4 (April 2005): 905–909.

Lee, Hilde Gabriel. *Taste of the States: A Food History of America*. Charlottesville, VA: Howell, 1992.

Lee, N. K. M. *The Cook's Own Book*. Boston: Munroe & Francis, 1832.

Lee, Virginia Carter. "A Flower Luncheon for the Bride-to-Be." *Table Talk* 23, no. 4 (April 1908): 155–156.

Leight, Robert L., and Alice Duffy Rhinehart. *Country School Memories: An Oral History of One-Room Schooling*. Westport, CT: Greenwood, 1999.

Lender, Mark Edward, and James Kirby Martin. *Drinking in America: A History*. New York: Free Press, 1982.

Lesley, Susan Inches. *Recollections of My Mother*. Boston: George H. Ellis, 1886.

Leslie, Eliza. *The Behaviour Book: A Manual for Ladies*. Philadelphia: Willis P. Hazard, 1854.

———. *Directions for Cookery in Its Various Branches*. Philadelphia: E. L. Carey & Hart, 1840.

———. *Miss Leslie's New Cookery Book*. Philadelphia: T. B. Peterson, 1857.

"Letter Carriers' Picnics." *New York Times,* June 18, 1893.

Letter to the editor. "Wants Peanut Cart Whistles Stopped." *New York Times,* May 6, 1900.

Levenstein, Harvey. *Fear of Food: A History of Why We Worry About What We Eat*. Chicago: University of Chicago Press, 2012.

———. *Paradox of Plenty: A Social History of Eating in Modern America*. New York: Oxford University Press, 1993.

———. *Revolution at the Table: The Transformation of the American Diet*. New York: Oxford University Press, 1988.

Levine, Susan. *School Lunch Politics: The Surprising History of America's Favorite Welfare Program*. Princeton, NJ: Princeton University Press, 2008.

Liberman, Sherri, ed. *American Food by the Decades*. Santa Barbara, CA: ABC-CLIO, 2011.

"Life in the White House." *Macon Telegraph,* July 2, 1886.

Lincoln, Jonathan Thayer. "The City of the Dinner Pail." *New Outlook,* February 9, 1907, 317–324.

Lipkowitz, Ina. *Words to Eat By: Five Foods and the Culinary History of the English Language*. New York: St. Martin's, 2011.

Literary Panorama. Vol. 8. London: Simpkin, Marshall, and C. Taylor, 1819.

Lockwood, Luke Vincent. *Colonial Furniture in America*. New York: Charles Scribner's Sons, 1901.

Loft's advertisement. *New York Times,* June 8, 1949.

Lovegren, Sylvia. *Fashionable Foods: Seven Decades of Food Fads*. Chicago: University of Chicago Press, 2005.

Lucas, E. V. "Concerning Breakfast." *Living Age,* March 12, 1898, 711–716.

Luchetti, Cathy. *Home on the Range: A Culinary History of the American West*. New York: Villard, 1993.

Lupton, Ellen, and J. Abbott Miller. *The Bathroom, the Kitchen, and the Aesthetics of Waste*. New York: Kiosk, 1992.

Lusas, Edmund W., and Lloyd W. Rooney, eds. *Snack Foods Processing*. Boca Raton, FL: CRC Press, 2002.

Maine Sardines advertisement. *Journal of Home Economics* 44, no. 8 (October 1952): 607.

Manring, M. M. *Slave in a Box: The Strange Career of Aunt Jemima*. Charlottesville: University Press of Virginia, 1998.

Mariani, John. *The Encyclopedia of American Food and Drink*. New York: Lebhar-Friedman, 1999.

Marjoribanks, Alexander. *Travels in South and North America*. 5th ed. London: Simpkins, Marshall; New York: D. Appleton, 1854.

Markham, Gervase. *The English Housewife*, edited by Michael R. Best. 1615. Reprint, Kingston, Ontario: McGill-Queen's University Press, 1994.

Marling, Karal Ann. *As Seen on TV: The Visual Culture of Everyday Life in the 1950s*. Cambridge, MA: Harvard University Press, 1994.

Marryat, Frederick. *Second Series of a Diary in America*. Philadelphia: T. K. & P. G., 1840.

Marsh, Margaret. "Suburban Men and Masculine Domesticity, 1870–1915." *American Quarterly* 40, no. 2 (June 1988): 165–186.

Martin, Susan F. *A Nation of Immigrants*. Cambridge: Cambridge University Press, 2010.

Mason, Laura. *Food Culture in Great Britain*. Westport, CT: Greenwood, 2004.

Matheson, Donna M., Joel D. Killen, Yun Wang, Ann Varady, and Thomas N. Robinson. "Children's Food Consumption During Television Viewing." *American Journal of Clinical Nutrition* 79, no. 6 (June 2004): 1088–1094.

Matthews, Glenna. *"Just a Housewife": The Rise and Fall of Domesticity in America*. Oxford: Oxford University Press, 1987.

Maurielle, Tani A. "Feed Their Vile Bodies . . . Starve Their Immortal Souls: Food as Moral Instructor in Nineteenth-Century Homes and Schools." In *Food and Morality: Proceedings of the Oxford Symposium on Food and Cookery*, edited by Susan R. Friedland, 194–206. Devon, UK: Prospect, 2008.

Mays, Dorothy A. *Women in Early America: Struggle, Survival, and Freedom in a New World*. Santa Barbara, CA: ABC-CLIO, 2004.

McCollum, Elmer, and Nina Simmonds. *The American Home Diet: An Answer to the Ever Present Question: "What Shall We Have for Dinner?"* Detroit: Frederick C. Mathews, 1920.

McDaniel, Rich. *An Irresistible History of Southern Food: Four Centuries of Black-Eyes Peas, Collard Greens, and Whole-Hog Barbeque*. Charleston, SC: History Press, 2011.

McFeely, Mary Drake. *Can She Bake a Cherry Pie? American Women and the Kitchen in the Twentieth Century.* Amherst: University of Massachusetts Press, 2001.

McHugh, Tom. *The Time of the Buffalo.* Lincoln: University of Nebraska Press, 1979.

McMahon, Sarah F. "A Comfortable Subsistence: The Changing Composition of Diet in Rural New England." *William and Mary Quarterly* 32, no. 1 (January 1985): 26–65.

McWilliams, James E. *A Revolution in Eating: How the Quest for Food Shaped America.* New York: Columbia University Press, 2005.

———. *The Story Behind the Dish: Classic American Foods.* Santa Barbara, CA: ABC-CLIO, 2012.

McWilliams, Mark. *Food and the Novel in Nineteenth-Century America.* Lanham, MD: Alta Mira, 2012.

Meacham, Sarah H. *Every Home a Distillery: Alcohol, Gender, and Technology in the Colonial Chesapeake.* Baltimore: Johns Hopkins University Press, 2009.

Meade, Mary. "Cereal Appears in New Forms on Daily Menu." *Chicago Daily Tribune,* September 21, 1933.

———. "Crackers Far Cry from Old Modest Selves." *Chicago Daily Tribune,* June 12, 1932.

———. "Easy Snacks for an Informal Gathering." *Chicago Daily Tribune,* November 15, 1953.

———. "Variety Takes Monotony Out of Breakfasts." *Chicago Daily Tribune,* April 2, 1933.

Meakin, Budgett. *Model Factories and Villages: Ideal Conditions of Labor and Housing.* London: T. Fisher Unwin, 1905.

Meckel, Richard A. *Save the Babies: American Public Health Reform and the Prevention of Infant Mortality, 1850–1929.* Ann Arbor: University of Michigan Press, 1990.

Mendelson, Anne. *Milk: The Surprising Story of Milk Through the Ages.* New York: Knopf, 2008.

Mennell, Stephen. *All Manners of Food: Eating and Taste in England and France from the Middle Ages to the Present.* 2nd ed. Chicago: University of Chicago Press, 1996.

Miller, Angela L. "Nature's Transformations: The Meaning of the Picnic Theme in Nineteenth-Century Art." *Winterthur Portfolio* 24, no. 2–3 (summer–autumn): 113–138.

Miller, David W. "Technology and the Ideal: Production Quality and Kitchen Reform in Nineteenth-Century America." In *Dining in America, 1850–1900,* edited by Kathryn Grover, 47–84. Amherst: University of Massachusetts Press, 1987.

Mintz, Steven, and Susan Kellogg. *Domestic Revolutions: A Social History of American Family Life*. New York: Free Press, 1988.

Moffat, Muriel. *Afternoon Tea: A Timeless Tradition*. Vancouver, BC: Douglas & McIntyre, 2012.

Montgomery, Rebecca S. *The Politics of Education in the New South: Women and Reform in Georgia, 1890–1930*. Baton Rouge: Louisiana State University Press, 2005.

Mood, Fulmer. "John Winthrop, Jr., on Indian Corn." *New England Quarterly* 10 (March 1937): 121–133.

Moran, Mary H. "Boston High School Lunches." *Journal of Home Economics* 2, no. 2 (April 1910): 181–184.

Morgan, Philip D. *Slave Counterpoint: Black Culture in the Eighteenth-Century Chesapeake and Lowcountry*. Chapel Hill: University of North Carolina Press, 1998.

Morton, Mark. *Cupboard Love: A Dictionary of Culinary Curiosities*. Toronto: Insomniac, 2004.

Moss, Michael. *Salt, Sugar, Fat: How the Food Giants Hooked Us*. New York: Random House, 2013.

Moss, Sarah, and Alexander Badenoch. *Chocolate: A Global History*. London: Reaktion, 2009.

Mudry, Jessica J. *Measured Meals: Nutrition in America*. Albany: State University of New York, 2009.

Mullen, Margaret. *An Arkansas Childhood: Growing Up in the Athens of the Ozarks*. Fayetteville, AR: M&M Press, 1989.

Mullins, Paul R. *Glazed America: A History of the Doughnut*. Gainesville: University Press of Florida, 2008.

Musick, Kelly, and Ann Meier. "Assessing Causality and Persistence in Associations Between Family Dinners and Adolescent Well-Being." *Journal of Marriage and Family* 74, no. 3 (May 2012): 476–493.

Napoleoni, Loretta. *Rogue Economics: Capitalism's New Reality*. New York: Seven Stories, 2008.

Nathan, Joan. *Jewish Cooking in America*. New York: Knopf, 1998.

National Center on Addiction and Substance Abuse at Columbia University. *The Importance of Family Dinners III*. National Center on Addiction and Substance Abuse at Columbia University. September 2006. http://www.casacolumbia.org/templates/publications_reports.aspx (accessed February 23, 2013).

———. *The Importance of Family Dinners V*. National Center on Addiction and Substance Abuse at Columbia University. September 2009. http://www.casacolumbia.org/articlefiles/380-Importance%20of%20Family%20Dinners%20V.pdf (accessed March 23, 2013).

Neat Treats and Royal Crown soda advertisement. *Good Housekeeping* 120, no. 5 (May 1945): 234.

Nestle, Marion. *Food Politics: How the Food Industry Influences Nutrition and Health.* Rev. ed. Berkeley: University of California Press, 2007.

———. *What to Eat: An Aisle-by-Aisle Guide to Savvy Food Choices and Good Eating.* New York: North Point, 2006.

Nicola. "Lunch: An Urban Invention." *Edible Geographies,* June 22, 2012. http://www.ediblegeography.com/lunch-an-urban-invention.

"Nutritionist: Snacking Leads to Poor Nutrition." *Chicago Tribune,* April 13, 1972.

Nylander, Jane C. *Our Own Snug Fireside: Images of the New England Home, 1760–1860.* New Haven, CT: Yale University Press, 2004.

O'Rell, Max. *A Frenchman in America.* New York: Cassell, 1891.

OECD. "Society at a Glance 2011—OECD Social Indicators." 2011. www.oecd.org/els/social/indicators/SAG (accessed March 1, 2013).

Offenbach, Jacques. *Offenbach in America: Notes of a Traveling Musician.* New York: G. W. Carleton, 1877.

Oliver, Garret, ed. *The Oxford Companion to Beer.* Oxford: Oxford University Press, 2012.

Oliver, Sandra L. *Food in Colonial and Federal America.* Westport, CT: Greenwood, 2005.

———. *Saltwater Foodways: New Englanders and Their Food at Sea and Ashore in the Nineteenth Century.* Mystic CT: Mystic Seaport Museum, 1995.

Oliver, Thomas. "Industrial Lead Poisoning." *Bulletin of the Bureau of Labor* 95 (July 1911).

Opie, Frederick Douglas. *Hog and Hominy: Soul Food from Africa to America.* New York: Columbia University Press, 2008.

Ott, Cindy. *Pumpkin: The Curious History of an American Icon.* Seattle: University of Washington Press, 2012.

Owen, June. "Food: Frankfurters: Despite Variation in Their Contents, Ubiquitous Hot Dogs Are Good Eating." *New York Times,* August 20, 1958.

Owen, William. *Diary of William Owen from November 10, 1824 to April 20, 1825,* edited by Joel W. Hiatt. Indianapolis: Bobbs-Merrill, 1906.

Panati, Charles. *Panati's Extraordinary Origins of Everyday Things.* New York: HarperCollins, 1989.

Parker, Arthur Caswell. *Parker on the Iroquois.* Syracuse, NY: Syracuse University Press, 1968.

Parkin, Katherine J. *Food Is Love: Advertising and Gender Roles in Modern America.* Philadelphia: University of Pennsylvania Press, 2006.

Patrick, Bethann, and John Thompson. *An Uncommon History of Common Things.* Washington, DC: National Geographic, 2009.

"Pen Pictures of All Sorts and Conditions of Kitchens." *New England Kitchen Magazine* 1, no. 1 (April 1894): 30–33.

Pendergrast, Mark. *For God, Country, and Coca-Cola: The Definitive History of the Great American Soft Drink and the Company That Makes It.* 3rd ed. New York: Basic Books, 2013.

———. *Uncommon Grounds: The History of Coffee and How It Transformed Our World.* 2nd. ed. New York: Basic Books, 2010.

Pendleton, Philip E. "Domestic Outbuildings." In *Architecture and Landscape of the Pennsylvania Germans, 1720–1920,* edited by Sally McMurry and Nancy Van Dolsen, 66–93. Philadelphia: University of Pennsylvania Press, 2011.

Pennell, Elizabeth Robins. "Eats." *North American Review* 215, no. 3 (March 1922): 353–360.

Perkins, F. B. "Childhood: A Study." *Atlantic Monthly* 18, no. 108 (October 1866): 385–395.

Petroski, Henry. *The Evolution of Useful Things.* New York: Vintage, 1992.

Phelps, Mrs. Lincoln. *The Educator, or Hours with My Pupils.* New York: A. S. Barnes & Company, 1872.

Philbrick, Nathaniel, ed. *The Mayflower Papers: Selected Writings of Colonial New England.* New York: Penguin, 2007.

"Picnic for Dr. Hill." *New York Times,* June 28, 1908.

Piernas, Carmen, and Barry Popkin. "Trends in Snacking Among U.S. Children." *Health Affairs* 29, no. 3 (March 2010): 398–404.

Pillsbury, Richard. *No Foreign Food: The American Diet in Time and Place.* Boulder, CO: Westview Press, 1998.

Plante, Ellen M. *The American Kitchen from 1700 to the Present: From Hearth to Highrise.* New York: Facts on File, 1995.

Pollan, Michael. *In Defense of Food: An Eater's Manifesto.* New York: Penguin Press, 2008.

———. "Out of the Kitchen, onto the Couch." *New York Times Magazine,* July 29, 2009, 26.

———. "The Food Movement, Rising: An Exchange." *New York Review of Books,* August 19, 2010.

Poole, H. Annette. "Dinner Pails and Lunch Baskets: How to Care for and Fill Them." *Good Housekeeping,* August 20, 1887, 182–183.

"Pop Pops—Popcorn Sales Net Farmers $9,000,000 in 1946." *Billboard* 59, no. 22 (June 7, 1947): 46.

"Popcorn Production Up." *Billboard* 68, no. 52 (December 29, 1956): 54.

Popik, Barry. "Hot Dog (Polo Grounds Myth and Original Monograph)." The Big Apple. July 15, 2004. http://www.barrypopik.com/index.php/new_york _city/entry/hot_dog_polo_grounds_myth_original_monograph.

———. "Hot Dogs at Baseball Games." The Big Apple. August 31, 2008. http: //www.barrypopik.com/index.php/new_york_city/entry/hot_dogs_at _baseball_games.

———. "Junk Food." The Big Apple. December 26, 2008. http://www.barrypopik.com/index.php/new_york_city/entry/junk_food.

Potato Chip Institute International. *Prize-Winning Recipes Starring Potato Chips.* Cleveland, OH: Potato Chip Institute International, n.d.

Powell, Adam Clayton, III. *Adam by Adam: The Autobiography of Adam Clayton Powell, Jr.* 1971. New York: Dafina Books, 1994.

Powers, Madelon. *Faces Along the Bar: Lore and Order in the Workingman's Saloon, 1870–1920.* Chicago: University of Chicago Press, 1998.

"Pretzel at Ninety." *New York Times,* May 9, 1951, 32.

"Pretzel Makers Work on Code." *New York Times,* July 9, 1933.

"Pretzel Minus Beer Acquires New Favor Backed by Science." *New York Times,* September 4, 1927.

"'Pretzel Town' Turns Out to Honor Native Product." *New York Times,* May 10, 1951, 10.

"Pretzel Vendors Fined." *New York Times,* February 23, 1930.

"Pretzel's Progress." *Kiplinger Magazine* 1, no. 2 (February 1947): 36–37.

"Pretzels in Upturn with Sales of Beer." *New York Times,* April 9, 1933.

Quaker Oats advertisement. *Chicago Daily Tribune,* April 13, 1894.

———. *New York Times,* December 9, 1891, 3.

———. *New York Times,* February 10, 1892, 3.

———. *New York Times,* February 13, 1892, 3.

———. *Washington Post,* October 5, 1893, 7.

———. *Washington Post,* November 23, 1898, 2.

Quinlan Butter Pretzels and Gulden's Mustard advertisement. *New York Times,* June 14, 1957.

Quinzio, Jeri. *Pudding: A Global History.* London: Reaktion, 2012.

Rainwater, Dorothy. "Victorian Dining Silver." In *Dining in America, 1850–1900,* edited by Kathryn Grover, 173–204. Amherst: University of Massachusetts Press, 1987.

Randolph, Mary. *The Virginia Housewife.* Baltimore: Plaskitt, Fite, 1838.

Reade, Charles. "A Simpleton." *Harper's New Monthly Magazine* 47, no. 280 (September 1873): 560–567.

Rees, Robert M. "Bite-Sized Marketing: Candy Bars." In *Chocolate: Food of the Gods,* edited by Alex Szogyi, 125–130. New York: Hofstra University, 1997.

"Related Tie-Ins Boost Sales." *Chain Store Age* 39 (1963): 311.

Rhode Island Board of Education. *Thirty-Second Annual Report of the State Board of Education.* Providence: E. L. Freeman, 1902.

Rice, Kym S., and Martha B. Katz-Hyman. *The World of a Slave: Encyclopedia of the Material Life of Slaves in the United States.* Santa Barbara, CA: Greenwood, 2011.

Richards, Ellen H. "The Food of Children and Young Students." *New England Kitchen Magazine* 1, no. 3 (June–July 1894): 147–152.

Richards, Laura Elizabeth Howe. *Abigail Adams and Her Time.* N.p.: D. Appleton, 1917.

Ridley, Glynis. "The First American Cookbook." *Eighteenth-Century Life* 23, no. 2 (May 1999): 114–123.

Riely, Elizabeth. "Sylvester Graham and the Origins of the Breakfast Cereal Industry." In *Oxford Symposium on Food and Cookery, 1989: Staple Foods,* edited by Harlan Walker, 198–201. London: Prospect, 1990.

Roberts, Calvin A., and Susan A. Roberts. *New Mexico.* Rev. ed. Albuquerque: University of New Mexico Press, 2006.

Roberts, William. *The Collected Contributions on Digestion and Diet.* Philadelphia: Lea, 1891.

Robinson, Harriet Jane Hanson. *Loom and Spindle: Life Among the Early Mill Girls.* New York: Thomas Y. Crowell, 1898.

Rogers, Ben. *Beef and Liberty: Roast Beef, John Bull, and the English Nation.* London: Vintage, 2003.

Rorer, Sarah Tyson. *Mrs. Rorer's Philadelphia Cook Book: A Manual of Home Economics.* Philadelphia: Arnold, 1886.

Rose, Mary Swartz. *Everyday Foods in War Time.* New York: Macmillan, 1918.

Rose, Peter G. *Food, Drink, and Celebrations of the Hudson Valley.* Charleston, SC: History Press, 2009.

———. *The Sensible Cook: Dutch Foodways in the Old and the New World.* Syracuse, NY: Syracuse University Press, 1998.

Roth, Rodris. "Tea-Drinking in Eighteenth-Century America: Its Etiquette and Equipage." In *Material Life in America, 1600–1860,* edited by Robert Blair St. George, 439–462. Boston: Northeastern University Press, 1998.

Rowlandson, Mary White. *A Narrative of the Captivity and Restoration of Mrs. Mary Rowlandson.* Cambridge, MA: Samuel Green, 1682.

Rubin, Nancy. *American Empress: The Life and Times of Marjorie Merriweather Post.* Lincoln, NB: iUniverse, Inc., 2003.

Russell, Howard S. *Indian New England Before the Mayflower.* Lebanon, NH: University Press of New England, 1983.

———. *A Long, Deep Furrow: Three Centuries of Farming in New England.* Hanover, NH: University Press of New England, 1982.

Russell, William Howard. *My Diary North and South.* Boston: T. O. H. P. Burnham, 1863.

Rutenberg, Ruth. "M-m-m, Ice Cream and Pretzels." *New York Times,* September 27, 2000.

Rutherford, Janice Williams. *Selling Mrs. Consumer: Christine Frederick and the Rise of Household Efficiency.* Athens: University of Georgia Press, 2003.

Rutledge, Sarah. *The Carolina Housewife.* 1847. Reprint, Columbia: University of South Carolina Press, 1979.

Ryan, Mary P. *Cradle of the Middle Class: The Family in Oneida County, New York, 1790–1865.* Cambridge: Cambridge University Press, 1981.

"Samuel M. Rubin, 85, Vendor: Put Fresh Popcorn in Theaters." *New York Times,* February 9, 2004.

Sawtelle, William Otis. "Father Pierre Biard, Superior of the Mount Desert Jesuit Mission of Saint Sauveur." *Sprague's Journal of Maine History* 10, no. 4 (October–December 1921): 179–191.

Scanlon, Jennifer. "Old Housekeeping, New Housekeeping, or No Housekeeping? The Kitchenless Home Movement and the Women's Service Magazine." *Journalism History* 30, no. 1 (April 2004): 2–10.

Scarcella, Nicole. *Made in Sicily—Born in Brooklyn.* Bloomington, IN: Authors House, 2011.

Schenone, Laura. *A Thousand Years over a Hot Stove: A History of American Women Told Through Food, Recipes, and Remembrances.* New York: Norton, 2003.

Schinto, Jeanne. "The Clockwork Roasting Jack, or How Technology Entered the Kitchen." *Gastronomica* 4, no. 1 (winter 2004): 33–40.

Schivelbusch, Wolfgang, and David Jacobson. *Tastes of Paradise: A Social History of Spices, Stimulants, and Intoxicants.* New York: Vintage, 1993.

Schwartz, Ruth Cowan. *More Work for Mother: The Ironies of Household Technology from the Open Hearth to the Microwave.* New York: Basic, 1983.

Schwarz, Richard W. *John Harvey Kellogg, M.D.: Pioneering Health Reformer.* Hagerstown, MD: Review and Herald Publishing Association, 2006.

Schweid, Richard. *Consider the Eel: A Natural and Gastronomic History.* Boston: Da Capo Press, 2002.

"Science Gives Pretzel Long New Life Lease." *Reading Eagle,* October 9, 1927, 28.

Shaftsbury, Edmund, Ralston Health Club. *Child Life: Before and After Birth.* Washington, DC: Ralston Club Press, 1898.

Shapiro, Laura. *Perfection Salad: Women and Cooking at the Turn of the Century.* 1986. Reprint, New York: Modern Library, 2001.

———. *Something from the Oven: Reinventing Dinner in 1950s America.* New York: Viking, 2004.

Shephard, Sue. *Pickled, Potted, and Canned: How the Art and Science of Food Preserving Changed the World.* New York: Simon & Shuster, 2000.

Shuey, Edwin Longstreet. *Factory People and Their Employers: How Their Relations Are Made Pleasant and Profitable.* New York: Lentilhon, 1900.

Sijs, Nicolene van der. *Cookies, Cole Slaw, and Stoops: The Influence of Dutch on the North American Languages.* Amsterdam: Amsterdam University Press, 2009.

Simmons, Amelia. *American Cookery.* 2nd ed. Hartford, CT: Simeon Butler, 1798.

Smith, Andrew F. *Drinking History: Fifteen Turning Points in the Making of American Beverages.* New York: Columbia University Press, 2013.

———. *Eating History: Thirty Turning Points in the Making of American Cuisine.* New York: Columbia University Press, 2009.

———. *Encyclopedia of Junk Food and Fast Food.* Westport, CT: Greenwood, 2006.

———. "Marketing Junk Food to Children in the United States." In *Food and Morality: Proceedings of the Oxford Symposium on Food and Cookery,* edited by Susan R. Friedland, 255–262. Devon, UK: Prospect, 2008.

———, ed. *The Oxford Companion to American Food and Drink.* Oxford: Oxford University Press, 2007.

———, ed. *The Oxford Encyclopedia of Food and Drink in America.* Oxford: Oxford University Press, 2004.

———. *Peanuts: The Illustrious History of the Goober Pea.* Urbana: University of Illinois Press, 2002.

———. *Popped Culture: A Social History of Popcorn in America.* Charleston: University of South Carolina Press, 1999.

Smith, Eliza. *The Complete Housewife.* Williamsburg, VA: William Parks, 1742.

Smith, James. *An Account of the Remarkable Occurrences in the Life and Travels of Col. James Smith.* Cincinnati, OH: Robert Clarke, 1870.

Smith, Sarah Francis. "'She Moves the Hand That Moves the World': Antebellum Child-Rearing: Images of Mother and Child in Nineteenth-Century Periodicals for Mothers." PhD diss., University of Minnesota, 2006.

"Snack Shop at Radcliffe: Students Sell Refreshments for After-Study Hours at Night." *New York Times,* October 16, 1938, 54.

Sobey, Ed. *The Way Kitchens Work: The Science Behind the Microwave, Teflon Pan, Garbage Disposal, and More.* Chicago: Chicago Review Press, 2010.

Sokolov, Raymond. *Fading Feast: A Compendium of Disappearing American Regional Foods.* Jaffrey, NH: Nonpareil, 1998.

Speth, John D. *The Paleoanthropology and Archaeology of Big-Game Hunting.* New York: Springer, 2012.

Spielvogel, Carl. "Pretzels Become Big Business Item." *New York Times,* February 5, 1956, 156.

Spigel, Lynn. *Make Room for TV: Television and the Family Ideal in Postwar America.* Chicago: University of Chicago Press, 1992.

Stavely, Keith, and Kathleen Fitzgerald. *America's Founding Food: The Story of New England Cooking.* Chapel Hill: University of North Carolina Press, 2004.

———. *Northern Hospitality: Cooking by the Book in New England.* Amherst: University of Massachusetts Press, 2011.

Stearns, Peter N. "Children and Weight Control: Priorities in the United States and France." In *Weighty Issues: Fatness and Thinness as Social Problems,* edited by Jeffrey Sobel and Donna Maurer, 11–30. New York: Walter de Gruyter, 1999.

———. *Fat History: Bodies and Beauty in the Modern West.* New York: New York University Press, 2002.

Steinhauer, Jennifer. "Snack Time Never Ends." *New York Times,* January 9, 2010.

Stowe, Harriet Beecher. *Oldtown Folks.* Boston: Fields & Osgood, 1869.

Strasser, Susan. *Never Done: A History of American Housework.* New York: Henry Holt, 1982.

Sturge, Joseph. *A Visit to the United States in 1841.* Boston: Dexter S. King, 1842.

Sudley, Granthorpe. "Luncheon for a Million." *Munsey's Magazine* 24 (1998): 834–845.

Sutherland, David E. "Modernizing Domestic Service." In *American Home Life, 1830–1930: A Social History of Spaces and Services,* edited by Jessica H. Foy and Thomas J. Schlereth, 242–265. Knoxville: University of Tennessee Press, 1992.

Sweet, John E. "Machine Designing." *Manufacturer and Builder* 20, no. 5 (May 1888): 110–111.

Symons, Michael. *A History of Cooks and Cooking.* Champaign: University of Illinois Press, 1998.

T. D. L. *A Peep at the Western World: Being an Account of a Visit to Nova Scotia, New Brunswick, Canada, and the United States.* London: J. R. Smith, 1863.

T. W. H. "Women and Men: The Decline of the Tea Party." *Harper's Bazaar,* May 22, 1886, 330.

"Table Manners." *Harper's Bazaar,* December 15, 1894, 1021.

Tarbell, Ida Minerva. *New Business Deals.* New York: Macmillan, 1916.

Tasty Chips advertisement. *New York Times,* June 8, 1945.

Taylor, Alan. *American Colonies: The Settling of North America.* New York: Penguin, 2001.

Taylor, Joe Gray. *Eating, Drinking, and Visiting in the South: An Informal History.* Baton Rouge: Louisiana State University Press, 1982.

"Tea Party Treats," *Woman's Home Companion* 83 (1956): 78–80.

Temple, Jennifer L., April M. Giacomelli, Kristine M. Kent, James N. Roemmich, and Leonard H. Epstein. "Television Watching Increases Motivated Responding for Food and Eating Intake in Children." *American Journal of Clinical Nutrition* 85, no. 2 (February 2007): 355–361.

"The Proper Hour for Dinner." *Good Housekeeping* 2, no. 12 (April 17, 1886): 345.

Theiss, Mary, and Lewis Theiss. "Fake Sweets and Soft Drinks to Be Dodged." *Pearson's Magazine* 26, no. 1 (July 1911): 79–86.

Theophano, Janet. *Eat My Words: Reading Women's Lives Through the Cookbooks They Wrote.* New York: Palgrave, 2002.

Thermo-Tray advertisement. *Daily Boston Globe,* December 4, 1956, 14.

Thong, Tracy. "Performances of the Banquet Course in Early Modern Drama." In *Renaissance Food from Rabelais to Shakespeare: Culinary Readings and Culinary Histories,* edited by Joan Fitzpatrick, ch. 6. Surrey, UK: Ashgate, 1991.

Thorne, John, and Matt Lewis Thorne. *Serious Pig: An American Cook in Search of His Roots.* New York: North Point, 1996.

Thwaites, Thomas. *The Toaster Project.* Princeton, NJ: Princeton Architectural Press, 2011.

"Times of Taking Food." *Godey's Lady's Book and Magazine* 95, no. 586 (1877): 344.

Toastmaster Hospitality Set advertisement. *Good Housekeeping* 130, no. 3 (March 1950): 180.

Tomes, Nancy. *The Gospel of Germs: Men, Women, and the Microbe in American Life.* Cambridge, MA: Harvard University Press, 1998.

"Topics of the Times: Snacks for Hikers." *New York Times,* October 1, 1927.

Toussaint-Samat, Maguelonne. *A History of Food.* 2nd ed. Chichester, UK: Wiley, 2009.

Trager, James. *The Food Chronology.* New York: Henry Holt, 1995.

Trollope, Francis. *Domestic Manners of the Americans.* 4th ed. London: Whittaker, Tracher, 1832.

Trubek, Amy B. *Haute Cuisine: How The French Invented the Culinary Profession.* Philadelphia: University of Pennsylvania Press, 2000.

Twede, Diana. "Uneeda Biscuit: The First Consumer Package?" *Journal of Macromarketing* 17, no. 2 (fall 1987): 82–88.

"Two Billion Pretzels Eaten in 1946." *New York Times,* July 26, 1947, 16.

"Two Pennsylvania Companies Join in Ice Cream, Pretzel Promotion." *Ice Cream Review* 42 (April 1959): 99.

Ukers, William H. *All About Coffee.* New York: The Tea and Coffee Trade Journal Company, 1922.

Underwood, Francis H. *Quabbin: The Story of a Small Town.* Boston: Lee & Shepard, 1893.

Unger, Harlow Giles. *American Tempest: How the Boston Tea Party Sparked a Revolution.* New York: Da Capo Press, 2011.

University Club. *The University Club of New York: A Souvenir.* New York: University Magazine Company, 1892.

Venema, Janny. *Beverwijck: A Dutch Village on the American Frontier, 1652–1664.* Albany: State University of New York Press, 2003.

Visser, Margaret. *Much Depends on Dinner: The Extraordinary History and Mythology, Allure and Obsessions, Perils and Taboos of an Ordinary Meal.* New York: Grove, 1986.

———. *The Rituals of Dinner: The Origins, Evolution, Eccentricities, and Meaning of Table Manners.* New York: Harper Perennial, 1991.

Volney, Constantin-Francois de Chasseboeuf. *View of the Climate and Soil of the United States of America.* London: J. Johnson, 1804.

Volo, James M., and Dorothy Deneen Volo. *Daily Life on the Old Colonial Frontier.* Westport, CT: Greenwood, 2002.

———. *Family Life in 17th- and 18th-Century America.* Westport, CT: Greenwood, 2006.

Voorhees, Don. *Why Do Doughnuts Have Holes? Fascinating Facts About What We Eat and Drink.* New York: Citadel Press Books, 2004.

Wansink, Brian. "Environmental Factors That Increase the Food Intake and Consumption Volume of Unknowing Consumers." *Annual Review of Nutrition* 24 (July 2004): 455–479.

———. *Mindless Eating: Why We Eat More Than We Think.* New York: Bantam, 2006.

Wansink, Brian, and Koert Van Ittersum. "Portion Size Me: Downsizing Our Consumption Norms." *Journal of the American Dietetic Association* 107, no. 7 (July 2007): 1103–1106.

Ward, Susan Hayes. "The Homelike House." *Chatauquan* 5, no. 6 (March 1885): 335–338.

Warner, Arthur. "Odd-Hour Munching in the Machine Age." *New York Times,* April 24, 1932.

Warner, Sam Bass. *Streetcar Suburbs: The Process of Growth in Boston, 1870–1900.* 2nd ed. Cambridge, MA: Harvard University Press, 1978.

Washington, Booker T. *Up from Slavery.* New York: Doubleday, Page, 1907.

Weaver, William Woys. *America Eats: Forms of Edible Folk Art.* New York: Harper & Row, 1989.

———. *The Christmas Cook: Three Centuries of American Yuletide Sweets.* New York: Harper Perennial, 1990.

———. *Country Scrapple: An American Tradition.* Mechanicsburg, PA: Stackpole, 2003.

———. *Pennsylvania Dutch Country Cooking.* New York: Abbeville, 1993.

———. *A Quaker Woman's Cookbook: The Domestic Cookery of Elizabeth Ellicott Lea.* Rev. ed. Mechanicsburg, PA: Stackpole, 2004.

———. *Sauer's Herbal Cures: America's First Book of Botanic Healing, 1762–1778.* New York: Routledge, 2001.

———. *Sauerkraut Yankees: Pennsylvania Dutch Foods and Foodways.* 2nd ed. Mechanicsburg, PA: Stackpole, 2002.

Weinstein, Miriam. *The Surprising Power of Family Meals: How Eating Together Makes Us Smarter, Stronger, Healthier, and Happier.* Hanover, NH: Steerforth, 2005.

Whitaker, Jan. *Tea at the Blue Lantern Inn: A Social History of the Tea Room Craze in America.* New York: St. Martin's, 2002.

White Ammunition. Produced by B. K. Blake. 1942. Sponsored by Borden's Farm Products. Prelinger Archives. http://archive.org/details/White Amm1942 (accessed December 4, 2012).

Wickman, Donald H., ed. "'Breakfast on Chocolate': The Diary of Moses Greenleaf, 1777." *Bulletin of the Fort Ticonderoga Museum* 15, no. 6 (1997): 482–506.

Wilcox, Estelle Woods. *The Original Buckeye Cook Book and Practical Housekeeping.* Chicago: Reilly & Britton, 1905.

Wilcox, Keith, Beth Vallen, Lauren Block, and Gavan Fotzsimons. "Vicarious Goal Fulfillment: When the Mere Presence of a Healthy Option Leads to an Ironically Indulgent Decision." *Journal of Consumer Research* 36, no. 3 (October 2009): 380–393.

Wild, Antony. *Coffee: A Dark History.* New York: Norton, 2004.

Wiley, Harvey W. "Milk." *Good Housekeeping* 66, no. 2 (February 1918): 49–50, 137–138.

Wilk, Richard. "Power at the Table: Food Fights and Happy Meals." *Cultural Studies ⇔ Critical Methodologies* 10, no. 6 (December 2010): 428–436.

"Will Put Cases on Pretzels." *New York Times,* May 4, 1930, N20.

Williams, John, and Stephen West Williams. *The Redeemed Captive Returning to Zion.* 1853. Reprint, Bedford, MA: Applewood, 1987.

Williams, Roger. *A Key into the Language of America.* 1643. Reprint, Bedford, MA: Applewood, n.d.

Williams, Susan. *Food in the United States, 1820s–1890.* Westport, CT: Greenwood, 2006.

———. *Savory Suppers and Fashionable Feasts: Dining in Victorian America.* New York: Pantheon, 1985.

Williams-Forson, Psyche A. *Building Houses Out of Chicken Legs: Black Women, Food, and Power.* Chapel Hill: University of North Carolina Press, 2006.

Willigen, John Van, and Anne Van Willigen. *Food and Everyday Life on Kentucky Farms, 1920–1950.* Lexington: University Press of Kentucky, 2006.

Wilson, Bee. *Consider the Fork: A History of How We Cook and Eat.* New York: Basic, 2012.

———. *Sandwich: A Global History.* London: Reaktion, 2010.

———. *Swindled: The Dark History of Food Fraud, from Poisoned Candy to Counterfeit Coffee.* Princeton, NJ: Princeton University Press, 2008.

Wilson, C. Anne. *Food and Drink in Britain: From the Stone Age to the Nineteenth Century.* Chicago: Academy Chicago Publishers, 2003.

Wilson, Mary Tolford. "Americans Learn to Grow the Irish Potato." *New England Quarterly* 32, no. 3 (September 1959): 333–350.

Wilson, Philip K., and W. Jeffrey Hurst. *Chocolate as Medicine: A Quest over the Centuries.* Cambridge: The Royal Society of Chemistry, 2012.

Winthrop, John. *The History of New England from 1630 to 1749.* Boston: Phelps & Farnham, 1825.

Winthrop, John, and Margaret Tyndal Winthrop. *Some Puritan Love-Letters: John and Margaret Winthrop, 1618–1638*, edited by Joseph Hopkins Twichell. New York: Dodd, Mean, 1894.

Woloson, Wendy A. *Refined Tastes: Sugar, Confectionary, and Consumers in Nineteenth-Century America*. Baltimore, MD: Johns Hopkins University Press, 2002.

"Woman Vendor, 80, Wins Court's Mercy." *New York Times*, November 15, 1927.

"Women and Men: The Decline of the Tea Party." *Harper's Bazaar*, May 22, 1886, 330.

Wood, Bertha M. *Foods of the Foreign-Born*. Boston: Whitcomb & Barrows, 1922.

Wood, William. *New England's Prospect*, edited by Alden T. Vaughn, 1634. Reprint, Amherst: University of Massachusetts Press, 1993.

Woodforde, James. *The Diary of a Country Parson, 1758–1802*. 1935. Reprint, Norwich, UK: Canterbury, 2011.

Woodward, George E., and F. W. Woodward. *Country Homes*. 5th ed. New York: George E. and F. W. Woodward, 1866.

Wright, Gwendolyn. *Building the Dream: A Social History of Housing in America*. Cambridge, MA: MIT Press, 1983.

Wright, Mary, and Russel Wright. *Guide to Easier Living*. 1950. Reprint, Salt Lake City: Gibbs, Smith, 2003.

Wyman, Carolyn. *Better Than Homemade: Amazing Foods That Changed the Way We Eat*. Philadelphia: Quick Books, 2004.

Yoder, Don. *Discovering American Folklife: Studies in Ethnic, Religious, and Regional Culture*. Mechanicsburg, PA: Stackpole, 1990.

———. "Pennsylvanians Call It Mush." *Pennsylvania Folk Life* 13, no. 2 (winter 1962–1963): 44–53.

Young, Lisa R., and Marion Nestle. "The Contribution of Expanding Portion Sizes to the U.S. Obesity Epidemic." *American Journal of Public Health* 92, no. 2 (February 2002): 246–249.

Young, William H., and Nancy K. Young. *The 1950s*. Westport, CT: Greenwood, 2004.

Zafar, Rafia. "The Proof of the Pudding: Of Haggis, Hasty Pudding, and Transatlantic Influence." *Early American Literature* 31, no. 2 (1996): 133–149.

Zanger, Mark H. *The American Ethnic Cookbook for Students*. Westport, CT: Greenwood, 2001.

———. *The American History Cookbook*. Westport, CT: Greenwood, 2003.

Zizza, Claire, Anna Maria Siega-Riz, and Barry M. Popkin. "Significant Increase in Young Adults' Snacking Between 1977–78 and 1994–96 Represents a Cause for Concern." *Preventive Medicine* 32, no. 4 (2001): 303–310.

Zuckerman, Larry. *The Potato: How the Humble Spud Rescued the Western World*. New York: North Point, 1998.

ILLUSTRATION CREDITS

Figure 1. Theodor de Bry, after watercolor by John White, in Harriot,Thomas, *A Briefe and True Report of the New Found Land of Virginia*, 1588. Courtesy of the John Carter Brown Library at Brown University.

Figure 2. Courtesy of Barbara Swell, Log Cabin Cooking, http://logcabin cooking.com.

Figure 3. In Maria Parloa, *Miss Parloa's New Cook Book and Marketing Guide*, 1880. Courtesy of the Michigan State University Libraries.

Figure 4. Between 1830 and 1900. Courtesy of the Library of Congress, Prints and Photographs Division.

Figure 5. Courtesy of the Historical Society of Moorestown, New Jersey.

Figures 6(a–b). In Thomas Hill, *New Revised Hills Manual Illustrated*, 1897, http://antiqueimages.blogspot.com/2012/03/vintage-graphic-of -victorian-dining.html.

Figure 7. Frank T. Merrill. In Ginn and Company, *The Common School Catalogue*, 1906. Clipart courtesy of the Florida Center for Instructional Technology.

Figure 8. Elizabeth Alice Austen, c. 1896. Courtesy of the Library of Congress.

Figure 9. c. 1896. Courtesy of the Library of Congress.

Figure 10. Lewis Hine, 1908. Courtesy of the Library of Congress, National Child Labor Committee Collection.

Figure 11. Lewis Hine, 1913. Courtesy of the Library of Congress, National Child Labor Committee Collection.

Figure 12. 1909–1920. Courtesy of the Library of Congress, National Photo Company Collection.

Figure 13. Photographs and Prints Division, Schomburg Center for Research in Black Culture, New York Public Library, Astor, Lenox, and Tilden Foundations.

Figure 14. Berenice Abbott. Photography Collection, Miriam and Ira D. Wallach Division of Art, Prints and Photographs, New York Public Library, Astor, Lenox, and Tilden Foundations.

Figure 15. Courtesy of the Library of Congress, Farm Security Administration/Office of War Information Photograph Collection.

Figure 16. Courtesy of the Library of Congress, Farm Security Administration/Office of War Information Photograph Collection.

Figure 17. Courtesy of the Library of Congress.

Figure 18. Courtesy of the Library of Congress.

Figure 19. Esther Bubly, Washington, DC, 1943. Courtesy of the Library of Congress, Farm Security Administration/Office of War Information Photograph Collection.

Figures 20(a–b). In Winnifred S. Fales, *The Easy Housekeeping Book*, 1923.

Figure 21. Gordon Parks, 1943. Courtesy of the Library of Congress, Farm Security Administration/Office of War Information Photograph Collection.

Figure 22. New York World's Fair, 1939–1940 records, Manuscripts and Archives Division, New York Public Library, Astor, Lenox, and Tilden Foundations.

Figure 23. Courtesy of the Library of Congress, Farm Security Administration/Office of War Information Photograph Collection.

INDEX